CW00695887

Solly Adam - Beyond Boundaries (UK Edition)

Hardcover   ISBN 978 81 971426 5 9

Paperback   ISBN 978 81 971426 9 7

E-book   ISBN 978 81 971426 3 5

Published in 2024 by Nirvana Publishers LLP.

3-2-172/PE/404, Pramod Elite,
Attapur, Hyderabad – 500048
www.nirvana-publishers.com
contact@nirvana-publishers.com

(The book is also available in India)
The view and opinions expressed in this work are the author's own and the facts are as reported by him, and the publisher is in no way liable for the same.

Cover page design by Satyanarayana Gorgi
Typeset by Laxman Tagili, at VIN Graphics

Printed and bound in Great Britain by
CPI Group (UK) Ltd, Croydon, CR0 4YY.

SOLLY ADAM

BEYOND BOUNDARIES

A PASSIONATE CRICKETER FROM YORKSHIRE

BY
VARA VANTAPATI

FOREWORD BY

SUNIL GAVASKAR &
JAVED MIANDAD

NIRVANA
PUBLISHERS

For my Mom, Ayesha Adam, and Dad, Saeed Adam, who always taught me that words have the power to change the world.

- Solly Adam

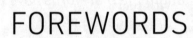

FOREWORDS

Solly Adam: The Star Behind the Stars

The game of cricket is fortunate to have so many genuine lovers who may not necessarily play at the highest level, or even the middle level, and yet make a huge contribution to the development and promotion of the game. Suleman (Solly) Adam is one such cricket lover who has made a significant contribution to the game though he has not even played first class cricket. A very enthusiastic club cricketer, he realised very quickly that playing cricket was not a career option, and so he focused his attention on developing his family business.

The family of Solly had migrated to UK in the late 1960s, and he has been a *pucca* Yorkshireman since then with the Yorkshire accent and all. What he has done though, despite not even playing cricket at the first-class level, is to keep his love for the game, even now, by opening a business that deals with sports equipment, specialising in cricket kit. For hundreds of Indian and Pakistani cricketers coming to England to try and play in the leagues, be it the Yorkshire league or the Lancashire league, Solly's house was almost the first visit on arrival in England. Here they were assured of food, warm clothes, and many times even a roof over their head. Because of the stringent foreign exchange conditions then, not a lot of these players had any spare money apart from the meagre amounts they would earn on weekends, playing for the club that had hired them. So, during the week, Solly would not only look after their food, but he would also arrange for them to get some employment to replenish their income. This was something quite extraordinary because almost all the cricketers that came to England were not related or known to him but recommended by someone he knew from India and Pakistan. Even those who did not know him would send a letter to Solly, along with the players, requesting him to look after them during their stay of almost six months in England. This kind of service to the game is unheard of, and unrecorded, and so Solly will not get the credit that he deserves.

I first met him on my first tour to England in 1971. The late Rahul Mankad, son of the great Vinoo Bhai Mankad, and brother of Ashok who opened the batting with me for India, would talk glowingly about Solly every time he returned from a season of league cricket in England. At first, because I was not aware that Solly was the nickname for Suleman, I was under the impression that he was an Englishman. But when I met him, thanks to Rahul, I was pleasantly surprised to see that he was of Indian origin. Our friendship took off from thereon itself, mainly because apart from the common love for cricket, there was a lot of commonalities in our likes and our sense of humour. Since then, I am hardly allowed to stay in a hotel in Yorkshire, unless it is of course for commentary work or when I was touring with the Indian team when it is mandatory staying with the commentary crew and the team.

One thing for sure is that the role of Maryam, his wife and simply Bhabhi to all of us, cannot be forgotten. She willingly and happily looked after all the cricketers from India and Pakistan, strangers to her, even when Solly was out at work and fed them like her own family. Solly's parents, his brother and the entire family were behind him as he looked after all the young, hungry cricketers from India and Pakistan. So, compliments to them as well as a big thank you for looking after these cricketers, some of whom later went on to represent their countries.

It is wonderful to know that the book featuring his life is being brought out which will inform the world of many of the details of his early life, which is not known to many, and throw a light about the struggles that he had to undergo. It would be terrific, if his services to the game could be recognised with perhaps an honourary life membership of his beloved Yorkshire County Cricket Club.

I am looking forward to reading the book, and the life story of my dear friend, Solly Bhai, as I call him.

Sunil Manohar Gavaskar
(Former Captain of Indian Cricket Team)
March 12, 2024

Solly Adam: Guardian Angel in True Spirits

I am greatly honoured to write a foreword for the biography of one of the rarest personalities in the history of cricket. Like several other cricketers of the sub-continent, I am also fortunate to be a friend of Solly. In fact, Solly is more than a friend to me; he is akin to my elder brother. Affectionately known as 'Solly Bhai' among the cricketing circles in Pakistan and India, Solly has played the role of a guardian angel for countless cricketers over the past five decades in England. Solly's impact was not confined to the sub-continent alone, as he swathed the hearts of English cricketers in the leagues as well, and in his protective guidance, numerous local young talents have been nurtured. His inclusive temperament has earned him the reputation of a true global citizen, as he extended his spirit of brotherhood far beyond regional boundaries, and belief systems. Hence, the title of the book, Solly Adam – Beyond Boundaries, is apt to represent the persona of Solly.

The life journey of Solly is marked by the personal struggles of his family since childhood. Having been a child of parents who were condemned to be refugees with absolutely nothing in hand, his transformation into a legendary club cricketer and a prominent businessman, would be a testament to the incredible power of human potential and resilience against adversity. With the heavenly blessings of the Almighty for giving me the opportunities to play cricket worldwide, I can certainly say with full confidence that Solly Bhai stands out as a unique figure in his selfless dedication to the sport, and for his support to his fellow cricketers. The contribution of Solly in shaping the careers of numerous Pakistani cricketers was so immense that many young talents have been elevated from domestic cricket to that of international eminence, under the guidance and support of Solly. There were countless occasions where Solly facilitated club signings, accommodation, and employment opportunities for cricketers from the sub-continent. Notably, some of the great luminaries like Abdul Qadir and Iqbal Qasim were initially inducted to league cricket by Solly during their early careers; the experience of playing in English conditions was so significant for them to sharpen their cricketing talents to achieve their triumphs on international stage in the subsequent years.

My affinity with Solly dates to 1975 when I visited England to play that year's world cup cricket as a member of Pakistan team. I had just turned eighteen then, and I subsequently joined the Sussex County cricket team, alongside Imran Khan, for the county championship. I continued staying in England to play league cricket, where I played for Bolton CC in the Lancashire League. It was during this period that I became involved in numerous testimonial matches organized by Solly in the northern part of England, and it was through these initiatives from Solly that a great bond of friendship blossomed between us. Those were truly enchanting days when cricketers of Pakistan and India seamlessly played together in various leagues and testimonial matches orchestrated by Solly. The friendship and unity among the cricketers of the subcontinent of the time resembled a close-knit family, and with Solly as the linchpin, we all rose to lead a life of brotherhood in England. I vividly remember Iqbal Qasim being integral to the family of Solly, and their bond has evolved into one that is akin to own brothers. Whenever Solly visits Pakistan, Iqbal would organize a gathering, and I would be honoured to be the first person to receive an invitation to join them; those moments were plenty, and I treasure them forever.

With great pleasure, I also extend my admiration to Vara Vantapati for taking up an arduous task of crafting this astonishing biography of Solly Adam. With his masterly artistic stroke, Vara gives a creative expression to the hardest struggles that Solly carried forth in his life, combining them with the sweetest fruits of his resultant successes and achievements. With this book, several known and unknown facts of history will see the light of the day, and I hope that through this book, Solly breathes a new life that enlivens him for the generations to come.

Lastly, I pray to God to bestow health, wealth, and happiness upon Solly Bhai and his family.

Javed Miandad
(Former Captain of Pakistani Cricket Team)
February 19, 2024

Table of Contents

PROLOGUE

Life is bouquet of experiences and knowledges. Every rise and fall in our lives present us with a mixture of joys, worries, curiosities, and desires. The greatest human inventions and achievements take place, when people preserve what they have, and struggle to explore for something new, and unknown. In this process, we come across the solutions to many unresolvable problems. This is the beauty of life – which is full of love and hatred, danger and daring, pain and pleasure, peace and violence, dreams and responsibilities, and destruction and creation. Life is a swing of fleeting moments and ever-lasting experiences.

The long journey of Solly Adam, whom all his near and dear ones, particularly his cricket fraternity, lovingly call as Solly Bhai, is a living account of existential struggle of an individual for humanity in its fullest form. He challenged the worst that was conferred upon him by nature and commanded the best of human potentials for leading a compassionate life for himself as well as for the world at large. In his presence, nature personifies as mother and guards her children, showering warmth of her love and affection, under her protective wings against her evil predators. He became a refugee due to circumstances, but only to become a refuge for countless people, living amidst common people; he is a commoner amongst commoners. However, his extraordinary zeal, compassionate heart and ever invigorating leadership is known to all those who have excelled in international cricket; he is a star of the stars.

No one would have thought that a boy of less than 7 years old, the young Solly, who had lost his home and everything, cursed by the circumstances of time, who became a refugee in one's own county, could be able to find his fortunes against all odds, to emerge as one amongst the best in his forties. Like lakhs of Muslim families in India during partition, the family of Solly Bhai too was deported to Pakistan in view of their religious identity and their familial connection with some of the relatives in Pakistan. Losing everything that their family inherited from his forefathers in India, the young Solly, with his younger sister and parents were destined to migrate to Pakistan; they endlessly walked through hot sands of Thar Desert for three long days and nights, till they reached Pakistan. On their way to Pakistan, they survived upon the benevolence of the country people, who provided them with whatever food and water they had and gave them shelter. After a formative period in Pakistan, against all odds, Solly and his family again migrated to England, and he finally found his fortune there both as a successful businessman and a star club cricketer, and emerged as a big brother to assist and guide all those from South Asia (India and Pakistan) who wanted to find their fortunes in England; he is a real brother figure for several Asians in England, and he is affectionately called Solly Bhai by all.

While historical circumstances compelled him to diverge from the path of cricket that was most dear to his heart, to find fortune in business as an entrepreneur, his heart continued to beat for cricket where he finally made his indelible mark as a player, mentor, and guide to cricketers across South Asia and even expanded his business into the domain of sports. He simultaneously fulfilled both the needs of his heart as well as the material needs of his self and family. While his business satisfied his everyday existential needs, cricket became next only to religion for him; he is equally successful in both the fields of business and cricket. In fact, Solly Bhai's world view for universal humanity has been shaped by his endeavour to nurture both his body and soul, and his struggles were directed in search of a home and a homeland for himself, and for his family.

Solly Bhai is the first Asian to start a petrol station business in England, and he sheltered and assisted several Asians to start such businesses in UK. A few amongst those who received his assistance in business, later, went on to emerge as successful businessmen. When he landed at Liverpool in England by sea in Caledonian Ship on the October 30, 1963, he was left with merely a £1 in his pocket. Ever since then, he began his struggles, and accomplished a remarkable feat of attaining an annual turnover of over millions of pounds from all his business firms combined—an endeavour which is beyond the reach of an ordinary man. He has also been a mentor and guide to several individuals to make their foray into several businesses and is now a prominent figure in business circles in the Northern England. More than a king, Solly Bhai is a king maker, who spreads the empire without becoming the king.

Solly Bhai, the name is also a signature reference for all those non-English cricket stars, mainly from Asian sub-continent, who played for league cricket in England; his house in England is a haven of cricket stars of the world for three decades. In this journey, most of the world-renowned cricket stars from India and Pakistan have been friends with Solly Bhai. They include, Sunil Gavaskar, Sachin Tendulkar, Kapil Dev, Gundappa Vishwanath, Mohinder Amarnath, Brijesh Patel, Syed Kirmani, Bishan Singh Bedi, Dilip Vengsarkar, Roger Binny, Dilip Doshi, Madan Lal, Mohammad Azharuddin, Kiran More, Vinod Kambli, VVS Laxman, Sourav Ganguly, Rahul Dravid, Chandrakanth Pandit, Abey Kuruvilla, Wasim Jaffer, Amol Majumdar, Paras Mhambray, Jatin Paranjape, Surinder Amarnath, Suru Nayak, Mohammad Kaif, etc., of India; and Imran Khan, Javed Miandad, Wasim Akram, Abdul Qadir, Iqbal Qasim, Majid Jahangir Khan, Wasim Raja, Anwar Khan, Sarfaraz Nawaz, Saeed Anwar, Shahid Afridi, Inzamam-ul-haq, Saqlain Mushtaq, and many others from Pakistan. Solly Bhai also cherished his friendship with some of the other renowned cricketers of the world; they include Geoffrey Boycott, Gary Sobers, Richard Hadlee, Alvin Kallicharan, Darren Gough, Chris Silverwood, Brian Close, Michael Vaughan, David Bairstow and many more. It is joyful surprise to know that Solly Bhai cherished fifty years of his intimate friendship with the two cricket legends and all-time greats, Sunil Gavaskar, and Imran Khan, who respectively led the teams of India and Pakistan. Solly Bhai also played with some of the greatest and most renowned cricketers of the world.

As 'only a jeweller knows the true worth of a diamond,' Solly Bhai discovered several young talents, and being a player, and leader-organiser, he had nurtured some of them into becoming cricket legends under his guidance. To that effect, he facilitated signing contracts for over 300 players from India and Pakistan into different clubs and leagues in England, and he would even accommodate many of them in his houses. His house was always flooded with cricketers, and there was a time when 15-20 cricketers used to stay in his house, while other players were accommodated by him in different places. With this, his popularity grew beyond England, and became more popular among the cricketers of the Asian sub-continent. Noticing his role and significance in signing cricketers for different leagues, a few senior cricketers who travelled with him in this long journey of life, recognized his contribution at par with Kerry Packer and his World Series Cricket (WSC). It was said that, while WSC was a professional commercial competition that staged many international cricketers across the world between 1977 and 1979, Solly Bhai volunteered to do the same in the same scale, or at an even bigger scale, yet in non-commercial terms. His contributions are not merely in the realm of cricket, but in all the other areas of human life, including business and social service. However, it was not such an easy task for him, as he had to engage in the struggles for his own existence, as he hailed from humble family, while extending his helping hand to those in need. While doing so, he transcended the boundaries of time and space, and hence the title of the book, 'Solly Adam - Beyond Boundaries.' In this context, the life of Solly Bhai exemplifies what Frederick

Douglass said, "You are not judged by the height you have risen, but from the depth you have climbed."

The interesting difference between him and other professional players is that most players do their best in their days of youth, and retire by their forties, while Solly Bhai did his best in his forties and continued to lead the team of youngsters towards winning the trophies. Solly Bhai did not merely nourish his best talents to become a good player, a good businessman and finally, a good human being, but he disseminated the seeds of talents and kindness across the world, particularly in the South Asian subcontinent. He recognised the best talents in cricket and inducted them into the cricket world of England. Solly Bhai's initiative in signing Sachin for the Yorkshire County is part of his attempt to broaden the scope in the county, as the admission to the county till then was exclusive to the cricketer of the Yorkshire region. With Sachin's signing to the Yorkshire County, he broke a century long rule, and for which Solly Bhai was referred by the media, as "the man who brought Sachin to Yorkshire."

Commencing in the Dewsbury and District League, Solly Bhai ascended to the role of a triumphant captain in both the Central Yorkshire League and Bradford League. His cricketing journey reached its pinnacle as he donned the colours of the Minor County team 'Cumberland' at the age of 46, marking a remarkable chapter in his cricketing odyssey. However, he again came back to play for league cricket, and has continued to be associated with leagues, till his retirement. In recognition of his services to cricket and business, he has had the rarest opportunity to receive an invitation from none other than 'Her Majesty Queen Elizabeth' herself for a Garden Tea Party at Buckingham Palace in 2015.

Hence, this biography of this rare generous has come into existence. Though it has been written with an intention to instil confidence among, otherwise wavering selves of today's generation, the book also helps in unearthing some of the buried histories of the cricket world. To that end, it is also an important source for understanding the history of cricket. For writing this biography, I depended heavily upon various source materials such as archives of newspaper articles and photographs, history books, biographies of other historical personalities, field notes, including interviews with his family members and cricketers. A major portion of factual details for this biography has been drawn from the hero of this book, Solly Bhai, who spoke at length about his experiences and recorded them, patiently responding to our questionnaire that was designed to meet the requirement of each chapter of the book. So, I chose to write this book in first person narrative, not merely as a token of respect to Solly Bhai for his contribution to the book, but this book also warrants a new method of writing biography in an autobiographical fashion. Despite its first-person account, I like to call it a biography, because its form, narrative structure, poetic imagery, symbolisms, and other aesthetic qualities of the book are purely mine. Hence, this is a biography of an ordinary man's extraordinary life account.

-Vara Vantapati

The Life of Solly Adam: In His Own Words

CHILDHOOD

Journey in Exile

Like a birds' nest hurled down in a whirlwind, my family had fallen apart due to circumstances of the time. At a time when light dawned upon the lives of millions of Indians with independence from British on August 15, 1947, darkness paraded in broad daylight among the lives of several others with the partition of the country into India and Pakistan. Ours was one such family thrown into the throes of partition. Like voyagers on board suddenly woken up from deep slumber to the sudden jerk of a smoothly sailing ship, we all tumbled. Overnight, we became refugees in our own country, even as my own grandfather continued to be a citizen of newly found India. I was barely seven-years old with a two-year old sister and healthy and unwavering parents, when we were all ripped apart from my grandfather and our ancestral home in a tiny village called Simlak in Gujarat of India today.

The moving images of a relentless police officer picking us all up, handcuffing my father around 5 or 6 o' clock in the evening, and dumping of all the four of us—my younger sister and I, my mother and father—by a police jeep right into the dreary sands of the Thar Desert in the same night of 1952, still haunts me. It is impossible to erase from my memory the tremors of the shock that I experienced as a child which continue to tremble me even to this day; I am now in my late seventies, and yet, these nightmarish memories are as fresh as if they are of yesterday's.

1

It was Khokhra Par, Karachi, I think, that borders India and Pakistan where we were finally dumped, our handcuffs taken off and asked to 'go back' to Pakistan. With this, from enjoying a more than moderately comfortable life that we lived until then, we suddenly became homeless and penniless without food, clothing, shelter, and national identity. At that moment, physical health, and unflinching determination to overcome all natural as well as man-made hurdles were the only wealth that our parents had, and me and my younger sister were their only hope for tomorrow. With my father carrying my little sister, Haseena, on his shoulder and I holding my mother's finger, we began our new sojourn as refugees to seek new fortunes against the vaulting tides of time. From right amidst Indian military check posts, piercing through the thickest of the darkness of night and breaking through the fear invoking silences of the desert, we started walking towards Pakistan.

Nature, the destroyer of glorious lives and preserver of the remnants of that destruction, consoled us in these worst times of our destitution. Like a mother hen to her chicks at a time of impending danger, mother nature took us all under her vast protective wings where we transcended every narrow domestic wall of destruction and emerged into truly universal beings. Free from every human construction of caste, class, race, religion and ethnicities of region and nation, with the limitless sky as our only limit, we continued our life's sojourn. The creaking of cricket and other insects seamlessly merged with the whisking sounds of our moving feet in the sand, consoling us. The cold touch of sand at night provided comfort to our untiring walking feet. We walked and walked, too tired to even find any human settlements to rest and shelter. Finally, we reached a small village and slept under a cattle-shed thanks to the kind reception of a poor peasant, who also provided us with some food to eat and water to drink. Without a penny in hand and no cloths other than those on our back, our uninterrupted journey continued, exclusively on the benevolence of villagers on the way, for three long hot and tiresome days and three long fearsome nights, till we finally reached Pakistan.

Life at Simlak, India: The Land of My Ancestors

Back home at Simlak, an exclusive Muslim settlement of just over fifty houses in Navsari District, near Surat town in Gujarat of British India, we were a very happy joint family enjoying great social respect with an economic status of a middle to rich class. My father, Saeed Adam, was the third child among six sons and three daughters of my grand-father, Ibrahim Suleman Adam, who owned a flour mill in a nearby small town, Dabhel; he was owned a car to be hired out for weddings and ran a local bus service. Into such a happy and prosperous family, I was born in 1945. Since I was the first grandson to be born in my paternal family, I was named after my grandfather Suleman, whereas my family name was Adam and hence my name became Suleman Adam. However, my mother called me Solly and so did everyone else. In due course I settled with the name Solly, and my near and dear ones call me Solly Bhai.

Except a mosque, there was no other public space at Simlak, no Madrasa nor school. The nearest school and Madrasa were at Dabhel, a cultural centre about a quarter mile away from Simlak. Those who know the importance of education, knowledge of Quran and Arabic language, would send their children to Dabhel for schooling once they grew up a little. Around 400 to 500 children from nearby villages used to attend school and Madrasa at Dabhel, which was also a centre of sports and games. I never attended school nor Madrasa, as I was a happy-go-lucky child and was also not yet old enough to attend school then. There were good open fields at Dabhel where the children and the youth engaged in sports and games, and where I had the earliest experience of playing and watching cricket. Meanwhile, my mother gave birth to two baby-girls, but they both passed away owing to ill-health. Deeply shaken by this tragic incident, my mother grew anxious about keeping us alive;

3

she would get anxious even if we were affected by a little cold or a fever. But my life at Simlak was extremely joyful with friends such as Rashid Desai, Laaki, Yousuf Naana and several others, with not a worry for tomorrow.

Failed Attempts to Find One's Own Home

The smooth playful life of my childhood at Simlak got interrupted with the sudden and unfortunate death of my grandmother, and then the consequent remarriage of my grandfather with another woman; later, they together had three daughters and three sons. Our stable joint family began to crumble, owing to this remarriage that brought upon a sense of embarrassment on our family members; by then my grandfather was old, and had children and grandchildren living in the same house. With this, all my uncles including my father began declaring independence, and eventually, everyone left our ancestral home. One of my paternal aunts named Ayesha Gardee, my father's sister, was then living in Lahore, owing to her marriage with a man from a rich business family of Gardee; they owned a huge factory, which required labour force, and had recruited several labourers from our village.

The workers in that factory were all provided with housing accommodation to stay, mosque to pray, and a school for their children to study and all other amenities such as hospital, sports-field, including a shopping centre, etc., for workers and their families; they had their own township called Gardeeabad, named after their family. So, except one uncle, who was next to my father, and two aunts who decided to stay back at home, rest of my four uncles, including my father moved to Lahore, in today's Pakistan, in 1950 to work in my aunt's factory. We were given accommodation in the residential quarters meant for the factory workers. After working for a while, my father began to feel uneasy about him being treated the same way as those of other workers; he might have expected some preferential treatment as the brother-in-law

4

of the owner of the factory and he was embarrassed, in specific, about being checked by the security every day after work.

So, my father decided to go back to India in 1951 and informed my grandfather of his decision. We were sailing back to Bombay with the intention of taking a road trip from there to Simlak. But before we reached India, somebody, probably a relative of us, complained to the Indian Government that we were trying to enter India illegally from Pakistan, because by then the country had been partitioned into two independent countries. It was 1951 I think, and there was a serious curb on the mobility of the populations across the borders by the police through informal means, and yet no proper formal system was in place to recognise citizenship, passport, etc. The police went to my house at Simlak, enquired about our coming back to India and asked our grandfather to inform us to report at Surat Police Station once we landed in India.

Fearing impending danger, my grandfather sent a communication to Bombay dock, warning us from going to our home; we were advised to go to Daman, an island located 2-3 hours of sailing distance from Bombay. Daman, by then, was under the jurisdiction of Portuguese, where there was no control of Indian Government, and hence we could find some temporary refuge there and avoid any form of untoward incarceration in the hands of the Government of India. My grandfather also arranged some money and other articles sufficient for us to live in Daman for some time. So, we went to Daman from Bombay, and lived there for quite some time, intending to wait till the situation in India had improved a bit. Our life in Daman was very happy, without much to say or do.

When we felt that there was some normalcy in India, we sailed back to India in 1952 and happily reunited with our ancestral family at Simlak. I was extremely delighted to reconnect with my friends and was immersed in playing with them. My father and uncle returned to working at my grandfather's flour mill and began looking after the occasional wedding car rental service. This joy continued for some time until one day we woke up to a knock on our door by a police officer; we had been called to report at Surat police station. To alleviate our fears and thereby comforting us to cooperate with them, the police officer gave us a suggestive nod that it was merely formal inquiry, and we had nothing to worry about.

So, the following day, we made plans to see the police at Surat in the early office hours so that we could catch a movie after the formal verification. We all were excited to watch the movie, *Aan*, that was made in 1952 and was being screened then in some theatre in Surat in the same year, starring Dilip Kumar and Madhubala. Accordingly, we reached the police station early in the morning in our grandfather's car, driven by our uncle Mohammed to report there. But the police officer made us wait; we waited and waited from morning till 7'o clock in the evening, when suddenly a jeep with some police personnel entered the station. As soon as the jeep reached the station, a bunch of policemen hurried us all to get into the jeep, handcuffing both hands of my father. This was how we were carried in the jeep and dumped in the India-Pakistan border, Khokhra Par, and from there we eventually reached Lahore on foot.

Life at Lahore

We went back to my aunt's place in Lahore. They were kind enough to give us shelter and a job, as before, to my father in their factory with a salary of mere 54 Pakistani rupees per month; it was probably some machine cleaning job. My other uncles, including the eldest one whose daughter I married later, also moved there. Gradually, we started leading a happy life. The temperature of summer in Lahore in those days was very hot, reaching nearly up to 50 degrees Celsius. As there were no fans nor air conditioners, I remember my mom pouring water on the walls in bedroom to cool down the room, and my sister and me playing with that water. I had always been playful, and my fascination for games grew more intense as I grew up. I never showed any interest in studies, despite my parents' insistence on studies and its importance for intellectual and financial progress. But I just watched and played cricket there, doing nothing about studies. Though occasionally I used to attend school that was meant for the children of the factory workers, I did not remember learning anything from there.

Meanwhile, my mother gave birth to two baby boys, and they were named Ibrahim and Afzal. Now, ours was a happy family of six, and I was joyous to play with my sister and two baby brothers, under the protective care, guidance and love of our mother and father. But, for the reasons explained earlier, my father was not happy to work in his sister's factory; he sought for self-respect. His thoughts began lingering around finding a way out. With the help of his friends in Lahore, he made contacts with someone in Karachi, and decided to move there. One night in 1954, we quietly took a taxi to Lahore railway station, and from there a train to Karachi, which was 5 hours away.

Life at Natal Colony, Karachi

Upon reaching Karachi, we again came back to ground zero with no shelter, nor a source of income for our livelihood. The contact on whose assurance my father moved to Karachi put us into a very tiny room of two square metres area beneath the staircase of a building, without any ventilation, where all six of us settled down. There was no bathroom, nor any toilets; just outside the room in which we stayed, there was a drainage covered with a square shaped lid, where we used to lift the lid off to defecate, and bathe there itself. As the house owner was from Dabhel, a village next to Simlak, there was some respite for us as he offered separate showering facility for my mother.

After a few days, my father joined as a worker in *Dadabhai Aluminium Factory* in 1954 for a monthly salary of 90 Pakistani Rupees. In his very first working day in the factory, my father had an encounter with the

7

boss of the company. The boss on his return from Japan tour reached the factory at late night when my father was on his night shift toiling very hard against the sweltering heat of the plant furnace. Sensing that my father was not a local Pathan as, unlike my father, Pathans were very strong and could work in any kind of an environment, he was curious to know who my father was and inquired. Hearing my father's name as 'Saeed Adam,' the boss asked whether he was in anyway related to Mr. Gardee. Since then, my father received good respect from everyone in the factory.

But we continued to stay in the same tiny room with poor living condition. Living in unhygienic conditions, both my brothers were infected with chicken pox. Due to his low income, my father could not afford proper medical treatment for my brothers. We took them to a local government hospital, but that did not help us; the infection spread more and more leading to the tragic death of both my brothers, just one week apart. Since it was a new settlement, there was not even a graveyard for Gujarati Muslims in the town. With the death of my brother, all Gujarati Muslims of Karachi came together instantly to purchase a piece of land, and then the bodies of both my brothers were buried in that land. This is how a graveyard for the Gujarati Muslims came to existence in the Nazimabad locality of Karachi. Around this time, they also formed a society called *Gujarati Muslim Welfare Society*. Somebody who felt sympathetic to our poor living condition that led to the death of both my little brothers, offered us with a little better accommodation, a room with a bathroom and a toilet, near Jiya Manzil of Bansroad, which was a few yards away from the room where we were living earlier. Meanwhile, a Gujarati couple from South-Africa came forward to build houses for factory workers of our community.

This couple built a colony with 54 houses, structuring it into four blocks, A, B, D and E, and by1954 all the houses were allotted to the Gujarati Muslims working for various factories in Karachi; they named it

Natal Colony, after a place in South-Africa from where they hailed. The houses were well built with a spacious room, kitchen, bathroom, and a toilet, along with the facilities like electricity and water; the colony also had a school, hospital, playground, etc. Since we were Gujarati Muslims, we also got a house to stay there in 1954. There were 15 houses in Block-A where we were allotted house no. 4, and all the 15 families used to live as one extended family, helping each other in need. The house was given for free, but one had to contribute a maintenance charge of Rs. 10/- per month. But many of the families could not afford to pay even that amount towards maintenance, which sometimes was waived off by the society on compassionate grounds.

Again, we were all living happily, and my father wanted to enrol me into a school, but he could not afford to pay the fee as his income was insufficient even to meet the living expenses of our family. Two neighbour aunts, one Zubeda Desai, wife of Ghulam Desai, who was the resident of the house no. 6 and Amanapa Sheik, wife of Khalil Bhai, of house no. 7 were of a great help to my mother in every way, including offering financial assistance. The salary that we got would run out by 21st of every month, and aunt Amanapa, whose husband was working in a bank, would lend some money to us every month without fail, which would be cleared upon my father getting salary in the following month. It was Aunt Zubeda who used to lend Rs. 10/- every month towards maintenance that also would be cleared on the first of every month. The three of them used to live like own sisters, each assisting in their care for other's families; they used to share food and shelter. Our neighbour in house no. 5, Yousuf Jasat had day shifts, while my father had night shifts in the factory. He was so kind-hearted that after his shift, Yousuf bhai used to lend his cycle to my father every day to go to factory, which was 4-5 kms from our house. It was in the Natal Colony that my mother again gave birth to another son in 1957 who was named Younus. The trauma of losing four children (two daughter and two sons) still haunts her; she was extremely concerned about the health of this newborn boy. She would feel frightened even if my brother caught the slightest hint of fever or cold and would immediately ask me to go to the nearby mosque and request every worshiper in the mosque to pray for the recovery of my brother from his ill-health. I was very sincere to her plea and act accordingly. I was extremely fond of my little brother and took the greatest care of him all through my life.

In such a vulnerable situation, it was difficult for my father to afford good education for my sister and me. But one day, I had the opportunity to attend one Madrasa that conducts evening classes for school children. Along with other children of our locality, I began attending classes there, and was fascinated with the teachings of the *Imam* of that Madrasa, Hafiz Patel, who later migrated to England and became very popular there; he established a big *Jamaat* (Markaz) of Europe in England. He was my first teacher, and Quran and other theological lessons were my first learnings. It was in Natal Colony and with the teachings of such a revered scholar that I was blessed to shape my moral, ethical, and intellectual being, and had really learnt how to read Quran there. Somehow, my parents finally admitted me to a school named Hosainy school in Nazimabad which offers free education for about 25 poor students in a year. I was admitted to that school in free quota as my father's income was very low. There was a playground opposite to the school where students and youth used to play cricket and other games; there was also a ground inside the school premises where we used to play cricket.

Despite my parents' desire and endeavour to give the best of education to me, somehow, I was not inspired by education; the heat beat to the rhythm of sports and games; I was particularly a cricket buff.

Though I was attending school, I was not good at studies; I picked up cricket with a lot of interest. Some youth of our colony like Ahmed Adam (Chacha), Yousuf Adam (Chacha), Yakub Darsot, Mohammad Darsot, Ghulam Desai, Nakhuda, Yousuf Bhai and Moosa Bhai, founded 'Natal Colony Cricket Club' whose members primarily had Gujarati origin, where Hafiz Patel, who was also the *Imam* of the *Madrasa* of the colony and my first teacher, was the captain of the team. I was extremely fascinated to be a part of the club, but I was not old enough to play for club cricket. Seeing my enthusiasm, the club team used to offer me a chance to play whenever there was a shortage of a player. Meanwhile I also founded 'Natal Colony Junior Cricket Club' for my age group of 10-13 years; several junior players joined the club and cricket emerged as a major game of the town. My interest towards cricket grew day by day, though I was also playing other games like *Gillidanda, Marbles, Pittu*, etc., and flying kites. We had several bright cricketers like Abdul, Saleem, Salahuddin, Bashir, Khayyum and Arif in our junior team, I used to have fun playing cricket with them. I enjoyed playing and watching cricket in my school days; I lead the junior club, while also playing for the seniors, and over a period I came to represent the senior Natal Colony Cricket Club as a captain of the team.

The Hosainy school in which I was studying was a girl's school, and boys could not continue their studies there after the fourth standard. After completing my fourth, I had to find a school for boys to further my education, for which I had to clear a test. Since I was not good at studies, I was not confident to clear the test to get promoted to fifth standard. A friend named Salahuddin was of immense help in clearing the test; he was originally from Deccan-Hyderabad and was staying in the House 9 of Block- B. Anyhow, I could save my admission and moved to the boys' school, otherwise I would have had to drop my studies after fourth standard. But, unlike the previous school, which was for free, in the new school that I got promoted to, I had to pay tuition fee. I was a bit hesitant to study further, but my parents wanted me to study. It was so difficult for me to adjust to the fifth standard, but I was doing my best. Alongside this, I also wanted to work to help my family and pay my school fee.

There was a place near us where they did the shoe work, and I took up a job there. This is how I tried my best as a boy to relieve some amount of the burden of my family.

Vacation at Aunt's Home in Lahore: A Few Good Old Days

After settling down in Karachi, we got reconnected with our aunt, Ayesha Gardee, in Lahore. During vacation, my aunt would invite us, and we used to visit her. Our aunt was so fond of children, all our cousins, Younus, Rashid, Yousuf, Mohammad Ali, Rukiya, Khatija, Fatima, Memuna and Zara would join there to spend the entire vacation. But unlike earlier when our father was a worker in their factory, now we were her guests and she, our host. It was an experience of luxury and thrill to spend time at her home in Lahore. The house had more facilities than that of a five-star hotel with several workers attending to us; there were about 20-30 rooms in that house, with several spacious halls, a huge garden, and a huge kitchen in which all the refrigerators were stuffed with varieties of fruits, ice creams, cold-drinks, etc. We used to eat and drink whatever and wherever we wanted and played; we had every freedom and there were no restrictions to eating and playing. Back home we were lucky to get even a biscuit and tea, but here it was in abundance, we used to get everything of our choice from cakes, biscuits, bread and jam, and ice-creams to fruits, eggs, and meat. I was eager to wait for the vacation to be announced, and I would love going there. As and when vacation was announced, we used to get a train from Karachi at night and reach Lahore by morning, and some car driver would pick us from station and drive us from there to home. My parents would visit occasionally, but I used to be there during every vacation without fail. I was fond of Coca-Cola and would drink as much as I could. Each time we passed by the kitchen, we would just open the fridge and drink aplenty. If we did not find an opener at times, we used to open it by using our teeth and drink. Beside the fridge, there was a stock of Coca-Cola bottles lying out in crates; in the absence of bottles in the fridge, we sometimes used to drink it in room temperature, directly from the crates; we were that mad about coke.

All of us children would sometimes go around the town and eat from bakeries and hotels. There were several cars, and drivers would take us wherever we want; I still remember us parking the car in front of the bakery 'Shezan' in Lahore and eating cakes from there. I had lot of fun playing with our cousins; once when we were playing in the cricket field of our aunt, the last toe of my feet accidentally fell under the lawn roller, when the daughter of my aunt tried to move the roller, I lost my last toe. Despite this, the vacations spent at my aunt's home in Lahore were one of the best times of my life, and even to this day we talk about those days with fond nostalgia whenever I meet my cousins.

Migration to England

Besides my studies and working, I continued watching and playing cricket as well. My natural love for sports and cricket was increasing and I was regularly watching and playing cricket. It was exactly the very beginning of my Matric year when my father was planning to go to England, upon the advice and assistance of my aunt, Ayesha Gardee, who had just then visited England and realised the abundant opportunities there for us to lead a safe and prosperous life. She called her brothers and said, "I want all of you to go to England and make your living there." She also offered air fare for all my uncles and my father and because of that all of them went to England one after the other, beginning with my uncle, Ahmed Chacha in 1962. Few months after my father reaching England and settling down there in a company, he made arrangement for me to go to England.

Finally, I got my passport ready, dropped my Matric studies in the middle of the academic year and went to England by sea. It was a great journey that took an entire fortnight; I boarded the ship on October 14, 1963, at Karachi and landed at Liverpool in England on October 30, 1963. It was very painful for me to leave my mother, sister and brother in the Natal Colony and go to England; eventually they also moved to England and happily joined us. Despite our happy and prosperous life in England, I miss Karachi and Natal Colony a lot because that was the lovely place where I lived the formative phase of my life. I still miss a lot the atmosphere near the school, hospital, playground, and the people of the colony who shared whatever little they had for each other's well-being. This shaped my consciousness in a way that I followed this belief throughout my life, *the pleasure of sharing is the best of all pleasures.*

MY VOYAGE TO ENGLAND

Leaving my mother, sister, and brother behind at Natal Colony in Karachi, I finally boarded the Caledonia ship to England on October 14, 1963, at Karachi Dock, with a heavy heart; one of my paternal uncles, Abdul Hai Adam, who later became my father-in-law, also came to see me off. In fact, it was this uncle, who arranged the ship ticket to England for me and gave me a currency exchange of 3 pounds with a free hand to spend the money as I wish. Three pounds was a huge thing in those days, as the currency exchange rate for each British pound then was 13 Pakistani Rupees. To meet out these expenses, my father must have sent some money to my uncle, who might have added some more money to it to make these arrangements for my journey. The ship was already crowded with several Indians, as the starting point of the ship was at Bombay, and Karachi was its second pick-up point. The neighbourhood uncle (Zubeda Apa's Father) in flat no. 6 of the Natal Colony was an Officer of the Customs at Karachi Sea port; he helped me in carrying the extra luggage, without any custom and handling charges. I got into the ship with loads of luggage, everything that were required for a house in England like clothes, blankets, pillowcases, dishes, and pans, including some cooking stuff for kitchen. Since there were luggage restrictions in the flight by which my uncle, my cousin, and my father, came to England, and even my aunt was about to fly after a few days, the burden of carrying the luggage of the entire family fell upon me. Keeping the luggage in its respective place, I settled down on my seat just to close my eyes, when the ship slowly moved.

My entire childhood miraculously flashed before my eyes, like a waking dream; everything and everyone at Natal Colony— neighbourhood uncles and aunts who were there to share the joy of our triumphs, offer compassion in our struggles for existence, my playmates with their fun and frolics, and their naughtiness that often led to intermittent tragedies during play, cricket tournaments in regular intervals, three factory sirens and five calls of Azaan, followed by the consequent movement of the workers in and out of the factories, and worshipers in and out of the mosques, every single day without fail, whatever happens, whoever dies and whoever is born etc.—including all my family members and friends at Simlak in India and Lahore in Pakistan, drifted before my eyes; for a moment, I felt as if it has happened yesterday. I remember it for ever, as I witnessed it, being an integral part of its making as well as its unmaking, and hence it is the story of my own, and the people with whom I cherished my life. Immersed in these thoughts, I did not get off my seat for the first couple of days, other than for daily routines of three meals a day and things related to nature calls.

However, as the ship proceeded through the Atlantic Ocean, cutting across Arabian currents of the Indian Ocean, I began realizing the splendidness of the journey that I was being part of. I began exploring the ocean around the ship in this journey by sea. In the past, I had sailed a couple times by sea between Karachi and Bombay, and once between Bombay and Daman. But that was a short journey, involving a couple of hours by ship, which was a little bigger than a boat; it was a whole lofty vessel, having only one hall like area with the benches for the passengers to recline on. But this voyage to England was completely different; it was an unbelievable and unforgettable journey, to sail for such a long time, and in such a huge ship that I had never imagined. I was amazed to see as huge a ship as this; it was a world-in-itself, being built in several floors; there were restaurants of all ranges, refreshment clubs, dancing halls, casino, and gambling centres etc., including common dining halls, toilets, and bathrooms; there was also a gym, cycling velodrome and a swimming pool on the top floor. It was an altogether new experience for me, and I either spent my time awestruck looking at them or retreated to the deck to silently sit in one place. This was my earliest exposition to the ways and views of a new world, the European world, and its inventions and infrastructural wealth.

Fear of strange circumstances, and not being aware of the passenger's privileged rights, I could not dare to move around freely and would couch in the corner of the deck to watch silently the movement of the people and observe the things in surprise. I was astonished to see the water that appear blue and transparent in the swimming pool and the dive of the people into it, but I never dared to join them to take even a dip. I was also not aware of how to take shower, nor using bathtub, as my knowledge of bath till then was only by using bucket and dipper; with this sudden appearance of shower and a tub in the bathrooms of the ship, I was perplexed, not knowing what to do. As a result, I hardly took bath in the entire ship journey. It was for the first time in my life that I had experienced eating from a restaurant of this kind as an adolescent. Before this I had an opportunity of eating from hotels and bakeries as a child at my aunt's place in Lahore. But I was not aware of the nitty-gritties of eating in European way, as being children, we had the freedom of eating whatever, however and how much ever we wanted and had never been trained with any table manners. With this new opportunity of eating from the restaurant in the ship, I would hurry to place an order for ice-cream first, before even the waiter asked for our choice of food, only then I would go for the main course, which was an unconventional way of eating. I would do that way because I was very fond of ice-creams, cakes and other desserts, and soft drinks, much more than regular food. The people in the restaurant would give an awkward smile; some of them would even giggle at me for being crude at my dining.

As the days went by, I came to know many people in the ship, and they became my companions; I shared some of the best moments with them. I used to join them in their dining, talking, singing, dancing and even in plays and merry making; it was also a learning experience in their association, where they would teach me not only the ways of taking shower, bathing in the tub etc., but also dining conventions of eating, beginning with soup, followed by main course and then dessert in the end. By then, we had just reached the Port of Aden (Yemen), where the ship had a break stop for a few hours. I got down from the ship, along with two friends and other passengers on board to see the Aden port and to do some shopping there, as I came to know that the port of Aden was known for imported goods available at cheaper prices; it was in this port that I bought my first watch, which was 'Favre-Leuba' brand, for 1.50 pounds. I had no knowledge of watches, nor its brands, yet I bought it with the advice of those two friends, whose names I now fail to remember. Then I was left with only 1.50 pounds more, which was more than sufficient till I reached England; I had nothing to spend for in the ship, since food and other expenses were included in the ticket price. Major expenditure in the ship was towards casino and other forms of gambling, and I never had any interest in such activities.

It was the day of Diwali by the time we reached Gibraltar port in Spain, which was just one stop before our destination at Liverpool port in England. Since there were many Indians, as the ship started from Bombay in India, the captain of the ship organized Diwali celebrations in the ship, involving singing, dancing, and all sorts of merry making; special foods and sweets were also served. By then I had made some friends from India, and joined the celebrations, to sing and dance upon their request; though I was not a singer, I made up some lines to sing only to do my part in the celebrations. A couple of days after Diwali, we finally landed at Liverpool port in England on October 30, 1963.

Upon landing, I collected all my luggage from the ship, and slowly stepped down on the platform of the Liverpool port. The officer of customs in the port charged its duty of 50 pence towards buying imported watch from Aden. With this, I was left with just only one pound. My father and my kaka (uncle), along with their three friends, Mr. Khan, Sadroo and Kaka Bismillah (from Simlak) came in a big van to the port to pick me up and to collect the heavy luggage. It was snowing heavily, downpouring of the snow that measure about 6 to 9 inches thickness on the ground. We do not see such heavy snow these days, but it was unimaginably high snow, during the October month of the1960s. I could not bear the freezing cold, despite wearing a very thick and long coat, that covered me from head to the toe. We loaded all the luggage into the van, and drove home to Dewsbury, where my father and uncles made their living. It was an amazing journey and I really enjoyed it. Just before I had landed, and in fact I was still on my way to England by ship, when my Aunt Hazra, wife of my youngest paternal uncle, flew to England, and landed on October 21; I had also carried her luggage on the ship. After a few months of reaching England, my mom, my sister, and my brother also joined us sometime in April 1964; they came here by flight. This is the voyage of my family to England, the journey of a refugee to discover a new home of one's own.

EARLY LIFE IN ENGLAND

When I landed in England, we already owned a house, as a collective property of my uncles and my father, since by then, both my father and my uncles were working in a plastic factory named *Burbees*. With my arrival, I became a helping hand to my aunts in cooking and other household works, besides my elder cousin, Masoom. While Masoom and I took over the task of rolling chapattis and toasting them, my aunt would prepare curries. Unlike in Karachi, where my mother would do every household work all by herself, here all the member of the house began to share the work in the house. Because there was no washing machine, nor dish washer in those days, we all had to wash our respective clothes and dishes, all by ourselves, without letting the burden to be fallen on any single individual. This was how we evolved a new way of life, of equal distribution of the labour, and nurtured a modern life, involving the sharing of equal responsibilities in all the matters, including the issues of domestic concern.

The weather in England during those winter days was very cold and freezing. Added to this, the house was also not so well furnished, and it was very difficult for us to withstand the numbing cold in that freezing weather. The floor was not carpeted, nor was there a centralized heating equipment in the house; there was just a coal fireplace in the front room, where all of us gathered to warm ourselves and talk; there were some paraffin heaters in other rooms as well. In that freezing cold, Masoom and I used to sweep and mop the house in every weekend. There was no shower, nor a geyser in the bathroom, so we had to heat water in a metal container on a kiln for bathing and other purposes, for which we used to use bucket and tumbler. Like a popular saying, grass is greener on the other side, I used to feel that all my dreams of a heavenly life in England was an illusion. It was intolerable for me, and I used to groan in the nights; often I resented my state and sought for the mercy of God, the Almighty, to save me from working in that cold.

But soon the remaining members of my family also started landing in England, one after the other, beginning with my mother and my two siblings, followed by my elder uncle and aunt, and their children, and second aunt and her children. By April 1964, all my family members reached England, and we all, my parents, me and my two siblings, along with my three uncles (Ahmed Chacha, Moosa Chacha and Mohammed) and their wives (Aunts) and children, began to live together as one single, large, and unified family of sixteen members. With this, most of the house-hold duties were again taken over by my mother and aunts, freeing children to have their life of freedom and learning.

However, the house was always crowded with people, and by night, we would use every single room of the house for sleeping, where different members of our family were adjusted in different rooms, in which I had chosen to sleep in the attic of the house. Slowly, but steadily, the signs of good days began to show.

My father and uncles were working in factories; they also bought vehicles of their own and used them as taxi to transport workers to the same factory in which they worked and dropped them back in some appointed places. While my father had one 12-seater minibus, my uncle had a van without any seats in it. When I got the driving license, I used to run that minibus for some time to relieve some burden of my father. Some of the weekends, the entire family together used to go for outings; we all used these two vehicles by which the entire family would visit some pleasant sites like Blackpool, Scarborough, Preston and Brislington, in seaside, or in some grasslands, to spend our holiday; we used to carry our food and water from home and eat there, and played and sang.

Socio-economic Life in England

Dewsbury was not yet completely urbanized by then, as the manufacturing industries had just begun to expand into the countries, from its old urban settlements and old centres of industrial production; the roads were well connected with airports, dockyards and to the cities of London, Yorkshire, etc. Dewsbury then was a semi-urban centre. However, there was also seasonal agriculture everywhere that gave an impression of the country. As per the English conditions, the entire plains in our sight were covered in the crops of wheat, that resembled the entire earth being carpeted in lush green during cropping seasons of summers that eventually turned into golden hue as the crop reached the stage of harvest during fall. There were also orchards of apple and other fruits in the hill side, with 'seasonal UK grown produce' such as beetroot, mushrooms, onions, red cabbage, etc. There were farms of cattle for milk and meat, and chickens and eggs; there were also bakeries around us.

In fact, the expanding industrialization and rapidly urbanizing conditions of England became a huge attraction for the people of the world, particularly from Asia and Africa. Since they were formerly the colonies of the British and immigration laws for them were not yet enacted as per 'English Laws and Rules;' nothing was required other than mere passport for people of these countries migrating to England. Because of this, there were several thousand families from these countries that migrated to England during the decades of the 50s and 60s of the twentieth century and found their fortunes here; ours was one such family. The family of the present Prime Minister of England, Rishi Sunak, also hails from these immigrant populations of the former colonies of the British.

There was no availability of the halal meat here, as Muslims had not yet gone into meat business in Dewsbury area by then. So, we used to buy live birds of chicken in lots (10 or 12 birds at once) directly from the farms nearby, or the local supplier would deliver the live chickens at home. I used to remove the skin of the birds clean and cut the meat into pieces. It was such an irritating job, yet it was a lovely thing to live together as one joint family and share the responsibilities equally; it was also a great entertainment for us, as there were so many children in the house with whom I could play and have fun.

Despite semi-urban conditions, wearing traditionally ethnic attires like *salwar kameez* and *pyjamas* by men, or women in *sarees* with blouses were not common in the 1960's England. The first thing that we used to do when we stepped out of the house was to put on trousers and coat and change into the clothes of our choice as and when we returned home. It was a bit uneasy to wear these English clothing, but as days went by, we got accustomed to wearing them, and came to be anglicized over a period, in food, clothing, language, manners, values etc. Now, other than retaining some mere customary practices, and religious rites and rituals in our private-personal spaces and familial gatherings, we have been totally anglicized and have become a proper national member of England; we now wear pants and coats, even in the house.

Life of Fun and Freedom: School Days in England

Since I had discontinued my schooling in Pakistan, I could not continue my studies as there was no parity of education between England and Pakistan. It was not me alone who suffered this situation, as there were increasing number of cases like that of mine, due to the increasing migration of the populations from the former colonies. To address such problem, community schools began to flourish around new immigrant settlements in England, with an objective to cultivate English ways among the children of these immigrants, and to make them equipped to be the citizen-subjects to make their careers in this new land. I was admitted in *Victoria School* (now runs as a primary health centre) that came up in our Dewsbury locality.

It was in this Victoria School that I first learnt my basic communication skills in English and about the fundamental rights and responsibilities as a citizen of England. Before I joined the school, English was an absolute alien subject for me, and I knew nothing other than yes and no. The same was the case with almost all the children of the school as they all hailed from the same/similar background as that of mine, and they were all Gujarati speaking Muslims from India and Pakistan. I used to speak Gujarati at home, having an excellent command over Urdu as well. Most of the correspondence among us was in Gujarati, however occasionally shifting to Urdu while talking to those from Pakistan. There were around fifteen students in the school, taught by a single teacher. The school would begin at 9 in the morning and close by evening 4. Slowly, I began having fun at school, as I was getting new friends, and learning English. I met Rashid Aswat, Shabbir Aswat, Ameen Lehar (we call him Baboo), Ghulam Lehar, Mohammad Ali, Ahmed Ali, and Rawat Brothers at school, and eventually also met some more friends like Mohammed Patel whom we used to call Mohammadu (who passed away recently) and his brothers, Ismail Patel and Yousuf Patel, and others, who used to stay at House 2 of Archibald Street in Bradford. In fact, Victoria School was my first means of finding a new social world in England.

In one of Easter vacations, Mohammadu took me to Bradford, and fed me in the Karachi restaurant there. It was my first ever outing in England, following which I frequently spent my weekends, and vacations with Mohammadu. There was also a Kashmiri restaurant in Bradford, which we also used to visit, and these two restaurants were two of the oldest ones that served South-Asian cuisines, were owned by folks of South-Asian descent in that area; they used to charge 20 or 25 pence for a meal. I often used to visit the house of Mohammadu at Archibald Street in Bradford during weekends when his parents were out of station, to have fun during weekends there with him and his brothers, and together we would go to the school on Monday directly from their house. Mohammadu also introduced me to his relative named Saeed Patel (who also passed away recently) and his friend Junaid Patel; all three were friends from the same village. During one vacation, Mohammadu took me to the house of Saeed, whose residence was at Dalaston, near Walsall in Birmingham, where Junaid also joined us; we went by bus from Bradford to Walsall. Saeed's mother gave us a warm welcome, and we were all cheerful and feasted the whole week together. This was the longest vacation that I ever spent in England; it was a real joy to travel across the cities, to have weekends with our loved ones. I always feel thankful to Mohammadu, but unfortunately, he is no more; I miss him so much.

I was also in correspondence with our friends and relatives from Karachi and Lahore in Pakistan, and Simlak and Dabhel in India. I got to know that Fathima Aapa (whom I call Bi Aapa as a mark of respect to elders) had been married off to Hashim Bhai (Hashim Mota), who belongs to the Desai Family, and they settled down in England with a little baby boy, Faisal; Hashim Bhai's mother and his brother, Saeed Desai was also staying with them. Fathima Aapa was younger sister of Zubeda Aapa, our neighbouring aunt, who was my mother figure and had been of immense help to us in Karachi. I visited Bi Aapa in one of the Christmas vacations at 16 French Wood Street in Preston, which was their residence. The whole family gave me a warm welcome and treated me like their own family member. We all got re-united, and we still meet up in all important family gatherings.

A few days before completing our schooling, I, along with Mohammadu and Baboo Lehar, planned a visit to Paris as part of our farewell from school. In Paris, we booked a hotel room in anticipation of staying there for few days. In the evenings in Paris, we left the hotel room to have a look around the city; like every tourist, we also began our visit witnessing the mystic splendours of Eiffel Tower, and other popular places. For supper, we entered a bar to have some food and soft drinks, and while having our drinks, three young girls not known to us, introduced themselves and joined us. It was quite strange, yet we invited them to join us, out of our curiosity to experience this new and unknown, and excitement to converse in English, since we did not get many opportunities to socialize in English until then; what all the life we had till then was confined amongst the Urdu speaking Muslim populace in England.

The girls ordered an alcoholic drink, and we were drinking coke; while conversing, they drank, drank, and finally left us by midnight. When we took out the purse to pay the bills, the bill was mind boggling: the price of coke was cheap, but the drink those girls ordered was so expensive that all our money that was to last our trip for days, had to be spent right there; we abruptly dropped our plans for further stay, and somehow managed to return to Dewsbury by the morning train. It was still an amazing experience, that we always share and laugh whenever we catch up; I still wonder what that drink could have been!

In Search of Career Opportunities

There were greater career prospects in textile industry in those days, and so my cousin, Rashid Gardee, joined textile industry as an engineer at Blackburn in England, after completing sandwich course in the discipline; he then went back to Pakistan to start textile industry there. Rashid was son of my paternal aunt from Lahore, on whose guidance and support my father and uncles came to England. Following Rashid, I too joined the textile industry as a labourer to work at a mill, Batley Carr Woollen Company; it was six working days a week for which I received weekly payment of 3.25 pounds. I had to do a very hard job of tufting, which involves cleaning the wool oil and dirt from the roller by hand. I was also doing over-time duty, to make more money, and often I used to earn cumulatively around 7 to 8 pounds a week, including my basic wage of 3.25 pounds. The money thus earned over time, I used to keep them with our company secretary named Dorothy Square with the hope of using that sum for some good cause.

I seriously attended the Sandwich course, while simultaneously working at the mills. I used to give the entire money to my mother, who in turn would give me 50 pence towards my pocket money, and the remaining amount she would give to my father as my weekly savings. I bought a bicycle by which I would go to work. Since I was not a spendthrift, though not a stingy person, I had no expenses, other than occasionally buying a chewing gum, or a Bittersweet, 50 pence were more than sufficient for me; in fact, I would save some money out of my pocket money, which I used for my fee towards learning car driving from a driving school, and toward application charges in obtaining official permit to drive.

Luckily, I passed my driving exam in the very first attempt, unlike my two uncle and cousins, all of whom had to undergo 2 or 3 futile attempts, before finally clearing their test; my father failed 4 times. With this, I started driving my father's van as a taxi during weekends, while continuing working in the mills. Eventually, I dropped my job in the mills, bought a van, and began working as a full-time taxi driver, running the taxi across cities, and along the Leicester motorway from Dewsbury to Heathrow Airport in London, through Batley, Bradford, right up to Wakefield that ends at Watford Gap, and from there to Doncaster, Nottingham, etc., and again back to Dewsbury. The journey time for one round trip would take 7 or 8 hours, and I would get 13 to 14 pounds for one round trip between London and Dewsbury; sometimes, particularly during weekends, I used to do double trips also, which amounts to around 26 pounds a day. I was busy during weekends, during which there were weekly flights to London from South-Asia, and when there were no passengers at airport, during weekdays, I had evolved a service taxi system, where I would charge £1 for each person, and fill the taxi with 10 to 12 people and ride them to nearby tourist places like Blackpool, Bolton, Preston, etc. This was profitable for me as well as cheap for individual tourists. I also used to extend the services of my taxi for the people to attend wedding, funeral rites, and other such occasions.

In this business, I was making good money, which I used to give in entirety to my father, who used to save it on my name. I hardly used to spend any money from that, other than for petrol, which was so cheap that it would cost just 11 pence a gallon (equal to 4 and 4.5 litre); there were no parking charges at airport in those days. My income had multiplied from earning 3 pounds a week to nearly 13 pounds in a day, and I was working seven days a week; there were times I even earned 26 pounds in a day. All my uncles, cousins and my father were also earning good money; they had a 12-hour work in the factory, from 7 to 7, having day and night shifts in alternate weeks, for which each of them was getting a weekly wage of 35 to 40 pounds. With this, we were all individually accumulating huge money, and were living together happily.

I was happy with this as I wanted to use my full energy when I am healthy enough to do so and bring greater comforts to my family members, particularly my parents in their old age. My parents were happy to see such huge money, and they spent liberally to meet out our daily comforts, without being spend thrifts, nor tight fists. While I was running taxi, I identified the failure of breaks and clutches was a frequent problem, and the repair of which was a heavy burden to the owner/driver to carry the vehicle all the way to the garage where one had to pay quite a lot to the mechanic. Identifying the profitability in mechanic field, I learnt the job of car mechanic, again as part of the Sandwich Course offered by the Government and began repairing vehicles in the backyard of my house. I was working as a driver in day and mechanic at nights; I also worked as a mechanic whenever I did not have passengers at hand, and gradually began I began shifting my focus on repairs, keeping my taxi service for occasional trips. Soon, I also opened a mechanic service to deliver repairs upon call, at the spot where the vehicle crashes. It was difficult to do this job in the freezing snowy open air in the midnights; however, I persisted doing it for amassing better profits.

Making our Own Home

Upon their landing in England, all my uncles together, including my father, took a three bed-room house on rent in Dewsbury, and began working in different factories. Seeing greater prospects in England to make better fortunes in life, they called all my family members, and we all settled down there. To that end, they gradually accumulated money and bought a house of their own in 1963 at 45 Leads Read in Dewsbury, for 600 pounds, by each having their share of 150 pounds. It was quite a huge house with 5 bedrooms, one kitchen, one dining room, one sitting room, one cellar and a loft; the house had a huge backyard and a front yard as well. We got such a big house for so cheap a price that everyone in that locality would visit the house to express their wonder. We renovated the house a little and moved in to live as a joint family; we also built one penthouse with a kitchen and began renting it for 50 pence a week which included charges on electricity, water, and cooking gas. One family friend of ours named Farid Usmani was also living in the same house with us. By now, I had saved sufficient money to buy a house; I pooled in all my savings, including the sum that was saved with Dorothy and singularly bought a house of my own, at 41 Leads Road, in 1968 and moved in along with my parents and siblings. The house was also quite big, as big as the one at 45 Leads Road, with a huge backyard and front yard, for the same price of 600 pounds. Eventually, all my uncles also bought houses of their own; while the house at 39 Leads Road was jointly owned by Mohammad Chacha and Ahmed Chacha; our family friend, Fareed Usmani also bought a house beside us at 43 Leeds Road.

It was during this period that I married Maryam Adam, daughter of my eldest paternal uncle, on April 14, 1968. We renovated the house with centralized heating equipment, well carpeted flooring, geysers, bathtubs, showers etc., for greater comforts and to withstand cold and other natural constraints. With this, I also moved my car repair shop behind my house and began working from there. When I married, my father gave a hike in my pocket money to 1 pound a week; he doubled the amount as there were two of us now. However, except some occasional outings with my wife, my hard work continued, and I was working very hard day and night. As said in a famous saying, 'bad days never stay, and good days always come back to you,' bad days did not stay forever in my life, nor did good days turn up naturally and suddenly; it took years of hard and collective labours to attain this desired objective of our family to lead harmonious living.

After years of working hard as mechanic and taxi-driver, I gradually moved into Petrol station business. Despite my hard labour, and busy schedules over all these years to empower myself and my family financially, the flaming desire for cricket kept burning in my heart. I used to play cricket during Saturdays and Sundays, or as and when I found a little leisure from work. Amidst finding fortunes in business, I never veered away from my desire to play cricket, though I had to sacrifice a great deal of my time for building career in business. I also never neglected attending my friends and relatives; despite our improved economic status, we never had forgotten our roots, and never turned our back against those who helped us in our time of need. In fact, I always believed that our hard labours, alongside cooperative co-existence of the people around us, was the main reason for our economic upliftment and social security; it had been culturally nurtured in us, and we continued to carry forth such lineage.

MY CRICKET LIFE

Life is like an unbelievable cricket track, ups and downs, seams, and swings; it is a strange circumstance, always caught between two polarities — security and freedom. In fact, the purpose of all our struggles is to find a pleasurable and meaningful life. But ironically, it is a sad fact that while attaining safety and security, we miss something true to our heart. My life, like those of several thousands of Asians in England, is one such case of a struggle to deal with this dichotomy—incessant labours for material development and my cravings for cricket.

Cricket in Natal Colony and Me as a Budding Cricketer:

Before I left for England, I was regularly playing cricket at the Natal Colony of Karachi in Pakistan. Having learnt cricket naturally, along with other boys of my age, I was a spirited child, highly enthusiastic to find every single opportunity to play, rather than study. We used to take the aid of a local carpenter to make a bat for us using the locally available plank of wood, and play with a rubber ball, without any pads, hand gloves and shoes. The passion for cricket that had just began to brew in the newly formed nations of Pakistan and India, took a giant leap with a tour of the West Indies team to Pakistan in 1959. In that tour, West Indies played three test matches with Pakistan—one, at the *National Stadium*, Karachi (our hometown), the second in Dhaka (in today's Bangladesh), which was then part of Pakistan, and the third was in Lahore Stadium.

Since the test-match that was held between February 20 and 25, 1959 was in our hometown, Karachi, we were all excited to watch international cricket. It was so fascinating for me to watch live match played by the cricket legends of the world like Sir Gary Sobers, Rohan Kanhai, Sir Wes Hall and Lan Gibbs from West Indies, and Little Master Hanif Mohammad, Imtiaz Ahmed, Ijaz Butt, Fazal Mahmood and Shujauddin of Pakistan. This fuelled my interest in cricket further, and I continued to play with increasing vigour; I soon emerged as a cricket enthusiast, excelling as a junior player.

Recognizing my interest and calibre in cricket, Hafiz Mohammed Patel (1926 – February 18, 2016), an Imam and the Captain of the Natal Colony Cricket Club, took initiative to mentor me in cricket during my early days. In his kind and compassionate mentorship, I was sometimes given an opportunity to play for their team as an extra-player. But my unsatiating desire to play cricket did not let me to go on endlessly waiting for my chance, as I was merely an extra-player. So, I, along with some friends, founded a club for junior players of the colony and named it as Natal Colony Junior Cricket Club, which served as an ancillary to the senior club in the colony. It was during these formative years of my life between 1959 and 1963, that I established myself as a player, leader of junior cricket team, and an occasional player for the seniors; eventually, I also played for the senior club of the colony. But this brief stint was cut short as I had to leave Natal Colony in 1963 for England.

Formation of Cricket Club by British Asians

Cricket had been a favourite game of Asians in England, and children in their respective localities would come together to play; they would pick up a plank of wood, get it shaped a little like a bat, draw some stumps on the wall with a chalk, or would keep a milk tray as stump, and play using a tennis ball. Amidst ceaseless labour and mundane life in this alien land, cricket was not merely a means of recreation for the workers in the industries around, but a main site of socialization for the Asian communities.

With this, some of the early Asians settlers in and around the Batley region of England, began randomly getting together to play in their nearby fields and parks during their weekends, after their week-long labour; they were exclusively Muslims of India and Pakistan, though most of them hail from the Gujarat region of India. These cricket enthusiasts, later, organised themselves to form a team in 1959, and eventually found a club, registering it as Batley Muslim Cricket Club (Batley Muslim CC) in 1961 to play under the Dewsbury and District League (DDL). The team began to play for the league cricket in England under the able leadership of Mr. Yousuf Dadhiwala, whom everyone would fondly call Yousuf Bhai. Batley Muslim CC, probably, is the first Asian cricket team that came to play for the league cricket in the United Kingdom.

My Entry as a Cricketer in Yorkshire Cricket League

Since Batley Muslim CC was already an established club for Asian community, I approached them in 1964 seeking a chance to prove my abilities to become part of their team. In the very first trial match, I played very well in which I scored 40 odd runs, taking 4 wickets. The club admired my performance, and they were glad to make me a part of the team. However, as per the club mandate, every team member had to pay 20 pence as match fee, for every single match they play, besides an annual subscription of £2. Since I was still a student with no earnings, and a dependent on my father, I could not afford to pay and had to unfortunately pass on the offer. Then upon learning that there was no match fee to play for the Birstall Trade Hall Club, which also played for the same Dewsbury and District League (DDL), I joined the Birstall club the same year in 1964.

The Birstall Trade Hall team was headed by Mick and Paul brothers as captain and vice-captains of the team, respectively. I played very well for Birstall for over a year in the warm company of these leader brothers and other team members. The club gave me good opportunities to play for them, where I performed so well that the Dewsbury and District League (DDL) honoured me with the best All-rounder prize, for my overall performance in the league, though our team could not register much success. It was with this team that I made my debut into league cricket in England, and got acclimatized to its weather, pitches, and players, etc. I was so happy that I was excelling in league cricket but was at unease as the club used to conduct its meetings in the pub attached to the club, where liquor consumption was common, whereas I had an aversion towards alcohol. Yet, I used to attend them in the pub as the team members were so kind and warm; unfortunately, most players of the team have passed away now. It was, however, for these nauseating pub meetings that I had to finally leave them; or else I would have loved playing for their team, and I miss them so much.

Batley Muslim CC [1965-69]

By now I had graduated from the school and had joined immediately as a labourer in *Batley Carr Woollen Company*, as a foremost necessary step to improve the living conditions of our family. When I did this, I also knew that I was sacrificing my soul, cricket, for the well-being of our family, as I wanted to give the best of material comforts to my parents, whom I saw restlessly striving throughout their lives; the incessant labours of my father toughened him as he worked days and nights alongside the machines in the factories, while my mother was doing everything at home. I did not want my parents to suffer anymore, and so I resolved to take some of their burden at the cost of sacrificing cricket.

However, I never veered away from training myself in cricket, which has been closest to my heart; it is next only to my religion. Besides working hard to make our living, I was also playing for Birstall Trade Hall during weekends, as and when I found some time, simultaneously looking for other opportunities in both cricket and business. As I began earning now, I decided to approach the Batley Muslim CC again in 1965, as there had better players, and they readily welcomed me. It was a fantastic team led by Yousuf Bhai Tilly, with brilliant cricketers like Yousuf Chunara (high-rated Batsman), Junaid Patel (all-rounder), Moosa Dawood and his two brothers, Rashid Dawood and Abdul Hai Dawood, among others; Saleem Dawood, father of Dawood brothers, was also a player in the club, and his grandson Ismail Dawood (son of Abdul Hai Dawood) later played for several counties before becoming an umpire.

Batley was a very good team, and I was doing very well there; I got the best all-rounder prize for every single year I played for them, also attaining the title of 'man of the match' several times, as I used to be the best in all aspects of cricket, including bating, bowling, and fielding. In one of the matches in 1967, I also won President Bowling Prize from the league for my best bowling where I took 9 wickets for just 19 runs against Wormalds & Walkers Ltd, outing everyone, except one batsman of the team. In another match against Birstall Carpet Company, I took 5 wickets in one over, missing merely one and only one ball, without even leaving a single run, while Saleem Dawood gave an outstanding performance as wicket keeper to make this record possible. Had I not missed that one ball, I could have got double hattrick in one over. Other players were also doing their best, and despite our best performances each of our individual capacities, our team could not win any major titles. This I noticed was due to the poor performance of the captain and learnt that the significance of the captain is immense in the winning of the team. However, I played a good number of matches there, and continued my association with them till I left them in 1969; I also served as a secretary of Batley Muslim CC from 1967-69.

Whitley Lower Club [1970-71]

In a brief stint between 1970 and 1971, I played for Whitley Lower team, before I found a desirable space in another important team named Cross Bank Muslim; Whitley Lower team had now been renamed as Hopton Mills. In Whitley Lower, Trevor Griffith and Ray Walmsley respectively acted as the captain and vice-captain of the team, and they had other players like David Farmer (whose occupation was farming), John Peters, including the fantastic David Peel with whom I developed intimate friendship that lasts even to this day. The atmosphere of the club was so friendly that, as I had married recently, I would often take my wife there to watch us playing, where she would be greeted by everyone. The club atmosphere was friendly where we would all look after one another and extend support to any one of us who happened to be need; it was so warm to be with them. During my stay there, we had the honour of winning the prestigious *Sheared Cup*, against Soothill team at Wormalds and Walkers' Ground in 1970.

Captaincy at Cross-Bank Muslim CC [1972-76]

In little less than a decade-long engagement with cricket in England, where I played for three different clubs, under the captaincy of various learned players, in the Dewsbury District League, I had not witnessed winning any championships, other than winning a few matches. Then again, in the same Dewsbury District League, I finally assumed the captaincy of the Cross Bank Muslim club in 1972. Then, Siraj Patel, one of my closest friends and a very good batsman at Batley Muslim CC also joined me. In Cross Bank, there were several experienced players like Noman Usmani and Rafiq whom we all fondly call Noman Chacha and Rafiq Chacha respectively, besides other brilliant players such as Qayat brothers (Ahmed Qayat, Moosa Qayat), Saeed Patel, Suleman Fadia, Masoom Chunara, Ahmed Nawab, Siraj Patel, Ibrahim Bhamjee, and Bashir.

I began learning the craftsmanship of captaincy, drawing immensely from the experiences of senior players like Noman Chacha and Rafiq Chacha, and with their advice and motivation, I drove the team towards a series of victories. We had very good fast bowlers like Qayat brothers, Ibrahim Bhamjee and Ahmed, besides having Moosa, a brother of Ahmed and one of the best all-rounders, and Suleman Fadia, one of the finest spin-bowlers who would spin the ball in miles speed; our opening batsman was Saeed Patel, who was also a wicket keeper, and we had with us other very good batsmen like Ahmed Nawab and Masoom Chunara. All these collectively contributed to the team achieving success.

Recounting Successes and Lessons Learned

In the very first year, under my captaincy, the Cross-Bank Muslim CC had won the prestigious title league championship, Dewsbury, and District League in 1973. In another match against Netherton, we experienced a phenomenal event in the history of Dewsbury League cricket. In that match, our team batted first, and we all got out for just 36 runs. While my team members had lost their hearts, my opponents were in a festive mood dreaming of carrying this historic victory home in the wee hours. But there was some hope lurking in the deepest chambers of my heart. During tea break, I called our two opening bowlers, Ahmed Qayat and Abdul Bhamjee, put my hands on their shoulders and told them: "Listen, imagine 36 runs are like 236 today, because it is a bouncy track that attracts wickets, and I want you to bowl your hearts out because I do not think you need to bowl more than 4 overs each, either to win, or to lose. To everyone's wonder, nine wickets fell just merely for 4 runs (all the 4 runs were extras!), thanks to the mind-blowing bowling of Ahmed Qayat and Ibrahim Bhamjee. Finally, when the tenth batsman was in the crease, I moved the fielders towards slip points, so that there will not be any chance for scoring any more runs. Despite the tight fielding, the ball took off the edge of the bat and went through between the slip fielders and they took a single; but the next batsman was clean bowled in the hands of Ahmed Qayat. It is a record in the history of Dewsbury District League, and probably will remain one in the history of DDL cricket. One of our brilliant bowlers, Suleman Fadia, who did not play for that match called me and expressed his extreme disappointment for leaving even that single run. With this, I learned a truth: *You cannot please everyone, does not matter whatever the best you do.*

Hearing the successes of the team, people began to show interest towards our team. The success of the Cross-Bank Muslims also attracted the Batley Muslim CC, particularly its founder and key functionary Mr. Yousuf Dadhiwala, who came to offer me captaincy to lead the team in one year from my date of joining them. Since it was a fairly established team, having the history of being the first Asian cricket club with necessary paraphernalia, I thought of going back to them, despite that the team had not registered much success in the past; and some of our close friends in Cross Bank like Qayat brothers had already moved there.

Return to Batley Muslim CC [1977-80]

Despite my bitter experience with Batley Muslim CC in the past, I chose to play for them again in 1977, upon prior unwritten consent from Mr. Yousuf Dadhiwala that assured to me of the captaincy in a year, after I joined them there. Along with me, Zahid Patel also joined us; he was a very good all-rounder and was playing for Hanging Heaton team, which was better in its standard than that of Batley Muslim CC. However, the team Batley Muslim CC refused to change, even after years of failing every *season* that they played; there was no change in the play, players, and the captaincy, including the director of the club and its secretary. Even then, I continued to play for Batley Muslim CC for four long unsuccessful seasons, and finally I had to leave them in 1980, when they continued to be dogmatic about not changing the captain and making other necessary changes in the team. It had always been my dream to lead Batley Muslim CC, as it had very good players and had a great scope for doing well, and still remained one of my unfulfilled dreams; the captain too was a good player but was unfortunately erring in building team spirit.

A Brief, but a Learning Experience in Thornhill Cricket Club [1981-82]

After leaving my dream club, Batley Muslim CC, in utter disappointment again in 1980, I approached Thornhill Cricket Club, which was just a few minutes away from our home, that was playing under Central Yorkshire League (CYL); CYL later merged with Bradford Cricket League in 2016, and was renamed as Bradford Premier League, and since then it has been designated as ECB Premier League. Seeing my profile, they readily agreed and invited me for a friendly match against Staincliffe in one of those Sundays, where I scored forty-six runs, took three wickets, and fielded well. Since the team we played against was already a first XI of Staincliffe Cricket Club of First Division, I was asked if I can play for the first team of the Thornhill CC, contrary to my expectation to play for its second team. So, it was a big surprise for me, and I was extremely happy to accept such a great offer to play for the first team of Thornhill. This was a new league for me, as whatever the matches and the clubs I had played for till then were all under DDL. But with this new opportunity in Thornhill CC, I moved out from DDL, and began playing for an altogether new league, CYL, which was a little better in standard than DDL.

The club had a better formal structure, and so did its league, than those of my previous ones. In this new club, we would have regular team meetings involving democratic discussions to improve our abilities of playing, inculcate team-spirit among the players, and to evolve strategies in leading the team towards the path of success; there was also a friendly atmosphere, and we all became good friends, and we remain so to this day. We had very good players in the team like Alan Hargreaves (senior player and former captain of the team), Mick Hargreaves (wicketkeeper and son of Alan), Peter Wood, and two fast bowlers—Roger and David Bruce—and the team was headed by Paul Brook and Ian Walmsley, the captain and vice-captain respectively; we also had other players like Collin Chapman, Collin Graham, and Paul Brothers. In this team, while David Bruce was the fastest bowler that I had ever come across in the club cricket of those days, captain Paul was a brilliant thinker and a good human being from whom I learnt how to be a good captain of a team. I was an opening batsman with Paul in the other end, right from the day one I joined, and had a great time playing with him.

In both the two seasons that I played after joining Thornhill CC, I did well where I scored few hundred runs, taking good number of wickets. Meanwhile, I met Raju Kulkarni, a budding player from Bombay who later represented Indian cricket team, in one of my tours to India, and had got him signed for our team. The club was very happy with my play as well as my enthusiasm to build a good team and had honoured me with some prize money at the end of the season; I was also honoured with life membership of the club, and I enjoy the same respect even to this day. The club performed very well overall, taught us good values, and produced many promising players, though it did not win any major trophies.

Promising Career in Batley Cricket Club [1983-87]

After a lovely second season at Thornhill Cricket Club, I got busy in all my businesses activities, looking forward to playing for the same club in the coming season as well. Then one morning at around 10 in October 1982, while I was working in the garage behind one of my petrol stations at Savile Road, two gentlemen walked into my petrol station, among whom one was Richard Illingworth, chairman of the Batley Cricket Club, and the other was Arthur Howden, member of the Batley CC, and owner of a newspaper shop in Batley town; they offered me the captaincy to lead the first team of the Batley CC. Here, some clarification about the club needs to be mentioned: Batley CC was different from Batley Muslim CC with which I was previously associated. While Batley Muslim CC was part of DDL, this Batley CC played under CCL, which is a premium league and higher in its standard than that of DDL.

Batley CC had a long and a successful history, as it was founded in 1863 as a successor to Prince of Wales CC, and soon rose to prominence in a short while, winning the prestigious Heavy Woollen Cup in 1894 as its first achievement. Thereupon, it achieved various victories and won several prestigious trophies. The Batley CC had a rich history. For instance, one of the All-time Cricket Greats, WG Grace, had visited Batley CC in May 1876 with his team 'The United South of England XI' to play a match against Batley CC team. This match attracted a huge gathering and was attended by 5000 people. WG Grace was an English amateur cricketer who was important in the development of the sport and is widely considered as one of its greatest players.

I felt so happy and honoured to receive such a great offer from Batley CC, and I accepted it immediately to take charge of leadership of such a prestigious club, and to walk in the trodden path of success that had already been set up by winning several trophies. I now feel privileged by the fact that I was the first and the only Asian in those days to lead a team as captain in the Central Yorkshire League (CYL). This was a turning point in my cricket career, where I got an opportunity to lead the team. When I took the captaincy of the team, Batley CC had some good players including David Bruce, David Tattersall, and bowlers like Barry Petty, Fillan, and David. However, the team was not performing well and had been thus relegated to Second Division from its glory of playing First Division and was struggling very hard to regain its lost status. To everyone's surprise, as soon as I took the charge of captain, luckily, one of the clubs in the league, named Wakefield CC was pulled out of the league in the last minute, as the club closed down, giving rise to the reinstatement of our team in the First Division. The Batley CC management felt that my entry into the club was a good omen which would bring successes to the team.

Rebuilding the Team

Bestowed with complete freedom, I began rebuilding the team with my own choice of players, shuffling, and reshuffling the team by inducting new players into it, both from other clubs and leagues in England, as well as from overseas. I identified two young and brilliant players named Arif and Paul Heaton in the second team of our own club and pulled them into the first team as an immediate measure. Then I began pooling good players from other clubs in England, beginning with a wonderful all-rounder, Paul Blakely, from Dewsbury Local, and another all-rounder, Martin, from Cleckheaton, besides other players like Luky Hans, Steve Wolfenden, Gary Brooks, including brilliant bowlers, Neil Haynes, and Terry Foy. While I was busy working on the team, one reporter of a reputed newspapers, *Dewsbury Report*, approached me and asked, "how much money had I offered to the club to assume the position of the captain of the team," to which I retorted, "money can get you into the team, but cannot buy championships and cups," and asked him to wait and watch.

While Neil Haynes was our opening bowler, Barry Petty was at his other end. Neil was an amazing bowler, but he would get tired after six overs or so, due to his sleep deprivation owing to his work at a nightclub. On the contrary, Barry was an energetic player who would easily bowl 20-25 overs, without being tired, even after travelling all the way from the other end of Leeds to play the match. When Neil got tired, I would motivate him to fetch all his energies to continue bowling. I would rarely pick up bowling, as I did not want to waste the greatest potentials of these bowlers, and on the other hand, I would exert all my energies in my captaincy, rather than in playing.

I continued looking for promising cricketers abroad as well. I focused on India and Pakistan to find new players for our team. The most important among them were some Ranji players in India, beginning with Chandrakanth Pandit from Bombay, followed by Barun Burman of Bengal, Abdul Azeem of Hyderabad, and Mehndi Shaik of Baroda, who later emerged to be a coach for famous cricket stars like Yousuf Patan and Irfan Patan. I also got two test cricketers, Masood Anwar, and Rashid Khan, from Pakistan to play for us. Several of the above players later became very popular players and represented their countries in international cricket. Abdul Azeem, for instance, sharpened his talents immensely playing league cricket in England, and when he went back to India, he scored a triple century (303 runs) against Tamil Nādu in 1986. In the end, I also signed for our team a charming, young, and gifted cricketer named David Dove from Cleckheaton team.

Our team had outshone all with our outstanding performances that brought a series of victories to our club. Batley team by then had got several brilliant players and had emerged as a very big and strong team comprising players, beginning with me as the captain, followed by David Byrns (Vice Captain), David Battye, John Prentice, Paul Blakely, Neil Haynes, Barry Petty, Rashid Khan, Barun Burman, Paul Heaton, David Dove, Paul Jarvis, Mehndi Sheik, Gary Brooks, Martin Evans, Bob Cooper, Richard Illingworth, Chandrakanth Pandit, Arthur Howden, Shaun Twohig, Abdul Azeem, Masood Anwar, Peter Jackson, Lucky Hans, Steve Derry, Paul Cooper, David Tattersal, A. Hampston, S. Woffenden, M, Bottomley, Mohammad Amar Arif, Colin Buzzard, B. Settle, Mohammad Dadhiwala, Robert Cooper, R. Varney, David Bruce, T Rukin, A. Lunat, Paul Taylor and Paul Wilman.

With this huge team of brilliant players, I was constantly shuffling the players considering factors like changing weather conditions, opponent team, and the condition of the pitch and the lawns. In those days, the role of money in cricket was minimal and most players would play merely for the love of the game, and not for money; we would find some sponsors for the very few who could not afford sparing their time for the game, yielding to the pressures of existence, just to meet out their needs. All the players were doing very well; particularly the balls released from the hands of our bowlers began to create tornadoes on the pitch, leading our team towards the path of success, winning several trophies and championships.

Jack Hampshire Cup - Champions [1983]

Winning the prestigious Jack Hampshire Cup / Knockout Cup against Liversedge Team at Ossett in 1983, in less than a year after I took up captaincy, was our first significant success in Batley. Chandrakanth Pandit was instrumental in winning this cup, as well as in the climb of our club to the first place; Chandrakanth scored 853 runs for the season that won him the CYL First Division League Batting Prize with the Batting Average of 53.31. Chandrakanth used to open his batting with another brilliant batsman, Sean Twohig; their partnership would score the best of runs leading the team towards its success. Chandrakanth also won the First Division League Wicket-Keeping Trophy in the year in 1984, for his excellence in wicket-keeping. In 1984, the club had also won league championship title, CYL Premium Championship. In 1985, Chandrakanth again topped the league, by scoring the highest at 1079 runs with an average of 53.95 runs, while Neil Haynes, with his splendid bowling, took 55 wickets for the season that fetched him the League Bowling Prize for the year, for taking the highest number of wickets in the league.

My Struggle to Retain my Position in the Batley Team

At this point of time, I was focusing more on captaincy, giving more opportunities to the competent players, disregarding my personal profile as a player. Our batsmen were credited with runs, and our bowlers with wickets, and so was their heightening personal profiles. I was so happy that all of this was happening under my captaincy, and so was everyone, as our team was winning trophies; my personal profile as a captain also rose high in the league. By now, the strength of our team had increased; we had a very big and brilliant team with competent players, always having several extra-players. I have been an all-rounder, with an excellent record in both batting and bowling. But, with an intent to motivate the young and rising cricketers, I used to keep my seat a bit backwards, only to promote the promising cricketers, while exerting my energies on captaincy. In due course, I would push myself into the 10th and 11th position in batting order, and rarely took to bowling, which unfortunately appeared as my incompetence to some of my team members.

One day, there were 12 players and one of us had to drop out; in our discussion pertaining to dropping one of us, there was one opinion that suggested me to stay out, as I was not supposedly batting, nor bowling. According to that opinion, the performance of each player in their respective individual capacities automatically brings successes to the team, disregarding the role of leadership. Here, individual occupies supreme importance over collective, thereby it denies the relationship between individual and collective in achieving success. But I believe that the success of a team does not lie merely on good players, nor upon a great captain; it lies in the combination of both the captain and the players; the same rule applies to success in business, family, social including national development.

After this incident, I also began sharing some of the bowling responsibility, besides sharpening the art of my captaincy, while continuing to privilege other good bowlers of the team. Initially, I was a left-arm-medium pacer with a good command over batting; I had been an all-rounder with quite a good record of successful bowling and batting that had earned me several rewards, including hattricks, man of the matches, and

45

championship trophies, for my performance in various seasons, both as a player and as a captain. I noticed that there were several pace bowlers already in the team, so I regarded myself redundant to do pace-bowling for the team, and thus, I began practicing left-arm-spin-bowling. I focused on practicing left-arm-spin-bowling whenever I got some time and opportunity and began experimenting with my bowling skills. With this rigorous practice in various clubs, I eventually emerged as a successful spinner in the later part of my career.

Winners of Heavy Woollen Championship [1986]

In the year 1986, Terry Foy played as an opening bowler, with John Prentice in the other end. In one of the matches in that season against Kirkheaton team, John Prentice bowled so well that he took 7 wickets for 31 runs, sending back our opponents to the pavilion with a total score of merely 66 runs, leaving the bat to us. In our turn, we batted so well that we could easily defeat them, winning the match by 9 wickets, with a score 67 runs for 1 wicket. With this fabulous victory, we were honoured with a prestigious Heavy Woollen Cup in 1986; with this cup, we could revive Batley CC's glorious past, as the last time that Batley won this cup was 25 years ago in 1961. Heavy Woollen Cup is the oldest cricket cup competition, that came into existence in England in 1883. The competition accommodates the maximum of 32 clubs, that lie within 18-mile radius of Batley Town Hall. From its inception, the Cup has got highest regards amongst English Cricketing fraternity. I began sharing significant responsibility of bowling, with not less than 40 wickets to my credit in every season in CYL, where in one of the matches against Heckmondwike, I bowled so well that I grabbed 5 wickets for 42 runs. In 1986, I also took the highest wickets, 64 wickets for the season, that earned me the League Bowling Prize, for the best performance in bowling in the league.

Winners of CYL Premium Championship [1987]

This form continued, and we again won CYL Premium Championship title in 1987; in the same year, we also scooped the Wheatley Cup 2nd XI Cup Competition. With this, we probably set the record of winning the trophies for almost every season, besides championships, man of the matches for our individual team members. Finally, our club embarked to the top position of our league and began representing the entire CYL teams in competition with other leagues in the Yorkshire region in the prestigious Yorkshire Council Championship. We reached the semi-finals in Yorkshire Council Championship, which used to be referred as 'Champion of Champions' trophy.

Both as captain of the team and as a player, I did so well that our club had won every major trophy that CYL presented, and with this, Batley CC had attained prestigious position in the Central Yorkshire League. Everyone in the league rated me so high that the management of CYL offered me with the position of the captaincy to lead the entire CYL against other leagues in Yorkshire. But I could not manage to communicate with the league in time, resulting in missing the opportunity of having the greatest honour to be the leader of one of the premium leagues in Yorkshire region. In this way, I had achieved everything as a player and captain of Batley CC and had kept my promise that I made to Dewsbury Report at the time of my induction as the captain of the club. In these five years of my captaincy, Batley CC had won almost every trophy in the Central Yorkshire League; we had won 9 trophies in total, including one Jack Hampshire Cup in 1983, two Central Yorkshire League Premium Championship titles (1984 and 1987), one Heavy Woollen Cup in 1986, and lastly, we stood as semi-finalist of Yorkshire Council Championship. Addressing the media in one of my interviews with the Dewsbury Report, I ascertained my success at Batley, and said, "I feel no challenge is left for me in Central Yorkshire League (CYL) as I have won every single title in CYL." With this, I finally bade goodbye to the Batley CC in 1988 only to explore something new, and a better standard of cricket, as I had always been inclined to set new challenges in life.

Preparations to Join Spen Victoria CC

Meanwhile, one of my good friends, Chris Pickles, who then was the captain of Spen Victoria, approached me and invited me to play under his captaincy, where he assured me that Spen Victoria which plays for Bradford League would be a better place for me to explore new grounds in cricket. Chris Pickles' intellectual insights convinced me so much so that I accepted his offer not merely for his promise of the provision for better space in the team for me to prove my calibre, but also because Bradford League was a better league in its standards than that of Central Yorkshire League (CYL), with which I was, at that moment, associated.

Having a long history of more than hundred years of its excellence after its inception in 1862, the club, Spen Victoria, which was originally associated with the Cleckheaton Wesleyan Chapel, had earned several prestigious trophies like Heavy Woollen Cup, Blacksheep Yorkshire Champions, including the esteemed Priestley Cup, and harboured innumerable players of international acclaim. The club initially had home ground at Whitecliffe Road, but later moved to its current home at Spen Lane in Gomersal; it was in 1931 that Spen joined the Bradford League and emerged the runners-up in their very first season with the league.

The higher standard of cricket you play, the better you improve your capabilities as a player, and consequently achieve personal progress and social respect. By now, I already emerged as one of the best and successful players and leaders in the league cricket in Yorkshire, and this gave me an opportunity to enjoy a new kind of experience—the glory of recognition as a cricketer. This motivated me further to explore new challenges in cricket, and hence I opted to be one of the players in a different league of higher standard under the leadership of somebody else, rather

48

than continuing to lead the same team in which I had already achieved the pinnacle of success. So, I left Batley CC as a captain and its CYL, to join Spen Victoria in 1988. When I was leaving Batley CC to join Spen Victoria, I suggested the management of Batley CC to offer the captaincy to David Dove as my successor, and to have Sean Twohig as vice-captain of the Batley team. The management respected my suggestion, and the said players were bestowed with respective positions. I am still in contact with Sean Twohig, Garry Brooks, and Paul Jarvis, who have been good friends of mine from my days at Batley CC.

Bradford League and its High Standard Cricket

Bradford League was, and still is, one of the best leagues in its standard of cricket in England. The league also attains its prominence owing to hosting some of the most acclaimed players internationally, in the early decades of the 20th century in England; they include the greatest of all times like Sir Leonard Hutton and Sir John Berry Hobbs (also known as Jack Hobbs), who was accredited with the title, The Master. The league also boasted of being represented by several later day renowned players like Brian Close (popular figure in Yorkshire cricket circles and known for his success as the captain of Yorkshire County Team), Derek Underwood, Matthew Hoggard, Darren Gough etc., including Herbert Sutcliffe. Herbert Sutcliffe, who was one of the greatest cricketers of England, went on to equate the standard of cricket in Bradford league to that of county cricket when he said, "From Land's End to John O'Groats of from Pudsey to Brisbane you would not find a better league than the Bradford League. No one can deny that the standard of cricket throughout the league has always been of the highest, in fact at one period it almost reached county standard."

The League also hosted several overseas players, who also attained international eminence at later times, from India, Pakistan, and New Zealand. They include Indian cricket stars, beginning with Dilip Vengsarkar, Suru Nayak, Yajurvindra Singh, Abey Kuruvilla, VVS Laxman, Mohammad Kaif, Jacob Martin, Anil Kumble, Wasim Jaffer, Lalu Rajput, Vinod Kambli, Rohan Gavaskar, Praveen Amre, and Sairaj Bahuthule, and Pakistan stars like Mohammad Yousuf, Iqbal Qasim, Abdul Qadir, Imran Nazir, Mansoor Akhtar, Shahid Mahboob etc., and the cricket stars from New Zealand such as Martin Crowe, Chris Pringle, Simon Doull, Nathan Astle etc.

Revival of the Spen Victoria CC as its Captain [1988-92 and 1994]

By the time I joined Spen Victoria in 1988, the team, despite having some of the greatest players, was struggling very hard to retain its former glory. Chris Pickles was our captain, and it was owing to his extra-responsibilities, as he was also representing Yorkshire County besides being the leader of our team, that our team had suffered some losses. Chris Pickles, otherwise was an excellent all-rounder, who played for both the first and second teams in Yorkshire County; he was a good human being, who later became my friend. Hence in 1988, all our efforts to retain the team's glory went in vain, Spen Victoria finished in 12th position in its performance in the order of merit out of 14 teams that were playing under Division-I of Bradford League, with East Bierley on its top, and Idle and Lightcliffe among the last two teams. By the end of the season in 1988, Spen Victoria had lost even its chance to play in the Division-1 of the league, being relegated to play in the Division-2 for the next season in 1989.

It was at this critical juncture when the team was about to be downgraded from Division-1 to Division-2 in the Bradford League, that the management of the Spen asked me if I can take up the captaincy of the team. But I felt that it was unethical to accept the position of captaincy since it would mean replacing someone who had initiated me to the same team; So, I suggested that the management take the consent from Chris.

But to my shock, I learnt from Chris that it was he who had suggested the management to offer me the captaincy. With this, I happily accepted the offer as the captain of the team, while Chris Pickles stepped down as vice-captain. It is in fact a great privilege for me that, I am not only the first Asian to have captained Spen Victoria, but perhaps, the only Asian to have captained three teams in the three major cricket leagues in Yorkshire; I captained for Cross Bank Muslim CC in Dewsbury and District League (DDL) and Batley CC in Central Yorkshire League (CYL) in the past, and I was now the captain of Spen Victoria in Bradford Cricket League.

As soon as I took the responsibility of the team, I began working towards improving the team by organizing friendly matches with various teams and leagues. I used all my experiences that I had gained in the Batley CC to improve the team here. Being impressed by my active engagement, the management of Spen Victoria, under the chairmanship of John Burton, sanctioned me with £1800 to rebuild the team with better players. By then, league cricket became more professional, where players were being signed on contractual basis. I started a talent hunt in different leagues and clubs, besides looking out in various local grounds.

Identifying the lacune in our team, I first signed Gary Brook, a wicket keeper from Drighlington, and Bethel brothers (Steve Bethel and Andy Bethel) from Barnsley. Then I identified a promising adolescent cricketer in his mid-teens, who had just turned 15, named Tim Walton, and offered him with £100 per season, an offer that was received with much excitement by both Tim and his parents. Then I signed up another young man, John Wood, in his late teens (19 years), Mike Smith for £25 per match, and Steve Foster with £300 worth cricket equipment as per his request. I also signed up Tushar Arothe, a Baroda based Ranji player, and an 'Overseas Pro' from India, for £1200 for the entire season. Finally, on the advice of Andy Bethel, I wanted to sign a brilliant bowler, Darren Gough, for £30 per match, as it was the only budget I was left with, after signing most of the players for Spen. I would have loved to have Darren in Spen team, but unfortunately, the deal did not take place, because Darren was looking for £35 per match. Because of that £5 difference the contract did not get materialized; how sad, and unfortunate it was!

However, we have always had John Burton, a very good player, and the chairman of our club, to play with us. With these brilliant players, I organized Spen Victoria into a strong team. I began studying the strengths and weaknesses of each player of our team, while utilizing their strengths to their optimum levels. I used to discuss with each player, and critically consider their suggestions, while I practiced bowling rigorously on different pitches. I also focused on nourishing team spirit among all the players of the team, instilled confidence in them, and utilized the best of their potentials. With this systematic approach and serious engagement of reorganizing the team for over little less than a year after I took charge of the captaincy, we began to see positive results for our team.

Priestley Cup Champions - 1990

In the season of 1990, we posed a stiff challenge against every team that played with us, and reached Priestley Cup finals, by defeating East Bierley in its semi-finals. An unbelievably huge crowd gathered for the semi-finals, as it was a home-ground for Spen Victoria, where an estimated record of the total worth of £1000 tea and coffee were being sold by the club, with each cup of tea and coffee costing 10 and 20 pence respectively. The same spirit continued, and by the end of the season in 1990, our team defeated Pudsey St. Lawrence (PSL) that was one of the strongest teams in Bradford League cricket, in its finals on August 12, 1990, at Bradford & Bingley CC. For this, Spen was awarded with the most prestigious Priestley Cup, also known as *Bradford League Allied Dunbar Priestley Cup*, for it was sponsored in collaboration with Allied

Dunbar, which is one of the largest British life insurance corporations. Priestley Cup is one of the most prestigious competitions in English club cricket, and was named after Sir William Priestley, who was the president of Bradford Cricket League when the cup-competition started for the first time in 1904, and since then, the Priestley Cup had continued in every season, without fail, honouring the team that wins the final match.

In the final match, we had batted first and scored 231 for 7 wickets in 50 overs, beginning with our opening batsman, Steve Foster, who scored 44 runs, followed by Andy Bethel at 30 runs and Tushar Arothe at 57 runs. In this match we lost 6 of our 7 wickets to one single bowler, named R Sladdin, of our opponents, Pudsey St Lawrence; they also had as great a player as Chris Pringle, who was already playing for New Zealand Team then. However, to everyone's surprise, we outed all our opponents for just 73 runs in 25.3 overs. For winning the final match, and hence this prestigious cup, John Wood stood to be the hero of the day, as he had used his fast-bowling skills to grab 7 wickets for just 20 runs in 13 overs; John was awarded with the man of the match for his best performance in the match, and hence he was also a determinant in winning the final cup. Mike Smith, a former bowler for the national team of England, joined Wood to take the remaining 3 wickets, and contributed his share in outing all the players of our opponents; just these two brilliant bowlers, Mike Smith, and John Wood, together got the entire PSL team out. With this, the young John Wood became 'the shining star' of the day and was hailed as 'Wakefield-based-Wood,' by the local media.

Sunil Gavaskar, a legendary cricketer from India and popular cricket commentator, who has been my best friend in life for more than 50 years, witnessed this cheerful moment as a delegate who had come to congratulate this young man, and the team under my captaincy, for winning the cup of this high stature. Upon this success, our teams grabbed the attention of the entire English cricket world. Following this success, the management of the Yorkshire County approached me for my recommendation to recruit John Wood and Steve Foster for their team, which I gave considering my great admiration for them.

With this glory, our team became very popular among Yorkshire circles; it was celebrated so much not only by the afficionados of the league cricket in Yorkshire, but also by the media, as Spen Victoria had won this cup after 45 years; the last that the team attained this cup was in 1944. I was so happy for the team attaining this lost glory under my captaincy, and often, I was proud for leading our team towards bringing back that glory. With this popularity, there began an unearthing of new talents that were buried under the dust till then; we all began receiving several opportunities, both individually as players and collectively as a team. Particularly, the three talented players who were crucial to our team, included John Wood, Tim Walton, Mike Smith, later went on to play first class cricket; they played for various counties in England. For instance, Tim Walton played for several major counties like Essex, Northamptonshire, Cambridgeshire, Canterbury, as well as England Under-19 Youth Team, while John Wood played for Durham and Lancashire County Teams, and Steve Foster for a minor county, and particularly Mike Smith, who later joined Gloucestershire County, and went on to represent the national team of England in international test cricket for one match. All these players had showered great respect and love for me all through their active careers, and some of them, particularly John Wood, continues his affectionate relation with me till date.

Bradford League Season 1990

As for our overall performance in the Bradford League season, Steve Foster with his scintillating batting, hit 879 runs, and scored his highest runs from Spen, followed by other fantastic batsmen, Andy Bethel at 764 runs and Tushar Arothe at 619 runs. I, on the other hand, with my left-arm spin-bowling took 49 wickets, followed by Wood who took 32 wickets; we together took the lion's share of the wickets for the season. In the end, I was honoured with Club Bowling Prize for taking highest wickets in the season. With this achievement, Spen took a huge leap by standing at the third position in the Division-1 of the Bradford League in 1990, behind only to Bradford & Bingley, and East Bierley, the top two teams in the league table.

Opportunity to Play for Cumberland Minor County

After winning Priestley Cup, I became more popular than ever, and my name spread across Yorkshire Cricket circles, that prompted me to receive an offer in 1991 to play for Cumberland minor county. I was 46 years old when I made my debut into minor county cricket in 1991, an age at which usually any first-class cricketer retired. But for me, it was a beginning, and I took to playing for Cumberland County, while simultaneously leading the Bradford league. However, I found minor county cricket much easier because they do not play cross-bat shots, instead they play according to the ball. But I did not get many opportunities to play for the Cumberland, as I played merely 6 matches in total, including my stints at both 1st XI and 2nd XI teams.

In the Minor County match against Lincolnshire on June 9, 1991, at Abbey Lawn, Bourne, I did not get a chance to bowl in the first innings, and I was the 9th batsman in the order, where I managed to score just 2 runs. Interestingly, however, in the second innings on June 10, the match got ended up in TIE, which was so rare and unusual. In that match, our Cumberland team was chasing a target of 134 runs, but we all got out for 133 runs in the last over which resulted in TIE; it was one of the most nail-biting matches I have ever played. In the second innings, I got the chance to bowl, and so I took 2 wickets in my share, while the rest of our bowlers took the remaining. Minor county cricket assumes a prestigious place in the cricket of England, since some of the popular players in the major counties also joined these minor counties in their later careers.

Overall, there was not much to share about my association with Cumberland, though the county wanted me to play for them again in 1992. But it was so hectic for me, as there would be matches continuously in the weekdays, right from 11 in the morning to 6 in the evening. In addition to these regular matches, I also had to play the league cricket during weekends, and this took a serious toll on my business. After finishing one season, I left Cumberland to focus on my business and my league cricket at Spen.

Returning to the League Cricket and Re-joining Spen Victoria

In those days, the county team used to grant a benefit year in which one player of their choice would be selected to play for the benefit match, where the resultant proceedings would be given to the selected player by the end of the match. From my days at Batley CC, I was one of the major initiators in organizing and playing these benefit matches, where several legendary cricketers like David Bairstow, Sir Geoffrey Boycott, Phil Carrick, and Richard Lumb who all played for Yorkshire County had their benefit matches played against Batley CC. This made me popular among the county and league circles, where I introduced some of the popular Asian cricketers from India and Pakistan. I introduced Sachin Tendulkar to Yorkshire County in 1992, and various other Asian cricketers from India and Pakistan to the English league cricket. For Spen Victoria, I signed up some Asian cricketers from India like Vinod Kambli, Tushar Arothe, Sairaj Bahuthule, Rohan Gavaskar, etc., and Mansoor Akhtar from Pakistan. With this, our team Spen became more stronger than ever.

Though we could not win the Division-1 championship of Bradford League for Spen in the 1991 season, having finished second (which is also a major achievement for Spen), my team members and I made several records. Though Vinod Kambli did not play for us from the beginning of the season, as he joined us in the middle of 1991, he performed very well in the season, where he scored five half-centuries in six consecutive innings, culminating in his record score of a total of 1,000 runs in the season from just 20 innings. With the highest score in one of the innings at 107 runs, and a mighty average of 58.82, Kambli became a star of our league, and later emerged as a popular player internationally.

I, on the other hand, showed the best of my bowling performance in this season: in a match against Bankfoot team on August 17, 1991, I took 7 wickets for just 42 runs, followed by my two other bests in the same season, where I took 5 wickets for 49 runs against East Bierley team, and 4 wickets for 38 runs against Undercliff team. My bowling performance continued all through the season with several bests: I took 5 wickets for 68 against Lowly Baildon team, where we won the match by 1 wicket, and in another match against Bowling Old Lane team, I took 4 wickets for 42 runs, in which John Burton did the best with 3 wickets for just 12 runs, outing all our opponents for just 121 runs.

In the most important match against Bradford & Bingley, one of the strongest teams of the league, bowling by Ralph Emsley and I became very crucial in defeating our opponents. While I took 5 wickets for just 30 runs, Ralph joined me with his best by taking 3 wickets for 29 runs, fetching our team victory by 63 runs. In this match, only three batsmen of our team batted to chase the total of 197 runs, each sharing their best: Steve Foster scored 63 runs (out), Andy Bethel with his 55 runs and Tim Walton with 46 runs, not out. For my excellence in bowling, I was once again honoured with Bowling Prize by the league. With these series of the best performances of various members of our team, we climbed to the second position from third in the Division-I of the league, just below Pudsey St. Law team who climbed to the first spot from the fourth.

And then for the season 1992, Spen Victoria finished fourth in Division-I, while Bradford and Bingley retained its first position. It was in this season that I signed up a brilliant bowler, John Carruthers. John played reasonably well in the first year at Spen, then he moved to Hanging Heaton team to do his best, where he took more than 1000 wickets in the Bradford league; he is referred as the 'Legend of Hanging Heaton' by the cricket lovers. We played very well, and in one of our matches against Bankfoot Team, Chris Pickles and Vinod Kambli together chased the target effortlessly, leading our team to victory. In this match, Chris with the pulsating strokes of his bat scored one century, while Vinod did his half-century (58 runs), and I took 4 wickets. In another match against Farsley team, Tushar Arothe showed his best performance by scoring 89 runs, when Steve Foster scored a 70; I did my best as usual in this match as well and took 6 wickets for 53 runs. I did very well with Spen, throughout all the seasons, and for my best performance in the league, I was awarded with Club Bowling Prize several times by Spen Victoria, almost every year I played there. I have heard that some people attribute greatness exclusively to me for putting Spen on the cricket map, but I think it was Spen, in fact, who put me in the cricket circles by giving me the best opportunity to lead her, as the club already has had a grand history.

Offer as the Chairman of Chickenley Cricket Club

It was around the end of 1991 when I was still with Spen Victoria that one day I got a call from Chickenley Cricket Committee; they asked me if can lead the club as, they said, they cannot run the club any longer as there were not many players left with the club, and to that effect, they even offered me with the chairmanship of the club. To be a chairman of a club, which has a historical and social significance, I thought, would be a great opportunity to build the bridge between the cricket clubs of Asians in England with those of English clubs, as these two clusters of cricket clubs have always been divided in the lines of ethnicity and religion. Apparently, Chickenley Cricket Club was founded about 133 years ago around 1850 behind the Crown Pub, and soon it became a member of the Central Yorkshire League (CYL). Then I took a while to talk to another club named Mount Cricket Club to know if they were willing to merge with the Chickenley club. While Chickenley was hosting players from all religions and racial backgrounds, Mount CC comprised of exclusively Muslims of Asian dissent in England, since it was founded in 1976 exclusively by some members of the local Asian community, under the initiatives of two young and enthusiastic cricketers, Mr. Hanif Mayet, and Mr. Farid Karolia, to play under Airedale-Wharfedale Cricket League, when there were very limited opportunities for immigrants to play and compete with the native English clubs. So, I took up the Chairmanship of Chickenley club in 1991, while continuing to play for Spen.

Building Bridges between Asian and English Clubs

At this juncture, I organized a very important meeting, known as 'Building Bridges,' on Jan 4, 1992, with the officials of Yorkshire County and the representatives of Local Asian clubs, as an attempt to fill the prevailing gap between English and Asian Cricket clubs. This historic meet witnessed the participation of some of the popular cricket figures in Yorkshire and English cricket circles; they include Sir Lawrence Byford, a former prominent police officer who then was the President of Yorkshire County Cricket Club, Brian Close, a former national cricket player of England and then the chairman of Yorkshire CCC, Chris Hassell, chief executive of Yorkshire CCC, John Holder, an Umpire in the International cricket, Phil Carrick, Former captain of Yorkshire CCC, Steve Oldham, Manager of the Yorkshire CCC, etc. with Adil Ditta, Ismail Dawood, Ahmed Loonat etc., serving as representatives of Asian Cricket Clubs in England; Mohammad Ali Siddique, the Pakistani Consulate from Bradford, served as the Chief Guest of the meeting. The noble intent and its endeavours behind this meeting had received public admiration, and it was widely covered in the local media, with me as the central figure of this entire process.

Though the meeting had a larger agenda of unity and inclusivity of the divergent cricket clubs, the immediate consequence of the meeting was that the Mount CC, agreed to be part of the Chickenley CC, despite that its league CYL was higher in its standard than that of Airedale-Wharfedale Cricket League. Thereupon, a mutual agreement was made on two counts: one, the name Mount will be included in the proposed team, renaming Chickenley CC into Chickenley Mount Cricket Club (CMCC) that would play for CYL, and the other was that the team would play under my captaincy, as I had experience in leading teams for CYL. Upon the mutual agreements of both the parties, I convinced the committee of Spen Victoria to release me just for one season, so that I can avail the opportunity to introduce these struggling Asian cricket enthusiasts to better standard cricket in England and help them in their progress. This, I also thought, would build a lasting impact on establishing a strong cultural cohesion between the so-called natives of England, and those of Asian dissent. It was with such a noble intention of seeing inclusive England, with equal opportunities for all the communities in it, and for realizing one unified community of citizens that, I took a short break to leave Spen Victoria for the season 1993 to play and lead Chickenley Mount Cricket Club for one year under my captaincy, only to re-join the Spen again in 1994. Since I was the only left arm spinner in Spen Victoria, I signed up another left-hand batsman and slow left-arm orthodox spinner, Rohan Gavaskar, who was an emerging player and good fielder from Bombay.

Futile Attempt to Build Chickenley Mount Cricket Club (CMCC)

I started building the CMCC team in 1993, and signed a few good players like Harvey Anderson, Ahmed Ali, Khalid Mohammod, Nazeer Rajiv, Patel (nephew of a very famous religious leader, Hafiz Patel) from Saville Star team, including Tom Chippy. I also signed up players from

Rochdale, Oldham, and Halifax. With these efforts, CMCC began doing well to moderate, if not emerge as one among the best, from its state of almost nothingness. But in the meanwhile, uneasiness began to crawl up in the club, probably, due to some religious mores. I think, unlike English men, the Asian guys were not spending money to buy Alcohol from the Bar of the club, and since alcohol was the main means of revenue of the club, and this culture of the Asians not drinking alcohol might have impacted the financial status of the club. The reasons were not known, but suddenly the CYL committee decided to remove Chickenley Team, and one day, our team was ousted off from the CYL League, without citing any reason, not even informing me, the chairman of the club, of such a decision. This abominable attitude and high-handedness of the league was widely covered and condemned across the media. But this crash blow of hammer by the league had already fallen like a last nail on the coffin of the struggling club, permanently crucifying the Chickenley CC; with this, more than 133 years of its glory was reduced to dust. Now, the club has ceased from existence, and its lands have been converted into residential/housing society. The main detriment of this sectarian act of the league, in fact, was upon the larger social life, that came up as menace to national integrity of England. Yet the Mount team, on the other hand, fell back upon its former league, Airedale & Wharfedale League, and went on to play for them under the able leadership of Hanif Mayet, whom everyone fondly calls Hanif Bhai, who was also known as Mr. Mount for he founded and guarded Mount CC; presently, Mount CC plays under the Halifax League in Staincliffe Cricket Grounds.

A Brief Period of Instability

During my absence in 1993, the Spen Victoria team played under the captaincy of a young, but spirited player named Andy Bethel. But unfortunately, the team suffered loses, as it fell to the bottom of the Division-I chart in the eleventh by the order of merit, while East Bierley went onto holding the top position. When I went back to Spen in 1994, I was again offered captaincy, but I opted to play under the young captain, Andy, who revived the team to its third position in the Division-I of the league. After playing for some time with Spen, I then resigned in 1994. In this way, except for1988, in all the years I played for Spen Victoria, the team had never gone bellow the 4th place, and had always maintained its status as one among the top four teams of the league. After leaving Spen Victoria in 1994, I joined Cleckheaton Cricket Club in 1995 upon the request of Abey Kuruvilla and played for one year there in Bradford League.

I again moved back to CYL in 1996, but this time to play for another club named Wrenthorpe for one year. In this club also, we as a team could not set any record, but I performed very well as a bowler, for which I won the *Club Bowling Prize* for my best performance in taking highest number of wickets for the season of 1996. After these couple of years of instability while changing clubs every year without attaining considerable success, I moved again in 1997 to play for Altofts CC, which was also a part of the CYL. In fact, the very first match that I played in CYL, when I joined Thornhill CC in 1980, was against this Altofts team; the team was so competitive that, on the same day, while playing against them, I wished that one day I should play for Altofts team, and it took so long a journey, almost 17 long years, to get a chance to finally play for this club in 1997.

In Altofts Cricket Club [1997-99]

When I joined Altofts as Vice-captain, the team was playing under the captaincy of Martin Bramley, with several other brilliant players like Tetley David, Gaza, Peter and a young wicket keeper, the famous Paul brothers (Paul Pemberton and his brother), and particularly the septuagenarian Clive Brook, who was called by everyone as Mr., Altofts for his dedication to Altofts. I have very good memories of all these players, particularly Clive who would be there in every single activity from cutting grass, preparing pitch, mentoring junior cricketers, playing, umpiring, and captaining both first and second teams, to organizing club meetings to carry out democratic dialogues and discussions; he was there as a substitute to any shortage of players; he was Mr. Altofts in true sense of the word. Captain Martin was a very cool man who would welcome the advice of every single player with equanimity and would give chances to all to show their talents, while sacrificing his own bowling opportunities. I began identifying with Martin, as I remembered my days in Batley CC as its captain, and in due course we both became good friends. I am glad that I met these great people, Clive, and Martin, and I am always indebted to them as I learnt immensely from them.

Clive got quite old, and unfortunately, he passed away in 2021 in his 90s. Peter was an unforgettable man, because of his bowling speed and consistency, in every over of every single match. In fact, the more he bowled the more speed he would attain in direct resemblance to a horse, so I used to call him 'Horsey.' It was a strange experience that although every player of the team was doing well in their own right, the team was not winning any season. However, I bowled very well for Altofts, during these 3 years of my association with them, between 1997 and 1999, that I took more than 200 wickets in all the three seasons combined and won the Bowling Prize in every single season I played there. In one of the matches against Staincliffe team in 1998, our opponents were playing well, and they were at 83 runs for 3 wickets, with several overs left to play, when I took to bowling. It was like a whirlwind; I took 5 wickets for just 6 runs in 28 balls, leading to the collapse of the entire Staincliffe team for merely 95 runs. It was a landslide victory for us, where we did not lose even a single wicket in our batting.

Slazenger Cricket Club and a Quiet & Relaxed Cricket Life

After leading the life of such a hectic schedule amidst increasing familial commitments, enhancing business activities, and with frequent travels to Altofts to play matches there, I now sought to lead a little relaxed life, yet continue to ally with cricket. Hence, I decided to leave Altofts in the year 1999 to join a club nearest to my home named Slazenger Cricket Club in 2000, so that it would be convenient for me to look after all the three important facets of my life—family, business, and cricket. So, I joined Slazengers in 2000, which was also part of Central Yorkshire League (CYL). In the very first year of my joining there, I won the 'League Bowling Prize' in 2000 for taking the highest wickets among all the teams in the premier division of the league. In a match against Wrenthorpe in the above season, an experienced batsman Robert Flack and I, as bowler, together led our team towards winning the match. Attributing our team's success to us, the media in those days hailed us as 'Slazengers' heroes' for our excellent performance. In that match, while Flack cracked his unbeaten 51 runs to steer our team's total score to 115 runs for 8 wickets, I took 6 wickets for just 23 runs to contain our opponents total score at mere 81 runs for 9 wickets.

After playing for a year, I took upon the captaincy of the team in 2001. By then, I had already entered sports business and launched a sport's equipment store on my name, Solly Sports. I also made an agreement with the Central Yorkshire League (CYL) to sponsor the League for 3 years, starting from 2001. But ironically, the team that I was heading as part of the CYL league was struggling very hard not to be relegated in its position. In one of the final days of the CYL-2001 season, when our team was in the verge of relegation, I made a self-satirical remark, with a smile, in a statement before the media: *It would not really be right if the sponsor's team was relegated, would it?* But I was wrong, and our team got relegated. After working for one more year as a captain of Slazengers, I finally took a retirement in 2002. After seven years of absolute disengagement with cricket, and complete involvement in familial and business affairs, I once again played a 40-over match for Yorkshire Over-60's against The Forty Club at Pinfold Lane, Fishlake on May 27, 2009, where our opponent's team won by 26 runs. So, Slazengers, in fact, came to be the last winning team in my cricket career, though technically it was not.

Summing up

After playing cricket passionately for 4 decades in Yorkshire, I finally decided to 'hang up my boots' in 2002. Ever since then, when I think of my entire cricket journey, I feel so blessed to be part of this most cherished sport to have been ever invented by humankind. When I started playing cricket in Natal Colony as a boy, I had not at once imagined that I would play this wonderful sport for such a long time. In these 40 years of my association with cricket in England, I never missed any chance to play cricket, except two matches owing to my daughter's marriage. I played every single match that knocked my door. This dedication had bestowed me with several laurels, and I was lauded by all and sundry for attaining them. Though I have a massive respect for all the clubs I played for, I specially thank Batley CC and Spen Victoria for giving me many opportunities and supporting me, and I will be forever grateful to them.

In this journey of my cricket life, I met some of the best people I have ever known, rubbed shoulders with several cricket legends, among whom some later became my intimate friends, with whom I shared some of the most beautiful memories for life. I also feel that I am blessed to have had an opportunity to be a mentor, to nurture various young cricketers in their early careers, many of whom later went on to represent their national teams at international levels; some of them also became very popular cricket legends of the world. All these things could have been possible because I consider cricket closest to my heart; it is next only to my religion. Cricket is not merely a game but has come to be a continuous source for learning the lessons of my life, to deal with everyday problems in life, including personal-domestic, socio-cultural, and professional problems. From the life experiences I gained from these years, I have shaped my world view that *difficult roads often lead to beautiful destinations.*

AIDING, MENTORING AND NURTURING

My natural drive to play cricket, my ardent desire to meet cricket stars and to be friends with them, and my ceaseless hunt for talented young cricketers, only to shower my unremitting affection for them had produced two mutually complementary formidable results: one, I had shown the young cricketers who were struggling to find a right place to prove their talents, in their desired path of progress of their careers; two, it had provided me in turn with ample opportunities not only to excel as a player and captain of various cricket clubs and leagues in England that earned me a popular status among the Yorkshire Cricket circles, but it had also bestowed me with warm reception as a loving member of a huge family of cricket stars and legends of the world. I provided several young and enthusiastic cricket aspirants, particularly Asians from India and Pakistan and its immigrants in England, with all the humanly possible help, and contributed my share in their successes, and in doing so, I got immense satisfaction. In a way, I have benefitted more from them, than the other way round. Among those hundreds of cricket-aspirants I aided in their path of success in varied ways, like signing contracts for them with various cricket clubs, and mentoring and nurturing them, were many who attained international eminence as star cricketers.

In my endeavours to extend my helping hand to the aspiring Asian cricketers, the support of some of the cricket legends and leaders from India was immense, particularly Sunil Gavaskar, Hemant Waingankar (Leader of a famous cricket club, Sun-Grace Mafatlal, in Bombay), and

Kailash Gattani (Founder and Manager of Star Cricket Club, from Bombay), and Rahul Mankad, who were instrumental in making my mission of identifying young talents to sign for the league cricket in England possible. Hemant, for instance, was a dedicated cricketing mentor, under whose stringent training promising cricketers such as Sachin Tendulkar and Vinod Kambli had been nurtured. Had it not been for these above stalwarts, it would not have been possible for many of the competent Asian cricketers to make their fortunes in England. The trust that managers of various cricket clubs in England have showered on me to sign contract with whomever I recommended, had also helped immensely to sign many Asian cricketers in England. In my life till date, I have aided more than 300 hundred cricketers from India and Pakistan and had them sign contracts with various cricket clubs in England.

In fact, the very idea of signing overseas cricketers for the club cricket in England, crawled into my imagination for the first time when I met a Bombay based Gujarati cricketer named Rahul Mankad, who had just been signed for Cleckheaton club, in 1976. Having Gujarati affinity, Rahul, and I became good friends, and through Rahul, I also met his other associates of Cleckheaton club like Suru Naik, Karsan Ghavri, Yajurvindra Singh etc., who were also from India, besides Vijay Mohan Raj. In fact, Rahul sought my help to find a contract for his brother, Ashok Mankad, whom I signed up for Dewsbury Cricket Club in late 70's. It became the starting point for my understanding of the nature of recruitment process in English cricket clubs, particularly in Yorkshire.

Meanwhile I was playing for Batley Muslim (1977-80), and during which I also organized and played several benefit/friendly matches with cricketers from India and Pakistan which resulted in establishing good contacts with them, and reputation spread in the overseas cricket circles, particularly in India and Pakistan. In this regard, I visited Bombay, India, in 1981, where I happened to see the net-practice of cricketers in the Cricket Club of India (CCI) grounds, as the CCI was just adjacent to a hotel in which I lodged. It was in the CCI grounds that I noticed the charm of four players, and with a little enquiry, I came to know that they were Chandrakanth Pandit, Raju Kulkarni, Lalchand Rajput, and Ravi Thakkar, and they were playing for a Bombay based team named Mafat Lal cricket team. All the four of them were young and talented with great potential and I thought that given an opportunity to play in English conditions, they would shine within no time with very little support. With the help of Ashok Mankad (Ashok Kaka), I checked about their interest for the league cricket in England. Sensing their enthusiasm and knowing about the rising demand for the Asian players in the league cricket in England, I immediately spoke to the two clubs—Batley CC and Thornhill CC—and upon their acceptance I called all four of them to England. While Chandrakanth Pandit was signed with Batley which offered him £25 a match, Raju Kulkarni was signed with Thornhill CC for £30 a match; the other two players - Lalchand Rajput and Ravi Thakkar—were respectively signed with Spen Victoria and Hartshead Moor.

The clubs in those days also had no restrictions/limitations, as to the number of the overseas players to be signed for each club, as several such restrictions were set in place in the later times. They reached England, and all the four were accommodated in one of my houses at Batley Carr and provided with lunch and dinner from one of our family friends, Saeed Desai, who lived in the neighbourhood of the house in which they stayed. In due course, they all played for several other and better clubs, which included their stint under my captaincy, and all of them proved their excellence in the league cricket in England; except Thakkar, who was also a promising bowler, the remaining three players went on to play for the Indian team later.

A few years after Chandrakanth leaving for India, I helped Masood Anwar from Pakistan to sign for Thornhill CC, and after a little while when I moved again to Batley CC, Masood also joined me to play under my captaincy. Meanwhile, I also brought Abdul Azeem, a Hyderabad based Ranji player to play for Batley CC. As soon as I took the captaincy of Batley CC, I began building the team by signing new players, or promoting the talented players in the 2nd team to play for the 1st team of the club. I signed various talented players, including Paul Blakley and David Batty of the 2nd Team of the club to play for the Team-1, besides signing two other Ranji players of India - Mehndi Shaikh from Baroda, and Barun Barman from Kolkata. Later, Mehndi Shaikh became a famous coach in India, upon whose training Pathan brothers—Yousuf Pathan and Irfan Pathan—attained star status as players of the Indian team. I also signed Rashid Khan and Masood Anwar from Pakistan during my tenure as a captain of the Batley CC; later, they both played for Pakistan team. Most of these players who were playing club cricket in England in those days, used to get a trifling amount of money that does not even meet their daily expenses, as their contract was performance based; the clubs would generally pay them merely 50 pence a run, 20 pence for a catch, and so on. However, they would still prefer to play, out of their passion for cricket only to attain mastery of the game; their dedication to the game earned them both wealth and fame as days went by.

Since there was not much involvement of money in Club Cricket, I used to organize Benefit Matches for cricketers by bringing different players together, whereby proceedings of the matches would be given to the nominated players. In this way, I organized more than 50 benefit matches. These matches were intended not merely to bring about democratic unity and inclusivity among the cricketers, and to instil sport spirit in the society at large, but also to offer the players with self-sufficient economic means to withstand themselves in their careers as sport-professionals.

Some of the cricketers who had no sufficient economic means for their survival would even look out for some part-time job opportunities, in between matches. I would either accommodate them in some of the business firms, whose management I was familiar with, or perhaps, sometimes I would offer them work within one of my own business firms. Likewise, many players, including some who rose to become cricket-stars later, such as VVS Laxman, Iqbal Qasim, Mohammad Kaif, Madan Lal, Abey Kuruvilla, Suresh Shetty, John Wood, etc., were accommodated to do some or the other part-time job in my own firms. I always feel proud of those players who made their living by working hard through their part-time jobs, while simultaneously sharpening their professional abilities to become star-cricketers. Interestingly, Iqbal Qasim was already an established international player in Pakistan by 1976, however, he would still prefer to play Club Cricket in England, when there were no international matches in the schedule. He was so fond of playing league cricket in England that, despite not having conducive weather conditions, he continued to stay in England, and eventually he became an intimate friend, loving brother-figure and member of my family. Such was the craze for club-cricket in those days. However, over the years, the clubs also began to bear both travelling and boarding expenses for overseas cricketers, at least once a player was signed with them. Of course, I had always been there to ease any one of them from any inconvenience caused due to cultural and other reasons, by inviting them for frequent dinners, or accommodation if required, or by offering them with part-time jobs, and even occasional financial assistance to some of them.

By the beginning of 1980s, my reputation grew much wider, and I became a single point of contact for all the clubs looking out for players from Asia, and for the sports manufacturers who look out for star-cricketers to endorse their goods. For many clubs, and for most of the times, my testimonial would suffice them to take any player I recommend. Hence, I used to help many Asian cricketers to sign for various clubs; often, many players would come to England on their own expenses, merely on my verbal assurance, and only then I would find some contract for them with some club, after their landing.

In January 1992, I organized a historic meet called 'Building Bridges' between the officials of Yorkshire league and Local Asian Cricket representatives to establish a bridge between English and Non-English cricketers. This meet did not serve its immediate purpose of establishing its stated objective, but it indirectly resulted in opening gates for the overseas players to sign for Yorkshire County. As an initial measure, the county invited an Australian cricketer Craig McDermott for the 1992 season, however, Craig could not join them yielding to his injury. Finding the right opportune moment, I immediately proposed the County to offer the same to Master Blaster Sachin Tendulkar, and which was agreed upon by both the parties. In this way, Sachin came to be not only the First Asian to play for the Yorkshire County, but he was the first one among any cricketer who played for Yorkshire County hailing from outside of its territory. Before Sachin, the County did never have a history of signing anyone born outside the Yorkshire region.

Sensing my increasing fame and influence in all the cricket circles, both at home country as well as in Asia, many sport equipment manufacturing companies like Crown Sports, County Sports, Slazengers, etc., also began approaching me to set the bat-contracts and endorsement deals with star cricketers as part of their respective brand promotion. Particularly, since the bat manufacturing company, Crown Sports had an account in my petrol station named AMOCO (American Motor Oil Company) to purchase petrol regularly from us, I used to promote crown-bats among all cricketers I know off. With this, several cricketers like Kapil Dev, Imran Khan, Abid Ali, Taslim Arif, Rahul Mankad, Ashok Mankad, Gundappa Vishwanath, Suru Nayak, Karsan Ghavri, Madan Lal, Brijesh Patel, Mudassar Nazar, and many others began to play with Crown bat in all their matches, both locally and internationally. This bat was also a favourite of our cricket legend, Sunil Gavaskar. The bat manufacturers, particularly the owner of the Crown Sports, George, would invite me to their factories, where I would visit along with popular cricketers from Asia like Mohinder Amarnath, Surinder

Amarnath, Abid Ali, and several others, who had an honour of picking any bat of their choice for free. In this way, many of them also got bat-contracts for £300 to £500 per season, which was quite a big amount in early 1980s.

Seeing the popularity that the above sport companies began to enjoy with these endorsements, another famous sports company Slazengers, also approached me around the same time in 1996, if I can help them finding endorsers; its director, Norman Hughes, came to offer handsome money, along with free kits, to its endorsers. For this, I first approached Sachin Tendulkar for a bat-contract with Slazengers; Sachin was glad, but by then he had already signed a better deal with another famous company named MRF. Then, I brought other emerging players of Indian team such as Sourav Ganguly, Rahul Dravid, Ajay Jadeja to sign bat-contracts with Slazengers during their tour to England in 1996.

My house had always been open to all the cricketers who made their debut into league/county cricket of England through me and became intimate family friends. As I had several houses in England, many cricketers from Asia, including Sachin, Vinod, Imran Khan, Iqbal Qasim, and many other would reside in one of my houses, during their tenure in England. Particularly, Imran Khan had been such a simple man, and was an inalienable member of my family. During his tenure at Wakefield Cricket Club in Yorkshire, Imran would stay in my house, and often sleep on the couch in the hall of my house. My wife, Maryam, had always been, and still is, there to host every cricketer, who comes to England through my contact, with equal warmth, and never let anyone leave without tasting her finest delicacies of Asia, and for that she would in turn receive the respect of all as the Bhabhi Ji; she was also a mother-figure for some of the young-stars to whom I extended my parental care and love. I feel the honour of assisting various cricketers from Asia, either through signing for clubs, or as a mentor for many a young cricketer, or by getting bat-contracts for the star-cricketers, or even by hosting several of them in my houses. My house was always crowded with several Asian cricketers, particularly before the beginning of a season, and many of them would go on staying in the house till they found some club-contract, and then some other accommodation to stay. There was a moment when 15 to 20 cricketers lived together, at once, in one of my houses waiting to secure some club-contract, before the start of a season. In this way, the list of the cricketers who are associated with me was quite a big (more than 300 cricketers), and it would be difficult to lay down the name of every single one I know. To recall from my memory, here are a few cricket stars who received my assistance in some or the other ways.

I took the initiative to sign Tushar Arothe, Vinod Kambli, Rohan Gavaskar, Sairaj Bahuthule, Lalu Rajput, Dhruv Mohan, Abdul Jabbar and Wasim Jaffer from India, for Spen Victoria CC that plays under Bradford League. I also assisted them when many of them later moved to play for other clubs, for instance Tushar with Treeton CC (South Yorkshire League), Sairaj with Stockton CC (North Yorkshire and South Durham League), and Wasim Jaffer with Scholes CC (Huddersfield League). I was also instrumental in signing Abey Kuruvilla, Kanwaljit Singh, Suresh Shetty, Noel David and Vivek Jaisimha from India for Cleckheaton CC that plays under Bradford League, and Dilip Vengsarkar, VVS Laxman, Sameer Dighe, Hoshedar Contractor, Rashid Patel and Abhijit Kale from India, and Abdul Qadir, Iqbal Qasim, and Suleman Huda from Pakistan to sign for Hanging Heaton CC, which too plays under Bradford League; some of them, later, went on to play for other clubs. While Laxman played for Pudsey Congs, under the captaincy of the legendary cricketer, Phil Carrick, who represented Yorkshire County, Sameer played for Ossett CC; Suresh Shetty also went ahead to play for Lidget Green CC later.

I initially signed Mansoor Akhtar from Pakistan for Chickenley CC, which he soon left to join Spen Victoria CC, upon my guidance. Abhijit

Kale, on the other hand, emerged unfortunately to be unsuccessful and controversial in the Huddersfield League, where he broke his contract with Scholes CC in the most critical juncture, that amounted to his breach of trust, for which he had to face the ban for life from playing with any league cricket in England; the ban, however, was revoked with my intervention.

I introduced Jatin Paranjape and Pranab Roy from India, and Rizwan-uz-Zaman from Pakistan to play for the Yorkshire Bank CC of Bradford League, Rashid Patel and Chetan Sharama to Scholes CC of Huddersfield League, Mohammad Kaif to Lightcliffe CC of Bradford League, and Daniel Manohar to Altofts CC, under Central Yorkshire League. I arranged contract for Jacob Martin, Ravi Thakkar, Shishir Hattangadi, and W. V. Raman from India, and Shahid Mahboob from Pakistan with the Hartshead Moor CC, that plays under Bradford League. Mirfield CC also accommodated cricketers like Badruddin Iqbal Khan and Ghulam Parkar from India, Nasir Ali Shah from Karachi in Pakistan, in their club, upon my recommendations. I also arranged contract for Vedam Hariharan, a Bangalore based Ranji player from India, with Slazengers team, when Hariharan moved to England; I did it upon the request of a journalist from Bangalore who was introduced to me by a close friend of mine named Brijesh Patel (a popular Indian cricketer, who later served IPL as chairman); Hariharan was supposed to be the brother of that journalist whose name I am not familiar with. Hariharan was a promising cricketer, who received applauds from Kapil Dev for his high potential in the game.

Besides Chandrakanth Pandit from India, I also signed Abdul Azeem, Mehndi Shaik, Faiz Fazal and Barun Burman from India, and Masood Anwar and Rashid Khan from Pakistan with Batley CC; Abdul later played for Shepley CC in Huddersfield League, when Masood moved from Thornhill CC to Batley CC. Later, I also signed Jatin Paranjape to Thornhill CC, and Aminul Islam (known as Bulbul) from Bangladesh to Birstall.

For inducting all these cricketers into different leagues in England, I had been their most supportive companion, adviser, and a guide; I was even a father figure for some of them. I had always been there to assist them in their every professional turn, as well as offering most of them with other kinds of support like food and accommodation when required. I never took even a penny for doing all these, instead I spent from my pocket when required; I now feel proud to look back, as almost all of them played for their respective national teams.

Besides the ones named above, I also arranged contracts for several other players with different clubs; some of them later achieved greater significance and became world stars and legends. In this line, I signed Imran Khan (former captain of the Pakistan cricket team), with the help of Hudson Insurance Company, for merely £50 per match, though it was the highest pay of the day for any cricketer playing for the leagues in the mid-seventies. A little later, I had set a contract for Madan from India for £1200 per season for playing for the Enfield Cricket Club (in Lancashire League), while he was expecting merely £600. Madan, then emerged a legendary all-rounder, and played his significant part in winning the World Cup for India in 1983.

I had helped range of players for signing various clubs, that include, Sulakshan Kulkarni, for Liversidge CC in 1990, whom I also guided in moving to East Bierley team in 1993, followed by a Hyderabad based Ranji Player named Madireddy Venkat Narasimha Rao (also known as Bobjee Narasimha Rao), Avinash Karnik and Connor Williams from India to sign for Birstall CC, Amol Majumdar for Lidget Green and Windhill cricket clubs in Bradford League, Nanda Kishore from Telangana, India for Woodlands Cricket Club in Bradford League in 1999, Rajesh Powar, Rajesh Yadav (brother of an Indian Test Player Shiva Lal Yadav) for Slazengers, Raju Kulkarni for Thornhill and then to Methley clubs, Sanjay Manjrekar for Stockton CC in North Yorkshire and South Durham League, Abhay Laghate for Soothill CC, Atul Ranade for Baildon CC, Prashant Vaidya for Heckmondwike CC, Manoj Joglekar for East Ardsley, Surya Baindoor and Nadeem Ghauri for Staincliffe, Rajendra Jadeja for Brighouse, Sanjay Bangar for Chickenley CC, Mansoor Rana (Player of Pakistan team) for Baildon CC, Saeed Azad from Pakistan for Chickenley CC, and then for Gomersal CC. I not only took initiative in getting all these above players in signing for all those above-mentioned clubs, but also extended my assistance in the change of their clubs. Vijay Mohan Raj (Tony), a popular cricketer among the Indian Ranji cricket circles, was inducted initially to Cleckheaton CC by Rahul Mankad. However, he and his family became my intimate friends in his later phase, as I signed him for Shepley CC under Huddersfield League. Sarfaraz Khan, on the other hand, approached me, through a friend, Dr Sameer Pathak, and I set the contract for him with Hull CC in Yorkshire Premier League; I also helped Sarfaraz to sign with Shenley Village CC later.

I also had a good connections with several clubs, playing under Huddersfield League, where I got the contracts for various players from India and Pakistan; they include, the signing of players from India such as Paras Mhambray for Skelmanthorpe CC, Amay Khurashia for Broad Oak CC, Atul Wassan for Marsden CC, Nilesh Kulkarni for Mirfield Parish Cavaliers CC, Atul Bedade for Golcar CC, Ameen Lakhani for Bradley Mills CC (the club is not in existence now) etc., and Syed Ali Raza Naqvi with Skelmanthorpe CC, Kashif Ahmed(Nephew of Tauseef Ahmad, who represented Pakistan team) for Townville CC, and Sajid Ali for Bradley Mills CC, from Pakistan; I also signed Robin Singh for the same league. While almost all these players later went on to represent their national teams, Paras Mhambray, for instance came to serve as bowling coach of the Indian team, after playing for India for a few years.

All these Asian cricketers apart, I was also instrumental in inducting several natives of England into the club cricket; they include Moham-mad Arif, Paul Blakely, and Paul Jarvis who were signed for Batley CC, while John Wood, Tim Walton, Mike Smith, Andy Bethel, and Steve Bethel were signed for the Spen Victoria CC; I also convinced John Car-ruthers, who was then associated with Birstall CC, and another brilliant player Steve Foster, to sign for Spen.

I exerted all my energies to do this talent hunt, that led me to get connected, thanks to Almighty, and during these four decades of my journey of life in cricket, I manged to sign more than 300 cricketers from India and Pakistan to league cricket in England. Out of them, at least more than 150 cricketers went on to represent, either their national teams in international cricket as players, captains, and some of them even emerged to be legends, coaches, referees etc., or played First-Class cricket. I often feel elated when, some of the senior cricketers would re-mind me of my invisible role in recognising original talents and initi-ating them to various clubs at right opportune moment, in the initial stages of their careers. It was a historical fact that there was a time when, out of the 11 players in the Indian Cricket team, 9 players took my assis-tance either for signing club contracts in England, or bat contracts with manufacturers, or some other help; it was the same with the cricketers of Pakistan as well.

For all my contributions to cricket and cricketers which conse-quently resulted in a surge of emotional attachment; I have the honour of being treated as Bhai (elder brother) by most cricketers I know of, and for some of the youngsters, I remain a father-figure.

For all these, I did not expect anything in return, nor did I act as a professional agent to earn my living out of them. In fact, there was no such profession called cricket agent during those days, as could be seen these days. I never took even a penny from any of the players to whom I extended different kinds of help, nor did I ever boast of my contribution. However, I invested every bit of my time and energies, including money for the professional and personal development of these cricketers, where my family members also extended their services and personal lives for the cause. As a saying goes, "Needing Nothing, Attracts Everything," I did this all out of sheer love for the game, and affection for the aficionados of cricket, without expecting anything in return, and so were these fantastic results of attracting a range of cricketers into the vast horizon of cricket.

BENEFIT/TESTIMONIAL MATCHES

My popularity as an Asian businessman in England and my excellence as a player and captain in leading all those cricket teams and clubs that I so far represented in England, had secured me the trust and confidence of various cricket clubs in Yorkshire. This apart, I also earned the affection of various cricket-legends in international cricket, particularly several star-cricketers from India and Pakistan. In fact, several young-cricketers whom I introduced to English club-cricket and county cricket from Asia, later rose to an international eminence. I always have cherished my affection with all of them, and some of them became my best friends in life. All this has been possible, because of my passionate commitment to cricket, and love for cricketing fraternity for over four decades; I love cricket, and I adore cricketers.

But the earnings from careers in cricket in those days in 1970s and 80s were so meagre, that the players had to live on bare subsistence. To address this challenge, I then proposed the concept of organizing benefit matches for those cricketers who had made significant contributions to the sport. The intention behind this idea was two-fold: Firstly, it aimed to foster unity, and fraternity among the cricket players across the globe, cutting across the ranges of players from local clubs to those who were part of first-class cricket, and even cricketing legends. Secondly, it also aimed to provide some sort of financial support to cricketers who had made significant contributions to the game. With this initiative, I tried to create some means of financial benefit to the cricketers who contributed to the game. While overseas club cricketers would get merely £25 to £30 per match, a single benefit match could generate a sum greater than what they would earn throughout an entire season. I also hoped that it would give a sense of satisfaction, for being honoured for their dedication to cricket, and their efforts for excelling in it.

It was with this above view that I began to organise several Benefit, Testimonial, Charity, and friendly matches in mid- 1970s, and by early 1980s, I had already signed numerous talented young cricketers from India and Pakistan to various clubs in England. In addition to these endeavours, I was also actively involved in fundraising activities for various sports, particularly cricket. On that account, I undertook talent hunt for the young promising cricketers, and would often sponsor those cricketers whom I considered had a great potential, or also assisted the less fortunate players with great potentials by providing them cricket equipment. I organised and played matches to raise funds for them. I also organized charity matches to support cricket-related causes, or other social empowerment initiatives.

I have successfully organized, played, and captained several benefit and testimonial matches in my cricketing career, and the list of these matches was quite extensive, and it is a bit difficult, if not impossible, to recall every event without the aid of technological tools, and online records. However, I began delving into for its details diligently partly from the archival sources, but mostly recalling from my memory, in which the untiring efforts of my young friend, cricket enthusiast and the author of this book, Vara Vantapati has been significant. The list of those benefit/testimonial matches are as follows.

List of Benefit/Testimonial Matches

- Asian XI vs DDL XI Invitation Match – Mirfield Cricket Ground - 1976

- Farokh Engineer - Testimonial Match at Mirfield Parish Ground - 1976
- Keith Goddard's Benefit Match at Hanging Heaton Club - 1977
- Shaukat Dudha (Gujarat) Benefit Match – 1977
- Solly Adam International XI Vs Hanging Heaton XI – August 6, 1978
- Avi Karnik - Benefit Match - Birstall Gavaskar XI Vs Select XI – August 10, 1980
- David Bairstow – Testimonial Match – July 27, 1982
- Richard Lumb - Testimonial Cricket Match – August 19, 1983
- Geoffrey Boycott - Testimonial Match at Batley – May 29, 1984
- Richard Hadlee – Testimonial Match – May 5, 1986
- Batley Vs Yorkshire CCC – Invitation Match – May 30, 1986
- Imran Khan - Benefit Match at Batley – July 5, 1987
- Suru Nayak - Benefit Match 1990-91
- Jatin Paranjape's Benefit Match – Thornhill CC- 1992
- Tim Robinson (Nottinghamshire) Testimonial Match at Batley CC – 1992
- Sanjay Manjrekar - Benefit Match – 1995 (Stockton Cricket Club)
- Sairaj Bahuthule - Benefit Match – 1996 (Stockton Cricket Club)
- Mansoor Rana Benefit Match - India XI Vs Pakistan XI – July 29, 1998
- Abey Kuruvilla – Benefit Match – August 20, 2000
- Mohsin Khan Benefit Match - Lancashire
- Mansoor Akhtar – Benefit Match at Huddersfield – (Sunil Gavaskar)
- Javed Miandad – Benefit Match at Preston - (Sunil Gavaskar)

- International XI Vs East Bierley Bradford League XI – 1992
- Kathiawar XI Vs Rest of the World XI - 1980
- Graham Thorpe – Benefit Match at Guernsey.
- Holland Centenary Cricket Match - Netherlands Vs World XI – June 14, 2003
- Yajurvindra Singh (Sunny Singh) - Benefit Match at Blackpool.

Asian XI vs DDL XI Invitation Match - 1976

The earliest match in this series, as far as I remember, was the one that I organised, probably in 1976, between Asian XI vs. Dewsbury and District League XI. This match holds significance, owing to historical reasons. As my petrol stations were sites of several coincidences, this match was also a result of one such coincidence at my petrol station in Huddersfield. One day, as usual, when I was working at one of my petrol stations in Huddersfield, I had an opportunity to have a general interaction with a customer named Goolam Abed. In our conversation, when he learnt that I was a league cricketer, he was curious to know about sports and cricket in the Yorkshire region, as he himself was a cricketer, and so we delved deeper into discussion on various topics associated with cricket, and our personal lives. From this conversation, I learnt that the family of Goolam Abed had hailed originally from South Africa, but migrated to England in the 1960s, owing to racial discrimination and oppression under the apartheid regime there. To my joy, I also learnt that his brother, Dik Abed, then was playing for the Enfield Cricket Club of the Lancashire League and was regarded as one of the most promising cricketers of the league. Eventually, our friendship bloomed, and one day I proposed the idea of organizing a cricket match, with the intention of unifying the immigrants and the natives. Goolam enthusiastically embraced the idea and began assembling players from different leagues.

In fact, it was while gathering the players for this noble cause that

Goolam Abed introduced me to Cec Abrahams, a renowned cricketer from South Africa; Cec gained recognition among the coloured community in Cape Town during 1950s as a talented fast-bowler, all-rounder, and a man of strong principles. Eventually, Cec and his family migrated to England, where he began playing in the Central Lancashire League in 1960; he later represented various clubs, including the notable Milnrow Cricket Club. I then also had the pleasure of meeting John Holder, who was playing in Huddersfield League. John Holder even tried to bring Joel Garner, a legendary cricketer from the West Indies who then was playing in Lancashire, for our match. But unfortunately, Joel could not join us, due to his other commitments. Cec Abrahams then proposed to bring in Gary Sobers, who was also in Lancashire and a good friend of Cec. Though Gary was a generous person who did not demand any money for playing the match, he would require £10 to cover-up his travel expenses, which I regretfully could not afford as £10 in those days was a significant lot. Thus, I missed out an invaluable opportunity to play with great Gary Sobers, where I was the captain, a regret that troubles my mind even to this day. However, it was from this idea, and endeavours to assemble immigrants in England that the team Asian XI was formed, and its match with Dewsbury and District League XI was finally held at the Mirfield Cricket Ground.

To the best of my memory, some of the players who participated in this historic match include, Dik Abed, John Holder, Cec Abrahams, Goolam Abed, Rashid Dawood, Baboo Karkun, Samad Vacchiyath, Haroon Hans, Abdul Hai Aswat, Philip Ackroyd, Colin Fretwell, Alec Joy, Kenny Blackburn, R. Dias (Sri Lanka) and myself. Some of them later embarked into international cricket. While Dik Abed served as the captain for the Netherlands team during ICC Trophy in 1982, John Holder later played for the Hampshire County team, and then went on to become a Test Umpire. Moreover, John Abrahams, son of Cec Abrahams, held the captaincy of Lancashire County team for several years.

Farokh Engineer (India) - Testimonial Match at Mirfield Parish Ground - 1976

A little while after this historic event (Lancashire XI vs Solly Adam International XI), in the same year, in 1976, I also organised a testimonial match for a Bombay based Indian test cricketer, Farokh Engineer. Farokh had an impressive career and had played 46 test matches for India, between 1959 to 1975, besides simultaneously playing for Lancashire County, during 1968 to 1976. This was the first benefit match that I had ever organised which was played for an International Player.

In recognition of his remarkable contributions to the Lancashire County cricket team, Farokh was granted a benefit season in 1976. But, contrary to general practice of the county, where they usually conduct its benefit-matches in their own grounds, unless somebody requests them to have it in those of other counties, the benefit-match for Farokh Engineer was scheduled to be played at 'Mirfield Parish' ground. The way in which the match was conducted was so informal that Farokh had to bring his own team from Lancashire, and I formed a team with a few players like Abid Ali, Brijesh Patel, Madan Lal, Rahul Mankad, and Ashok Mankad, who were playing club-cricket in Yorkshire at that time, and a couple of other players from Pakistan, and John Holder (Test Umpire) and some local cricketers. Added to this, there were hardly any Asian spectators to watch cricket matches in England of the 1970s, and so the chances for its success were too meagre. But, to everyone's surprise, the event was a massive success, as there was huge turn out; cricket-fans of the Yorkshire region thronged in large numbers as they were excited to see their international cricket-stars come to play in their native grounds.

I was so happy that my very first initiative for the benefit match became a huge success. Having attained this success, given a large fanbase in England and my association with popular cricketers, several clubs expressed their appreciation for my efforts in organizing these kinds of matches and bringing in international stars to participate. It was an immense gratification for me to witness the positive impact these benefit/testimonial matches had on both the players involved, and the clubs that were hosting them. As the managements of various cricket clubs in England were well-aware of my extensive connections with international players and star cricketers from sub-continent, they considered me to be a suitable candidate to assist them in organizing these matches. It was so great a success that, even county players from Yorkshire, Lancashire, and Nottinghamshire would also approach me to arrange benefit matches for them during the benefit seasons of various players.

Keith Goddard's Benefit Match at Hanging Heaton Club – 1977

In 1977, I received a request from the committee of the Hanging Heaton, asking me, if I can organize a match for the benefit of their player named Keith Goddard. Fortunately, most players of international eminence whom I knew, and were friends with from India and Pakistan were at that moment playing for various clubs in the Yorkshire region. I spoke to Jimmy (Mohinder Amarnath), his brother Surinder, and other Indian stars like Madan Lal, Abid Ali, Rahul Mankad, Sunny Singh (Yajurvindra Singh), and those from Pakistan like Shafiq Papa (Shafiq Ahmed), Mohsin Khan, Aslam Qureshi and Imran Khan, including some local league cricketers, and they all happily agreed to join me to play under my captaincy, against Hanging Heaton. With these players in hand, I formed a team named after me as *Solly Adam's International XI*.

The match was scheduled to be played at Bennett Lane in Hanging Heaton; it was a wonderfully bright sunny day, that attracted massive crowd who were curious to watch all their favourite cricketers. Just before the match, Imran joined me to go and see the pitch and grounds. It was so brilliant! The pleasant sunlight enhanced the green glow of the grounds, as the pitch and the grounds were covered with lush green grass which aids the ball to have a good swing and bounce. Stunned by the appearance of the pitch, Imran said, to my recall: "Solly Bhai, for God's sake, please do not give me bowling; this pitch is amazing for a fast bowler, but their batters might get injured if bowled in full pace," and then he said, "they are all local club cricketers; so, I don't want to hurt them." Then I said to Imran, "the crowd would be excited to watch you bowling, and if you do not bowl at all, they might get upset. So, please bowl one or two overs and see how it goes, and if the batsmen are unable to play your ball, then you can bowl slow, or I will get someone to bowl in your place." Imran said, "okay."

At that time, Imran Khan had just moved from Worcestershire County to Sussex County in 1977, but a general practice/rule of the counties was that there must be a gap of at least 10 weeks before one begins to play for a new county. Hence, during those 10 weeks, Imran wanted to play some club cricket to keep himself fit and active. So, I got him signed for Wakefield Cricket Club, where he would play on Saturdays. Since he was free on the remaining days of a week, he was generous enough to play for us, whenever I organized any benefit/testimonial matches that honours other players. Likewise, he played two matches under my captaincy against Hanging Heaton. By then, Imran Khan was already an established international player, and was also playing county cricket in England. But, to honour my friendship, and to extend his solidarity to his fellow cricketers, he would always be at my beck and call and would join us to play whenever I invited him.

Having several international players, my team (Solly Adam's International XI) took to batting first, after winning the toss. In this match, we scored 238 runs in 40 overs, which was a big score in those days for a 40-over match. We thought it was almost impossible for a club team to chase that score, against all the International Bowlers in our team. Amidst the cheers from audience, Imran started bowling first over, and I set fielding according to Imran's wish and asked the keeper to stay slightly distant from usual standing place, as the ball has too much swing and bounce. The opening batsmen of the Hanging Heaton, on the other hand, were Hudson Brothers, among whom Ronnie Hudson was one of the best batsmen in the league. Imran started off the over with fast bowling as usual, and we were all worried as to how these guys were going to face Imran. But it was unbelievable; Ronnie hit back-to-back boundaries, while his brother hit a sixer in the last ball of the first over itself. It was a shock to everyone, and worst so, for Imran. Abid Ali bowled the second over which went reasonably well, leaving the 3rd over again to Imran. Imran was furious and wanted to take a wicket at any cost. But the faster he bowled, the faster the ball was going out of the ground. Both the Hudson brothers played astonishingly well on that day; one of them scored a century, while the other did 70 odd runs. Despite having all the international and top bowlers, we lost the match merely to a club team, Hanging Heaton; they could chase our score more than comfortably.

Imran's words, after the match, are still reverberating in my ears: "Personally, I learned a big lesson that you cannot predict anything, and you cannot say big words that I can do this, and I can do that; you never know what happens to you in the minute. Moreover, we should never underestimate the opponent's capability!"

Shaukat Dudha (Gujarat, India) Benefit Match – 1977

Again, in the same year in 1977 within few months after the above match, I organised and played a benefit match for Shaukat Dudha at Durham, upon his personal request. Shaukat was formerly a Baroda Ranji Player, and then a club cricketer in Durham; we became friends, owing to Gujarati affinity. So, when Shaukat asked me if I can play and organise popular cricketers for his match, I agreed, and immediately contacted my best friend, and younger-brother figure Iqbal Qasim, who had just then returned from Australian tour; it was a successful tour for Iqbal as he had managed to get the wickets of the best of the Australian cricket-ers like Chappell Brothers, and all other top players. As expected, Iqbal readily agreed to play. Then I approached Rahul Mankad, Yajurvindra Singh, Madan Lal, Ashok Mankad, Karsan Ghavri, Abid Ali, etc., to play; they all expressed their joy to be part of the match.

There was a big turn-out of the crowd; mics & speakers were ar-ranged for the match commentary, and it was a full vibrant atmosphere at the ground. At the registration of our names, just before the match, I registered my name as Iqbal Qasim in the scorecard, replacing him with that of my name (Solly Adam), just for fun. Since Live cricket on TVs in those days were not accessible to the masses, the spectators mistook Iqbal Qasim for me, and vice versa. But they were all aware of the fame that Iqbal Qasim had attained as a Pakistani test cricketer who had re-cently tasted success in Australian Tour. It was also confusing for both audiences, and the players in the opponent's team alike, that we both (Iqbal and I) were left-arm spinners, and so they could not actually dif-ferentiate between us. So, when I went to bowl, I was referred in the announcement, as 'Iqbal Qasim,' a renowned Pakistani Test player.

The psychology of the batsmen was such that, on hearing my name Iqbal Qasim, they showered a mix of attitudes—respect for me, and their pride for playing against a star cricketer. In their over cautiousness, they played straight and could not actually hit the ball, that credited me with a maiden over. On the contrary, when Iqbal Qasim went to bowl, they perceived him as Solly Adam, a local cricketer from Dewsbury and Dis-trict League (DDL). Then, the batsmen started hitting him black and blue, as they were free from any inhibition since they thought that they were just playing against a local club cricketer, and not against a crick-et star; they keep hitting the balls of Iqbal all over the ground. All my friends—Rahul Mankad, Shaukat Dudha, etc., —who noticed this fact could not control laughing, while the rest were in a shock and confu-sion. When I went to bowl the next over, the batman at the non-striker end who played my first over maiden, was telling me, "Iqbal, we are so fortunate to play your bowling today, particularly, after you had a great tour in Australia; you bowl to all the cricketers of Australia—Ian Chappell, Greg Chappell, Rodney Marsh and other top batsmen." He then also told me that he was so pleased that he was facing a Pakistani Test Cricketer. Seeing the batsmen hitting cross shots in a few overs of his bowling, Iqbal shouted at me, while we were all laughing, "Solly Bhai! go and tell them that I am Iqbal Qasim," It was a great and memorable event for all of us. Moreover, this match was a lesson for me that, psychology makes a huge difference in sports. This experience helped me a lot when I later captained the teams in better standard cricket.

Solly Adam International XI Vs Hanging Heaton XI – August 6, 1978

Inspired by the popularity that these benefit/testimonial matches enjoyed, Hanging Heaton CC once again approached me some time in 1978, asking if I could organise an invitation match for them against my team, an offer which I readily accepted. By now, my team, Solly Adam International XI had been already familiar to all the cricket lovers among the Yorkshire league circles, as my team enjoyed the privilege of hosting several world renowned International and first-class cricketers in it. Since most of our team members were busy playing internationally, I had to check their timings, and only then I could confirm their participation. So, as the captain and organiser of my team, I began approaching all the players who were previously part of my team. Most players gave their confirmation to play.

This was our 2nd match against Hanging Heaton XI, and the match was scheduled on August 6, 1978, in their own grounds at Bennet Lane. While preparing the program card, Imran was not sure of his participation, as he felt that he might have other commitments, and yet expressed his love for being the part of it. But fortunately, he could join us on the day of the match. Then, I formed my team with such star players as Imran Khan, Rahul Mankad, Rajendra Jadeja, Karsan Ghavri, Madan Lal, M.V. (Bobjee) Narasimha Rao, Subrata Guha, Suresh Shastri, Rajinder Amarnath, Abdul Jabbar, Hari Haran, Surya Baindoor, Mohammad Dadhiwala, Haroon Rasheed, and Dilip Doshi. The team, Hanging Heaton XI, on the other hand, comprised of their own club players; they included players like Ruel Hudson, Ronnie Hudson, A Jackson, C Beilby, D Bruce, M Wrigglesworth, D Haigh, David Legood, and G Ford, with David Garner as its captain along with Malcolm Preston in their team.

Though it was an invitation match, all the players played with a sporting spirit, and it turned out to be a huge success. The Indian and Pakistani cricketers enjoyed a lot, playing together, and the joy got heightened when we emerged victorious. In celebration of the unity of the players, and success of the match, we all shared a delightful dinner; it was a memorable evening, and all the proceedings of the match, including its dinner party, were all sponsored by my own group of companies named Adam Brothers.

Avi Karnik (India) - Benefit Match at Birstall - August 10, 1980

On August 10, 1980, we organized an invitation match at Birstall Cricket Club in Batley for the benefit of Avinash Karnik. Avinash was formerly a first-class cricketer who played for the Bombay team; he was, at that moment, playing for Birstall CC team in Central Yorkshire League. He is also known as Avi by all his friends and was a good friend of Sunil Gavaskar. In fact, it was with the recommendations from Sunil that I helped Avi get recruited to Birstall CC. It was also a time, when Sunil was the captain of the Indian Test Team, besides being a player for Somerset County as a replacement for Sir Viv Richards. This match was aimed at enhancing sport-spirit among the league cricketers, and to that effect, attempts were made to involve international cricket stars, particularly legendary Sunil Gavaskar, besides other star-cricketers like

Karsan Ghavri (an Indian Test Player) and Iqbal Qasim (a Pakistani Test Player).

As a commitment to their friendship, Sunil gave his assurance to Avi that he would join his team. Initially, we were slightly apprehensive about Sunil's participation in the match, as he had a hectic schedule with the Somerset County. But we all knew that, once he made a promise, Sunil would never fail to meet that promise. Accordingly, Sunil flew from Somerset, and landed in Leeds-Bradford Airport. I picked him up from airport, and we directly went to the grounds. Once the participation of Sunil was confirmed, I decided to join the opposing team, and till then, I was thinking of playing in Avi's team.

Finally, we all formed two teams and named them Birstall (Gavaskar) XI and Select League XI. We inserted the name Gavaskar in the title of the former team, as a token of respect for Sunil who represented the team of the benefitting player (Avi). While Avi captained the Birstall (Gavaskar) XI, having Sunil Gavaskar, P. Ingham, R. Wright, M. Walmsley, D. Sadler, G. Hobson, W. Finch, A. Bordman, C. Manby, D. Jones, D. Johnson, M. Ellis and D. Gill in his side, I formed Select League XI team, with players, like J. Woodford, R. Jarrett, E. Loxton, A. Dennison, B. Mason, G. Parkes, M. Laidler, R. Hirst, including me, and world renowned players like Iqbal Qasim, Vijay Mohan Raj (Tony), Barun Burman and Karsan Ghavri, with P. Hudson as our Captain.

I was excited to bowl Sunil, as it was the dream of my life to bowl him. When I got the chance to bowl, I utilised all my skills and experience as a spin-bowler and tried to drift the ball to trouble him. The first ball, I managed to bowl on the leg-side, which swiftly drifted off-side. Sunil missed it, and in great disbelief, he said, "Solly, what are you doing.?" Then, I replied to Sunil that I was doing my best to take his wicket. To my reply, Sunil again said, "never mind the wicket, first try to beat me again." After that, he left no ball untouched and played tremendously well, leading their team to win the match. I felt honoured to be defeated by my best friend, Sunil, who is an all-time cricket legend; it was a delightful challenge for me to have bowled Sunil. Overall, the match was successful, and it presented Avi with some benefit; over time, Avi became my close friend.

David Bairstow (England) – Testimonial Match –July 27, 1982

Given the large fanbase that Batley CC enjoyed, to which I was previously associated, and my extensive connections with Asian cricketers who were playing for various clubs in Yorkshire region, several players from Yorkshire County approached me to organize testimonial matches for them at Batley CC. By early 1980s, though I was an active part of Thornhill CC, I continue to have a good rapport with the management of Batley CC. Since both the players and managements of the Yorkshire County were aware of my connections with renowned cricketers, they chose me to be a suitable candidate to assist them in organizing these matches.

When Yorkshire County granted benefit year for David Bairstow in 1982, to honour his long-standing service to the county team, David approached me to organise the match for him at Batley CC. David was a highly regarded cricket personality in Yorkshire, and his son, Johnny Bairstow, is currently a key player in the England team. So, I was happy to extend my assistance to him, and along with the county, we organised a testimonial match for him on July 27, 1982, at Mount Pleasant of Batley CC, featuring David Bairstow Yorkshire XI and Batley Select XI. Both the teams comprised renowned players; while Yorkshire County comprised several renowned players like David Bairstow, Richard Lumb, Phil Carrick, Jim Love, Arnie Sidebottom, Kevin Sharp, Peter Ingram, Neil Hartley, Peter Whitley, and Paul Jarvis, Batley Select XI, on the other hand, had players like Ghulam Parkar, Barun Barman, Chandrakanth Pandit, Mehndi Shaik from India, Shahid Mehboob from Pakistan, Ronnie Hart from New Zealand, and Ronnie Hudson from the Hanging Heaton CC.

Sir Geoffrey Boycott was originally slated to be a part of the Yorkshire Team, and his name was even included in the program card. But he dropped out at the last minute, due to unknown reasons. Then, the renowned New Zealand cricketer, Martin Crowe, took his place to play for the Yorkshire team. I was offered the captaincy to lead Batley Select XI team, even though till then, I had only played league cricket at the Central Yorkshire League (CYL) and Dewsbury & District League (DDL). So, I felt a bit hesitant about leading the team against a county-level squad, and suggested John Burton, whom I regard as one of the best players in the Bradford League, to captain the team, keeping myself as a regular player of the team.

Among the benefit matches I played in and organised, this was the first benefit match at Batley CC that was intended for a county player. It was also my first experience in bowling to Martin Crowe. I was amazed by his exceptional skills and impeccable timing. The event turned out to be tremendously successful, attracting a large crowd to the ground. Inspired by this match, I went on to organize and play several benefit-matches for various Yorkshire County players in the following years. Fortunately, when I took up the captaincy of the Batley CC in 1983, my task of organising the benefit matches for the cricketers concerned became much easier and conducive for me, and to its participants. With the presence of passionate cricket enthusiasts in the Dewsbury area that ensured a large crowd turnout for these special matches, the hosting of testimonial matches at Batley CC proved to be mutually beneficial for both benefiting players and the hosting club.

Richard Lumb (England) - Testimonial Match - August 19, 1983

The match that was intended for the benefit of Richard Lumb on August 19, 1983, at Mount Pleasant, a Batley CC grounds, is worth mentioning. Richard Lumb is an English first-class cricketer, who had a remarkable career of playing for Yorkshire County from 1969 to 1984 and had emerged as a key player for the Yorkshire team; his son, Michael Lumb, also followed his footsteps to represent Yorkshire, and then went on to play for the England team.

To honour Richard for his contribution to the Yorkshire County, its management had granted him with a benefit season for the year 1983. We set up two teams, Richard Lumb Yorkshire Select XI and Batley Select XI. While the former team was under the captaincy of Richard Lumb, and comprised of players such as Geoffrey Boycott, C.W.J. Athey (Bill Athey), Martin Moxon, Jim Love, Kevin Sharp, G. Stevenson, S. Dennis, Arnie Sidebottom, Phil Carrick, A. Ramage, and N. Taylor, and for the latter, I had the honour of leading players that include Chandrakanth Pandit, Mehndi Shaik, Dilip Doshi, Raju Kulkarni and Barun Burman from India, besides a few local club players like S. Lax and Ronnie Hudson from Hanging Heaton, and G. Gill (Shepley), B. Haigh (Ossett), John Burton (Spen Victoria) and Ali Zai.

As anticipated, a massive crowd turned out at the Batley grounds, that indicated their high regard for this gifted player of the Yorkshire County. The entry ticket for the audience was £1 per adult, and 50p for children; refreshment drinks and snacks were sold inside the grounds. Following the match, we organized a raffle for a bat autographed by the cricketers, which contributed additional funds to support the event. Overall, it proved to be yet another successful benefit match for a county player at Batley CC.

Geoffrey Boycott (England) - Testimonial Match at Batley CC - May 29, 1984

One morning in the following year in 1984, I received a phone call from Geoffrey Boycott, who expressed his interest in having a benefit match at Batley CC grounds, and for which, he sought my help. Sir Geoffrey Boycott was a cricket legend from England, and he holds a prominent place in Yorkshire's cricket history due to his exceptional batting skills. For his remarkable contribution to county cricket, Yorkshire County in particular, he was already honoured with a benefit season for the year 1974, by the Yorkshire County; with this benefit match, he became an exception to have been credited with two benefit years in one's active career. Interestingly, my association with Geoffrey started off on a bitter note, which will be further elaborated in subsequent chapters. However, gradually things turned softer and friendly, only with this benefit match, when Geoffrey called me one day to seek my assistance in organising it for him at Batley CC. By then, I was already leading the Batley team as its captain and was busy organising benefit matches. After consultation with the management of the club, I organised a benefit match for Geoffrey on May 29, 1984, at Batley, involving several prominent cricketers.

As Geoffrey was such a popular cricketer in English County circles, the news of the testimonial match for him being held at Batley CC created a huge buzz among the cricket lovers in our local town. Amidst standing ovation from a huge crowd of audience, the highly anticipated match between Geoffrey Boycott XI and Batley Select XI took place at Batley CC on May 29, 1984. Captained by Geoffrey himself, his team comprised mainly of Yorkshire County players, but also two Australian players, besides one player named Sean Twohig of our club; its players included, Martin Moxon, Jim Love, Phil Carrick, Richard Lumb, David Bairstow, Stevenson, Arnie Sidebottom, Steve Oldham, R. Spencer, and D. Taylor (Australia), and Sean Twohig (Batley CC). On the other hand, I headed its opponent's team, Batley Select XI, that comprised a few international players from India and Pakistan, adding further excitement to the match; our players included Chandrakanth Pandit, Mohinder Amarnath, Suru Nayak, Masood Anwar, Barun Burman, Shahid Mehboob, B. Haigh, A. Blain, N. Haines, A. Mitre, M. Omiuddin, and Ravi Thakkar. The match proved to be a tremendous success, that had left a lasting impression on the minds of audience, who had an opportunity to witness both county players and international stars together in action at Batley CC. Personally, I felt deeply honoured to captain the Batley Select XI, and to play against Geoffrey and his County team; I still cherish this happiness to this day.

Richard Hadlee (New Zealand) – Testimonial Match at Batley CC – May 5, 1986

In 1986, Nottinghamshire Cricket County had honoured Richard Hadlee for his outstanding contributions to their county, by granting him with a benefit season. Sir Richard Hadlee was a former New Zealand cricketer and was widely acclaimed as one of the greatest all-rounders, and a fast bowler in cricket history. In my personal view, he stands amongst the most exceptional all-rounders to have ever graced the game. He represented Nottinghamshire County for a large part of his career from 1978 to 1987, besides playing for the New Zealand team.

Given my acquaintance with some of the players in Nottinghamshire County team, particularly through my friend, Tim Robinson, they approached me to organize a benefit match for Richard Hadlee at Batley CC. I diligently made all the necessary arrangements to ensure the match took place without any constraints, for which a local travel company named Bharat Travels generously stepped forward to sponsor the event.

The match was scheduled on May 5, 1986, to be held at Mount Pleasant Grounds, Batley CC, between Nottinghamshire XI and Batley International XI. Headed by Richard Hadlee himself, Nottinghamshire XI comprised regular county players such as Tim Robinson, Chris Broad, Clive Rice, Derek Randall, Paul Johnson, Duncan Martindale, Bruce French, Eddie Hemmings, Kevin Cooper, Kevin Saxelby, Andy Pick, and Peter Such. On the other hand, I again had the honour of being the captain of Batley International XI, which consisted of players as diverse as Vivek Jai Simha, Abdul Azeem, Suresh Shetty, Abdul Jabbar, Barry Petty, David Dove, Sean Twohig, Mohammad Dadhiwala, Michael Fen, John Prentice, Robert Cooper, and Paul Blakeley.

In this match, Nottinghamshire XI won the toss, and chose to bat first; their opening batsmen, coincidentally, was the opener of the England Test cricket team for that year, Chris Broad (father of Stuart Broad, another cricketer of England's national team), and Tim Robinson took the crease. However, after scoring just 4 runs in the first 4 overs, the game was interrupted by rain, leading to its unfortunate abandonment. This turn of events was a disappointment for all the cricket enthusiasts in Batley, but they were still overjoyed by the presence of Richard Hadlee, and his county team at the Batley CC Ground.

Imran Khan (Pakistan) - Benefit Match at Batley - July 5, 1987

Imran Khan is an internationally popular cricket star from Pakistan, who played for Worcestershire County between 1971 to 1976; later, he also served Sussex County for several years. To honour his great contributions to Sussex County, the management of the county had granted him with a benefit season for the year 1987.

He is a very good friend of mine, and when Imran called me up one day to ask me to organise a benefit match for him at Batley CC, I was elated to attain such a privilege. He also informed me that the Pakistan Team was scheduled to visit England for a test series, in which one of its matches would be held at Headingly Stadium in Leeds, which is just 30-minute drive away from Dewsbury. So, we planned to keep the same Pakistan test team intact, to play against our Batley Select XI team.

When I shared this with Batley Committee, they too expressed their joy as Imran by then was already a renowned player in England, and the entire Pakistan team would be here, that would amount to be beneficial for Batley CC with its additional funding.

As the test series was scheduled in the summer of 1987, the Pakistan Cricket team visited England to play a series of matches. Accordingly, they played five Test-matches and three One-day Internationals, with the third test-match scheduled at Headingly Cricket Stadium in Leeds, between July 2, 1987, and July 6, 1987. The test matches in England, in those days, would be held during six-week days, with Sunday off. So, we organised the match on Sunday, that was July 5, 1987, and the entire Pakistan Test team arrived at Batley CC grounds on the scheduled time to participate in the match for Imran Khan. The Pakistan XI Team comprised Imran Khan (captain), Ijaz Ahmed, Shoaib Mohammed, Mansoor Akhtar, Manzoor Elahi, Wasim Akram, Asif Mujtaba, Salim Yousuf, Zakir Khan, Azeem Hafeez, and Iqbal Qasim.

By then, I was the captain of the Batley Select XI team; the players of our Batley team had already assembled, besides some of the star players from India and Pakistan like, Dilip Vengsarkar, Mohinder Amarnath, Masood Anwar, Rashid Patel, Anwar Khan, Azeem Khan, Tanveer Ali, Atique Rahman; Collin Buzzard was also included in our team. There was a massive turnout of cricket fans, as they were excited to see their favourite international players from both teams, particularly the entire Pakistan test team, playing against a club-team.

Imran had won the toss, and Pakistan XI team chose to bat first in the match. Asif Mujtaba with his impressive performance, scored 57 runs, while other batsmen also did their best, leading the Pakistan Team to score a total of 215 runs for 9 wickets in 30 overs. I was so overjoyed that I took the wickets of both the stars, Imran Khan, and Wasim Akram, and it was one of the most memorable events of life.

And when our Batley Select XI team began to bat, except Ronnie Hart who hit the top score of 59 runs with his notable innings, and Anwar Khan's 26 runs, we all struggled to face their bowling, and none of us could do much. As a result, we were all bowled for just 151 runs, with Pakistan Team winning the match. This match remains one of the greatest events that Batley CC ever organised, and the testimonial match turned out to be a tremendous success. Following the match, the Pakistan Team happily returned to Leeds to continue the rest of the test match against England.

Suru Nayak (India) - Benefit Match 1990-91

Suru Nayak was a former Indian cricketer hailing from Bombay and is a good human being. He is a very good friend of mine and would visit me often at my home when he was playing for Bilton CC under the Airedale & Wharfdale League. I played my role in arranging a bat contract for him with County Sports, thereby our bonding had strengthened further.

In 1990-91, I had the pleasure of organizing a benefit match for Suru Nayak at Bilton CC in Harrogate. For this benefit-match, Suru brought his club team as its captain while I formed a team that comprised of young, and yet promising cricketers from India like Sachin Tendulkar, Vinod Kambli, Sanjay Manjrekar, Sameer Dighe, with Atul Wassan as the captain of our team; our team also included other talented cricketers from India such as Sulakshan Kulkarni, Suresh Shetty, Yakub Vali, Iqbal Khan, Atul Wassan, Sameer Dighe, and Abhay Laghate. At that time, as far as I remember, Sanjay Manjrekar and Sachin Tendulkar were already playing for Indian team, and Vinod, Atul, and Sameer joined them in the Indian team later. It was an incredible experience for me to captain these young cricketers, and to witness them growing from emerging talents to international superstars, and cricket legends.

Jatin Paranjape (India) - Benefit Match - Thornhill CC- 1992

Within a year after the benefit match for Suru Nayak, I organized a special match in 1992 for the benefit of Jatin Paranjape at the Thornhill Cricket Club. My affinity with Jatin began when I helped him in signing for Yorkshire Bank CC in Bradford League. Jatin was a Ranji player who represented the Bombay team; he then also had the opportunity to play for Indian team for the Sahara Cup (1998) at Toronto against Pakistan team. Jatin's father, Vasoo Paranjape, was also a venerable cricketer for mentoring some of the all-time greats, including Sunil Gavaskar, Dilip Vengsarkar, Sanjay Manjrekar, Rohit Sharma, and several others.

Fortunately for Jatin's benefit-match, I managed to gather very renowned players like Sachin Tendulkar, Vinod Kambli, Tushar Arothe, Venkatapathy Raju, Ajay Jadeja, and Raju Kulkarni, including my all-time favourite Sunil Gavaskar.

Sachin was part of Jatin's team, and I was leading the other team, when Sachin approached me and jokingly said, "Solly Bhai, I want to give your bowling a good thrashing!" Knowing Sachin's extraordinary skills, I started to worry of how I would handle him with my bowling. Unlike Vinod, whose strengths and weaknesses I knew as he had played several matches under my captaincy in the Bradford League, I never bowled Sachin in my life and so my fear got heightened. Added to it, Sachin was on a different scale altogether, and I knew he could effortlessly launch my deliveries out of the park. Fortunately, Sunil now was in my team, and so I did not have to worry.

While waiting for such an exciting moment of my life, I learnt that, unfortunately, Sachin sustained minor injuries while playing for Yorkshire. Despite injuries that left considerable pain on his body, he remained confident and committed to his promise and had participated in Jatin's benefit match, having his arm wrapped in bandages. Though he could not even grip the bat properly, he embodied such a dogged spirit that he showcased remarkable performance against all the bowlers and managed hitting a boundary or two during my bowling as well. Recently, when I happened to meet Sachin, he reminded me of the time and said with a smile on his face, "Solly Bhai, there's one ambition of mine that still remains unfulfilled—I wanted to hit you for sixes in Jatin's match but couldn't accomplish it." Sachin's unwavering dedication exemplifies how true legends approach the game, and how deeply passionate they are to play even in the face of adversity; Sachin is undoubtedly a genuine legend of the game.

There was a massive turnout of cricket fans eagerly waiting to watch their favourite players, and the most noteworthy moment of the match was that Sunil hit a few sixes, which was so unusual for him as he preferred to time the ball well for boundaries instead. It was an unforgettable moment for me, an experience that holds a special place in my heart, because Sunil played this match under my captaincy. Overall, the match was a resounding success, and everyone went home with cherished memories of the day.

Tim Robinson (England) - Testimonial Match at Batley CC - 1992

In the same year in 1992, I had another opportunity to participate in a benefit match for a former England player Tim Robinson, who was granted a benefit season by his county team Nottinghamshire. Tim had been my friend from my early days in cricket, and I was then serving as the captain of Spen Victoria. The match was planned at Batley CC grounds, which holds a special place in my heart, as I had played numerous testimonial matches there for various county players. In this Batley grounds, over the years, I had the privilege of organizing and playing testimonial matches for several esteemed county players like David Bairstow (1982), Richard Lumb (1983), Geoffrey Boycott (1984), Phil Carrick (1985), and Jim Love (1989) from Yorkshire County, as well as

Richard Hadlee (1986) from Nottinghamshire, at Batley CC. Therefore, when Batley CC extended its invitation for me to be a part of Tim Robinson's benefit match, I felt deeply honoured that the club continued considering me even after my departure from the club. Moreover, in this match, I had the privilege to be the captain of the Batley team, against Tim Robinson's Nottinghamshire team. The event was a great success, and it was memorable occasion for all the cricket enthusiasts gathered to support Tim and celebrate his remarkable career. I cherished the same as I had been actively involved in such an esteemed event and played my part in its success.

Sanjay Manjrekar (India) - Benefit Match – 1995 (Stockton Cricket Club)

Again in 1995, I had the honour of organising a benefit match for Sanjay Manjrekar at Stockton Cricket Club. Having known Sanjay for a long time and having had the opportunity to captain him in a couple of benefit matches in the early 90s, we decided to organize a benefit match in his honour. He played for Stockton CC in Durham and had emerged as one of the most prolific batsmen in that league. Sanjay's remarkable achievements included scoring an impressive 1,735 runs that broke the club record, besides his magnificent knock of 181 runs against Bishop Auckland in 1995.

For his benefit-match, I managed to gather a few test-cricketers from Asia, particularly India; they included notable players such as Mohammad Azharuddin, Abey Kuruvilla, Subroto Banerjee, Sairaj Bahuthule, Raju Kulkarni, Lal Chand Rajput, Paras Mhambray, RP Singh Senior, and of course, Sanjay himself; Umar Rasheed from Pakistan and Clayton Lambert from the West Indies had also joined us to make it a star-studded event to remember.

As far as I remember, Azharuddin was playing for Derbyshire County at that moment, and despite his busy schedule, he made a special effort to travel all the way to Durham, to participate in the match for Sanjay. His presence was not merely an excitement for his fans, as he was very famous by then, but was a huge challenge for me to bowl him. As I reached bowling crease to bowl, Azhar greeted me with a smile and asked in Hindi, "Solly Bhai, *kidhar maroon?* (Where should I hit you?)." Knowing his exceptional skills and his reputation as a great cricketer and captain of the Indian team, I was taken aback a little and responded—I would be bowling on the off-side, with an intention to avoid him playing a shot on the leg-side. In my strategy to block his shots, I also positioned six fielders on the leg-side. But to my surprise, Azhar effortlessly found the gap between the fielders, and had hit a boundary on the leg-side. His wristwork and ability to execute on-drives and flick shots were truly remarkable. Throughout the match, I continuously shuffled the fielders, positioning them between the leg-side, and then off-side, to restrict him from hitting shots, but to no avail. Azhar proved to be a rare genius; he displayed impeccable placement with his remarkable wristwork, effortlessly driving the ball precisely to wherever he wanted it to go; it did not really matter to him however I bowled. This match was one of the most interesting matches for me, and overall, it was a big success.

In this way, I had the privilege of bowling to numerous legendary cricketers, including Sunil Gavaskar, Sachin Tendulkar, Imran Khan, Javed Miandad, Geoff Boycott, and many others, and now to Mohammed Azharuddin. However, I personally feel that the two most challenging batsmen I have ever bowled to were, the New Zealand cricket legend Martin Crowe, and Mohammad Azharuddin; their unique batting styles and exceptional skills fumbles any bowler. Nevertheless, I consider these challenges as valuable experiences that taught me numerous lessons of my life as a cricketer and helped me enrich my cricketing journey.

Sairaj Bahuthule (India) - Benefit Match - 1996 (Stockton Cricket Club)

In the same grounds of Stockton Cricket Club, I also took an active role in organising a benefit match for Sairaj Bahuthule in 1996. Sairaj was an Indian cricketer from Bombay known for his exceptional skills as an all-rounder. I signed Sairaj for Spen Victoria in 1994 in Bradford League, and with his performance as an all-rounder, he had proven to be an asset to the team; later, I also signed him for the Stockton Cricket Club in Durham. During his association with Stockton CC, Sairaj emerged as an outstanding performer, where he achieved a double record in 1996; he scored an impressive 1,297 runs and took 123 wickets in the season and had come to be known as the first player that had ever accomplished this all-rounder record in both bowling and batting in the history of North Yorkshire & South Durham League.

In recognition of his committed contributions to cricket, this benefit match was organized for Sairaj. The match featured a star-studded line-up with Abey Kuruvilla, Paras Mhambray, Nilesh Kulkarni, Amol Mazumdar, Salil Ankola, and, of course, Sairaj himself. The opposing team was led by West Indies star cricketer Clayton Lambert, who added excitement and prestige to the match.

During the match, an intriguing incident unfolded: When Clayton as a left-handed batsman stepped up to bat, I strategically positioned myself to pitch the ball on the offside and had it drift into the wickets. When I did so, I anticipated that Clayton would try to play on the leg side, and so I placed most of the fielders in that area, with an aim either to dismiss him, or restrict runs. However, Clayton's response left us astounded; he executed a remarkable 'reverse sweep' shot, nearly hitting the ball for a six. The surprise and awe among the players, including myself, Abey, Sanjay, and others, were indescribable; it was the first time that any one of us had witnessed such a shot and we looked at one another in astonishment. In this way, Clayton managed to hit me for three boundaries using the same reverse sweep technique, with one of them almost clearing the boundary for a six. In the context of T-20 cricket today, the reverse sweep shot has become quite common, but back in those days in 1990s, it was almost unimaginable to witness such unorthodox strokes. Even to this day, whenever Abey and I meet each other, we fondly reminisce about Clayton's reverse sweep shots. The event, as expected, turned out to be a resounding success, and we all returned to Dewsbury after the match, filled with memories of the day.

Mansoor Rana (Pakistan) Benefit Match - India XI Vs Pakistan XI -July 29, 1998

Among the several matches I had organized so far, the benefit match for Mansoor Rana in 1998 stands out to be a rare and memorable one. Mansoor is the son of the renowned former Pakistani cricket umpire, Shakoor Rana. Mansoor has later emerged as a cricket-coach in Pakistan, and currently serves as the manager of the Pakistani Cricket Team.

When Mansoor approached me with a request to arrange a benefit match between India and Pakistan for him, I gladly accepted his proposal. I took responsibility for assembling the Indian team, while Mansoor worked diligently to bring together the Pakistani players. The match featured a line-up of established international players in both the teams, with some players having already achieved great success, while others were on their way to achieve international eminence.

Wasim Akram being the captain, the Pakistan XI team comprised of players like Saqlain Mushtaq, Rashid Latif, Asif Mujtaba, Shahid Mehboob, Mansoor Rana, Manzoor Elahi, Ata-Ur-Rehman, Zahoor Elahi, Maqsood Rana, Shahid Anwar, Nadeem Khan, and Iqbal Sikander. On the other hand, I had the honour of captaining India XI with players like Abey Kuruvilla, Sameer Dighe, Sairaj Bahuthule, Amol Mazumdar, Wasim Jaffer, Atul Ranade, Kiran Powar, Iqbal Khan, Moinuddin Kadri,

Nanda Kishore, R. Sridhar, Rohan Gavaskar, and Tushar Arothe. The match took place at Baildon Cricket Club on July 29, 1998.

It was a season for Wasim Akram, who then was serving as the captain of the Lancashire County team. Since their team, unfortunately, got defeated in the quarter finals of the Benson & Hedges Cup, by the Surrey Team at The Oval, Wasim wanted to focus his practice on batting in this match. Prior to the start of the match, he expressed his wish to me that he would keep to his wicket, and bat at least ten overs. In response, I jokingly said that he should hope to make some runs, but if he gets out early, he should not blame me. Then Wasim won the toss and had chosen to bat first as it was his preferred choice for the day. I informed our team that Wasim Akram was wishing an extra batting practice, and so I urged everyone to allow him to play a few overs before taking any decision of outing him, as it would be a batting practice for him to participate in the county matches in the upcoming weeks.

Atul Ranade opened his bowling from the top end in the first over, while Abey Kuruvilla had to bowl from the other end. Atul was thrilled to bowl Wasim, who by then, was already a legend in the cricket world. Wasim played the first two balls and on the third ball, Atul Ranade dismissed him for a score of zero. Wasim was extremely disappointed as he had hoped to bat for at least 10 overs but was out on the third ball without getting any runs. When I asked Atul, "What have you done, man?" Atul exclaimed, "Solly Bhai, that's a remarkable achievement! I will cherish the memory of dismissing Wasim Akram for zero as long as I live." We bowled out the Pakistan Team for the total of just 136 runs.

During the innings break, Wasim approached me for a friendly chat and teasingly said, "Solly Bhai, you ruined my plans. I wanted to have an extensive batting practice today, but you guys got me out for zero. Now, let us see if you can even score a hundred runs, and you all will witness my fury." Wasim Akram began the bowling innings, and I have never witnessed such incredible speed and swing from a bowler before.

He bowled aggressively, leaving our top-order batsmen apprehensive to face him. Unfortunately, we lost five wickets with just 36 runs on the board. Among us, only Wasim Jaffer managed to play Wasim Akram effectively that day, while none of our other batsmen even reached double digits. After taking six wickets, Wasim Akram came up to me and remarked, "Okay, Solly Bhai, I will leave the rest to Shahid Mehboob and Saqlain Mushtaq; they will finish off your team. As he said, we were all out for just 96 runs, with only Wasim Jaffer contributing a respectable score of 40 runs.

It was an incredible match, and I had the privilege to be a part of it. Despite it being an unofficial international match between India and Pakistan, the game was played with a remarkable blend of aggression, true sportsmanship, and yet in a cordial atmosphere. Mansoor Rana was delighted with the impeccable organization of the match, and I must extend my gratitude to Wasim Akram, who is undeniably one of the greatest bowlers the cricket world has ever witnessed, for gracing this match with his presence on behalf of Mansoor Rana. This benefit match served as a testament to the unity and goodwill that cricket can inspire, bringing together players from rival nations for a common cause. It was a memorable event, that highlighted the spirit of sportsmanship, and the shared love for cricket that transcends boundaries.

Abey Kuruvilla (India) – Benefit Match – August 20, 2000

To honour the excellence and contribution of Abey Kuruvilla in attaining successes for several years for his team of Southport & Birkdale CC, which plays under Liverpool League, we decided to organize a benefit match for him. I know Abey as I had signed him for the Cleckheaton CC in 1994, to play in the Bradford League. Ever since then, our friendship grew so intimate that he became part of my family, much like an elder son. He also became very popular among Indian and Bombay cricket circles as a brilliant bowler of Indian team during 1990s, and he is the

General Manager of Board of Control for Cricket in India.

To organise the benefit match for Abey, I approached many young Indian cricketers who were playing for various clubs in England, and they were glad to be part of the match. The match took place on August 20, 2000, at the Southport & Birkdale Cricket Club that featured two teams: S&B XI and Overseas XI. The S&B XI team consisted of players of their own club; they include, Mark Warren (captain), Ryan Pitts, Dave Barlow, Marlon Black, Asif Jan, Colin Maxwell, Toby Miller, Nick Gallimore, Simon Sutcliffe, Neil Rimmer. On the other hand, I had the honour of captaining the Overseas XI, that comprised several promising Asian cricketers associated with various clubs in England; they include Sameer Dighe, Wasim Jaffer, Amol Mazumdar, Ameya Khurasiya, Amit Dani, Nishit Shetty, Robin Morris, Rajesh Pawar, Atul Ranade, Shawn Petafi, and of course Abey Kuruvilla. Among these players, Sameer Dighe, Wasim Jaffer, Amay Khurasiya, and Abey Kuruvilla, by then, had already represented the national team of India. The S&B team enjoyed playing against these international players, and the match turned out to be a resounding success with the presence of good crowd, having been sponsored by Prompt International. Abey expressed his delight for the way in which the match was being organized.

Mohsin Khan (Pakistan) Benefit Match - Lancashire

The benefit match for Mohsin Khan occupies significance, because, I was the only cricketer, among all the payers in both the teams, who had not played either major county, or any international matches; all the cricketers of both teams were mainly international cricketers, but there were first-class cricketers at least. I was included in the match, because of my extensive experience in Yorkshire League Cricket. Though I did not organise this match, I arranged a few Indian and Pakistani test players for the match.

Mohsin was a former Pakistani cricketer, a cricket coach, cricket administrator, and even Bollywood actor. Being a prominent cricketer of Pakistan, Mohsin was known for his role as an opening batsman. Mohsin was also a Pro cricketer (1976-89) for Todmorden CC in Lancashire League. In recognition of his great services to cricket, both at Todmorden CC and internationally, the management of the Todmorden CC organised a benefit match for Mohsin Khan. Mohsin asked me in person, if I could arrange a few players from Indian team to play, besides inviting me to be part of the team. Given his stature as a glamorous cricketer internationally at the time, the match attracted a star-studded line-up. I vividly recall notable players such as Sir Clive Lloyd (Former West Indies captain), including Mudassar Nazar, Salim Malik, Rameez Raja, and Anwar Khan from the national team of Pakistan, besides Martin Crowe, the renowned New Zealand cricketer, David Hookes, an Australian Test cricketer, and many other accomplished test cricketers participated in this match. I felt honoured to be part of these world-class star-cricketers, and to play amidst them, despite myself being not even a first-class cricketer.

In this match, I played under the captaincy of David Hookes, and was given an opportunity to bowl Martin Crowe. By then, Martin was an established international cricket star, and I had previously bowled to him in 1982 during David Bairstow's testimonial match at Batley. Just before I took to bowling, our captain David Hookes approached me and asked, if I wanted any alterations to the fielding setup. Particularly, considering Martin Crowe's proficiency in playing elegant leg-glance and on-drive shots, he suggested the possibility of adding more fielders on the leg-side. I said, in response to him, that I would like to bowl a middle to off-stump line, and therefore, we might not necessarily require additional fielders on the leg-side. I said this with a view to bowl a few deliveries, however, only to assess the situation.

To our astonishment, it became apparent that it did not matter where I bowled. Martin Crowe effortlessly played his shots wherever he pleased, be it on the leg-side, or in the off-side; his precision in shot placement and timing was unparalleled. Despite all my efforts, Martin played a few boundaries in my bowling and played magnificently well throughout his innings. David Hookes attempted various changes in fielding, but Martin's exceptional skill and natural style of play could not be curtailed. This benefit match turned out to be a resounding success for Mohsin Khan, and personally, it was truly an immense honour for me to have played in this match alongside such distinguished international cricket stars.

Mansoor Akhtar (Pakistan) – Benefit Match at Huddersfield – (Sunil Gavaskar)

Besides the above benefit-matches which hold great significance in my life, I also had some more matches to my credit which were of a little lesser significance. However, it is relevant to make a mention of them here, as they were all great learning experiences for me.

The benefit match for Mansoor Akhtar stands out as an interesting one. After playing for Huddersfield CC at Fartown for some time, Mansoor joined Spen Victoria CC to play under my captaincy in the Bradford League. When Huddersfield CC wanted to organize a benefit match for Mansoor, he approached me with a special request to convene some international players, particularly my friend and legend Sunil Gavaskar, to play the match. Knowing Sunil's readiness to assist fellow cricketers, and being his friend, I approached him, and as expected, Sunil happily expressed his consent to the cause; several notable players from Pakistan, including Shahid Mehboob, Ali Raza, and Assad Rauf (former international umpire), also joined us.

The match was convened at Fartown Cricket Ground in Huddersfield, to where I travelled along with Sunil in my car. It was the time in 1983 that Sunil had just achieved the remarkable feat of securing the world record of highest test runs in the world-cricket, surpassing

Sir Geoff Boycott's record. Despite this highest achievement, Sunil's passion for the game remained unmitigated; he would approach every match, be it international, or benefit or a friendly match, equally, perceiving them with same seriousness.

From the beginning of his batting, Sunil, as usual, played his steady game. But when he reached a score at 67, he elegantly flicked the ball towards square-leg, where a young fielder dived and executed an exceptional catch. We all thought it might be the best catch of his life. However, on our way back to home at Dewsbury, Sunil remained unusually quiet in the car, not saying anything. I expressed my concern at what happened, and if everything was okay. I was surprised to hear Sunil's response, "Solly, I threw my wicket away unnecessarily!" When I tried to remind him of the exceptionality of the catch by that young fielder at square-leg, Sunil continued insisting, "Yes, but if I had played the ball a little later, it would have stayed on the ground; I was in a bit of a hurry and played it a bit early, which resulted the ball to go up in the air."

I coaxed him to take it easy and said, "it was just a benefit match, and we don't have it take it so seriously." Then Sunil responded much more emphatically and said, "It doesn't matter if it's a benefit match, a friendly match, or a test match. You should never make a habit of throwing your wicket away carelessly. No bowler in the world will come to you and ask you to hit for a boundary, even in a friendly match. Then why should I give away my wicket so easily? If I had played the ball a bit later, it would have been ideal; at best it could have gone for a boundary, or at the very least, I would not have been out." This incident was a great lesson for me, that revealed how the legends are made, and how serious they are about their matches. This remained to be one of the most valuable lessons that I ever learned during my cricketing journey.

Javed Miandad – Benefit Match at Preston – (Sunil Gavaskar)

In the early 1980s, Javed Miandad, my close friend, and the star cricketer of the Pakistan team, announced a benefit-match by the Preston Club with which he was associated in his early days. Upon request from Javed to convene Sunil to play for his match, I checked with Sunil for his convenience. The response of Sunil, as usual, was a joyful gesture. On the appointed date and time, I again travelled along with Sunil to Preston to play. The match went well, and we were happy to be part of such a noble cause of expressing our solidarity to our fellow player. I believe that it would be the warmth of the players that unites the players of the world and help and support each other to live with harmony with all for the betterment of the sport; it is motivational for anyone to know of such solidarity for each other in cricket, and it can have a healing effect for many of the problems of the world at large.

International XI Vs East Bierley Bradford League XI – 1992

In addition to organizing and playing several benefit/testimonial matches for various cricketers, I was also actively involved in fundraising activities for various sports, particularly cricket. I often would help sponsor talented young cricketers whom I believed to have had great potentials, and I also had assisted less fortunate players by providing them with cricket equipment. In this line, the match I organized and played to raise funds for the East Bierley Pitch building project holds great significance. Being friends with members of the East Bierley CC, they approached me for such a help. Then I planned this fundraising match with several Indian players associated with Yorkshire and Lancashire Leagues at that time.

The match was held at the East Bierley Cricket Club that featured two teams: the International XI and the East Bierley Bradford League XI. I had the honour of captaining the International XI, which included prominent Indian players such as Vinod Kambli, Tushar Arothe, Sameer Dighe, Iqbal Khan, JP Yadav, Prashanth Vaidya, Sulakshan Kulkarni, Jatin Paranjape, S Sajjad, Nilesh Kulkarni, and Abhay Laghate. Interestingly, more than half of the players from this team later went on to represent the Indian Cricket Team.

The match proved to be an enormous success, and I had expressed my heartfelt gratitude to all the cricketers who invested their valuable time and energies in making the match a huge success and thereby extending their helping hand in building the pitch for the club.

Kathiawar XI Vs Rest of the World XI – 1980

In addition to the benefit matches and other matches for raising funds for several sports causes, I also organized charity matches to support cricket-related and other social issues. In the summer of 1980, I had the idea of organising a charity match with international players at Dewsbury, as it was the time, when many players from their respective national teams of India and Pakistan were playing for various clubs and counties in England. Using the right opportune moment, I invited all those Asian players of international eminence in English clubs, and fortunately, all of them happily agreed to participate in the match. There were deliberations to name the teams for the match. Recognising significant number of players hailing from Kathiawar region of Gujarat in India, I proposed the name of one team as 'Kathiawar XI' having the other team as 'Rest of the World.' This creative team division was admired by all, particularly a good friend of mine named Yajurvindra Singh who described it as 'ingenious.'

The Kathiawar XI team comprised notable players mainly from Kathiawar region of India, but also some of them were then living in Pakistan having been the descendants of the region. Having the best talents from the region, the team included eminent players like Rahul Mankad, Karsan Ghavri, Ashok Mankad, Dhiraj Parsana, Uday Joshi,

Yajurvindra Singh, Mushtaq Mohammed, Iqbal Qasim, Sadiq Mohammed, Javed Miandad, and Taufiq Ahmed. On the other hand, the "Rest
of the World" team boasted of cricket legends like Imran Khan and Sunil
Gavaskar, along with several other international players. Unfortunately, the match was interrupted by persistent rain in Yorkshire. However,
the atmosphere that this charity match created had resounded in the
region hopes for creating camaraderie and friendship. In fact, it was the
time for the cricketers from the sub-continent in England to cherish
the opportunity to meet and build strong friendship in this moment of
solidarity. Personally, I hold best of my memories from during 1970s and
1980s, as they were marked by building genuine friendship and joyful-
ness among Asians in England; these moments were truly special and
will always be treasured.

Graham Thorpe – Benefit Match at Guernsey

Even after retiring from club cricket, I continued to receive requests
from various clubs and players to participate in several benefit or testimonial matches. They were aware of my extensive connections with
international players, and so they would seek my help at least in securing popular players for their matches. To that end, immediately after
I retired from playing cricket, I had taken upon the role of a manager
(unofficial) and continued accommodating players for several matches.

In this regard, I recall an instance of a testimonial match for the renowned England cricketer Graham Thorpe, organised by the Guernsey
CC. One day the club committee approached me, seeking my help, to
arrange popular players from India and Pakistan to participate in the
match. Then, I corresponded with all those players whom I knew of in
their respective countries, and from them I managed to secure Sameer
Dighe, Amay Khurasiya, and Iqbal Khan from India, and Kashif Ahmed
from Pakistan. To these players, the club had added some more players like Nasser Hussain, former England captain, and Jimmy Adams,

former West Indies captain, to play in the match alongside of Graham Thorpe.

Unlike other clubs where I so far organised our matches, Guernsey CC is quite far from where I reside, as it is near the French coast in the English Channel. As a result, we all flew from Manchester to Guernsey to participate in the match. I felt deeply honoured to still be involved in the sport, even after retiring from cricket. It was a privilege to contribute to the testimonial match and continue to support the cricketing community.

Holland Centenary Cricket Match - Netherlands Vs World XI – June 14, 2003

As part of the Centenary celebrations of cricket in Netherlands, the Holland Cricket Association planned a special match titled, "Netherlands vs World XI." One day, the association contacted me and sought my assistance in securing international players for the match. I promptly organized three players from my connections, and they include Shahid Afridi from Pakistan, and Sameer Dighe and Dinesh Mongia from India. Besides these three players, the World XI team had an impressive line-up, featuring renowned international stars such as Gary Kirsten, Daryll Cullinan, and Justin Kemp from South Africa, Chris Harris and Andre Adams from New Zealand, Neil Johnson from Zimbabwe, and Jimmy Adams from West Indies. Having their own team of players, the Netherlands team had the memorable opportunity to play against this star-studded World XI.

The match took place on June 14, 2003, at De Diepput in the city of Hague, Netherlands. My wife, Maryam, and I travelled from the UK to the Netherlands to watch the match and had a fantastic time enjoying the match as a spectator; we also spent a couple of days exploring the local attractions and had immersed ourselves in the travel experience. It was a memorable event for all of us to be a part of the Centenary celebrations, and to witness the match. On a lighter note, I recall that Dinesh Mongia had recently gotten married at that time, when I approached him for the match. He was amidst planning his honeymoon, and when I contacted him about participating in the Netherlands match, he readily accepted; it seems it was a wonderful opportunity for him to combine cricket and his honeymoon in the Netherlands.

Yajurvindra Singh (Sunny Singh) - Benefit Match at Blackpool

During those days, cricket was all our life, and it would bring us all together, as the sport would forge strong bonds among us. I vividly remember organizing a benefit match for Yajurvindra Singh (Sunny Singh) in Blackpool when he was playing in the Blackpool League. It was pleasurable to reminiscence that despite achieving so much in their respective careers, all the players, who had represented India and Pakistan at the international level, had come together to participate in the event upon my invitation. The unity, friendship, and happiness that characterized our lives during that time were not influenced by status, but upon our unity and fraternity. Cricket was the common love that had bound us all; no money, nor power and prestige can buy that love and happiness.

Summing Up

It gives an immense pleasure that amongst the cricketing fraternity, players come forward of their own volition to aid their colleagues and demonstrate solidarity across nationalities. I am fortunate to be a helping hand to all those cricketers whom I come across in life. Of all the matches I organised and played, each benefit match holds its own significance, and had provided me with an opportunity to support and celebrate the careers of talented cricketers. It is a source of great satisfaction for me to have played a part in organizing these matches and contributing to the success and well-being of my fellow players. I feel so glad, when players from the subcontinent express their gratitude and say, "Thank you, Solly Bhai, for organizing a benefit match for me."

Moreover, with these benefit matches, I had an extraordinary opportunity and a privilege to play alongside cricket legends like Sunil Gavaskar, Sachin Tendulkar, VVS Laxman, Mohinder Amarnath, Dilip Vengsarkar, Madan Lal, Karsan Ghavri, and Azharuddin from India; Imran Khan, Javed Miandad, Wasim Akram, Mudassar Nazar, Iqbal Qasim, and Abdul Qadir from Pakistan; Sir Richard Hadlee and Martin Crowe from New Zealand; Sir Geoffrey Boycott from England; Sir Clive Lloyd from West Indies; and David Hookes from Australia.

And for most of the benefit matches that I organised and played, my entire team would travel together in my 12-seater van, and most often, the van would be filled with my Indian and Pakistani cricket friends heading to the benefit matches; the joy of camaraderie we shared during these trips, singing songs together, and our friendly banter, still echoes in my ears. I am blessed to have several great stars as my friends, to travel with them, play with them, and dine and cheer with them. I often expressed my desire to my friends that if given a chance, I would love to relive those moments of my life in cricket with these cricketing legends.

QUEST FOR MORE

My Sojourn into the Holy Land

For a soul that is driven by an unsatiable zest to explore something more and new, asking to relax and relish upon whatever the best we have, in fact, is a real torture. The greatest pleasure of such people is the pleasure of embarking into new challenges of life. I think, I am a mystic being to feel an immense kick in exerting all my potentials for some productive cause than mere idling and relishing. By the time I married Maryam, in 1968, I had already made England my home, and all my extended family too, one after an another, joined us to settle down around us. We had already bought a huge house in England, and was making good money, involved simultaneously in multiple occupations—I was a worker in a factory, besides being a motor mechanic and a taxi-driver at my will, and had just begun to advance my endeavours into league cricket as well.

Then one day, I came to know that Fareed Warsi, a cousin of Shakeel Ahmad, was also in England and had made his stay at Nuneaton. Though both Shakeel and Fareed were my classmates from Hosainy School in Karachi, Shakeel was one of my best childhood friends who helped me in many ways, including my studies. I took Fareed's address from Shakeel and went to Nuneaton to see Fareed. He was a tenant in a house owned by Zakariya Bhai from Bombay and was sharing his flat with his friend named Abdul Rahman also known as Makki. We call him Makki, because he hails from Mecca in Saudi Arabia, and has come to England to pursue higher studies. Makki was a compassionate person, and his father was a wealthy businessman who owned several business firms. I also met his father along with his younger brother, Saifullah (Saifu) at Nuneaton, and had a good time with them all. Eventually, our friendship grew strong, and we would often call, and meet up one another. In 1969, Makki invited me and Fareed to Saudi Arabia, and described his travel plan by car, taking a long ride to Arabia, by covering the entire continent of Europe.

At first, I was fascinated by the notion that there would be greater prospects in Saudi, though I was a bit hesitant, as Maryam had just conceived our first child and was in the seventh month of her pregnancy. However, when Maryam encouraged me to pursue my interests which might provide me with opportunities for a brighter career, as she always wished the best for me, I assented to his proposal. Maryam also assured me that she would be fine staying with my parents, in my absence. Moreover, Mecca is a holy place for us Muslims, and so I even thought of settling down there with my family, if things turn out in our favour. I also wanted to go on this continental tour by road and experience the ways of the world.

Thereupon, Makki bought a new Vauxhall Estate Car for £600, and with little money in my hand, the five of us — Makki, Saifu, Fareed, and me, along with Makki's father embarked on our journey. Leaving England on March 1969, we set off to Belgium first; from there, we went on to Germany, Switzerland, Austria, Yugoslavia, Bulgaria, Turkey, Syria, Iraq, Kuwait, and then finally we reached our destination, Mecca in Saudi Arabia. It was an amazing journey which took us 28 days— we shared driving, mostly stayed in, and ate from hotels whenever or wherever we wanted some rest or felt hungry. However, most of our expenditures were all borne by Makki; he was insistent on paying everything and had never given us a chance to pay. We stayed in Switzerland for a couple of days, as Makki's family owns a perfume business there. The journey was quite exciting, safe, and explorative for us, till we entered Ankara in Turkey. In Turkey, for some unknown reasons, the police in their national boarders grew suspicious of us. They escorted us till the border of the country, and then handed us over to the police of Syria, who in turn did the same and left us to the border security forces of Iraq. When we finally entered Saudi and reached Kuwait, crossing the borders of Iraq, we were quite relieved. I had some friends in Kuwait, so we stayed with them for a couple of days, and from there we resumed our journey to Riyadh. Then we went on to Jeddah, the principal gateway to *Mecca*, the holiest city in Islam, followed by Medina, the second holiest city; finally, we reached our destination.

In Jeddah, we received a warm welcome from Makki's parents and siblings, and soon I became integral part of their family. After enjoying their warm hospitality for a couple of days, I attended an interview with *Bin-Zakar company*, a dealer of *Vauxhall Motors*. As I had expertise in repairing Vauxhall cars in England, I was offered a job as a mechanic at Bin-Zakar with good wages (£120 a week), with a car under my custody. I immediately accepted the offer, as 120 pounds a week was a big amount in those days.

But Saudi was so hot in those days that the temperature often would shoot up to 50 degrees Celsius. So, the company planned our work schedule from early morning to 12 noon, and again from 4 pm to late evening, keeping a break of four hours in the afternoon. My workplace was on the main road to Mecca. Unable to tolerate the scorching heat of the sun, I would drive from Jeddah to Mecca to pour some *Aab-e-zamzam* (sacred water) from the well that was most pious for all the Muslims of the world. I would pay just one or two *halalahs* (Saudi Riyal currency) for one leather bag full of water and pour on myself just to cool my body. And then I would go inside the mosque and perform Tawaf (walk around Kabbah). In those days hardly a few dozen would perform tawaf, and fortunately I was one among them. So, despite the scorching heat, I was glad for such a sacred opportunity to bath in Zamzam and perform tawaf every single day at the holiest mosque for the entire Muslim fraternity; I was also earning a significant amount from my job. But I began to miss England and my home—mom, father, brother, and my wife.

Then one day while doing Tawaf at Mecca, during my usual break from work, a hefty man on a wheelchair, assisted by some men, came in. As they entered from one side of the Kabbah, one of his assistants rushed to the other side, and requested a devotee worshiping there, "Can you move a bit to your right? Maulana Zakariya Saab is coming". I was totally ignorant of who Zakariya Saab was, and his connection to the Mosque. Then I learnt that his name was Zakariyya Kandhlawi, and people reverently call him as Maulana Zakariya Sahib for his knowledge on Islamic theology, and his spiritual leadership in the Islamic world; he had written several books, and significant among them were Fazail-E-Amaal, Fazail-E-Hajj, etc. They were treatises widely popular across the Islamic world, particularly among the Tablighi sect of Muslims, as they brilliantly recount the tenets for leading the life of a true Muslim. Then I witnessed a surprising incident: Zakariya Saab called the same man who had asked the devotee to move aside, and explained, "This place does not belong to me, nor to my father; this is a place of God and on which all of us have equal rights; you have no right to deprive other's right to praying." I was awestruck after hearing this as I wondered how he, sitting on one side of the Kabbah, could know of something that had happened on its other side. Then I thought, it could be due to his spiritual potential and social commitments that might have endowed him with an extraordinary capacity to see and hear something that he did not witness. I thought I must spend a great deal of my time with Maulana Zakariya Saab and take his spiritual blessings, and accordingly, I was fortunate to receive his spiritual preaching. However, after a few days of his stay at Mecca, Zakariya Saab, and his followers moved back to Medina.

Meanwhile, I received a letter from my home in May 1969 which had carried the happy news of my wife's delivery of a baby boy; He was named Ebrahim Adam, after both my deceased brother, Ebrahim, who had died of Jaundice, and my paternal grandfather whose name was also Ebrahim. By then, I had completed 4 months of my stay in Saudi, and I was already missing my wife and parents, amidst the terrible hot weather and the lonely life in Saudi. Now that with this cheerful news of the birth of my first child, I could not take it any further; I was desperate longing to flying off to England. But, before I leave Saudi, I wanted to make a visit to "Al Masjid an Nabawi" in Medina (the holy tomb of Prophet Mohammad), and live there in the holy auspices of Zakariya Saab for some time.

As soon as I received my wages for the week, I resigned from my job, took leave from Makki and his family, and moved to Medina, to leave for England from there by hitch-hike; Aziz Khan (another brother of Makki) also joined me as he too wanted to come to England. I was excited to get a chance to live in Medina, under the sacred guidance of one of the most influential theologists and religious teachers of our time; in such a heavenly bliss, I felt the divine touch. Zakariya Saab with his heavy physique, would always be on his wheelchair and will never step down from it. But, as he set to pray, God knows where all he got this energy, he turned out to be as swift as a young man, and reverted to his wheelchair as soon as he finished his prayer; he was a miraculous soul who amazed everyone around him.

After a few days of my stay at Medina, when I went to take leave from Zakariya Saab, he asked me whether I would leave for England by car. Though I was not sure of how I would go by, I just said 'yes' to him, to avoid further explanation. Then he said, "Suleman!" as he would call me, "I will give you some khajoor (dates) and some Zamzam water, you take them to England and deliver it to one of my students named Maulana Yousaf Saab in Bolton." Though I was worried of how I would take them all in that unplanned journey, I quietly agreed to oblige. Sensing my concern for the safe delivery of the items, he said, "don't worry, you will have a safe journey."

When we took leave of Zakariya Saab, Azeez expressed his concern about taking the heavy lot—bagful of *khajoor* and ten litre tin full of water—besides our own luggage. In those days, there were trucks which would carry watermelons to Medina from Jordan, and they carried passengers for 10 riyals on their return; it would take more than 48 hours to reach Jordan. We had no clear plan of our journey; we just we jumped into the truck with all our luggage. Travelling through hot desert sand of Arabia in that topless truck, we were exhausted by the time we reached Jordan; our bodies pained like a soaring wound, and we felt it impossible to carry ourselves any further. We thought of taking a flight, with whatever little money we had. But when we checked for tickets in Lebanon (from Jordan to Lebanon, we travelled by hitch-hike), its price was mind boggling; we learnt that each ticket cost 300 pounds, where our money put together would not even exceed 300 pounds. We do not know of what to do; I kept reminiscing Zakariya Saab's words, "don't worry, you will have a safe journey."

Hearing our conversation, one gentleman gently laid his hand on my shoulder and asked, "do you want to go to Paris (France) by air for 20 pounds?"; he said he had 2 tickets to Paris on his sons' names, and he could just get the names changed to ours. I was shocked and then began to suspect him of tricking me. But he explained to us that his sons dropped their plans of visiting Paris at the last minute, and if we share our names and other details, he will change the tickets to our names. I think, in those days, probably still, people who work for airlines would sometimes get complementary air-tickets, benefitting one's family members to travel, and some of them would sell those tickets to others. These tickets also must have been of a similar kind I suppose. He also left his house address with us and asked us to collect 2 tickets in our name the next morning from his house, in exchange of 20 pounds each.

Next morning, we went to his house and collected the tickets to Paris on our names, for a total of merely 40 pounds, and took the flight to Paris, the very next morning. And from Paris, we took a train to London, and reached home safely.

My happiness knew no bounds in seeing my newborn child and reuniting with my family, and so were my wife and parents. The house was filled in an atmosphere of celebration, where Aziz also joined us. After a few days of my reaching home, I went to Bolton as sought by Zakariya Saab, and handed all those holy things (Zamzam water and dates) over to Maulana Yousaf Saab, who was a preacher at a mosque there. Since then, Yousuf Saab became a good friend mine. There lies a divine company among those who are in the service of God and having an affinity of the spiritual gurus like Zakariya Saab and Yousaf Saab, I feel that I too cherish the divine bliss forever.

BUSINESS ESTABLISHMENT AND CAREER

Beginning my career as daily-wage worker in a woollen factory, I quickly rose to become a mechanic, then a taxi-driver, and over a period, I finally embarked on the journey to gain an eminence as one of the first amongst a very few Asian immigrants to curve a niche as an entrepreneur in Yorkshire. Amidst every challenge, both natural as well as socio-political, to attain these life fortunes, I never veered away from sharpening my talents in cricket, and to be one of the popular cricketers and leaders in Yorkshire league cricket as well. In fact, both these pursuits, business and cricket, have mutually complemented each other in my career building, and now, I am an established businessman, and a former cricketer in Yorkshire, England.

Venturing into Petrol Station Business

After working at Batley Carr Woollen Company as a labourer for over a year, I completed Sandwich Course in 1965, from Leeds Govt. Training College, to be trained as a 'Motor Mechanic,' and to start my own mechanic works. Then, I joined a small garage at Ossett where I worked for some time repairing only one model of a car named MINIS. Since it had a limited scope to work only on one model, I soon left to join another garage, Mirfield Motors, and then, in yet another garage, Rowland Wind (an official dealer of Vauxhall). The latter two garages gave me exposed to repairing all kinds of vehicles, and it was during this period that I also had acquired the craft of selling and buying second-hand cars.

After working for five years as an employee in these garages, repairing various kinds of vehicles, I finally left Rowland Wind in 1970, to start my own mechanic garage, to be independent, and to explore new businesses. When I left working at Rowland Wind garage, I got £120 in total from my savings on overtime work there, out of which I spent £100 to buy a small plot of land, along with a parking garage, from a person called 'Collins'. The plot was in Thornhill Street of the Savile town, where I did not even do my firm registration, and yet I started repairing vehicles from there. Since its former owner, Collins, was a milkman, who used to park his Milk Van there, the locals would call my garage as a milkman's garage.

Having a garage and a taxi of my own, I intensified my mechanic work, for which I would buy petrol from our adjacent petrol station AMOCO. When I learnt from its proprietor, of his decision to close his AMOCO petrol pump, incurring to losses, I thought that it could be a great opportunity for me to lease it, as I can look after both my mechanic job as well as petrol business from within the same compound. Immediately, I contacted the manager of the AMOCO to know the terms and condition to run the station. The manager, Mike Sanders, came down to my house the next morning, and agreed to hand over the station for free for three years, without any rent, including the space around it, except for the cost of petrol that amounts to £2000 a bond.

Though I did not have that huge lot, I accepted the offer in a view to pool the money from different sources. None of my family members, except my father, was happy with this new venture of mine, as all the people who held on to that specific station till then had all gone bankrupt. As planned, I pooled the required sum of £2000 in a short-while, and deposited the same in National Westminster Bank, for which I had to sell out our family car for £800 and borrowed another £800 from my father. After doing all this, to my surprise, I came to know from Mike that I had to deposit £2000 more (total of £4000), as I was told that, the company did not have trust on Asians, and I was the first Asian to make such a venture into petrol business. I had absolutely no clue, of what to do and whom to seek help from. At this critical juncture, I went to the Lloyds Bank, where my father had an account, and sought a loan of £2000. I explained about my business plans to the manager, Mr. Robinson, that I would transfer £2000 that was deposited in National Westminster Bank, to their bank, if they could lend me the amount as loan; I also showed him the agreement letter from the petrol company as proof. The manger was impressed with my plan but was not ready to pay me in cash as their bank rules did not permit him to do so. Instead, he extended his help by giving me a letter of assurance that warranted me with the lease.

I was glad, but I still needed some more money to buy Engine Oil, De-Icers and some accessories like breaks and clutches for the garage. I bought all the required materials, when fortunately, Moosa (Bhai) Aku-di, brother-in-law of my friend from Victoria School Babu, helped me by lending me £600, and then another £1000 by Rasheed Desai, who is a close relative to my family. I also borrowed £1000 from another friend of mine named Ahmed Isa, but on condition that the amount would be returned in a couple of weeks. Anyway, the entire amount was ready, and I deposited the same in the bank. Finally, I made my niche into petrol business as the first Asian to do so in Yorkshire. We planned to inaugu-rate the station on Friday, as it was not merely an auspicious day as per our religion, but was also the last working day of the week, where all the bank transactions for the week would get closed on that day. This was the pragmatic concern, as the reason for inaugurating business on Friday was due to the lack of sufficient funds to buy petrol on cash. I would buy petrol on bank-cheque for £2000 a tank on every Thursday, sell them during the entire week, and deposit the thence received money on sales in the bank during early hours of next Tuesday. I would do this hoping that the cheque that I issue them on Thursday, would get clear-ance by next Tuesday, and accordingly the cheque always got cleared on time. All my calculative plans in this regard had not been failed yet, and hence no cheque that I deposited in the bank till date got bounced out. As planned, Petrol, Engine Oils, and other related stuff reached our station by Thursday, and the business was inaugurated on Friday morning in the hands of my mother.

As soon as I took the AMOCO garage in 1972, I asked my father to quit his job and join me assisting in this new business. But he was not sure of its worth, as he was already earning £40 a week, which was quite a good amount. When I persisted, he took sick leave for one week on sick note, only to verify its profitability, as it was the only way he was entitled to take such as long leave. When I was doing the mechanical work, my father served petrol for 1 week. He was amazed to see the turnover that amounted to more than £200 in a day. With this, he never went back to join his job in the factory. Petrol business had worked well, and in a couple of days, I returned £1000 that I owed to Ahmed Isa as an immediate measure and resorted to work 7 days and nights a week rigorously in the garage, repairing cars both during days and snowy nights, and simultaneously looked after the petrol business. I also got MoT license (Vehicle Fitness Test) during this time that gave me an authority to ratify vehicular fitness. For this, I built repair bay, ramp, and everything to conduct the tests for the fitness of vehicles, and issue certificates accordingly. I kept the bay open for seven days a week, where I would charge £1 for testing each car, and would test 10 cars per day, which meant a considerable amount of money.

In those days, the petrol stations in England used to operate from 8:00 in the morning to 6:00 in the evening, and there was no station, except Leicester Café motor way, that operated for 24 hours in that part of the city. We would also keep it open during holidays and on festival days, including Christmas, Boxing Day, Good Friday, etc. Availability of petrol in the nights was convenient for the commuters, and all the taxi-drivers began opting my petrol station. This was being aired both by oral means as well as by radio, television, and other mass media, resulting to people queuing up at my petrol station. Slowly, the business picked up, and in a short while, I cleared all the money that was borrowed from all, including Moosa Akudi, Rasheed Desai, etc.

I was so happy that my business began ushering in profits, and the company too was happy with my work that I was selling Engine Oil, De-Icers, and some accessories like brakes and clutches in my garage, alongside of petrol, as they were not available in the motor outlets, nor were there accessories shops in those days. The untiring efforts, and committed participation of my father in these struggles, had been inalienable in my struggles, and had made my job not only possible, but also given me a flexibility to venture in multiple businesses. My father was so punctual in his job, that he would open the garage at 8 in the morning and look after the business till it closed at 10 in the night, without fail, except a half-an-hour between 12pm and 12:30pm for lunch. His devotion to work for three decades, without desiring to have even a leisure for a day to lead a life of his own, assured me with a time and space to look after multiple tasks, including cricket. I also began to devote sufficient time for cricket amidst my busy schedules.

And one day, on my way back to home, I happened to see an office of an old-age home. An idea struck in my mind to plan a holiday trip for all the old-age inmates of that home, and then decided to sponsor them all the expenses for one day outing. All the inmates were so happy to join the outing, and its manger was so pleased to hear this plan, as it was first of its kind, and no one had ever done this before. Immediately, I booked a coach (bus) to Blackpool from Dewsbury for the next Friday and took all the 52 old-age people. We set off at 8:00 a.m. and were back by 10:00 p.m. I bore all the expenses of the trip. Hearing the news of the trip, reporters from various newspapers thronged to the spot to take photographs, and the next morning it was widely published in the print-media, including Dewsbury Reporter, Bartley News, Yorkshire Post, and others. The media lauded me and my act in bold letters, as Solly Adam being its proprietor, "Adam Bothers" organized a free holiday trip for old people from Dewsbury; 'All old people from Batley went to Blackpool for a day, paid all by Adam Brothers' Garage in Savile Road, etc. This led the people of our city and its surrounding areas to give a nod of admiration to me for my compassion for old people, and that became a huge advertisement for my business too.

The news of my hard work, punctuality, and goodwill spread around, leading to several other petrol companies approaching me, beginning with AMOCO (American company), and two French companies named TOTAL, near Huddersfield in Bradley, and VIP at Bradford Road, to know if I could run their petrol stations in different parts of the country. Since many of these companies were struggling hard to function well, they offered them to me free of charge for years. While all the above companies offered me a contract for free for years, and kept renewing the contract in the stipulated period, some of them like VIP not only did a free contract with me for 4 years, but also paid me an honorarium of £13,000 for running the site; I owned this site after a while. Likewise, within a year, or so, I made contract with all these petrol companies in 7 different sites altogether, having two Petrol Stations on Saville Road, one in Leeds, one on Bradford Road, Batley, one at Bradley in Huddersfiled, one on Halifax Road (Staincliffe) and one in Heckmondwike.

There was also a time that witnessed dislocation of populations, involving rapid migrations across countries and continents. This situation gave rise to the sale of several old houses in our locality. Since I had already amassed a huge sum of money, those natives who were moving out of their native towns, would approach me to sell their houses. I began buying house after an another, that amounted to the owing of 25 houses to my credit. I was involved simultaneously in various businesses. One day, while attending to a car break-down at Birstall in Fieldhead state, I had to visit a shop to wash my hands, after repairing the car. It was a massive super-market, yet surprisingly had almost nothing in it. I was a bit curious to know the reason for not keeping good stuff in its gigantic and well-built supermarket. To my wonder, I learnt from its owner that they were old couple and were left with no one to look after the shop, and so they intending to sell it. Since it was at a prime location, and it was a good building, I showed an interest to buy it, left my telephone number with them, and returned home. By the same evening at around 6:30 p.m., I got a ring from that old gentleman, who was ready to sell the entire supermarket, including whatever the little stock it had for £16,000. I accepted the offer, took over the shop and named it 'Pick N Pay' supermarket.

At this moment, I also found a lot of scope for making money in the car hiring business, besides petrol business. I started buying cars, and mini-buses and would hire them out. Since my brother, Younus Adam, was still young, and my children were school-going kids, so I was like a headless chicken running from one petrol station to another, of course assisted by my wife, while my father was looking after one of my seven sites. With this, my profits mounted so high that my annual business turnover had already hit millions of pounds, from all these 7 petrol stations together.

I employed two persons to look after my supermarket: one was Ibrahim Naana, whose mother was a good friend and relative of my mother from our village in India, and the other was Saeed Desai, my neighbour in Karachi of Pakistan. I would get £4000 to £6000 turnover in a week from this shop, which amounted to more than £20,000 a month. It was at this moment that I stopped working as a mechanic, as I had too many businesses to look after. My wife, Maryam, would accompany me to the supermarket every day in the evening at 6:30, from there, we would go to the Petrol Station at Pudsey around 8:30pm, followed by another petrol station on Saville Road (which I still own); we also had our own takeaway food business called 'Royal Sweets', where we together would help workers until 9 pm, or sometimes even as late as 11 at night, depending on the intensity of the customers, and only then we would return home to do all cash counting and stock checking just before going to bed. After a while, we also recruited two more storekeepers, Mary and Andrea sisters.

In this way, day by day, my business continued to grow, and at the peak of my business career, I possessed 7 Petrol Stations and a garage, Kirklees Taxi, 20 plus hire-cars and over 8 mini-busses, 20-25 houses to rent, and a huge super-market 'Pick N Pay' and Takeaway food business named 'Royal Sweets' and with a support drawn from my father, mother, and wife, I had undertaken all these businesses simultaneously. Eventually my brother, Younus Adam, grew up and began sharing some of my business responsibilities; both my sons, Afzal, and Ebrahim, completed their university education and they too joined us, and I shared job responsibilities to each one of them. I also recruited more personnel like Hashem, Shaukat, Pauline etc. for the smooth functioning of business, and to carve out some time for me to play cricket. My business was going very well, and I was minting a good deal of money in each business that continued for more than twenty years. But as the saying goes, 'as you rise, so will you fall,' everything has time and space to rise, as well as to fall. The time of decline began, along with its changing conditions. All the petrol companies began changing their policies from keeping tenants, to opening their own company outlets, or to sell their companies to others. With that I gave up all my sites back to the respective companies. I had to undergo huge losses in this fiasco, as Amoco sold all its sites to SALE company. But I could retain one of the petrol stations that I bought from JET company.

My Entry into Sports Business

After a little while, when I was playing for Slazenger's CC in 2001, which was the last cricket club that I ever played for, I started a sports business named "Solly Sports," along with its in-house embroidery/printing facilities, having its headquarters in Dewsbury, Yorkshire. I started this business, having gained knowledge of the manufacturing sports-equipment from some of its manufacturers, as world's top manufacturers of cricket equipment were all mainly from India, and I have been friends with almost all of them.

Ever since I started sports equipment business, I have been a major supporter of league cricket in the Yorkshire region, and supplied Cricket Gears to hundreds of players, including international cricketers and local league cricketers, and had sponsored many leagues/competitions in the last two-decades through "Solly Sports." The prominent among the leagues/competitions, I sponsored on behalf of Solly Sports include:

- Quaid-e-Azam Sunday Cricket League Cup Competition
- Dewsbury & District Cricket League
- The Solly Sports Heavy Woollen Cup (For 20 years, and still on)
- The Solly Sports Crowther Cup (For 20 years, and still on)
- Heavy Woollen Junior League (for 3 years)
- The Solly Sports Central Yorkshire Cricket League (for 12 years)
- Yorkshire ECB County Premier League – League Sponsor (for 10 years)

Solly Sports not only manufactured bats and other cricket equipment but was also a specialist in design and embroidery of the logos on sports dresses, and track suits. I proudly owned an extensive range of clothing and equipment of our own brand, along with products from the biggest brands in cricket such as Gunn & Moore, Asics, and Kookaburra. With this, we provided a wide range of embroidery, printing and customised clothing services for sports, clubs, businesses, and individuals. I joined this sports business, out of my knowledge and personal identity with the game, and not even had any remote motive to exploit my association with cricket stars and legends for my benefit. In fact, some of my friends, even asked me, "having several cricket legends like Sunil Gavaskar, Imran Khan, Sachin Tendulkar, etc. as my friends, why did not I ever try to endorse my bat," the fact of which I always abhorred taking advantage of friends. I have always been a staunch professional about my professional life, untampered by my personal relationships, and vice versa. I love to be associated with Solly Sports, which is my sole identity as a cricketer and businessman. It is for this reason that, though all my businesses were being looked after by my all the four children (three sons—Ebrahim, Afzal, Sohail, and a daughter, Asma), I still held on to Solly Sports throughout my retired life, having two workers at hand. Yet, I feel elated and joyous to open the shop on my own at 10 am, and close it by 5 pm every day, except for an hour during lunch.

IIFA 2007 - Celebrity Cricket Match

One day when I was busy in my sports shop, I got a phone call from a lady, who introduced herself as an event manager for the IIFA (International Indian Film Academy) 2007 cricket match. She asked me, if we can supply Cricket Gear, Equipment, clothing, and other accessories required for the match. IIFA 2007 was a celebrity cricket match that was held on June 8, 2007, at Headingly Carnegie Stadium, the venue of some of the greatest test matches ever, in Leeds, Yorkshire, between IIFA Celebrity Cricket Team (also known as IIFA XI), and UK Celebrity Cricket Team (also known as Yorkshire XI). I was delighted not merely because it was a great honour for me to be part of such an event of historic glory, with a noble purpose, but also because of its hosting city, Yorkshire to which I belong. By then, Solly Sports was already popular in the league cricket of the Yorkshire region, as we were able to produce our equipment that was no less than that of international standards. I immediately agreed to sponsor the required quantity and quality of the equipment and had expressed my allegiance to the match. I personally went, along with my two assistants (workers in my company), to take the measurements of all the Bollywood Celebrities, who were to participate in that event, and had carefully tailored required dresses for them. I managed to deliver everything before time, though there was not much time in hand.

While the IIFA celebrity team comprised Asia's cricketing greats and top-rung film-stars of Bollywood combine, its counterpart, UK Celebrity Cricket Team consisted of English cricketers, British TV stars and musicians, including two members of the Parliament of England. Captained by the then young film star, Saif Ali Khan, the IIFA celebrity team boasted of cricket stars like Kapil Dev, Mohammed Azharuddin and Ajay Jadeja. The team was also star-studded by various film personalities that include, Rakesh Mehra, Shaan, Emran Hashmi, Sohail Khan, Dino Morea, Fardeen Khan, Sunny Deol, Bobby Deol, Aftab Sivdasani, Tushar Kapoor, Arshad Warsi, Boman Irani, Hrithik Roshan, Chunky Pandey, Kunal Kapoor, Zayed Khan, Sunil Shetty, Riteish Deshmukh, Anil Kapoor and Abhishek Bachchan. The team Yorkshire XI, on the other hand, displayed talents like Nick Knowles, Rosalie Birch (England Women Cricketer), Former England Players Gladstone Small, Devon Malcolm, Chris Lewis and Ajmal Shahzad; Jay Sean, Sherwin Campbell (West Indies Test Player), Danny McGuire, Harry Gration, Greg Wise, Manish Bhasin, Andrew Gale (Yorkshire County Player), Colin Salmon (British Actor), Oliver Milburn (British Actor) and two members of the parliament of England named Keith Vaz and Shahid Malik. The match also saw the return to the square of the ever popular and highly respected Yorkshireman, (Harold) 'Dickie' Bird, who umpired with Jack Hampshire.

Amidst cheering applauds from both cricket and cinema fans, the match was inaugurated by acting legend and IIFA brand Ambassador, Amitabh Bachchan. Before being joined by celluloid superstars, Salman Khan and Shilpa Shetty for the toss of coin; the jest-filled commentary for the match was being provided by actor-comedians, Chunky Pandey and Boman Irani, with a special commentary, marking the signature elegance of Preity Zinta and Urmila Matondkar. The stadium was overcrowded, and vibrant atmosphere prevailed, as there was already a huge fanbase for Bollywood stars in the Yorkshire region. The event hosted over 28,000 visitors from India and Pakistan during the weekend, boosting off the region's economy by more than £9.5 million, and had also attracted 30,000 extra visitors from all over the world. All this was being broadcasted globally by STAR TV, to reach nearly 500 million viewers from 110 countries.

I reached the stadium a bit early to make sure all the arrangements for the event, delivered dresses to respective players and organizers, and transported the cricket equipment for the day to the stadium. My family members, however, had joined me a bit later, as they all had to attend Namaaz-prayers, owing to Friday. I introduced my family members to all the Bollywood film stars and cheered-up some of the finest moments with the celebrities of the Bollywood and star cricketers; they all treated me and my family with great respect. My grandson, Mohammad Adam, at that moment was just 3 years old, so all the stars, particularly Salman Khan, Chunky Pandey, Sohail Khan, Kapil Dev, Saif Ali Khan, Arjun Rampal, Azharuddin, etc., pampered him so much and played with him. I already knew the cricket-stars as my colleagues and friends in the past, like Kapil Dev, Ajay Jadeja and Mohammad Azharuddin who represented the Bollywood team, and Sherwin Campbell, Gladstone Small, Devon Malcolm, Ajmal Shahzad and Chris Lewis, who represented Yorkshire team. With this event, I also happened to know several Bollywood stars as well.

Interestingly, the Birthday of Shilpa Shetty, also coincided with the day of this charity match (June 8, 2007), so all the celebrities had joined for her birthday celebration on the same evening. I was glad that I was also an invitee, along with my wife, for her birthday party at night, the celebrations of which converged with the celebration of winning the

Bollywood team in that match. I also felt glad to recount myself for being invited as a VIP for the IIFA awards function that took place on June 10, 2007, in Sheffield, near Dewsbury, as a final event of its weekend activities. I attended this function, again, along with my wife, Maryam Adam. We were greeted warmly by all the Bollywood stars present there, including Big-B (Amitabh), Dharmendra, Saif Ali Khan, Akshay Kumar, Salman Khan, Shilpa Shetty, Preity Zinta, etc. The honour and respect we received from those film stars on that day, jostled with the love and affection I had been cherishing with hundreds of cricket stars in my 42 years of cricket and business life combine.

The popularity of excellence that Solly Sports enjoyed in English league cricket till then, began to expand into international cricket as well, and by 2010, we had got ratification from *International Cricket Council* (ICC), as "an approved manufacturer for clothing and equipment," that could supply its equipment to any ICC cricket events and matches. With this approval from ICC, a few players had used my company equipment in International and First-Class Matches; they include, besides Saeed Ajmal, Kamran Akmal, Mohammad Asif, Shahid Afridi, Steve Foster, Sameer Dighe etc.

Presently, I am still looking after Solly Sports all by myself, as I have always been, as it remained a favourite affair in my retired life, while the rest of my businesses were looked after by all my four children. All of us sit in the same building on Saville Town, which has a petrol station, Londis supermarket, dessert centre, food takeaway and mobile store. My elder son, Ebrahim Adam, is looking after the accountancy business and meat factory, while my second son, Afzal Adam, is with a mobile phone store, and third son, Sohail Adam, a real estate, and development company named Adam Estates, and my daughter, Asma, is associated with a travel business called, Travel Tonight. I often wonder, whether it is real, or was I daydreaming. When I landed in England in 1963, I was left with only £1 in my hand. But now, having gone through the toughest times as a day-wage labourer in a factory in 1964, followed by a vehicle mechanic, taxi-driver, and then finally my emergence into a successful businessman and a cricketer in Dewsbury, at some point of time, I had millions of pounds as turnovers annually, having my children now looking after multiple business establishments. I feel that all this would not have been possible, without support from my parents and wife, who have been an invisible force in every respect, and they stood like strong pillars in all my achievements and successes. More than a successful man, today I feel that I am a fully-satisfied human being to be born and have walked on earth, to be one of the first Asian entrepreneurs in Yorkshire region, and upon my support and motivation several other Asians also established themselves as businessmen; hundreds of people, including several cricketers had worked in my firms, before their rise as star cricketers. In this way, I have been truthful to both my business and cricket life, and so I feel that I am now reaping its fruits of attaining greatest satisfaction in my life.

MY SPECIAL MOMENTS WITH CRICKET STARS

Sunil Gavaskar: A Friendship to Treasure

Like every other human being on earth, I too met innumerable people in my lifetime. However, I have had the rarest opportunity to be blessed to have friends with hundreds of cricketers, including its stars and legends around the world, out of which some of them became my friends for life; I also have been friends with several prominent businessmen in England. Among those best friends of my life, there are two people who came to emerge as an integral part of my family; they are none other than the legendary cricketer Sunil Manohar Gavaskar from India, and the other, a cricket star Iqbal Qasim from Pakistan. They have been my family friends, as they both share their warmth of affection and friendship with all the members of my family. So, my affinity with Sunil has been one of the longest and the most formidable one.

I met Sunil for the first time at Old Trafford, Manchester, in England during a Test match between India and England in 1971. Just a few months before his visit to England, he scored 774 runs with his remarkable batting feat against the sturdy team of West Indies in their own home turf during his debut test series with them. This batting performance is widely regarded as one of the greatest in the history of the sport, and so, Sunil was a great attraction for all of us. However, our interaction then, was just casual and mere exchange of greetings. As the presence of Asian cricket audience in English stadiums in those days was very few, as compared to the present day, it was relatively easier for the cricket

140

fans of Asian origin to meet any cricket star from India and Pakistan. In those days, the cricketers themselves would also be delighted to see their fans of Asian origin in England. It was an exhilarating experience for me to meet all the players of the Indian cricket team together, but I had not even imagined that this cricket legend, Sunil, who is one of the finest human beings with great intellect and a noble heart, would one day become my friend, and that our friendship would last forever.

Ever since I met Sunil for the first time, we became friends. Eventually, over the years, our bond had strengthened and penetrated each other's families, and by mid-1970s, the bond strengthened more than ever. Sunil visited England multiple times and each time, either on his cricket tour, or due to personal reasons, we would meet up and then he would prefer to stay with us at my house in Dewsbury. I always would love his company as it entailed great emotional bonding, but also each moment spent with him, was a great learning experience. Sunil and his family have been so intimate that, all my children grew up before his eyes; he has a genuine love and concern for me and my children and had always been my guide to advise and assist me in need; he had attended the marriages of all my children, who affectionately call him Sunil Uncle. Sunil's wife, Marshneil Gavaskar, whom we all affectionately call Pammi, also shares a close bonding with our family, particularly with my daughter, Asma. Their son, Rohan Gavaskar, has been the loving kid for all of us, and they have all been integral to my family. In fact, when Rohan was born in 1976, Sunil was not in India, as he had to go out on a tour to New Zealand. Owing to telephone connectivity issues from India, the Sunil's family was unable to reach out to him to share the happy news. Knowing that Sunil and I would be in contact with each other, regardless of the location of our stay at any given moment, Sunil's family approached me to inform Sunil about the birth of his son, and of the well-being of both the mother and the child. In this way, I had the privilege to inform Sunil about the birth of his son, and I was the first person to share his happiness.

Sunil had never been treated, nor he himself behaved, as a guest in my house; he has always been like a brother, a member of my family. If any of his friends needed an accommodation in England, he would assure them before even taking any confirmation from me, and then inform me of the need for their accommodation. One such occasion had arisen during the tour of the Indian cricket team to England in 1979 led by Venkata Raghavan, on a test series against the English team; a few months before this cricket series, the team also had participated in the 1979 World Cup. I have a vivid memory that, CD Gopinath was serving as the manager of the Indian team for that test series.

As scheduled, one of the matches was to be held at Headingly Stadium, and the cricketers had landed in England along with their wives, for this tour. But the team manager CD Gopinath made a rule that the wives of the cricketers would not be permitted to stay with them in the hotel rooms, for he believed that their families would be a distraction. Considering the safety and well-being of the women, Sunil rang me up to accommodate all the women in my house in Dewsbury and provide them with the comforts of a home in England; he also assigned me with the job of taking them all to the Old Trafford stadium to watch the following match there. At that time, I had a mini car which could accommodate only four persons. But besides me, there were five; they included Kavitha Vishwanath (Sunil's sister and the wife of Gundappa Vishwanath), Jyothi Gaekwad (w/o Anshuman Gaekwad), Ranjani Raghavan (w/o Venkata Raghavan), Toral Patel (w/o Brijesh Patel), and of course Pammi (Sunil's wife). Having Pammi seated in the front seat beside me, while the other four occupied the backseat, all the six of us began travelling together in my car to my home in Dewsbury. But our unusual arrangement did not go unnoticed; a police officer stopped us on account of breaking the law, as we were six persons in a car that was designed only for four. Then I explained to the officer that they were wives of Indian cricketers, and of the situation they were in. Fortunately, the police officer himself was a cricket enthusiast, and so he allowed us to go further without being penalised, and yet with a gentle warning. They all stayed at my home, while their husbands were in the hotels. My wife and children had a wonderful time with them; they cooked, ate, shopped and had lots of fun in the warmth affection of each other; I would also take them to the Old Trafford stadium on the days of the match, apart from helping them in shopping and other activities. This is one of the lasting memories, that we often recollect whenever we meet up.

I also would receive the same warmth of reception from Sunil and other cricket stars in India, whenever I happened to go there. One such event was a tour of the England cricket team to India in 1981, on a test series with the Indian team. To my memory, it was Keith Fletcher who was the captain of the England team, and Sunil was heading the Indian team. I was excited to watch the matches, and immediately wrote a letter to Sunil, asking him to arrange 7 tickets. But Sunil did not acknowledge my letter due to his busy schedule. Undeterred by this, I went to India along with my wife, Maryam, and our three-year-old son, Sohail.

Upon our arrival at Bombay, Rahul Mankad graciously came to the airport to receive us; he took us to their house, and we had a wonderful time there. During dinner, Ashok Mankad, the brother of Rahul, asked me about the tickets for the match. I told him about my letter to Sunil, and Ashok said, he would look after the tickets. The next morning, by the time I went to the Wankhede Stadium, the Indian team was in practice for the match, and Sunil was addressing the press. Not wanting to disturb Sunil, I stood a few yards away from him. But the moment Sunil spotted me, to my astonishment, he called me out from amidst the reporters and said, "Hey Solly, come here! Your three passes are in my hotel room 224 at the Taj Hotel." He also asked me about my wife and son. I was glad that Sunil had a genuine concern for me, and his usual way of silently doing everything for the wellbeing of all his loved ones. This incident has deeply etched in my heart and has enhanced the respect and love for him that had already there in me.

Three historic moments occupy significance in the life of Sunil, and I was fortunate to witness all the three of them in person. The first remarkable occasion was India's triumphant victory in the World Cup-1983, against formidable West Indies team in the finals that was held at Lords on June 25, 1983. The second notable milestone was Sunil's distinction as the first cricketer ever to attain the incredible score of 10,000 runs in the test matches; he reached this milestone during a test series against Pakistan in 1987 at Motera Stadium, Ahmadabad in India. The third one was his exceptional Century (188 Runs) in the MCC Bi-centenary match, which took place between MCC and Rest of the World XI at Lords on August 21, 1987.

In fact, I travelled all the way to India just to witness Sunil's world record of 10,000 runs - first ever by any cricketer in the test matches. After the match, Sunil affectionately autographed several T-shirts, caps, and bats for me and my family members, which we still treasure to this day. We also had a great time together in India, and then travelled back to England. And for both the 1983 World Cup Final and 1987 MCC Bi-centenary matches, Sunil arranged tickets for me and my family. We were all incredibly fortunate to witness these truly historic events in Sunil's career. The quality of the TV broadcast during 1980s and 90s was not so good. So, Sunil would supply me with all the video cassettes recorded by the broadcasting team for all the matches he played. During my leisure time, I loved watching him play on the TV at home, and I still possess all those collections of cassettes. In addition to his involvement in international and first-class cricket, Sunil also had participated in 5 benefit matches upon my request, in a view to support his fellow cricketers; it was a memorable experience for me, as I played in all the five matches with Sunil.

I was a special guest for the wedding of Sunil's son, Rohan in 2003, along with two other close friends of Sunil, Chandresh Patel (England) and Vinoo Bhai (Narottam Vadgama). All three of us, along with our families, and his family friend Raju Mehta, had stayed at 'Saahil Apartments' in Mumbai. Several Bollywood celebrities, cricketers, and politicians attended the wedding, and to many of them, we were introduced proudly by both Sunil and Pammi as their own family members. After the wedding, all the three families were honoured with gold, as part of the family customs. This treatment from Sunil and Pammi further reinforced the warmth and affection among our families.

In a view to bring together all the friends of Sunil, a lavish party was organised, the next week after the marriage, at a prestigious 5-star hotel in Mumbai by one close friend of Sunil named Kishan Gehlot, who was also a well-known businessman in Kenya. Of course, I attended the party along with my family, and during the event, Sunil graciously introduced us to several Bollywood celebrities, including renowned film stars like Dilip Kumar and Saira Banu; it was a fun-filled moment for all of us.

It gives me immense pleasure to know that Sunil desired my presence in all the moments which he considered to have some significance. One such event was the retirement of Sachin Tendulkar with his final and 200th Test Match of his career in 2013. Sunil invited me to Mumbai so that we could watch this final and historic match of Sachin together. In fact, he had gone an extra mile by writing a letter to the Consular Officer, Mr. Parmanand Sinha, requesting a visa on my behalf. In his letter to the officer, Sunil explained the deep bonding that our families had shared over years. I was so glad to be in Mumbai to watch Sachin's final Test match along with Sunil; Sachin also expressed his pleasure for having me there for his farewell match.

When Sunil was in England, he used to receive invitations from several rich businessmen for dinner parties, and we often attend them together. One such occasion was an invitation from a businessman of

Manchester. Sunil accepted their invitation, and we together went to Manchester in my old Datsun Car, heading towards a hotel where we were to meet our host, and from there we would proceed to a Private Guest House for the party. Upon our arrival, we found one brand-new Rolls-Royce car awaiting us. The hosts wanted Sunil to be chauffeured in the luxurious vehicle to the party venue. However, Sunil preferred a ride in my humble Datsun car, suggesting that we follow the Rolls-Royce. Both the hosts and me were taken aback by this sudden reply of Sunil. As we trailed behind that extravagant car, I could not help but ask Sunil that he could have gone with them, while I follow him in my car. In response, Sunil said, "this party was just for a day, but our friendship would be for life." With this, one can understand how immense the value and respect that Sunil holds for our bonding; I felt proud of having him as the rarest friend of my life.

Similarly, Sunil also displays respect for everyone's faith and demonstrates his humility towards different religious beliefs. I recall an incident when Sunil had a meeting with Dr Ali Bacher, the former South African cricketer and administrator, that was scheduled at 4:30 pm at Kings Cross Railway Station in London. After having lunch at my home in Dewsbury, I was getting ready to drop Sunil off at Wakefield Railway Station. Unaware of Sunil's appointment with Dr Ali, my wife asked me in Gujarati if I was going to perform Namaaz prayers. Sunil understands, and even speaks, a bit of Gujarati as well. Upon hearing our conversation, he swiftly suggested that he would take the next train and arrive in London by 5:30 pm and asked me to continue with my prayers. I tried to explain Sunil that I can attend the next session of the Namaaz prayers, after dropping him off. However, Sunil persisted me to go on with my prayers, and only then he would go out, as he said, Dr. Ali can understand the delay.

There are several incidents that illustrate how Sunil cherished his friendship; they have left a profound impact on me. Sunil enjoyed shopping; he explored the stores whenever he visited England, often buying books and other articles. One day, when we were out shopping, I noticed that he deliberately avoided shopping from a popular store called Marks & Spencer in Sheffield. I was a bit curious to know of why he avoids such an important shop, and on our way back, I asked him about that. Then Sunil recounted the reason. In 1974, during a test series against England, Sudhir Nayak, a former Indian cricketer who opened the batting line-up with Sunil, had a troubling encounter at that store. Sudhir tried on the socks but forgot to take them off while checking other clothes, for which Sudhir was falsely accused of stealing two pairs of socks, worth 50p. Despite repeated pleadings for his ignorance and apologies for his unintended act, Sudhir had to face legal proceedings and had to appear before the court; the Indian High Commissioner also had intervened to address this issue. Sunil knows Sudhir as a wonderful human being with a compassionate heart. This incident haunted Sudhir and the Indian team for years. Since Sunil knew that one of his colleagues had been wrongly accused of theft by the staff of this store, he made a personal promise to himself that he would never enter Mark & Spencer store for life. However, he took this decision, not due to his ill will towards the M & S store, but only to impart an immense value to his friendship. This shows how principled Sunil is.

Sunil had a special bonding with our family; he fondly refers my wife, Maryam, as Bhabhi. Despite caring for and looking after numerous cricketers from the sub-continent, Maryam does not have any interest about cricket; she never watches cricket, and so she cannot even recognise cricket legends. She has other interests—taking care of our family, supporting me in our business, and to honour the guests by serving them with home-made delicacies; often she engages in the discussions about shopping, cooking, and places of travel. In fact, this aspect of Maryam and other members of my home makes Sunil feel at home, because he can come out of the world of cricket and freely live here, talking about non-cricketing topics with his Bhabhi.

Once, I, along with Maryam, attended a party organized by a well-respected London-based businessman, Saeed Ahmad, whom I affectionately call Ahmad Bhai. It was a party that was also attended by Bollywood celebrities such as Dilip Kumar, Saira Bhanu, Mumtaz, and Usha Mangeshkar (Lata Mangeshkar's sister), and one Indian High Commissioner, along with several other cricket stars like Gary Sobers, Avinash Karnik, etc.; Sunil was also present. As Gary Sobers entered the hall, just before the commencement of the party, he drew the attention of everyone. Many cricket-fans began taking pictures with him. Noticing the special attention of Gary, Maryam quietly approached Sunil and enquired who Gary was. Amazed by this, Sunil asked her if she really did not know him. Then she admitted her ignorance of Gary, that she had never seen him before, and then, she expressed her wonder, if he was an actor or a politician. Amused by her enquiry, Sunil took Maryam to Gary Sobers and asked him, "Gary, do you believe that everyone in the world knows who you are?" Gary responded with a smile, saying, "I think so." Sunil then explained to Gary that his Bhabhi cannot recognize him, and with a huge laughter warned Gary, "Remember! not everyone recognises you." Gary, wearing a big smile on his face, took a picture with my wife, Maryam, making it a memorable moment for all.

My children too, have a special attachment with Sunil, and whenever they visit India, they stay at his place. Sunil enjoys their company and treats them like his own children. He takes out time for them despite his busy schedule; he often takes my children to film studios and sites of entertainment. During her teenage years, my daughter Asma was a big fan of Bollywood movies, particularly Madhuri Dixit. On one occasion when Asma visited India, Sunil took her to a Bollywood film party where Madhuri Dixit was also present. Asma was thrilled to see Madhuri Dixit and expressed her desire to Sunil that if she could take a picture with Madhuri Dixit. Sunil quietly approached Madhuri and requested her if she would be willing to take a picture with Asma. Madhuri, surprised by this request from none other than Sunil Gavaskar, who is one of the biggest celebrities in India as a cricket legend, publicly announced with her exclaim, "Look, everyone! Sunil Ji is requesting a picture with me!" This is how he cares for our children, as his own.

Sunil is remarkable in his humility and integrity. Once, we returned to our home after a match, and my wife had prepared biryani, as Sunil had a fondness for it. While arranging food on the dinner table, she also placed poppadom and yogurt. We were in conversation while sitting down to eat, and Sunil began eating poppadom and some yogurt, which I thought was a starter. But, by the time the biryani was served, he quietly said he had finished his dinner. I could not help but express my astonishment, and said, "Come on Sunil! Bhabhi has prepared biryani especially for you, and now you say you finished your dinner?" Sunil explained his cultural habit of eating only one item at a time and shared the story behind this practice.

As recounted by Sunil, during the reign of Lal Bahadur Shastri as the Prime Minister of India, the country had faced a severe famine caused by war, resulting in scarcity of food. By November 1965, the situation had become so adverse that Shastri addressed the nation, asking all the citizens, "if each person can give up one meal in a day, the rest of the population gets their only meal of the day." This message of Shastri was seriously taken up by the family of Sunil and it was made a familial practice, which he continues to this day. It looks strange, but Sunil steadfastly practices it for decades; he is an exceptional human being, who is committed to a life of principles, fairness, and compassion for humanity; I have never come across anyone like him in my life.

After his retirement from cricket, Sunil began working as a commentator for BBC and other broadcasters of Sports in the UK for a few years. Despite being provided with luxurious hotel accommodation in Headingly, or Manchester, with all his expenses borne by the company, Sunil would prefer to stay at my home. During this period of his stay at my residence, we had shared numerous wonderful memories with him as a family. In fact, one of our bedrooms were exclusively reserved for Sunil, and that room is still his.

Sunil has been a valuable source of advice and assistance for my business as well, on multiple occasions. In fact, it was his suggestion that had led me to start 'Solly Sports,' which allows me today to have a connection with the sport that we together cherished during the best part of our lives. It is still afresh in my memory when Sunil would spend hours of his time in my office at Dewsbury, diligently writing articles for various journals and magazines. He is a true example of a hard-working man, and he had a firm conviction that nothing comes in life on its own, but success requires effort and dedication. He always encourages us all to work hard, and to attain our goals. To cherish our long and enduring friendship, we organised an event on attaining the 50th year of my friendship with Sunil in 2021, when he visited us in Dewsbury. In that regard, my family members arranged a special cake with letters adorned on it as, 'Sunil and Solly - 50 Years of Friendship.' We together cut the cake joyfully, while all my family members cheered the occasion.

Sunil occupies a special place in my life, and he has been so significant in all important occasions of our familial lives as well. One such occasion was of my house-warming ceremony at our ancestral village, Simlak, near Surat in the Jalal pore Taluka, Navsari District in the state of Gujarat of India. Since I was born in my ancestral house at Simlak, I feel deeply emotional about the place, its people, and my house there. Having become quite old and almost on the verge of dilapidation, a couple of years ago, I resorted to building a new house, demolishing the structures of our old ancestral building. Accordingly, we rebuilt the house, drawing contributions from some of our family members. I shared all my plans with Sunil in the very beginning of its construction and sought his presence for the occasion to inaugurate the house which he was glad about. A few days before finishing of its construction in November 2023, I once again reminded about it to Sunil. Sunil was happy but it was the time of world cup, and so he was busy with it until the final match on November 19, 2023. So, I checked his dates, and scheduled my house-warming ceremony on November 28, 2023, as per his availability.

Accordingly on the scheduled date, Sunil took a flight to Surat from Bombay, via Bangaluru, and reached Surat by 2:00 in the afternoon. I waited for him, along with my friend Ahmed Mame from Simlak, at the Surat airport, and from there, we all went to Simlak by car. In the evening of the same day, Sunil inaugurated our house, with which our long-awaited dream of rebuilding and reclaiming our ancestral house has finally come true. After the ceremony, Sunil visited our village school and interacted with the students, gave his autographs to them, and posed for photographs with them. The village was small, as it comprised hardly 100 houses, but even people from the villages nearby came to see Sunil, who interacted with them, and even had dinner with some of them at my house. Those who joined Sunil for dinner at our Simlak house include, Dr. Iqbal from Dabhel, Suleman Nana (Teacher of our village school), Imran Kurawalla, Ahmed Mame, Ahmed Daya, and Rashid Desai.

Sunil is so committed to his friendship, and just to cherish his friendship with me, he came all the way from Bombay to this tiny village and stayed with us for the night there. Despite being a legend in cricket, Sunil was humble enough to be associated with common villagers, and people were amazed to see Sunil in their own village and to have spent their moments with him. The next morning, I arranged a car for Sunil, assisted by two of my friends from Simlak, named Imran Kurawalla and Yousuf Daya, who drove him straight to Bombay by road. It would generally take 5 hours to Bombay from Simlak by car, and it was a great moment for those two friends who travelled to Bombay with Sunil. Upon reaching Bombay, Sunil fed our friends sandwich and coffee, and only then, they returned to Simlak; they treasure their moments with him and reminisce whenever I meet them.

Meanwhile, on his way to Simlak from Surat, we happened to see a railway station named *Sachin*, which is named after an industrial town called Sachin, and which had nothing to do with cricket legend, Sachin Tendulkar. Amused by this coincidence, Sunil got down from the car, and took a photograph posing on the railway platform, with the sign board of the station, Sachin, as his background. He, then, posted the picture along with his heart-warming note on his Instagram handle, which reads, "what foresight of those in the last century to name a railway station near Surat, after one of the all-time greats of our game and my favourite cricketer but more importantly my favourite person." The news went viral and was widely published in the media, describing the entire episode of Sunil visiting Simlak, his connection with me and my house-warming ceremony there.

Sunil is a rare genius, who has a vast knowledge on various subjects that he acquired through his voracious reading and keen observation of society. Each time we speak to each other, he shares something that is new and enlightening to us. He is so neat and systematic that, within the short time he stays in our house, he tries to organise the house in order, instead of simply sitting; he even takes time out to iron his own clothes. He prefers to stay active, keeps himself healthy and the house, neat. He believes that time is the most precious asset in our lives, and so he utilizes it for productive endeavours. Sunil's simplicity in life is truly unparalleled and serves as an inspiration to all; he has particularly left a profound impact on my life. He is my true friend, brother and philosopher who has always been there with me, both in the times of happiness as well as in adversity. I learnt many valuable lessons from Sunil, particularly on the questions of friendship, family, ethics, etiquette, etc. All through our lives, we stood for each other, and no week passes without us talking to each other; we talk a few times at least in a week. It makes me feel great that I walked with him in his long cricket journey from a promising cricketer to becoming one of the all-time greats; he is, according to me, *the legend of legends*. All through these 50 years, the persona and character of Sunil have remained consistent in every re-spect, despite his tremendous achievements in life. Personally, I feel that I am honoured to have a wonderful friend like Sunil. In his association, I have preserved a treasure of memories, which I would cherish till my last breath.

Imran Khan: The Natural Leader

During our existence, we traverse a rich tapestry of things, persons, and events, and each one of them is characterized by a unique blend of factors, that include racial, ethnic, linguistic, and religious cultural traditions. But, only a few of us can attain the pinnacle of mastery in life. Imran Khan stands out to be one such extraordinary genius who transcended the boundaries in the realm of cricket and had emerged as a legend among the cricketers. He is exceptional, and I saw that brilliance in him right from the nascent days of his cricketing career in 1970s. The radiance of his charisma was not confined to the world of cricket alone. Instead, it has spread into the larger world of politics in Pakistan. The resonance of his team spirit and his exceptional captaincy in leading the Pakistan team towards path of successes has been creatively channelled into politics, and he later emerged the captain of the entire nation when he was chosen to be the Prime Minister of Pakistan in 2018 by its own citizens. With this, the name Imran Khan has been etched in the annals of the history of Pakistan as the most influential figure of immense sig-nificance in both the sporting and political domains.

My encounter with Imran Khan was a sheer coincidence, yet a pro-found sense of inevitability pervaded right from the very moment of our first meeting, culminating into a strong bond of friendship. During my visit to Headingly Stadium at Leeds in England to attend the first day of the third Test match on Thursday, July 8, 1971, I had the opportunity of sitting beside a person named Mr. Shah Saab. From our conversation, I was surprised to know that Shah Ji had travelled all the way from the

USA to here, just to watch that match. I also learnt from Shah Ji that both Imran and he were best friends from their school days as classmates at Aitchison College in Lahore. During the lunch break, Shahi Ji accompanied me to the dressing room of the Pakistan Team where I was introduced to Imran and other players. Apparently, Imran at that moment was a student at The Royal Grammar School Worcester (RGSW) in England and had just made his debut into test cricket as a player of the Pakistan team against the team England at Edgbaston stadium (Birmingham) in June 1971; it was the same year in which he also signed for Worcestershire CC to play county cricket.

But for the third Test at Headingly, Imran was not included in the final XI, and so after the lunch break, he sat beside me to watch the match. Since I was an active player of league cricket in Yorkshire during that time, Imran was curious to know about league cricket, as well as about my own cricketing pursuits there and my personal life. After the match, Imran asked me if he can get some Asian food for dinner. Delighted by his desire to eat Asian food, I invited Imran, along with Shah Saab, Mushtaq Mohammad, Asif Mohammad, and Majid Jahangir Khan (Majid Bhai) to my home, and to have dinner there. I immediately called my mother and asked her to prepare food for six people. As Dewsbury was just a 30-minute drive from Leeds, we all got adjusted in my car and drove home. After the delightful dinner that also involved conversation on various issues, particularly about our personal lives and cricketing careers, I again drove them back to their hotel.

The next evening after the match, Imran asked me if I knew of any good night-club around? I fulfilled his wish, and after the dinner at my house, I took Imran and Shah Saab to the Batley Variety Club, which was quite famous in West Yorkshire for hosting stage concerts and theatrical performances. Unfortunately, this was not the sort of the club that Imran was looking for; he was looking for one with a dancing floor where people turn up to dance and have fun; he wanted a discotheque.

I laughed at myself for my ignorance as I had never experienced the night club, nor did I have any idea of it. Then, I contacted a couple of my friends in that locality, and upon their suggestion, I took them to a night club in Leeds. As we stepped into the night club, I was shocked to see a complete change in Imran. Having studied in England, he was adept in both dancing and English language, and was accustomed to English ways of living. Recognizing him as a cricketer, some people approached Imran, asking him to join them in dancing. Imran rejoiced their invitation, and immersed himself in the dance, showcasing his remarkable dancing skills. I was captivated with his dance moves, and it remains one of the most cherished memories of my life. Meanwhile, Shah Saab and I sat in a corner, ordered some soft-drinks, and cherished watching the vibrancy of the club. With this incident, I realized that Imran could adapt to any atmosphere, regardless of spatial and cultural peculiarities in the world. In this way, all the three of us celebrated the entire test-series every single day. And as Sunday was a rest day, I invited the other members of the team, including Mushtaq Bhai, Asif Bhai, Sadiq Mohammad, and Majid Bhai, along with Imran, to my house for lunch; it was a festive atmosphere for us where we had cheered together until evening.

Ever since then, I had regular interactions with Imran. He pursued his studies in Economics and Politics at Keble College, Oxford in 1972. And in 1974, he became the captain of Oxford's cricket team, which led to more frequent interactions between us; he was also playing for Worcestershire County during that period between1971 and 1976. Then he decided to move to Sussex for the following season. But it was customary for the counties of the time that statutes a mandatory wait period of 10-weeks as a transit time to move from one county to another. As a result, Imran had to wait for 10 weeks before joining Sussex County in 1977. One day, Imran called me to find a way out to utilise this gap, so that he could continue playing cricket to stay fit and to keep himself in active practice. Then I suggested him to play for Wakefield CC, which played under Central Yorkshire League, and it was just a 20-minute drive from Dewsbury. Tony Greg, who was already a player in Sussex County by then also suggested Imran to play for Wakefield CC. But Imran did not want to leave London, to move to Wakefield. Then I suggested that he travel to Dewsbury on Friday evening, stay at my house, play the matches on Saturday and Sunday, and then return to London on Monday. Imran was happy with this idea and agreed to sign for Wakefield Cricket Club. I then signed him with the Wakefield CC with the help of Hudson Insurance Company, for £50 per match, which makes him the highest-paid cricketer I had ever signed up anyone till that day. Despite being an established international cricketer, Imran displayed remarkable dedication to club cricket. He displayed the same intensity of passion in every single match he had played for the club in his 10-week tenue.

During weekends when he would stay at my house, he would enjoy the company of my family members; he held a deep respect for my mother, who took great care of him. Imran was a charming and joyful person who upholds his humility, and yet exhibits his passion for life. Though I arranged a separate bedroom for him in my house, I never saw Imran sleeping on the bed. He would always prefer to sleep on the couch or even on the floor. His simplicity and down-to-earth nature often impress us all. Imran had a fondness for *Dal Chawal* (lentils and rice), and he often express his desire for Dal Chawal which either my mother or my wife would prepare it for him. We had a great time together in those 10-weeks.

Imran's performance in all the matches he played for Wakefield CC were exceptional, and there are two instances that stand out to reflect his incredible character and attitude. In a match against Liversedge, Imran displayed his all-round abilities where he had scored 50 runs in his turn of bating, besides taking a couple of wickets in his bowling spell. In those days, a notable tradition of the English Club Cricket was that the spectators, at the end of the match, would contribute money of their will, to honour exceptional performances of the players. This reward from the spectator's end would serve as a gesture of motivation for the players to strive for excellence in their later matches. The money thus collected by the club representatives would either present it directly to the player or allocate it for the club development. In some cases, the money would also be spent to cheer up the team that wins the match, by organising drinks for them. In that match, the club received a substantial amount of money from the spectators, and it was decided to present the lot to Imran as a mark of his best performance. But to our surprise, Imran declined the reward on moral ground that its success was a result of the collective efforts of the team, and not based on his individual performance; his decline of the offer was also because he did not want double advantage, as he was already being paid by the club for his participation, and so, he suggested the club to keep that lot for its own development. With this, my respect for Imran got doubled as he is a man of principle.

In another match against Ossett, while he was bowling, Imran had a heated argument with the batsman of his opponent's team, yet he tried to keep his cool. But when the batsman crossed his limits and resorted to racially abusive remarks, Imran got angry and decided to respond with his bowling. The very next ball, he bowled with such great force that it almost broke the batsman's arm. In a fit of anger, Imran said, "Go and get an ice pack for your arm, mate!" But a little later, he again felt sympathetic to him, and after the end of the match, he took initiative that the issue be resolved amicably, as he also recognized the significance of resolving conflicts as a marker of sportsmanship; he set aside his ego for the larger good and believed in the power of dialogue in resolving conflicts. In this way, he was busy with his club matches on Sundays, and so was I. Imran also played two benefit matches under my captaincy against Hanging Heaton upon my invitation—one in 1977, and the other in 1978. It was my privilege to have him in those matches, as his presence added immense value to the events.

For the 1979/80 season, the Pakistan cricket team visited India, which coincided with my vacation there with my wife, Maryam, and our three-year-old son, Sohail. While we were waiting outside the stadium for one of our family friends, the Pakistan team arrived in a coach headed for the stadium. From the coach window, Imran spotted us and called out to me, inviting us to join them; I felt deeply honoured by his invitation. By then, I had several friends in both the teams, and particularly my best-friend Sunil Gavaskar was leading the Indian team for that series. It was a great experience for me, as players of both the teams would visit us during their breaks, to spend time with me and my family. It was a privilege for my family to sit with them and enjoy the game in India during our holidays there.

Having known me as the one who had good connections with several international players, the owner of the County Sports, a well-known sports equipment manufacturer, Steve, approached me in 1981 with a request of promoting his products. He asked me if I could get two international players to use their cricket gear, including bats and pads, and to endorse them. For that, Steve offered £450 together for 2 players, along with providing them with free County Bats. By then, the sports advertising was not so advanced, and the players did not play for endorsing the sports brands. Unlike today that involves so much of paperwork to make a formal agreement, everything in those days was informal, and was based on mutual trust. At that time, Kapil Dev was playing for Nelson Cricket Club in Lancashire, and I know him through another cricketer friend from India, Mohinder Amarnath. I spoke to Kapil about the offer, which he had gladly embraced; Kapil received £250 from the County for endorsing their bats, besides a few free bats. Later, during a casual chat with Imran, I told him of the endorsement offer for the remaining sum of £200, which he too was glad to accept; Imran, at that time, was playing for Sussex. After a few weeks, Kapil Dev and Imran crossed paths in one of the matches where they both were using the same County Bats. It must be possible that Kapil might have told

Imran about the deal, but one evening, Imran passed a teasing remark at me for him being paid lesser than Kapil, when both were playing the same standard of cricket. Though it was a lighter moment, I explained him the deal.

In 1987, the Pakistan Team embarked on a tour to England, marking it as a momentous event in the history of Pakistan's Cricket. This tour proved to be a highly significant one, as Pakistan team had achieved their first-ever test series victory in England, under the captaincy of Imran Khan. In the same year, a little later, Imran had been granted a benefit season by the Sussex County; it was to honour Imran's exceptional contributions to the county. I took the initiative to organise the benefit match for Imran on July 5, 1987, at Batley Cricket Club. It was an extraordinary situation where several international players representing Pakistan also participated in this benefit match, attended by the rest of the players, as it was a coincidence that it was the time for the third test of the Pakistan team against England at Headingly. The local spectators were thrilled to see the entire international team playing at the Batley Cricket Ground. In the same year, Sunil Gavaskar called me up and asked me to approach Imran, to know whether he could appear in Thums Up advertisement alongside Sunil. I immediately called Imran; he expressed his joy of being part of the Ad with Sunil. The photograph capturing Sunil and Imran together for the advertisement stands out to be a delightful memento for cricket enthusiasts, and so was it to me.

Amidst these glories of his stardom, Imran came to become the shining star of the world, when Pakistan team, under his captaincy, achieved a momentous victory against England in 1992 by winning the ODI World Cup final in Australia. I was overjoyed to see its triumph and extended my congratulations to Imran, and his team. On that occasion, Imran generously gifted me a bat adorned with the autographs of all the winning team members. During our conversation, following that cheerful moment, Imran had informed me that he would be visiting

England soon to organize several events to raise funds for charity to establish a Cancer Hospital in Pakistan; he sought for my presence there. I vividly recall one such charity event which was held at the *Holiday Inn* Hotel in Bradford, attended by several renowned stars from cricket and film, including Sunil Gavaskar, Dilip Kumar, Saira Bhanu etc. Eventually, Imran inaugurated the hospital in Lahore, under Shaukat Khanum Memorial Trust (SKMT) in honour of his mother, marking it a significant milestone in his philanthropic efforts. In fact, Imran was widely recognised for his involvement in several charitable events worldwide over the past four decades, and his reputation grew every day as a philanthropist.

A few years ago, Imran was a special invitee for a charity event organized by the Savayra Foundation at the Akash Restaurant in Dewsbury, which he graciously attended. The Foundation was established by Baroness Sayeeda Warsi in 2003 which supports vulnerable women in Pakistan. I also attended the charity event and presented an idea to Imran that we could auction the bat that was gifted to me by Imran on the eve of winning world cup, and contribute that money for the charity. Imran was greatly impressed by this idea of mine, and in an auction, the bat was procured by an avid cricket enthusiast named Sajid Butt for £3700. Thereupon, the entire money thus raised was donated to the charity foundation.

His fame grew bigger and bigger, and between 2005 to 2014, Imran Khan served as the Chancellor of Bradford University. During this period, he frequently visited Bradford, and I would often attend the events that were meant to honour him by the university and other forums. If I was absent in any of the events, he would call me up to know the reasons for my absence. Imran then ventured into politics that culminated in him eventually becoming the 22nd Prime Minister of Pakistan on August 18, 2018. But with his political rise, our interactions gradually decreased. In fact, it reached a point where I did not have the opportunity to talk to him at all for several years due to his busy schedule with the issue of political concern. Watching his swearing-in ceremony on live telecast brought me with flood of memories. I reminisced about the times when Imran Khan would visit my house and lie down on the couch to have long chats with me, or of the moments we played together, and the humorous banters we shared; all these memories and nostalgic visions floated through my eyes just like a passing cloud.

And at last, when I visited Pakistan in March 2023, I contacted Imran's office to arrange a meeting with him to which he readily responded with great pleasure at the prospect of meeting me after such a long time. But unfortunately, that did not happen owing to political unrest in Pakistan, in which Imran Khan was arrested on the same day when I had secured the appointment. I lament his woeful plight and feel deeply compassionate about him. I found a natural leader in him, and I wish he would resurrect one day into normalcy and continue his philanthropic deeds; I pray Almighty! presents Imran good health.

Sachin Tendulkar: A Natural Prodigy

Sachin Tendulkar is yet another legend in the world of cricket as a batsman of the highest order of his time and has come to register his mark of brilliance among the lineage of the sporting luminaries and legends, beginning with Don Bradman, Gary Sobers, Sunil Gavaskar, Imran Khan, Ian Botham, and Viv Richards. Sachin is as unparalleled in cricket, as Muhammad Ali in boxing, the trailblazing Jesse Owens and Usain Bolt in athletics, the soccer maestros Pele and Maradona, the baseball icon Michael Jordan, and the tennis virtuosos Roger Federer and Serena Williams. Sachin stands tall, and emerges as the all-time greatest cricketer, for which he was hailed as the God of Cricket by millions worldwide. He unequivocally deserves a place among the greatest of all-time athletes and undoubtedly is the most revered cricketing icon in the history of cricket.

By the time I met Sachin, along with Vinod Kambli for the first time in 1989, on my visit to Bombay, India, they both were widely recognized as exceptional young talents by the media. At a very young age of 15, Sachin had already made an impressive beginning into the first-class cricket with a century to his credit, in his very debut match against Gujarat in 1988. This outstanding achievement made Sachin to be the youngest Indian ever to achieve such a feat in first-class cricket. Notably, Sachin holds yet another unique distinction that he scored one century in each of all his three debut matches in domestic first-class tournaments—the Ranji, Irani, and Duleep Trophies. Sachin's rapid rise to fame in India was extraordinary, and so was he to rise up soon to be part of the international cricket fraternity.

In the same year in 1989, Sachin visited England, as part of a youth team that plays under *Star Club of India*. Led by its club-founder Kailash Ghattani, the team comprised of other young players such as Sourav Ganguly, Vinod Kambli, Ajay Jadeja, Jatin Paranjape etc.; they toured England to play against English youth teams. Since Kailash knew me well before, I got yet another opportunity to watch these young talents, but this time, when they were playing in my home country. By then, I knew numerous Indian cricketers, particularly those hailing from Bombay, as I was quite popular in Bombay cricketing circles for assisting skilled players in securing contracts with local clubs in England. Like several others, Sachin also approached me for my assistance to find an opportunity to play for some club of good repute in Yorkshire, and to get accustomed to English conditions. Accordingly, I recommended Sachin to Chickenley CC, which too was very glad to sign him. But unfortunately, it did not happen owing to budgetary constraints, as the club could not afford the amount that Sachin desired, and so I got Sanjay Bangar signed as a substitute to Sachin. Sanjay later went on to represent Indian team; he later served as the head coach of the RCB team in the IPL.

Sachin Tendulkar, on the other hand, made his debut into international cricket with a match against Pakistan on November 15, 1989; his extraordinary batting skills caught the eye of everyone, where he performed very well and became the centre of media attention. In 1990, I had an opportunity to meet the entire Indian team during their second test match at Old Trafford, Manchester; the match was held as part of their test series against England. Sachin being the youngest of the team, as he was just 17 years then, had showcased his brilliance by scoring his first-ever test century in international matches, and for which he received accolades across the English media, who hailed him as a 'teenage prodigy.'

In 1991, Sachin visited England again to play a few benefit-matches here, in which the significant among them was the one which was organized for my friend, Suru Nayak. In that match, Sachin, Sanjay Manjrekar, and Vinod Kambli played for 'Invitation XI' team under my captaincy, against the Bilton CC headed by Suru. At that moment, Sachin's cricket mate and best friend, Vinod Kambli was playing for Spen Victoria CC under my captaincy. During this visit, Sachin asked me one day, 'Solly Bhai, why didn't you play for County matches?' and then he said, "You are one of the best left-arm spinners I have ever seen." I was delighted to hear such words of praise from Sachin. I replied, "It's really kind of you to say that, but there's a century-old rule in Yorkshire that anyone, whether an Englishman or an Asian, born outside Yorkshire is not eligible to play for their county team. This rule aside, I couldn't leave Yorkshire to play for another county team due to my business and family commitments."

But in 1992, when that century-old rule was removed in Yorkshire, giving rise to their open resolve for the inclusion of all players not only across England, but also across regions and nationalities, I tried to introduce Asian players such as Sachin Tendulkar, Javed Miandad, and Inzamam-Ul-Haq into the Yorkshire County team. And when the Yorkshire committee members finally agreed to recruit an Asian in their team, I suggested the name of Sachin Tendulkar to them. The then committee looked down upon the capacities of Sachin, and to put it in their own words, "he is only a young kid." Meanwhile, the Yorkshire County tried for the legendary Malcolm Marshall of Hampshire County, and then a famous Australian cricketer, Craig McDermott, to sign for their team. But none of them worked out due to some reasons. But I seriously persisted recommending Sachin, and had explained them how the cricket legend, Sir Don Bradman himself had held Sachin in high regard, by comparing the bating style of Sachin to that of his own. With my continuous persuasion, in this way, the committee members had finally convinced to sign Sachin for their team.

At that moment, Sachin was on the Australian tour, playing for the 1992 World Cup. And when I shared the news with Sachin over phone, he, however, sought for some time to think of his decision to accept the offer, as he was by then busy playing extensively, including in the upcoming Ranji matches in India. But I did not want him to miss this opportunity, and so I contacted Sunil Gavaskar, who happened to be in the same hotel in Australia that Sachin was lodged at that moment. Since Sunil knows the value of playing County cricket, as he personally witnessed it in his time as a player of Somerset County in 1980, he suggested Sachin to play for Yorkshire, to which Sachin finally conceded. After his Australian tour, Sachin returned to India to spend time with his family. Then one day, Chris Hassell, the Chief Executive of Yorkshire, asked me if I could accompany him to India to finalize the formal contract agreement with Sachin. But, due to my busy schedule and family commitments, unfortunately I could not join him in his trip to India. Chris, however, went alone to Bombay and secured Sachin's agreements signed for the County, probably, on April 3, 1992.

It was remarkable that, a couple of years ago, the same person who was curious to know, of why I did not play for Yorkshire County, has now himself become part of the same county and broke a century-old tradition. The news of his signing with Yorkshire created a sensation in English media, as he was the first overseas player ever signed for Yorkshire. Though I signed numerous cricketers for various clubs in the past, none of them had been as exceptionally sensational as that of Sachin's, because of its historical significance. With Sachin's signing, the age-old privilege that was exclusive only to its regional cricketers, had now been amended, and its floodgates were being opened to all the cricketers of the world. With this, the attention of the media shifted to me, enhancing my popularity further. The English and Indian media turned around me, for my interviews to explore the details of Sachin's signing, and they were curious to know how I managed to convince the Yorkshire committee, and to bring change in this century long historical rule. All the media referred to me as "the man who brought Sachin to Yorkshire," and some channels went further to describe Sachin, using a biblical reference to 'Adam's Apple,' presenting me (Adam), the man behind that juicy and attractive apple (Sachin).

In England, Sachin wanted to stay close to my house, as he saw a kind of a guardian in me who would extend ready assistance to him at any moment. I too was glad to see Sachin in close quarters, and so I arranged a house for him at 34, Wakefield Crescent, which was just a short walk from my own residence. Sachin also wanted me to be present on his first match for the County, as he told me how I would be his surrogate elder brother, Ajith Tendulkar, who would always be there in all the matches that Sachin ever played in Bombay. It was so sweet to hear such affectionate words from Sachin and so I gladly accompanied him to his debut match for Yorkshire County against Hampshire on May 7, 1992, at Headingly. Sachin displayed his brilliance by scoring 86 runs in that innings, yet it was a great disappointment for him, because he could not do a century on his debut in the County. In that match, one of the greatest bowlers of all-time, Malcolm Marshall, also played for Hampshire, and Sachin could play him comfortably. During his time with Yorkshire, Sachin had a fantastic experience; he amassed 1070 runs in total from 16 matches; he won the hearts of Yorkshire cricket fans who embraced this prodigious talent, making him feel at home in this foreign land. The 1992 county season had contributed immensely for the growth of Sachin as a batsman, as mentioned by Sachin himself, it was "one of the greatest four-and-a-half months I have spent in my life."

Sachin would frequently visit our house as it was at a walking distance from his house, and so would his cricketing friends from India such as Vinod Kambli, Jatin Paranjape and Amol Mazumdar, who were then playing for different clubs. Therefore, my house became a site of assembly for them to celebrate and to feel the touch of their own home in England. In due course, Sachin had developed a great friendship with my sons and daughter. In fact, he attended my first 2 sons' weddings in August 1991 as he was at that moment playing exhibition matches in England. I still remember, how Sachin, along with his cricket friends, attended my sons' weddings on August 24 and 25, and had stayed till late nights with us in our party celebrations, despite that they had a match on the very next day. Sachin however was so dedicated that, he got up early in the morning, after the party, and drove the car all the way to Wales (4 hours' drive from my house at Dewsbury) to play the match 'Glamorgan Vs Rest of the World XI' in which both Sachin and Javed Miandad scored half-century each.

One night, just as we are all set to bed at around 11:30 pm, I heard a knock at our door; it was a bit unusual to have people visiting us at that odd a time. When I opened the door, to my surprise, it was Sachin. He told me that he would be leaving back for India by early morning flight, and before he leaves, he wanted blessings from me and my wife. I felt greatly emotional about him leaving us, and I woke my wife up from sleep to bless him and see him off. Then Sachin touched both our feet, and we blessed him to have the best and happy long life. I will remember his humble gesture as long as I live. He was such a cute child who has now embarked such great heights that were extraordinary even to imagine; I cherish all the memories of affection that we had showered upon each other.

Today when Sachin has emerged to be the greatest of all-time in the world, I recollect the happy days of him growing from a boy to a man amidst us in England; he is like a son figure for me and to my wife, and a brother for my children. In fact, it was when he was playing for Yorkshire that he began learning so many things pertaining to household chores like washing, drying, and ironing his own cloths and dish washing. To recall a funny thing, one day Sachin called my wife, Maryam, to know how to use a washing machine. Then, she instructed him, explaining in detail, asking him to put clothes and detergent in the machine, and then switch it on. He then did everything as she instructed and gone out for a practice session, but by the time he came back to collect his clothes to put them to dry, the entire house had filled up in soap foam. Terrified, Sachin called my wife again frantically to explain what all the mess up that had happened. In a cool temperament and with an intent to comfort Sachin, Maryam asked him how much soap he had put into the washing machine. Then Sachin replied, "The Entire Box." It was now Maryam's turn to get shocked and she regretted not telling him how much detergent was needed for the clothes; it was a fun-filled moment for all of us, and we still cherish this memory whenever we think of Sachin. After this incident, his clothes were always washed, dried, and ironed at my place. He would love eating food prepared by my wife, whom he affectionately calls 'Bhabi Ji,' and she always treated him like her own son. My younger brother Younus and his wife Rukhsana also treated him with care and affection; they three became good friends within a short period of time, and Sachin would love Asian cuisines prepared by Rukhsana. Anjali was his girlfriend then who later became his life partner by marriage; she used to live in Gloucester and would visit him at our place. Over a period, Anjali also became member of our family, particularly she has got a great bond with my daughter Asma, and still, they treat each other like own sisters.

Sachin, by nature, is quick at grasping everything. One day, I took my family to Blackpool on an outing, where Sachin, Vinod, Jatin, Sairaj and Sameer also joined us. We had lots of fun and played billiards there. Though Sachin did not play the game ever before, he picked the game within 20 minutes, and began performing better than every one of us. He did the same in tennis as well. One day, when I took him to tennis court, in a few minutes, he began hitting shots better than the person who was teaching him, though he had never played tennis before; it was a wonder for me. Sachin has a great appetite for Pizza and Kentucky Fried Chicken (KFC); he enjoys eating them like a kid. I also arranged a Honda Car with Sachin's name emblazoned across and several Cricket fans in Yorkshire took pictures posing next to the car; the car was sponsored by one of my close friends, Simon Bowett.

Sachin gives supreme importance to practicing cricket; he never leaves any scope for fun during his practice sessions, and he plays during his practice hours with the same seriousness that he plays the real matches. He never missed practice even during weekdays, when he had to play for the Yorkshire. After the match with the county, he would drive his car from Headingly to reach Spen Victoria by 6pm, and then he practised there. I remember him putting a 'Pound coin' on the stumps and challenge the bowlers if they can hit the same. Those days, a pint of beer used to cost a Pound, and bowlers would vie with one another to get him out, to get a free beer. But no one had ever bowled him out during net practice. Apparently, Sachin never lost that coin, and he used the same Pound coin throughout his 4 months of stay in Yorkshire. Sachin also bowled to all the batsmen, and he would be the last person to leave the nets, and never left the net in the middle of practice. No wonder, with such dedication and determination to cricket, one can emerge oneself to be the all-time greatest, and Sachin did it with great commitment and passion, and so he is the 'God of cricket.'

Even after attaining such high a status as the world's biggest cricket star, he remains to be the same humble Sachin that we witnessed in the early '90s. It has become customary for Sachin to visit us whenever he travels to England, whether it is a cricket tour or on a personal trip. His humbleness, down-to-earth attitude, and unwavering loyalty to his friends, sets him apart from the rest of the people I met so far. Sunil too had a great affection for Sachin; he personally invited me to attend Sachin's farewell Test match at Wankhede Stadium in Bombay in November 2013, and I had cherished watching that match with Sunil.

After the match, I shared with the press, "It will be the final glimpse of a genius. I do not believe cricket will witness another Sachin Tendulkar. He was destined to play cricket and bring joy to the people." Sachin's greatness goes beyond mere statistical records. Over two decades of his play, he had left behind a profound impact on the game, emerging as the most adored cricket icon the world had ever witnessed. While my dearest friend Sunil Gavaskar popularized cricket in India during the '70s and Kapil Dev continued the trend in the '80s, Sachin elevated the sport to an entirely new level in the '90s until his retirement in 2013; he was the heartbeat for one billion Indians for more than two decades.

Interestingly, now, the intriguing story behind writing my own biography has, in fact, unfolded from the pages of the autobiography of Sachin. Vara Vantapati, a voracious reader of sport literature, particularly about cricket, as he himself is a club cricketer in England, came across my reference from one of the chapters in Sachin's autobiography, *Playing it My Way*. In that chapter, Sachin described our family bonding with him, and the support he received from me during his brief stint in England. Then amazed Vara, who turned curious to know more about me, and then connected with me through Facebook. He then came to discover that I live in Dewsbury, which is in the closest proximity to his house in England. Out of my conversations with Vara that the initial idea of writing my biography has been sparked, and from his initiatives of recording my voices, and transcribing and editing them, with the help of his friend in Hyderabad, that my biography has finally taken its shape. So, I am greatly indebted to Sachin for acknowledging me and my family in his autobiography, and Vara for unearthing several forgotten incidents from my life, and in persuading me to engage in this task of writing this book. Finally, I wish Sachin, Anjali and their children Sara and Arjun to have good health and happiness.

Iqbal Qasim: My Younger Brother

In this journey of my life, I met hundreds of cricketers, among whom several cricketers had become my friends, but there are two persons who have been closest to my heart and part of my family. One being the star-cricketer from Pakistan, Iqbal Qasim, and the other is none other than a legendary cricketer from India, Sunil Gavaskar. Iqbal is such an emotional being that he has a very few friends like Dr. Jamil, Taslim Arif, Rakib Zarif, Abdul Qadir and Shamuddin. He is intimate with all his friends, and yet he treats me more affectionately than anyone else, including his own brothers.

When a Pakistani Test Cricketer Shafiq Ahmed (Shafiq Papa) introduced me to Iqbal over phone in 1977, Iqbal had just finished his debut test cricket tour to Australia in 1976-77 as part of the Pakistan team. Right after the tour, Iqbal joined his teammates who came to England for a month on a holiday visit to find a career in league cricket, as many of his colleagues like Taslim Arif, Shafiq Ahmed and Abdul Rakib, by then, were already playing for various clubs in England. It was his dream, like many Asians in those days, to get an opportunity to play in English conditions, and to attain expertise upon that experience of playing here. They all together took a house on rent in Manchester and had begun playing for their respective clubs. But young Iqbal felt home sick and was bored, as he had to sit in the room all alone when all his colleagues were busy playing during weekends. It was in these tough times that Shafiq, who by then was playing for Black Burn Club, rang me up and asked me to take Iqbal to my home, and provide him with the comforts of our home. So, I took him to my home at Dewsbury. On our way to my home in my car, during our conversation, I realized that both Iqbal and I share several commonalities—both of us are Gujarati speaking immigrants who have had a history of being refugees in the Karachi of Pakistan. In fact, the family of Iqbal would reside in the closest vicinity of our Natal Colony, and his two elder brothers had attended the same school that I did during my schooling in Karachi. Interestingly, Iqbal Qasim was also a left arm spinner just like me.

Having such a common affinity, particularly our language, but of course our identification as immigrants in Pakistan, he became a loving child of my parents, particularly my mother, and my dearest younger-brother, in the very first short-stint of his stay at my home; he is now an integral part of my family. I feel so emotional about Iqbal, because he was of around the same age of my two younger-brothers, whom I lost, along with two younger-sisters, to a fatal disease in my very childhood. Then, Younus was the only surviving brother of mine with whom I never shared any brotherly relation. Instead, I always treated Younus as my loving kid and had given him every care that generally a father would offer his own child. As I missed a life of sharing brotherly emotions in my childhood, Iqbal came to play such an emotional role in the rest of my life. Iqbal is a star-cricketer and a celebrity, hailing from a well-to-do and well-educated family, but none of them strikes to my mind; he is just my brother. Unlike my other friends who mostly share their professional issues with me, Iqbal takes part in my every personal and familial issues, just as every other member of my family. I have preserved some of the best memories of my life with Iqbal, out of which, some of them I would like to share here.

During his stay at my house, while having food one day, I saw a brand-new watch on his wrist. It was so beautiful and a unique one which he had just bought from Australia, and so I appreciated the beauty of the watch. After staying in my house for a few days, I again took him back to Manchester. Knowing that he would leave for Pakistan in a few days, I gave him Rs. 5000 and asked him to hand them over to my parents-in-law who were still living in the Natal Colony of Pakistan, and he quietly took the money and left. One day, after a few days of Iqbal leaving for Pakistan, somebody knocked the door of my house; it was the host of Iqbal and his friends where they had stayed at Manchester, and so I warmly welcomed him into the house. He then handed me over an envelope and said that Iqbal asked him to give it over to me. But to my wonder, the envelope contains both the watch that Iqbal bought from Australia and the Rs. 5000 that I asked him to deliver to my parents-in-law. Added to this, I got a call from my parents-in-law the next morning; they said that Iqbal visited them and handed them over with the money of Rs. 5000. I was happy with the watch but was a bit confused and had tried to return the money to Iqbal when I visited Pakistan later, which he refused to take. I wore that watch for the most of my life, and I still possess it in my safe.

In my personal visit to Pakistan that had lasted eight weeks, I contacted Iqbal to check if I can get a car on rent for the entire tenure I planned to stay with my parents-in-law in Karachi. He was glad about hearing the news of my Pakistan visit, yet quietly asked for the details of my flight. When I, along with my wife, landed in Karachi airport, Iqbal was promptly waiting for me near the exit gate of the airport, and stretched out his arms as a gesture of warm welcome. Then he set it upon himself to load all my luggage in his car, left his own car keys in my hand, and asked me to keep the car with me as long as I stay in Pakistan; he then quietly called a taxi-auto and went back to his work. On my departure to England, he again visited me and sent me off, till I got checked in. That is how he treats me, and had never failed attending to me, mostly in person, but arranged somebody at least to look after me, each time I visited Pakistan till date. He does this for me, not only when I visited the city of Karachi, but wherever in Pakistan I go, whether it is Lahore or Islamabad, he would arrange all the comforts for me, including transport and boarding accommodation. Even in my recent visit in March 2023 to Pakistan, he did everything for me; he arranged a car and even a driver who looked after me for the entire trip I stayed there, till the last minute, when I departed back to England.

He was, and in fact still is, so kind and compassionate towards me, but was equally cranky, if he gets hurt even remotely. I experienced one such instance of him getting angry with me, when I went to Pakistan for a few days to sell out my property in Karachi. As usual, I called Iqbal before I start from England, and he made all the arrangements for me. But when I landed, another person who was also known to Iqbal came to see me in the airport and persuaded me to go to his house to take his hospitality. So, I had to skip meeting Iqbal, and had stayed in the house of that new host for the night. I rang Iqbal the next evening, but no response. After ringing him a few times, I turned out a bit suspicious, and immediately rushed to see Iqbal at his home. But to my surprise, he refused to see me and had not even opened the door. With great difficulty, somehow, I managed to talk to his wife, Samina Behan, who finally told me that he had been upset with me from the time I left him to stay in the house of someone else. I did not know that Iqbal would be so cross with me. But I realized my mistake only later when Iqbal got so infuriated at my act of neglecting him. He is fine with me staying in a hotel as it entails my privacy, or I can stay with my in-laws, otherwise only with him, but not with somebody else. I reached his house at 9:00 in the night and was incessantly pleading him to forgive me for my mistake, with the mediation of his wife, till 11:00, and at around 11:10 he finally came out of his bedroom. The moment I saw him, I could not control myself, and fell on his shoulders to weep out a lot; it was after such a long a time that I came back to normalcy, that too after repeated consoling from Iqbal.

I was so desperate that I did not want to miss Iqbal at any cost, that too due to my mistake, because he is indeed my younger brother. Yes, it was my mistake alone, not remotely his, and so his anger was rightful. From then on, whenever I visit Karachi, I never dared to stay in anyone's house; either I stayed in the house of Iqbal, or in a hotel arranged by him.

In the meanwhile, I wanted Iqbal to play for the club cricket in England, to get him used to English conditions and to sharpen his skills in cricket. So, I helped Iqbal in getting contract for various clubs. First, he joined Spen Victoria CC and played there for two years from 1980; it was this club that I was formerly associated with, and it was also near my house in Dewsbury. Iqbal was very happy at the club, and was performing very well, because he could stay in my house and have the comforts of his own home here; he would love eating Gujarati dish, *Kadi Kichidi*, prepared by my mom. It was during this time that he had won the love and affection of all the members of my family, particularly my mom, but also my father, and got integrated into my family. He was busy playing in weekends, and during weekdays he was a big helping hand to my mom at home, to papa at the businesses, and to me in every respect. My mom would miss his absence and recall his name several times in a day when he leaves for Pakistan for a while; he was a loving child of my parents, a younger brother for me, and another uncle for my children, besides my own brother Younus. He would sit with my parents and talk till late night, having tea with them, wake up late in the morning, while all of us go to bed early and wake up early; he would eat only with my parents, and would lead a life of joy with them.

But he began experiencing loneliness in England that had resulted in severe homesickness only when he moved to Thornaby Durham CC, which was quite distant from our home, for a year in 1982. I got him signed for Thornaby CC because the club pays more than double of the money that we generally get in the clubs of our locality. I wanted him to make good money for himself, besides sharpening his cricket skills.

But he did not like the living conditions there, as in his own words, he was accommodated in a farm like ambiance where he was surrounded by cows and sheep, with no humans in his sight. He would call me every day and would curse me for deserting him in such a remote place. He then would call my mother to complain to her for the worst state he was in, thereby my mother would scold the hell out of me. Unable to stay there, he would rush to our house to stay with us at Dewsbury during weekdays and go back only to play cricket in the weekends. In that way, he managed somehow for a year, and insisted me to find another club in our vicinity so that he can live with us. It was in such a situation that I had to sign Iqbal for Hanging Heaton (1984), by replacing Ali Zia in his place at Thornaby; Ali enjoyed playing there, and Iqbal too was happy with Hanging Heaton.

At Hanging Heaton, Iqbal did very well; he again rejoined us and had been happy and made us all very happy. It was when he was in Spen Victoria that he wanted to bring his wife to England, and so I accommodated the couple in one of my houses in Bradford; they would stay in that house, and he would play for the club during weekends. To escape from boredom during the weekdays, and to utilize his productive time, I asked him to look after my *Pick N Pay Supermarket* at Batley. He then turned to be very punctual and hardworking there and would look after my supermarket during weekdays. He was so helpful, and the couple would often come and stay with us whenever they felt bored and would go back to Bradford. After playing for Spen for two years, he had moved to Hanging Heaton CC in 1984, again in the same Bradford League and played there for two years. He did very well there as well, while continuing to stay in the same house at Bradford. In that way, he played for four clubs in England during 1978 and 1985 and had made his significance felt in all the clubs he played here. Besides these clubs, he was also playing international cricket, and had shown his significance there as well, as a member of the Pakistan team.

When Iqbal was in Bradford, he started preparing for bank exams, as he wanted to settle down as an employee of a bank. As he hails from a well-educated family, he too wanted to lead a life like that of his family; his wife was a teacher and his father-in-law an officer in some high Commissionerate. He never intended to make much money, but to have friends and relative of his kind to have an affectionate living, and to lead a life of joy. As intended, he got recruited as an officer of the National Bank of Pakistan in 1987, and settled down there, while simultaneously continuing to play for his national team till his retirement.

Despite him settling in Pakistan, my relationship with Iqbal had not worn out; we would correspond each other over phone, and occasionally meet up when either of us go to each other. But ever since I started my sports business, Solly Sports, in 1999, I frequented my visits to Pakistan as I got the necessary equipment for my business in Karachi and Sialkot. Though Iqbal was very busy with his bank job, he would still arrange a hotel room, a car, and his own driver to assist me during my stay. For the weddings of both his children, his son and daughter, I went to Karachi along with my wife, Maryam. We were accommodated in a very nice hotel there, keeping a separate car and driver for us. Iqbal did not treat me like his guest, but the host and the elder member of his own family. In fact, he has two elder brothers—one in South Africa, and the other was in Karachi—yet he presented me as the host of the function. To that end, on the day of weddings, Iqbal asked me to stay just beside him all through the event and introduced me as his own *Bhai* (elder brother) from England; he also introduced Maryam to them as his *Bhabhi* (sister-in-law). I cherish such an intimate relationship with Iqbal. I continued visiting Pakistan on this sports business several times in a year for almost 25 years, till recently, when I had to stop going anywhere owing to a health issue of my wife, in which she lost her leg in 2018; I cannot leave Maryam alone. When Maryam got hospitalized, Iqbal would call me several times in a day to know her condition, to cry, and to console me from crying. And when her leg got amputated, I cried so much, and

Iqbal had to console me for days. He said, it was difficult for him to talk to his *Bhabhi* in such a state, but when she rang him up to talk after her recovery, Iqbal could not control crying. He is my true brother, and I wish him every day after my prayer that, one day, he should come along with his wife to England, and stay with me for the rest of my life.

Javed Miandad: The Man of Confidence

Javed Miandad is an epitome of stability and consistency, as he has been the only player, alongside of Herbert Sutcliffe, whose test average had never faltered below 50 runs, having played a total of 124 Tests matches in his illustrious career as a professional cricketer. He has amassed several records and achievements, firmly establishing himself as one of the greatest cricketers in the history of the world cricket.

My association with Javed dates back into 1975 with his debut into ODI World Cup in a match against formidable West Indies team. Being acquainted with several player in the Pakistani Cricket team, I had the privilege of meeting Javed just a day before his 18th birthday. But we became intimate friends with each other when Javed signed for Sussex County (1976-79), following the World Cup, and had begun to stay in England. During this period, Javed also played club cricket in Preston, which is just an hour's drive from Dewsbury by car. Javed would love visiting my home during his free time and would spend good time having fun with my children. Both Imran and Javed together visited my home several times, and we used to have a celebratory atmosphere at my home when they would stay with us, and we all together would relish delectable Asian cuisines lovingly prepared by my mother and my wife. With time, this bonding with him grew stronger, and that endures even to this day.

In 1980, Javed joined Glamorgan County, and had played for the club till 1985. It was during this period that, he again represented the Pakistan team for the World Cup in England for the year 1983. In the early

80s, I travelled to India to watch a test series between India and Pakistan. Since I was friends with many cricketers from both the nations by then, including Javed, I had a privilege to join them before and after the match, to share the best moments with them. I would be an invitee to all the parties organised for both the teams by various sponsors, including the match-organisers. It was during these parties and gatherings that I noticed what a fun-loving person he was. He would mingle with the players of both the teams, and would spontaneously crack jokes, creating an atmosphere incredibly friendly and animated. Everyone would undoubtedly love his company and cherish his friendship. His charisma and vivacious nature made him not only a brilliant cricketer, but he was truly a good human being.

During my visits to Pakistan, Iqbal Qasim would graciously arrange parties in my honour, inviting cricketers and friends to come together. On many occasions, Javed would also be present, adding vigour and pleasure to the event with his joyful talk. In these gatherings, we would recall the best moments of cricket and share our happiness, an atmosphere that invokes a great passion for the game.

I distinctly recall a day when Javed called me to seek my help in organising a benefit match for him at Bolton; he asked me if I could talk to Sunil and see him to be the part of the match. Though both Sunil and Javed were prominent figures in international cricket and were known to each other, Javed approached me, considering my intimacy with Sunil. When Sunil came to me, I spoke to him about the benefit match of Javed and his wish for Sunil to be part of the match. Sunil happily agreed to participate in the match and said, "Javed is my colleague and a member of the cricket fraternity. I would be delighted to play the match." Sunil and I together travelled to Bolton for the match, which turned out to be a resounding success.

I learnt valuable lessons from Javed; he recognised the significance of confidence in achieving success, specifically in the realm of sports.

Javed illustrated this in his life experiences as a cricketer; he fearlessly stepped out of the crease and effortlessly dispatched deliveries even to face as deadly a bowler as Richard Hadlee. But he also knows the fact that when one loses one's confidence, it will be impossible even to face ordinary club-level bowler. This was a profound insight which had always worked like a guiding principle in every critical juncture in my life.

To cherish our bond of friendship, Javed gifted me a Gray Nicholas bat. This bat holds a special significance in his life, as it was the very instrument with which Javed scored several centuries for both the Pakistan Team and Sussex County. I possess that precious object, and have carefully secured it in my vault, as a tangible memory of our enduring friendship and the remarkable moments that we had shared together.

Even after his retirement from his illustrious career as a world-renowned cricketer, Javed Miandad has continued his contributions to the sport in various forms and capacities. He held significant positions in the Pakistan Cricket Board and had served as the coach of the Pakistan cricket team on three separate occasions. In 2009, Javed was inducted into the prestigious ICC Cricket Hall of Fame. I felt very happy to hear this news, and immediately called Javed to congratulate and admire him; he had warmly cherished this newfound status with me.

Of late, Javed has also developed a tendency towards spirituality and an inclination towards welfare activities. Whenever someone needs any assistance, be it a social or financial matter that involves donations for some social cause, he would reach out to me. I have always been ready for such measures, and I promptly respond to him, doing to the best of my capacities. He is not only a cricket legend but a good human being. I wish him good health and wish for him to be an inspiration for the cricketers of this time and the generations to come. Javed's legacy will forever be etched in the annals of cricketing history, an inspiration for the generations to come.

Abdul Qadir: An Enigmatic Spin-bowler

It was widely acknowledged that Abdul Qadir has been a major influence in keeping the art of leg-spin alive during the late 1970s and 80s, for which he received admiration of all, and gratitude from the entire cricket community. Being one of the greatest leg spinners of all time, he was hailed as the torchbearer of an enigmatic wrist-spin technique. His mastery over spinning the ball became an inspiration for numerous aspiring spinners of the subsequent generations who had delved into the intricacies of leg spin. In the 80s, Abdul played a pivotal role in bringing several victories for the Pakistan team, including his remarkable performance against the team of England in Lahore where he created a world record, by taking 9 wickets for just 56 runs in a single inning. Graham Gooch, who faced him on that memorable day, praised Abdul's bowling and remarked that his skills had surpassed even those of Shane Warne, who himself drew inspiration from Abdul Qadir's mesmerizing wrist-spin, and went on to become one of the all-time greatest bowlers in the history of the game.

During my visit to Lahore in the early 1985, I happened to spot Abdul Qadir playing for Habib Bank under the captaincy of Abdur Rakib, who was known as Rakib Sir across cricket circles in Pakistan. Noticing his impressive wrist-spin bowling, I predicted that Abdul would one day become one of the best spinners in history. Through Rakib Sir, I inquired if Abdul was interested in playing for an English club. When I asked Abdul of his interest to play cricket in the English Leagues, he humorously expressed his desire to visit England, partly fuelled by the Marks & Spencer (M&S) brand of T-shirts which his friends brought from England. Abdul was enthusiastic about the offer, as he knew that representing League cricket enhances his scope not only for sharpening his bowling-skills, but also enhances the chances of being selected for the Pakistan team. Abdul had previously played a few years for Pakistan team but was dropped from the ODI team after the New Zealand tour in January 1985.

After my return to England, I learnt that Hanging Heaton CC was looking for an overseas player for the 1985 season. Then, I immediately contacted its chairman, Brian Wilkinson, and informed him about Abdul and his high potentials for the game. Brian knew me very well, as I had signed a few cricketers like Iqbal Qasim and Hoshedar Contractor (the son of former Indian Captain Nari Contractor) for their club in the past. But Brian was a bit doubtful about Abdul. Then I gave my personal assurance to Brian because I had complete faith on Abdul Qadir's abilities and convinced him to sign Abdul for the club. When Abdul arrived in England, I accommodated him in the house of my friend, Majid Patel, and his wife Rabia, as their house was near to the club.

But unfortunately, the first three matches turned out to be a big failure for Abdul; he conceded numerous runs without taking any wickets. Then, Brian called me and expressed his unhappiness about Abdul. I tried to explain to Brian about the need for the player to get adapted to the changed climatic conditions, as confessed to me by Abdul himself that he had a difficulty to grip the ball in those cold conditions. Unfortunately, the weather too was freezing with snow at that time, posing an altogether new challenge before him. I personally requested Brian to give Abdul a couple of more chances to see if he could adapt and improve. Brian agreed, but insisted me to pay Abdul's match fee, if he fails to perform, which I agreed with full faith on Abdul's potential.

Fortunately, in the week that followed, the light of hope began to flicker, with the turning of cold and snowy weather into little warmer and sunnier days. Abdul delivered a sterling performance in which he took 5 wickets for less than 30 runs. He continued the same performance in the week that followed as well where he claimed 7 wickets, conceding merely a few runs. And in the subsequent week, Abdul again showed his exceptional performance by taking 6 or 7 wickets in a match. Then I contacted Brian and asked him (in a light-hearted manner), whether he could consider sending him back to Pakistan. Brian expressed his joy, "No, Solly! He is a magician; I want to keep him for the rest of the season."

While Abdul was unleashing his series of successes in this way, he encountered an unfortunate incident during a match against the Undercliff team. In this match too, Abdul was in his full-swing, and had already taken a few wickets, including that of Haroon Rashid (Pakistan Test player). But suddenly, his captain, David Garner, asked Abdul to bowl from a different bowling-end than he was bowling, which Abdul refused to do, because he was not comfortable bowling from that end. The captain was not happy with such response from Abdul, who discounted Abdul from bowling, and sent him to fielding at fine leg, to which Abdul had to concede. Because of this dispute, they had lost the match, despite having good chances of winning. In review of this incident, the club management had resolved to suspend Abdul, abruptly terminating his contract for the season. Though he was paid for the entire season by the club, I feel that it was a small issue that had unnecessarily spurred up, else it could have been resolved amicably during the match itself. Abdul expressed his gratitude for all the support, but was sad about the unfortunate incident, as he wanted to leave the club in good terms.

Surprisingly, on the same Saturday at around 7:00 pm when Abdul Qadir's contract was terminated, I received the news from Imran Khan at 9:00 pm that Abdul Qadir had been selected for the Pakistan team. Imran had a great liking for Abdul; he would call me every Saturday night to know about Abdul's performance during his tenure at the club and would express his happiness about his best performance there. I noticed Abdul's unwavering commitment and strong work ethics throughout his career. He took practice sessions very seriously, and we would often practice together either at the Hanging Heaton club, or at Batley.

After his retirement from cricket, Abdul assumed the role of a Chief Selector for the Pakistan Cricket Board. When I called Abdul to congratulate him on his new position, I remember him saying, "Solly Bhai, I will try to ensure my selection is based purely on merit and talent, and not remotely on recommendations (Parchi), or nepotism." I knew Abdul was sincere and committed person, but unfortunately, he had to resign from the position relatively quickly.

Finally, the unfortunate death of Abdul in September 2019 came as a shock to me. In my eyes, Abdul Qadir always remains to be a magician and one of the greatest bowlers in the history of cricket. His legacy continues. Abdul's son, Usman Qadir, also followed in his father's lineage as a leg-break bowler. I got the opportunity to sign Usman to the Yorkshire League cricket in his very young age; he later played for the Pakistan team and had also played for the Big Bash Cricket League (BBL) in Australia.

VVS Laxman: The True Gentleman

The phrase, 'Gentlemen's Game,' resonates in true spirits, when I think of VVS Laxman; he is not only one of India's greatest cricketers but embodies all the qualities of a gentleman. Laxman is widely recognized as one of the most stylish batsmen of the modern era, known for his unwavering spirit to stand against every odd, particularly when the team encounters difficulties. This undaunting spirit in him has earned him the *moniker of a Saviour*. Laxman gained immense recognition when he played an extraordinary innings against Australia at Eden Gardens, Kolkata in 2001, where he scored 281 runs, and was credited for his role in the team's win; the iconic innings rose to be ranked sixth in the prestigious Wisden's list of the top 100 Test innings ever in the history of the game.

My acquaintance with Laxman dates to 1994. During a vacation in the early 90s, I went to Hyderabad, India, on a holiday visit, and had met one of my close friends named Vijay Mohan Raj (Tony). During our conversation, Vijay spoke words of praise about Laxman as a promising young talent in Hyderabad cricket and had anticipated a bright future for him; he was certain that one day Laxman would find place in Indian cricket team and would become an asset to the nation. However, I did not get to see him at that time, as there was no discussion about Laxman joining Club cricket in England, and he was still playing Under-19 team for India.

Again in 1994, when Indian Under-19 cricket team embarked on a tour to England, which included a match against the England Under-19 team at Headingly in Leeds from August 24 to 27, the name Laxman flashed in my memory. Sandip Patil, a former Indian cricketer, was the then team's manager for that tour, and I had known Sandip for a long time. Sandip would meet me whenever he visited England and would join me for dinner at my place. Sandip introduced me to Laxman, and then Laxman said that he had heard about me a lot, as my name was very much talked about in Hyderabad cricket circles; Laxman also expressed his interest in playing for club cricket in England.

Since then, I kept looking out for an opportunity for Laxman, and as and when I learnt that Brian Wilkinson, the then Chairman of Hanging Heaton club, was in search of a talented overseas batsman, I immediately recommended Laxman to Brian. Brian readily accepted my recommendation, and Laxman was signed for the 1995 season. I found a house for Laxman close to my house where he would live single, though he would frequent my house. In that season, Laxman, however, did not play as great as I had anticipated, but he was not bad either. It was a reasonably successful season for him, in which he scored a total of 619 runs, though Laxman himself was not happy with his own performance there.

Over time, he became part of my family; if he felt hungry, he would come, and my wife would serve him some food. But he was a vegetarian, and we eat meat almost every day. I remember one day my wife went to the market, and I was watching television, when Laxman came in suddenly and was hungry. He went straight into kitchen, served food for himself, ate, and came out saying, 'Oh! what a tasty dal fry!' I had not eaten that curry but was happy that he liked the food. Then my wife came back from shopping and said, "oh! Laxman is here, shall I cook some veg curry for him?" Then I said, "no, he has already eaten." Then she exclaimed, "How come! It is keema fry, which he cannot eat." We all started laughing, including Laxman, though with a bit of embarrassment, for mistakenly taking minced meat fry for dal fry.

For the 1996 season, Phil Carrick, the then captain of Pudsey Congs CC approached me to know whether Laxman had any interest to play for his team. Phil found something great in Laxman, and so he wanted to sign him. Laxman liked the offer and joined Pudsey Congs. The club had also offered Laxman with a flat to stay in, and so he moved to that flat. But he was single and was feeling lonely. Therefore, I accommodated Noel David to stay with Laxman in his flat so that there can be a companionship for each other. David was formerly a colleague of Laxman, when they together represented Hyderabad team for Ranji trophy, and now, David had signed for Cleckheaton CC, and Laxman for Pudsey Congs. During weekdays they both would come to my house, and we would spend happy moments together, and then one day, I learnt from David that Laxman had a habit of walking and talking in his sleep. It was due to his sheer mad love for the game that Laxman sometimes would even walk out of his bedroom and often talk about cricket while he was in deep sleep, and David had to take him back to his bed.

Laxman is such a person who would always keep himself busy and could not stand an idle life. Though he was reasonably well off in India and was getting money sufficient for him from the club cricket, he

wanted to do some work, did not want to idly languish in the flat without doing anything during weekdays, when there were no matches. I
could have accommodated him in one of my businesses, had he been
in Dewsbury, but then he was in Pudsey. So, I spoke to one my friends
and a businessman in Pudsey named Mahesh Patel, who arranged a job
in his petrol station for Laxman. Mahesh's brother, Manish Patel was
also a cricketer and was playing for Cleckheaton CC. Then, Laxman set
to work hard in the nights for the entire week and played for the club
on Sundays. Occasionally, Laxman used to help me in my petrol station
business as well whenever he got free time. Laxman was equally serious
about practising cricket, and we together practised regularly. Bowling
him in nets was an amazing experience, as he was a wonderful batter,
and I would love bowling him. If there was no match on Sundays in his
club, then I would invite him for some benefit/friendly match.

One day, an interesting incident took place when we were about to
start my car for a friendly match at Wrenthorpe CC which Laxman still
remembers and might probably have mentioned it in his autobiography.
On that day, there were only 10 players, with a shortage of one player to
make our team for the match. I remember a boy named Aamer Ishaq,
who was young but a competent player. Since Aamer was a young boy,
I presumed that he would be idle and joyfully asked him to get into the
car on our way to the match, and he just followed my call out of respect
for me. Then I drove my car to the grounds, gave him shoes, trousers,
shirts, bat, pad, gloves, everything, as I had several spare ones in my van.
The match went well, and when we started our car back to our homes,
Aamer sitting in the back seat of my car beside Laxman, began crying.
Shocked by this sudden cry of the boy, Laxman asked Ameer, what has
happened? Why are you crying? Have you got hurt? But the boy continued crying, and finally opened his mouth, saying: "Bhai, my aunt asked
me to get milk to make tea for this morning, and I was on my way to buy
them, but you took me here to play the match; my aunty will kill me now
when I go home. Laxman and I laughed at this and consoled him that I

will explain it to his aunt and take the entire burden of responsibility on his behalf. Later, Aamer played first-class cricket for Pakistan National Shipping Corporation (PNSC) for several years; I recently signed him for Thornhill CC.

In this way, we were very informal, and yet would play with utmost seriousness, embodying the spirit of the game. In fact, it was during this season that Laxman joined Indian team and had made his debut in the test series in November 1996 against South Africa, where he scored half-century in his very first test match. Laxman then went on to play 134 Test matches, and during his long tenure as a test player, he performed very well and contributed immensely for bringing several victories for the Indian team.

Laxman is kind and affectionate at heart; he has been ready to extend his help to all in need, particularly to his loved ones. His humbleness never deterred him from meeting me whenever he visits England, despite him now being a world star cricketer. On his tour to England in any test series, he would call me as soon as he lands in England to say, "Solly Bhai! How are you and Bhabhi?" He would then affectionately invite us to watch the matches and give us complimentary tickets. He never failed to visit me during his breaks and would spend time with all my family members; he was particularly close to my son, Sohail. In January 2018, when he came to England on some personal visit to London, and learnt that my wife got hospitalised, he rushed to the hospital all the way from London. He often calls and enquires of my well-being, and he is a real gentleman with a kind heart. I wish Laxman and his family a good health and happiness.

Vinod Kambli: From Stardom to Obscurity

The life of Vinod Ganpat Kambli exemplifies a strange combination of poverty, neglect, and lack of respect and love, besides the indomitable spirit to excel. Vinod is a former Indian cricketer who unfortunately had to face tragic circumstances in his life despite possessing extraordinary cricketing talents that could have earned him a place among the greatest cricketers in history. The reasons for Vinod's downfall could be both personal and familial, as well as social and political. Whatever the reasons, sadly, his greatest potentials were not properly channelled, nor his exceptional talents utilized properly, resulting in his tragic decline. Otherwise, he was someone who could have emerged as a cricket legend.

But Vinod's family was not financially well off, nor did they enjoy any social respect. Vinod was destined to live virtually in one of the small rooms of an almost dilapidating chawl at Kanjurmarg in the suburbs of Mumbai. Having been left behind with no property from his ancestors, his father, Ganpat had to feed the family of seven; the only means of survival for him and his family was his acquired skill to repair motor vehicles, as he was a mechanic, for which he had to exert all his physical labour throughout the days and nights. Vinod developed interest for cricket in his very early days, and as a young boy, Vinod had to endure traveling in crowded local trains from Kanjurmarg to Shivaji Park with his cricket equipment for practicing the game. Against all odds, Vinod's dedication to the sport shone through. It is said that he was an active child with great potentials for the game, and so his cricket talents helped him to secure free admission to the prestigious Sharadashram Vidyamandir school where he studied with Sachin Tendulkar in the same class. It was from this school in Bombay that these two young boys became friends, and together emerged to be the promising cricketers later.

The name, Vinod Kambli registered in my memory, along with the name of his colleague and friend Sachin Tendulkar, when they together created history with their unbroken partnership of 664 runs (Vinod 349 and Sachin 326) in the Harris Shield Trophy in 1988. In the following year in 1989, both Vinod and Sachin travelled to England as part of their cricket tour to play against English youth teams, in which they represented Star Club of India led by its founder, Kailash Ghattani. Following this, these two young players quickly gained international attention in the world of cricket. However, while Sachin went on to represent India in the Pakistan tour later in that year, Vinod made his debut in first-class cricket against Gujarat in the Ranji Trophy in November 1989. In his debut match in this Ranji trophy, I recall Vinod making a brilliant start by hitting a six to the very first ball he faced. This feat was sensational in those days, particularly because he was just 17 years old at that time. Vinod continued the same form in first-class cricket as a representative of Bombay Ranji team and had achieved a world record by scoring a cumulative total of 1006 runs from just six innings. Possessing natural talents, Vinod emerged as a brilliant player with a rare combination of aggression and skill to drive the ball effortlessly towards boundaries and had demonstrated his splendid performance from the very beginning of his career.

Sunil Gavaskar was a great admirer of Vinod's talents, and so was Ravi Shastri. Ravi would often share stories about Vinod and his potentials for the game. One such story, as recounted by Ravi, was about an incident during semi-final match of the Duleep Trophy against the South Zone team. Vinod went to bat just before the lunch hour, when Anil Kumble, who by then was already a renowned bowler in the opponents' team, took to bowl his final over. Ravi being the captain of the team, advised Vinod to be cool and play defence till the lunchbreak. But Vinod hit a six for the very first ball, leaving everyone in surprise, particularly Anil. Tensed by Vinod's aggressive movement, Ravi approached Vinod to urge him to remain composed; he warned Vinod of not risking his wicket so that he could score more runs. But Vinod continued the same pace, and to everyone's awe, he hit a series of boundaries.

Having such a wonderful track record, and upon the recommendations from Sunil and Ravi, I signed Vinod for Spen Victoria team to play for the 1991 season, where I was the captain of the team. When Vinod landed in England, I went to the Heathrow Airport in London along with my teammate, Steve Foster, to receive him. When Vinod joined Spen Victoria, he was just 19 years old, with a frail and skinny composure. Many of our teammates, including Chris Pickles, were sceptical about his cricketing abilities, though I was completely aware of Vinod's exceptional talents; Chris would often comment that 'his arms look like chicken legs.'

But all their doubts were dispelled in the very first match he played against the Yorkshire Bank team. The match took place just a day after his arrival in England, and so thinking that he might have undergone jetlag owing to his journey across continents, I asked Vinod to bat at number 4, although his usual position was number 3. He batted very well throughout, and by the time the last ball of the innings approached, he was at 49 runs. He then struck the ball to a point, anticipating it would reach the boundary. However, the fielder made a brilliant stop and quickly threw the ball to the wicketkeeper. In a calculated move, Vinod deliberately ran slowly in the middle of the pitch, putting pressure on the fielder to throw the ball quickly. As anticipated, wicketkeeper missed the ball, leading to a boundary, that made his inaugural innings with an unbeaten 54 runs. I was intrigued to know why he slowed down his pace of running, and Vinod explained that, if he had continued running, he would have easily secured one run and would have got his personal milestone of reaching 50 runs. But by confusing the fielder and by pressurising him to throw the ball quickly, there was a chance for the team to score five runs, if the wicketkeeper misses the ball. Vinod had prioritized the team's score over his personal achievements and had stated that his individual score was not as important as winning the match. I was totally amazed and was so happy for his selfless commitment to the cause of the team.

I also have a vivid memory of another match against the Yorkshire Bank team, where we had to face one of the renowned bowlers in the

Bradford League, Paul Grayson, a former cricketer from team England, who had played for multiple county teams, including Yorkshire and Essex. Vinod, however, started hitting Paul's deliveries out of the ground repeatedly, causing Paul to stop bowling position himself as a fielder at the fine leg. At the end of the match, I asked Paul why he abruptly stopped bowling. Paul replied candidly, "Solly, I have upcoming county matches to play in, and this young lad is effortlessly hitting me out of the ground, even against my best deliveries. I did not want to shatter my confidence!" This showcases the calibre of Vinod, who can strike the ball with incredible power, that leaves even the seasoned players in awe.

In a match against Hanging Heaton, Rashid Patel, an Indian test bowler, was in our opponent's team. There was a heated exchange of words between Vinod and Rashid during the game. In a fit of a rage, Vinod threw an open challenge to Rashid, 'If permitted, I can play your bowling without even pads;' fortunately, the issue got resolved with the intervention of the umpire. And when Rashid took to bowling, Vinod responded by hitting 4 consecutive boundaries. The captain of Hanging Heaton understood the fierce determination of Vinod and sensing the impending danger of Vinod's aggression to Rashid's confidence, he assigned him to field at fine-leg, despite Rashid's insistence to continue bowling. Vinod often thrived on challenges, and any bowler who dared to challenge him would often witness his explosive batting display, although sometimes, he had to taste bitter results, owing to his raw aggression.

Vinod is such an impulsive person; it is sometimes difficult to discern his mind. In a match against Bradford & Bingley Team, there was a star bowler named Richard McCarthy from Australia in their team. McCarthy was held in high regard in the league by all, and even Vinod himself had expressed this fact several times that McCarthy was the most challenging bowler he had ever faced. During our last match against them, I informed Vinod that if he can score 71 runs, he would reach 1000 runs in the season for the club in Bradford League and Priestley Cup combined, and he could also secure the best batting average prize in the league. Prior to his innings, Vinod asked me, "Solly Bhai, how many runs do you want me to score today?" I then replied, '71.' He played his brilliant innings with his frequent shots, that included the boundaries he hit against McCarthy's balls. But, as soon as he reached exactly 71 runs, Vinod gave away his wicket deliberately. Shocked by his unexpected return, I could not help but shout at him furiously, "Are you stupid, Vinod? If you had carried on, you would have won the best batting average prize in the league." With a smile, Vinod replied nonchalantly, "Solly Bhai, you asked me to score 71 runs, and I accomplished that; my job is done, and I don't concern myself with personal accolades." I was shocked and speechless, hearing his response.

In this season in 1991, Vinod showcased exceptional batting performance, in which he scored 943 runs from 19 innings with an average of 58.94 runs per inning in Bradford League. With this outstanding performance, he earned a total of £700 from match fees and other financial rewards for the 1991 season. It was quite a lot of money in those days, around 60,000 Indian Rupees. I travelled to India to hand over the entire lot to his father. His father was so happy and said, he had never seen that lot in his entire life. However, Vinod, when returned to India, he took all the money from his father and spent it with his friends. For some reason, Vinod never cared money, nor did he have any respect for commodities. At the end of each season, Vinod would generously give away all his cricket gear—bat, pads, and gloves, including his mementos and trophies at my home, before returning to India.

Vinod had the same incredible track in the Ranji Matches as well, with which, he made his debut in the Indian One-Day International (ODI) team against Pakistan at Sharjah on October 18, 1991. A little later, just before the end of the year, the Indian team was preparing for a tour to Australia for Test matches, and there was widespread anticipation that Vinod would be included in the squad, as he had a brilliant track record in the first-class matches. In a trial match that was held before the tour, Vinod scored 116 runs, and Pravin Amre scored 120 runs. It was almost certain that both Vinod and Amre were selected; Vinod had even been asked to provide measurements for Official BCCI blazers and other clothing, suggesting his expected inclusion. But when the final selection list was out, it was to everyone's surprise, Amre was selected for the tour, but not Vinod, which left Vinod in deep dismay. This decision by the selection committee drew strong criticism from all quarters, including renowned cricketers like Sunil Gavaskar and Kapil Dev, which got published widely by the press. Withstanding this hurdle, Vinod continued to pursue his cricketing career. He was selected to play for Indian team for Benson & Hedges ODI (One-Day International) World Cup, held in Australia in 1992. Following this World Cup, he came back to England to play again for Spen Victoria for the 1992 season in the Bradford League. He showcased his batting talents in that season as well, where he scored 683 runs.

During two seasons when he was with Spen Victoria in 1991 and 1992, Vinod became an integral part of my family. He would stay at our house and seamlessly blend into our regular family routines, like any other member of my family, like buying things for the house from the market, joining us for meals and to be a part of family gatherings. Over time, Vinod developed a close friendship with my youngest son, Sohail.

Vinod had a unique approach to batting practice. Unlike other professional cricketers, Vinod never did his practice sessions in the grounds with other cricketers, and I had never seen him practising. Instead, he would ask Sohail to throw a few balls at him, just before the match, and that was his practise; he would not even wear pads, nor head gear, for this. And yet, surprisingly, he would score tons of runs in all his innings and maintain his consistency. Given his impressive performance, I never felt the need to insist him to go for formal batting practice.

In fact, for the 1992 season, Vinod also received contract offer with better package from yet another club, which played under a different league. I even suggested him to move there as it was more lucrative for him. But he wanted to remain with Spen Victoria, as this club played under Bradford League which provides higher standard cricket than that of that new offer, so that he could sharpen his cricketing talents for international test cricket. Though he hailed from a socio-economically underprivileged family, without even proper housing, money never held any importance for him; the only aim for him was to find a place in Indian test team. Vinod often expressed his strong desire and committed will to be a part of the Indian test team. One day, when a group of Bombay cricketers were having lunch at my house, they asked Vinod, why would he not consider working on weekdays when there were no matches. To that, the response of the Vinod was loud and clear: "I will earn money when I play test matches for India, and I don't want to divert my focus into part-time jobs." Some admired his confidence, while others remained silent. I was so happy to see such a strong will and commitment in him for the game, as I knew that Vinod was naïve but possessed talents in abundance.

True to his words, Vinod was selected for the Indian Test team in 1993. Ever since then, Vinod was occupied with international matches and would call me whenever he got some free time to share his cricketing experiences there, but mainly to check upon the well-being of me and my family. On the midnight of February 21, 1993, I woke up to a telephone ring at my home; it was Vinod, and he was on his test innings with England team at Wankhede Stadium in his hometown, Bombay, India. I heard his voice with great excitement, "Solly Bhai, today I scored a century against England. As soon as I reached hundred, I thought of you and all the help you had extended to me." He also confessed that his experience in Spen Victoria helped him in enhancing his abilities. I admired his achievement, and yet I expressed my disappointment to him remarking that he had almost threw his wicket at 119 runs; he apologetically admitted, "Yes, sorry Solly Bhai! I was so exhausted that I played a lazy shot. But I will be a little more focused and would aim for a double century tomorrow." As promised, Vinod went on to score 224 runs in that test match, which is still regarded as one of the finest innings ever played by any Indian cricketer in the 1990s.

In addition to cricket, Vinod had a passion for dancing and sing- ing, and he would delight us all with his performances at home, keeping everyone happy. When we were all free and assemble in the evening, I sometimes would ask him, Vinod! *Thoda Gaane Suna Dena* (Vinod! Would you please sing a song for us), and he oblige without any further ado and begins to sing and dance passionately. His mimicking of several crick- eters and actors was amazing, and we all would have cheerful moments with Vinod; he was truly an amazing person.

Several years later, Vinod came to England to participate in a series of exhibition and charity matches. One of the charity-matches which took place in London was organized by Sunil Gavaskar, and featured by renowned cricketers such as Imran Khan, Javed Miandad, Sameer Dighe, Sanjay Manjrekar, and of course Vinod and other international players. Following the match, Vinod approached me seeking my hospi- tality at my home, and I gladly invited him. But to our surprise, Vinod came to our house with a good-looking girl; he introduced her to me and to my wife as his girlfriend, Noella Lewis, about whom we had not even heard. Vinod told us that they were in love for quite some time, and so we warmly welcomed the young couple and hosted dinner for them. After dinner, I accommodated them in one of my houses at 27 Cowper Street and asked them to stay there for as long as they wished.

However, a few days later, I was startled by a phone call at 3 am. Given my habit of going to bed early, my friends rarely call me after 10 pm and before 6 am, unless it was urgent. Sensing something serious, I picked up the phone. On the other end, I heard the voice of a gentleman, trembling in supreme anxiety. He said, he was calling from Pune, India, and told me that his daughter had been missing for several days. Then he said someone had told him that she might be in England with Vinod Kambli, and so he was urged to reach out to me. The worried father was also told that if his daughter was indeed at my place, she would be safe. Then I reassured him that she was safe and staying in my house with Vinod, though I was unaware of the full story. I also promised him that I would inform his daughter by morning and ask her to call him; the father expressed his relief upon hearing this news.

Noella was a tender-hearted woman, and Vinod and Noella together stayed in my house for over three weeks. During this period, they were happy, and Noella became close to all the members of my family. However, they had some issues, and often would be falling-out with each other. One midnight, I heard an unexpected knock at my door. To my surprise, it was Noella; she complained that she had some small argument with Vinod, for which he left her all alone in the house and went off. I got worried, and immediately went out in search of Vinod. I then found him to be sitting on the steps of Dewsbury Townhall and persuaded him to return home. On another day, another midnight knock, but this time it was a knock from Vinod, and Noella had left home. Again, I had to look out for her, found her sitting on a bench in Dewsbury City Centre, and then took her back home. This was a recurring pattern for them all through the period in which they stayed with us, and they would re-join and live happily with my intervention. I always had a great concern for Vinod, and often would worry about their relationship.

However, after their return to India, I learnt that Vinod and Noella eventually got married. I lost contact with Vinod after their marriage, but I came to know that they unfortunately could not continue together for long, their marriage ending up in separation. Worse still, I was extremely saddened to hear that Vinod was depressed and had become addicted to alcohol. In fact, Vinod was a complete *teetotaller* and was a quiet personality; he would simply greet everyone with a hello and then silently retreat into the background. This change in him was a shock and I cannot help but pray to GOD, the Almighty!

The cricketing journey of Vinod Kambli was short-lived, and yet one of the most brilliant ones. He made his debut into international test cricket when he was nineteen and he disappeared totally from test cricket by the age of just 23. In this short stint, he played a total of 17 test matches, and displayed the best of his performance in all the innings he had played; his performance was so magnificent that he scored consecutive double centuries for India, solidifying his position as one of the top players. Notably, he holds the distinction of being the fastest Indian cricketer to score 1000 runs in test cricket, and to accomplish this feat he played just 14 innings. Vinod's astonishing performance amassed the appreciation of cricket lovers of the world and made its headway into the headlines of cricket news worldwide in 1993; he quickly became a popular cricketer in the world. I cherished all his victories and fame as my own, as I consider him to be one of my most endearing children. Vinod too, always treated me with utmost respect, and had extended all his gratitude publicly before the media, for whatever the little help, support and love I showered upon him during the short time he stayed with me. My heart melts when I recall Vinod's address before English media, where he referred to me as his 'fatherly figure.'

My tears begin to well up when I think of the tragic story of this bright child, who could have had a promising career in cricket. I feel that Vinod possessed immense talents and had the potential to become one of the greatest players in cricket history. He would have been no less than his friend and cricket-legend, Sachin Tendulkar; he would have been as great as any other modern day legendary figures in cricket like Brian Lara, and Ricky Ponting. Even to this day, when I think of Vinod, I travel back to the early '90s, and his silent, yet flamboyant character, his stylish batting, and above all, his inherent innocence plays out like a silent film just before my eyes. But I cannot blame anyone for his decline, as its reasons might be as dark and varied as it could be, which even the rays of the sun cannot penetrate through. Any way, it is futile to do autopsy at this hour, as his demise as a cricketer while he was still young and alive is impossible to revive. This story often leaves a pessimistic image on us, as life is not always as colourful and joyful as rainbow, but sometimes it would be as ugly and dreadful as a Mare in the Norse Nightmare.

Of late, I have attempted several times to contact Vinod, but unfortunately, I have not received any response from him. If by chance Vinod gets to see this at least, I want him to know that we have a lot of love for him, and every member of our family, would love to see him and talk to him, to reunite with him. Vinod, we all miss you, my dear!

MY MEMORIES OF CRICKETERS

As the saying goes, "Nothing ever grows without a seed," Rahul Mankad, whom his loved ones call Jiga, was central to the building of my connection with Indian cricketers. Rahul was a league cricketer in England, when I first met him at Cleckheaton Cricket Club that plays under Broadford League; he is a son of Vinoo Mankad, who was one of the greatest all-rounders that India has ever produced. Ever since I met him, we became very good friends; our common Gujarati ethnicity had also prompted us to gel with each other, as we both speak in Gujarati. Eventually, Jiga developed his bonding with my parents as well, and he began frequenting our house whenever he craved for our traditional cuisines of his choice, and he would spend talking endless hours, while dining with us. Our frequent meets and discussions on cricket, followed by my tours to India, has only brought me closer to a range of Indian cricketers of supreme brilliance in first class cricket, as well as those of international eminence from India and Pakistan; Jiga introduced me to so brilliant players from India as Vijay Mohan Raj, Yajurvindra Singh (Sunny Singh), Suru Naik, Avi Karnik, Padmakar Shivalkar, Karsan Ghavri, and several others, including his own brother, and a brilliant test cricketer, Ashok Mankad. In fact, my niche in introducing several Asian cricketers to English league cricket also took shape, during my affinity with Jiga.

Jiga once asked me to find an opportunity for his elder brother, Ashok Mankad, in English league cricket; Ashok, who is also known as Kaka, by then was a renowned test cricketer and was representing Indian national team. I began looking for clubs in our Yorkshire region, and finally I secured a deal for Kaka at Dewsbury Cricket Club. With this, I discovered an increasing number of opportunities for Asian cricketers to play in English leagues; I had also figured out that there were no professional consultants to aid Asian cricketers to recruit for the clubs in England. So, I started volunteering to assist cricketers from India and Pakistan in signing contracts with various clubs in England. Eventually, I had emerged to be a single point contact, for most cricket clubs in Asia and England, as well as to the individual cricketers who were aspiring to find opportunities in English leagues. This marked a beginning of my journey to be a volunteer to secure contracts for numerous cricketers from India and Pakistan with various cricket clubs in England. Ever since then, I have been a well-known and respected person among the most Asian cricketers and cricket clubs in England, though not popular among the cricket fans. I am fortunate to meet hundreds of cricketers from India and Pakistan and had befriended them; I also have friends among English cricketers, and those who played for counties in England.

This is not a compendium of cricketers of the world; it is just a recollection of the personal memories of a league cricketer, who had lived through cricket for decades, having his base in England, the cultural centre for cricket world. For structural reasons, first I divide the list of players into three groups—Indian cricketers, Pakistan Cricketers, and English Cricketers—based on their nativity. Each of these groups are further divided into three—Test Cricketers, One-Day International cricketers, and the First-Class Cricketers. Though it is difficult to lay down every detail of every single cricketer I met in my life, I would like to recall the best of my memories about some of the cricketers, with whom I had cherished intimacy, from India, Pakistan, and England; some of them are still in touch with me, and the treasure of memories that they have left with me are so invaluable in my life that I would cherish them forever.

My Memories of Cricketers from India

My assistance in securing club contracts to Indian cricketers in England took its roots in the late 1970s. Thanks to Almighty! I never veered away from this noble task of helping the bright minds from India for decades, and during my active cricketing career, I had managed to successfully sign nearly 150 Indian cricketers to various clubs in England. Among them, some had already represented India, while many others went on to play for the country in the subsequent years. I recollect a period when 9 out of 11 Indian Test players had either obtained club contracts or cricket equipment (Brand Endorsement) deals through me or were personally associated with me. It brings me immense joy to witness a fact that there were several young talents, whom I helped in securing club contracts in England, before they evolved from promising play-ers to international cricketers. Seeing my role in aiding several Indian cricketers to get contracts with English clubs, some media, then, lauded me as an 'Unofficial Indian Selector,' a title, however, I humbly disagree with. I just assisted them to the best of my capacities, and it was their individual hard work, discipline and talents that had ultimately shaped them as excellent cricketers. The following is a list of Indian cricketers, with whom I had an affinity with, and the memories that I cherished with them during my long journey, as an active player, captain and an organiser of cricket matches in Yorkshire.

They include, Nari Contractor, Salim Durani, Farokh Engineer, Ha-numanth Singh, Bishan Singh Bedi, Subrata Guha, Syed Abid Ali, Ashok Mankad, Gundappa Vishwanath, Mohinder Amarnath, Sunil Gavaskar, Madan Lal, Brijesh Patel, Karsan Ghavri, Surinder Amarnath, Syed Kirmani, Dilip Vengsarkar, Yajurvindra (Sunny) Singh, Kapil Dev, M.V (Bobjee) Narasimha Rao, Yashpal Sharma, Dilip Doshi, Shiva Lal Yadav, Roger Binny, Sandeep Patil, Kirti Azad, Ravi Shastri, Krishnamachari Srikanth, Ashok Malhotra, Pranab Roy, Ghulam Parkar, Suru Nayak, Rakesh Shukla, Maninder Singh, Balwinder Singh Sandhu, Laxman

Sivaramakrishnan , Navjot Singh Sidhu, Chetan Sharma, Manoj Prab-hakar, Mohammad Azharuddin, Lalchand Rajput, Kiran More, Chandrakanth Pandit, Raju Kulkarni, Bharat Arun, Raman Lamba, Arshad Ayub, Sanjay Manjrekar, Narendra Hirwani, WV Raman, Rashid Patel, Salil Ankola, Sachin Tendulkar, Venkatapathy Raju, Atul Wassan, Anil Kumble, Javagal Srinath, Subroto Banerjee, Praveen Amre, Ajay Jadeja, Vinod Kambli, Vijay Yadav, Nayan Mongia, Paras Mhambray, Vikram Rathour, Sourav Ganguly, Rahul Dravid, VVS Laxman, Abey Kuruvilla, Nilesh Kulkarni, Debasish Mohanty, Ajith Agarkar, Robin Singh, Ashish Nehra, Wasim Jaffer, Murali Karthik, Mohammad Kaif, Saba Karim, Sairaj Bahuthule, Samir Dighe, Virendra Sehwag, Sanjay Bangar, Yuvraj Singh, Dinesh Karthik, Pragyan Ojha and Naman Ojha.

This is quite an exhaustive list, and so, I will try to talk about only a few players with whom I have cherished some special moments; hope, others will not get offended!

1. A. Test Cricketers of India:

Mankad Brothers (Ashok Mankad and Rahul Mankad)

As Jiga (Rahul Mankad) had been my family friend in England, eventually I too became intimate with all the members of his family in India; with my assistance in signing contract for his brother, Kaka (Ashok Mankad), with Dewsbury Cricket Club, our family ties strengthened further. In 1981, during my visit to Bombay to watch India vs. England test series, I had the pleasure of meeting all the members of Mankad family, including their younger brother, Atul Mankad, who was also a cricketer. Kaka, then, generously arranged an accommodation for me at CCI (Cricket Club of India), and it was during this visit that Kaka introduced me to four promising young cricketers, Chandrakanth Pandit, Raju Kulkarni, Lal Chand Rajput, and Ravi Thakkar, whom I later helped get recruited for different clubs in Yorkshire.

My ancestral home at Simlak, Gujarat, where I was born. Lots of fond memories!!

During my school days at Natal Colony, just before leaving for England.

Lifting Priestley Cup for Spen Victoria, August 12, 1990; one of the most cherished moments of my life!

I was with Avi Karnik, Sunil Gavaskar, Vijay Mohan Raj (Tony), Karsan Ghavri, Iqbal Qasim, Junior Sohail Adam (my youngest son); taken just before Avi Karnik's benefit match at Birstall on August 10, 1980.

Captains of both the teams shaking hands; Sir Richard Hadlee and I during Richard Hadlee's testimonial match at Mount Batley on May 05, 1986.

PICTURED with the Cup are two of the stars of the Spen side skipper Solly Adam and pace bowler John Wood whose 7 for 20 performance earned him man of the match award. Offering congratulations is ex Indian Test player Sunil Gavasker, now a cricket commentator with the BBC.

The Pristley Cup Trophy presentation event became much merrier with my dear friend, Sunil's presence. Indisputably, the star of the day was John Wood for his sterling perfomance of 7 wickets for 20 runs.

That's my team against Suru Nayak's team, during the latter's testimonial match; I as the Captain with Sanjay Manjrekar, Sachin Tendulkar, Sulakshan Kulkarni, Suresh Shetty, Yakub Vali, Vinod Kambli, Iqbal Khan, Atul Wassan, Sameer Dighe, and Abhay Laghate.

Asian XI vs DDL XI Invitation Match-1976 at Mirfield; players of both the teams combined-Dik Abed, John Holder, Cec Abrahams, Goolam Abed, Rashid Dawood, Baboo Karkun, Samad Vacchiyath, Haroon Hans, Abdul Hai Aswat, Philip Ackroyd, Colin Fretwell, Alec Joy, Kenny Blackburn, R. Dias (Sri Lanka), and I (Captain).

During a Benefit Match, Asian XI team Vs DDL league team, at Woodkirk; Harun Hans, Yakub Vali, E. Raje, V. Banerjee, M. Saeed, Barun Burman, S. Basu, Karsan Ghavri, Mohsin Khan, Sohail Adam (My son), M. Javid, and I(Captain).

I was with Mr. and Mrs. Barry Wood, and Batley Muslim Club officials, during the club awards event. Later, my photograph was apparently removed from its publication in the newspaper.

With both the teams, Geoffrey Boycott XI (Yorkshire county team) Vs Batley Select XI, for the Geoff Boycott testimonial match at Mount Batley on May 29, 1984; Geoff Boycott captained his team, and I captained Batley Select XI.

With Glorius Batley CC team - Sean Twohig, Masood Anwar, Abul Azeem, Paul Blakely and other team members

My Batley team with Central Yorkshire League Championship Trophy - 1987; David Bruce, Barry Petty, Dave Tattersall, Rob Cooper, Paul Blakely, Mohammed Arif, Tim Ruskin and Neil Haines.

Spen Victoria Priestley Cup winning team on August 12, 1990 - A joyful moment for all of us.

Former president of the Bradford League Bruce Moss presents Solly Adam with a trophy at Spen Victoria Cricket Club presentation night. They are seen with the secretary, Tom Horkin (centre). Pictured back are:- Robert Burton, Kevin Denham, John Burton (Cricket chairman), Bill Garside and Steve Bethel. Photo by Barry Mounsey.

Spen Victoria Club Awadrs night; receiving a trophy from Bruce Moss, former President of the Bradford League.

WEDNESDAY 24-6-98   STEVE RIDING

● **BATTLE OF WITS:** Batley's Solly Adam (above) sends one down against Altofts in their Central Yorkshire League clash, while Alftofts' Steve Hodgkiss (right) hits out.

Back to Central Yorkshire League in 1998; bowling in a league match

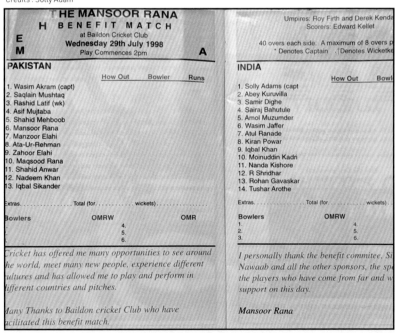

The Mansoor Rana Benefit Match, India Vs Pakistan, at Baildon CC on July 29, 1998.

Solly Adam, the area's 'Mr Cricket' (right).

'What we need is a better mix... We don't want all-Asian or all-white teams. We want people of all backgrounds to mix together'

The purpose of sport is to unite the people, and I am always vocal about it. (left)

My good old Batley CC friends catching up at my house in Dewsbury - Chandrakanth Pandit, Paul Heaton, Sean Twohig, David, and I. (right)

Sir Gary Sobers, Sunil Gavaskar, my wife (Maryam), and I in a party.

Candid moment when friends (Sunil Gavaskar, Gundappa Vishwanath, Dilip Vengsarkar, and Suru Nayak) visited my petrol station - AMOCO; gifting a Parker Pen as a gesture of my friendship (funnily, Sunil made it as an awards event)

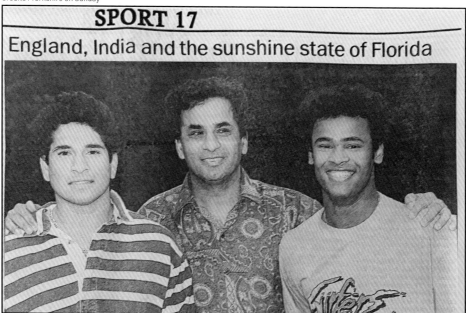

From Sunday newspaper in Yorkshire when Vinod Kambli scored a famous double century against England in February 1993 at Wankhede Stadium, Bombay.

Catching up Imran Khan and Javed Miandad for a dinner at my house during their tenure at Susesex County team in 1970's.

With Iqbal Qasim - my younger brother indeed!

Imran Khan's Benefit Match at Mount Pleasant, Batley, July 05, 1987.

SOLLY Adam (left) tosses up under the watchful eye of Pakistan captain Imran Khan to start Sunday's match at Mount Pleasant, Batley. — (0507/3).

At a cheerful moment with Chandresh Patel, Kavitha Vishwanath, Kapil Dev, and Gundappa Vishwanath.

Sanjay Manjrekar, Sunil Gavaskar, my wife, Maryam, and I

Vijay Mohan Raj (Tony) and Farida Raj visited us in Dewsbury; such a lovely couple!

Another good friend of mine from 1970's, John Holder (Test Umpire).

With Sir Ian Botham during an event.

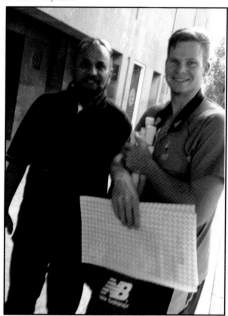

Bumped into Former Australian Captain Steve Smith during my trip to India on a business tour.

The warmth of VVS Laxman in my difficult times at Pinderfield Hospital, Wakefield, when my wife faces the hardest battle of her life.

Meeting friends and famillies is forever a cherishable moment; Dr. Farida, and Jimmy and his wife, Dr. Bikku. (left), Mohinder Amarnath, my good old friend, and the hero of the 1983 World Cup, visiting us in Dewsbury. (right)

Catching up with Shahid Afridi after a long time

Rameez Raja (Former Pakistan Captain) with us during breakfast.

Meeting this rare genius, Vishy (Gundappa Vishwanath), is always a cherishable moment. (left), I miss my brother-figure, late Rahul Mankad (Jiga). (right)

Musthaq Mohammad (Former Pakstani Cricketer) and I, during an event.

Saqlain Mushtaq, a Great human being; what a fabulous spinner he was!

While Mankad brothers started living in Dewsbury area, followed by Kaka signing his contract with Dewsbury CC, we would meet almost every single day, and would discuss a lot on cricket. Kaka had the temperament to assist young enthusiasts in the club, and given his international cricket experience, we gained invaluable insights from him. Kaka would also join practice sessions at Batley Muslim CC, and I had a pleasure of playing several friendly matches with him. In one such friendly match, Kaka taught me a life lesson. After the match, Kaka expressed his displeasure about the match, as some players were too casual about the game which he detested. He said, "if you play cricket for fun, you'll lose its true spirit, and will never be able to grasp its depth," and he continued with a metaphor, "playing cricket itself is great fun, but if you put too much sugar in a cup of tea, it will spoil the tea." He sought 101 percent effort to win the match, whether it is a friendly, or a first-class game, and had taught me to have fun in attaining excellence in the game, rather than merely cheering it. It clearly shows his seriousness and dedication for the game, and it was a great learning experience for me to treat every game with equal seriousness. Many players from Bombay acknowledge that, Ashok Kaka and Vasu Paranjape are the best captains Bombay had in those days. I was deeply touched by his commitment to the game, and clarity in his thought process. His wise words had a great impact on my life, and he made his contributions for my success.

Jiga, on the other hand, gives a lot of priority to friendship, besides his play. Though Jiga could not rise to represent Indian national team in test cricket, like his brother, Kaka, he was a brilliant player and a nice human being. Whenever he would call me from India, he would never fail to ask about all our mutual friends in Batley. Of late, Jiga had settled in Dubai with his wife. When he learnt about my holiday in Dubai, he warmly picked me from airport, and I was hosted for dinner at his beautiful house. Though I booked a hotel room in advance, he insisted that I stay with him. During my stay there, Jiga took us to several places like Papa Roti, Gazebo, and various shopping malls; it was fun to be with him, and it was truly memorable. Unfortunately, Jiga passed away on March 30, 2022; he was one of the finest human beings I have ever known, and all my family members miss him so much.

Nari Contractor

I got acquainted with Nari Contractor through Ashok Mankad when I visited Bombay in 1981. Nari Bhai, by then, had already represented Indian test cricket, and was affiliated with Sun-Grace Mafatlal Cricket Club in Bombay. Having a common Gujarati descent, we started speaking in Gujarati, and became close to each other. In the brief time that I spent in Bombay, he spoke at length on cricket, and had shared his knowledge and experiences as a senior cricketer. He loved my company and curiosity to learn things, and warmly welcomed me, along with my wife and my youngest son (Sohail), to his home for dinner. It was a very warm reception, and I loved his company too. He also admired my endeavours in league cricket in England, and I felt elated, hearing such pleasing words from so learned person as Nari Contractor. One of those days, he took me to Hindu Gymkhana, where he introduced me to Salim Durani, an aggressive left-handed batsman. Later, I signed Hoshedar Contractor, son of Nari Bhai, to play for Hanging Heaton CC.

Farokh Engineer

Farokh Bhai had an impressive stint playing for Lancashire County from 1968 to 1976, while simultaneously playing test cricket as a member of the Indian team. He possesses an extensive knowledge of cricket and is known for his noble character. When he visited Yorkshire for county matches, I had an opportunity to get to know him through our mutual cricket friends. Eventually, he made England his home to serve Lancashire, and we became good friends. Over time, our friendship grew stronger, and we frequently met to discuss cricket and have dinner together. During benefit season with Lancashire in 1976, I not only played, but was an organiser of his benefit match at the Mirfield Parish ground, featuring 'Lancashire XI' against 'Solly Adam International XI' Team; the match turned out to be a huge success. Then one day, during our interactions, Farokh Bhai expressed his desire to watch me bowling, as he said that he heard a lot about my left-arm bowling. I felt glad to hear such pleasing words from none other than such a great player as Farokh Bhai himself. I also had the honour of being part of a party that Farokh Bhai once organized for Indian cricketers at his house in Lancashire.

Bishan Singh Bedi

Bishan Singh Bedi, whom the Indian cricketing fraternity would affectionately call Bishan Paaji (elder brother), was a fantastic person. I remember Bishan Paaji visiting Dewsbury to meet Madan Lal, who was a son like figure for Paaji. Interestingly, at a time when Bishan Paaji signed for the Northampton County, players like Mushtaq Mohammad and Sarfraz Nawaz also part of the team, and it was a learning experience for me to watch them play. Given my acquaintance with Mushtaq, the trio—Paaji, Mushtaq, and Sarfraz—would frequent our house and dine with us as and when they had matches in Yorkshire region. I would call him with great respect as Bishan Paaji, and in turn, he would greet me warmly, "my friend, Solly." I always held him with high regard for both his talents as a bowler, as well as his noble character. Unfortunately, Bishan Paaji passed away recently, leaving the cricket fraternity in grief.

Syed Abid Ali

Abid Bhai was not only a fantastic cricketer, but a wonderful person. He played in the Lancashire League for Rawtenstall CC, and I know him through our common cricket friends from India. We played several benefit-matches together in Yorkshire, which had brought us closer to each other. Our friendship deepened over time, leading to a very good familial bonding between us. Abid Bhai, along with his wife, used to visit my

205

house during the week, when we had to play matches in weekends. He would treat every single match with same seriousness and had expressed his devotion to cricket. I facilitated a sponsorship for him from Crown Sports, and we would often go together to Crown Sports in Dewsbury, where he would choose his choicest bats and other equipment. When he was a coach for the UAE team, I met him the in Dubai, where he graciously invited me for a meal; we also went for shopping there and had a wonderful time together in Dubai. On my return journey, he also extended his help regarding extra luggage, and he was there with me till the last minute of my stay there. He now has settled down in America, and we occasionally catch up and reminisce our good old days.

Madan Lal

Though I knew of Madan Lal right from his debut into test cricket for Indian team in 1974, I got a chance to meet him only in 1975, after he began playing for Meltham CC in Huddersfield League. In fact, I learnt about Madan's contract with Meltham club from Bishan Paaji, when Paaji joined me for dinner at my home; Paaji, being his father figure, had also requested me to help Madan, if needed. Then one day, I went to Meltham CC exclusively to watch Madan's play, and to befriend him. It was around the same time, I also got connected to two other club cricketers, Tanvir Shah and Jasbir Singh, who were playing for Queensbury CC; Madan, then, was sharing his house with Jasbir Singh. Eventually, we four became good friends, and together played several matches in Yorkshire. As matches would be held only during weekends, Madan sought out some part time jobs. So, he would occasionally work in my shop, and when a friend of mine wanted a full-time employee to work in his petrol station, "Graham of Dewsbury," I accommodated Madan there, to serve petrol during the weekdays. I remember him earning 50p to £1 per hour, which was a respectable wage in 1975.

Madan was an outstanding player whose performance in Meltham

CC earned him with the batting prize from the club in the same year he had joined the club in 1975. He continued playing there for two years and had proven his track. Meanwhile, Dik Abed, my close friend, and a cricket stalwart associated with Enfield CC in the Lancashire league, had to move along with his family to Netherlands in 1977. So, Dik suggested the club management to seek my recommendation to find a skilled all-rounder, as his replacement, and then he called me to seek my help in that regard. Since, Madan was already a proven all-rounder in Test cricket as well as in league cricket, I promptly suggested his name to its club chairman, whom I had known for a long time. In a meeting that was intended to sign contract between Madan and Enfield CC, the chairman of the club asked for our expected honorarium per season. To that, I looked at Madan, and then he whispered to me (in Hindi), saying that he would be content with £600 plus an air ticket. However, knowing Madan's true worth, I took an initiative to negotiate it for £1200 per season, at which Madan was taken aback but was quiet. Though the chairman did not budge initially, I persuaded him to agree to the cited amount, and we sealed the deal with a handshake. Madan was supremely elated, and I was happy to see him being placed well.

Madan would frequent our house, along with his wife, Anu Lal, and they had become our family friends; Anu hails from an affluent family of Mohan Meakin, which held on to the lineage of owning one of the oldest and renowned breweries in India. During our holiday in Delhi, they warmly invited my family for dinner at their residence; Anu also took my wife out for shopping, fostering a greater bonding between our families. After retiring as a player, Madan became the coach for Indian cricket team during the 1996-97 season. In this season, when the Indian team was on its West Indies tour, my family was also on a holiday visit in the Caribbean Islands. So, I had the opportunity to meet him there, alongside the Indian cricket team, and had a great time with them. Even to this day, Madan never fails visiting us whenever comes to England and we all have a great time together. His humility, hardworking nature, and thankfulness to others, are remarkable; he once acknowledged to me that he owes much of his success to Bishan Paaji.

Brijesh Patel

Brijesh is more of my family member than a cricketing friend. I met Brijesh for the first time in the mid-70's, while he was playing for the Elland cricket club, under Huddersfield league. During his stint in this club, he would visit my house for dinners, along with other Indian cricketers. Eventually, we became very good friends, and then he went on to become an integral part of our family. But what truly deepened our bonding was Brijesh's amiable nature and his proficiency in Gujarati language. Brijesh was so endearing to my parents that they would spend hour after hour talking to him. Brijesh's wife, Toral Patel, was also dear to us all; she would visit us often, along with Brijesh, and my children affectionately call the couple, Uncle and Aunty. The parents of Toral would reside in Leicester, and so whenever they visited their daughter, they would not miss visiting us in Dewsbury; often they would stay with us for days. Toral would call Maryam and talk for hours and enquire about each member of our family.

Whenever I visit Bangalore, I would stay in Brijesh's house, where he would introduce me to several young cricketers who were aspiring to play League cricket in England. Brijesh was in India at the time of my daughter's wedding, and so, I just informed him, without expecting him to be present for the occasion, as I knew Brijesh was busy during that time. Brijesh too was quiet and did not show any sign of accepting my invitation. But, on the day of the marriage, he made a surprising knock at the door of our house, making us all happy; he travelled all the way from India to England, along with his family, just to share the happiest moment of the marriage of my daughter. The couple stayed with us all through the two days of celebrations, where he even drove my daughter to the wedding hall in a Rolls-Royce car, which was generously lent to us by Saeed Ahmad Bhai for the occasion. We were also special invitees for his daughter's wedding. But I could not make it, as unfortunately my mother had just been diagnosed with cancer and had passed away after a few days. I am glad that Brijesh has been there in every important moment of my life, and I am fortunate to have him as my best friend.

Gundappa Vishwanath

Though I knew Vishy (Vishwanath) through Indian cricket team, our friendship had deepened due to Sunil Gavaskar; he is the brother-in-law of Sunil. If I may share my views about Indian cricket, I would say that India has produced three finest batsmen ever in history: Gundappa Vishwanath, Sunil Gavaskar, and Sachin Tendulkar. I recall Sunil once telling me that if Sunil could play one shot for one ball, Vishy had the ability to produce different shots for a single ball. This succinctly encap-sulates the exceptional skills and versatility that Vishy brought to the game. During the tour of Indian national team to England in 1979, a sit-uation arose where the wives of the cricketers were not permitted to stay with their husbands in their hotel rooms. Then I hosted all their wives in my home, among whom Vishy's wife, Kavitha Vishwanath, was also one. Then Vishy and other cricketers, would join us at my home after the play every day of the Test match, and then, we all would have dinners and fun together by sharing the happy moments. Vishy is a true gentle-man and is remarkably soft-spoken. He is quiet, but once considers you a friend, he unleashes a repertoire of jokes, showcasing his great sense of humour. Personally, I believe that the cricket world did not give him the credit he truly deserves. However, he occupies a place of high esteem in my mind; we also had a great time together during Rohan Gavaskar's wedding in Bombay.

Mohinder Amarnath

There was a period when it was a customary practice for the Indian team to visit my house for lunch, or for dinner, in each of their tour to England, if they had a match in the Yorkshire region. I met Mohinder Amarnath, fondly known as Jimmy, for the first time in one such occasion in 1976, when the Indian team visited my home. Then Jimmy told me that he had signed with Lowerhouse CC in the Lancashire league and was planning to come to England the following year, in 1977. Once the season commenced, Jimmy gave me a call, and had left his phone number, and other details of his contact, as he was a *paying guest* in the house of an elderly woman. Jimmy also told me that he would come to Dewsbury, as some common friend in India had entrusted him with a parcel to be handed over to a lady doctor at Dewsbury Hospital which was just 5 minutes away from my house.

The very next day, I received Jimmy at Dewsbury railway station, and we together went to the hospital to meet a lady doctor named, Dr. Inderjit (Biku). Dr. Inderjit greeted us warmly and offered us a cup of coffee. After some conversation, I took their leave, as I had some important commitments, asking Jimmy to give me a call once he is done. But Dr. Inderjit assured me that she would drop him off at the railway station a little later and asked me not to worry about Jimmy. I did not know when Jimmy made his way back, but I called his landlady the next morning to enquire about Jimmy. The landlady told me that Jimmy had gone to Dewsbury to meet someone named Solly. I waited for him, anticipating him to join me for lunch. But Jimmy did not show up. Then I thought that he might have dropped his plan of visiting me. After a couple of days, I called his landlady again, and she replied the same, that Jimmy went to Dewsbury to see his friend, Solly Adam, and had not returned home in the past three days. I was puzzled and had no idea where Jimmy had gone.

And then suddenly, one day, while I was working in my mechanic garage, Jimmy called me, and hurried me to come to Dewsbury Hospital. When I went there with a bit of surprise, he asked me to take him to some nearby Asian store. I then took him to Batley Cash & Carry, where he began to pick some drinks, food, cups, plates, etc. Intrigued by this, I asked him of the reason. To my surprise, Jimmy revealed that he had been in love with Dr. Inderjit, and they had decided to tie the knot. The next day, Jimmy, and Dr. Inderjit, whom he affectionately calls Biku got married at the Dewsbury Registration Office. The same evening, I, along with my wife, attended the wedding party where Biku introduced us to her friends. This incident cemented the bonding between Jimmy, Biku, and our family. They were regular guests at our home for dinners and gatherings.

Another aspect of Jimmy that has intrigued me, was his concern for fitness. He once advised me, "Solly, if you want to have a long career in the game, you must exercise regularly." Jimmy introduced me to some exercises that had proven beneficial in maintaining my fitness through-out my playing years. I distinctly recall an incident in Wakefield, en-route to Wrenthorpe where we went to see to our family friend and a sister figure, Doctor Farida. It was a few miles away, and Jimmy said, "Solly! you guys go by car, and I'll join you by running." Reluctantly, I agreed. But to our surprise, Jimmy joined us on foot shortly after we arrived the spot by car. I have never seen anyone who maintains his fitness the way Jimmy does.

Jimmy played for the club from 1977 to 1981, and during his stay in England, I had arranged several bats and other sports equipment for him through *Crown Sports*. Whenever Jimmy and Biku visit England, they never fail visiting me; they are such a fantastic and loving couple, whose affection for me and my family remains strong to this day. Recently, on October 6, 2023, they visited us in Dewsbury, and we had a wonderful time reminiscing about the incredible moments in our lives.

Karsan Ghavri

I got to know Karsan Ghavri through Rahul Mankad, and when I met him, he was associated with Ramsbottom CC (1978-82) in the Lancashire League. Rahul, at that time, was residing, along with Avi Karnik and Vijay Mohan Raj (Tony), in a house near Dewsbury. On Saturday evening, after playing the league match in Lancashire, they all would join and visit my house. Karsan being a Gujarati, he would love eating our traditional cuisines, particularly Kadi Kichidi. In a short while, he became very close to me, as he not only spoke Gujarati, but was very jovial, easy-going, and kind-hearted person. Karsan played many friendly and benefit matches for my team, and he would never miss a match. However, Karsan was casual, simple, and straight forward. Despite reminding him repeatedly to bring his cricket kit to play the match, he would invariably come in his shirts and trousers, and then we would borrow the kit from others for him. Whenever I visit India, he warmly invites me to his house, and we would reminisce about the good old days we spent together in England.

Surinder Amarnath

Cricket enthusiasts often describe Surinder's talent as a gift from God, and I share that view as he was a fantastic player. I knew Surinder as my family friend, as he is the brother of Jimmy (Mohinder Amarnath). Surinder is an easy-going person with a good sense of humour; he played for Burnley CC in the Lancashire League for the 1977 season. I would attend several matches at Burnley to watch Surinder play, and during the time, I had also got acquainted to the club chairman. And then one day, during my interaction, the club chairman asked me, if Surinder is interested to be a coach to the youngsters in the club, and to train them to be competent players. When I shared the same with Surinder, he refused the offer with his humorous words, 'I wish there should be someone, who could first train me, before me assuming the position of a coach' as he, by then, was still grappling with hard English conditions. However, when Surinder took to the field for matches, he always gave his 110%

attention and did his part so well. Surinder also played in a couple of testimonial matches for my team in Yorkshire; he too has been my close associate, and this bond remains strong to this day.

Syed Kirmani

As a customary practice, Indian cricket team visited my house for dinner in 1982, during their tour to England. Being a team member of the time, Syed Kirmani, whom I later call Kiri Bhai, was also present. In the evening, when we were all casually chatting, as there was still time for dinner, Kiri Bhai asked me if there was any mosque near us for him to perform Namaaz. As there was no mosque as such in a traditional sense in our locality, I took him to Markaz, a gathering place for Muslim devotees in Dewsbury. Kiri Bhai was impressed with the atmosphere there, particularly, the system of serving food on non-commercial terms which invited individuals to pay 50p or £1 for a meal of their own volition. Kiri Bhai loved the place and its practice so much that he chose to have his dinner at Markaz, rather than at my home, to which I wholeheartedly conceded. After his prayers, followed by a quick meal, I introduced him to Hafiz Patel, the founder of Markaz.

Kiri Bhai expressed his joy for everything, particularly for the food, and for meeting Hafiz Patel. Kiri Bhai shared a close friendship with Abid Ali, who was so dear to me, and whenever I visited Lancashire to meet Abid Bhai, I would also catch up with Kiri Bhai there. Their bonding deepened further when Kiri Bhai's daughter married a son of Abid Ali. At my request, Kiri Bhai also played in an India vs. Pakistan Veterans Match at Sirsha in 2004; his son, Sadiq Kirmani also expressed his desire to play league cricket in England. Over the last 40 years, Kiri Bhai has been a great friend, and our bond continues to endure to this day.

Dilip Vengsarkar

Like many other Indian cricketers, I met Dilip Vengsarkar also for the first time during his tour to England. However, our friendship grew through common connections in Bombay. During my Bombay visit in mid-80's at Wankhede Stadium, I went for a meal with Hanumanth Singh and Vasu Paranjape, where we had discussed about English league cricket. Then, Dilip also joined us, and expressed his interest to play club cricket in England. I was surprised to see such interest in Dilip, as by then, he was already the World No.1 batsman, as per the Coopers and Lybrand rating in 1986-87, who could have easily played for any county team in England. Then I spoke to Brian Wilkinson, who was my friend and the then chairman of Hanging Heaton club, about it, and Brian too could not believe it, as Dilip by then was already a world star, and a heartthrob of English cricket fans; he was known for his sensational batting record, with his three centuries at Lords.

Then, Brian, along with Andy Hindel, outlined their budget for a professional cricketer, and yet, they were not sure whether it pleased Dilip. But Dilip was happy with the offer and signed for Hanging Heaton in Bradford League to play for the 1987 season. The cricket community of Bradford League was overjoyed to see Dilip playing in the league. Dilip, along with his wife, children, and a servant, initially stayed at my home for a couple of weeks before they moved into a house provided by the club. It was a Ramadan season, where we were all in fasting, and yet, my wife looked after day-to-day meals for Dilip and his family.

Throughout his stay in England, Dilip and his family would visit us, and we would have great family moments; we would also do net practice together. Interestingly, however, on the very first day of his practice session, just before his first match in the league, there was a young left-arm spinner in the opposite team. Pointing at that spinner, Dilip leaned at me and whispered, "Solly, if this bowler were in Bombay, I wouldn't even let him bowl in the nets." I was shocked to hear such words from Dilip, about a player who was regard as one of the best bowlers in the Bradford league.

214

But I maintained reticence, as I knew that he was speaking from his international experience, which is different from those of English leagues. And when he started playing for the league, he began to face the reality of the league cricket. Dilip had a very tough time all through the season. With great difficulty, he could score a mere 478 runs in the entire season, when the total score of an average batsman in the league was between 800 to 1000 runs in a season. Interestingly, however, Dilip lost his wicket on three occasions to the same left-arm spinner whom he had regarded unqualified to play. In this case of Dilip, it would be apt to recollect a Chinese proverb, which Abdul Azeem, my friend in Batley CC, would often say, "when you have bad times, dog bites a person sitting on a camel." Despite being the world-class batsman, Dilip had a tough time, even to face the bowlers of the local leagues in England. This was a lesson for us, particularly, for Dilip. I still have very good contact with Dilip, and when I visited India recently, he affectionately came to see me in my hotel room.

Yajurvindra Singh

Sunny Singh, as his near and dear call, hails from the erstwhile princely family of Bilkha in the Junagadh district of Saurashtra. Besides being a talented cricketer, Sunny is a wonderful person; he was a professional player in the Blackpool League. I first met Sunny when he came to visit Rahul Mankad. Gradually, we became friends, and he would frequent my house, along with Rahul; often, we would also go out together to meet friends, and to have dinners. We together played many friendly and benefit matches in the Dewsbury region. I had also organized a team and played in Sunny's benefit match, where I took all the players of our team in my 12-seater van, from Dewsbury to Blackpool; it was one of the most memorable events in our cricket journey. Sunny was a committed player, with his exceptional fielding skills, notably, he is the joint holder of two world records in fielding. During my visits to India, I stayed at his place in Bombay a few times, and I can say that Sunny is one of the best human beings I have seen in my life; his humility and kind-hearted nature leave a lasting impression on anyone who know him.

Kapil Dev

Kapil Dev, undoubtedly, is one of the best all-rounders of all times; he had played for the Nelson CC in Lancashire for the 1981 season. I knew Kapil through Mohinder Amarnath and had visited Nelson CC several times to watch Kapil's play. In Lancashire, my Indian cricket friends such as Abid Ali, Madan Lal, and Mohinder Amarnath, and others would organize parties frequently in their homes, where I was a constant invitee. It was at these gatherings that I would often meet Kapil and his wife, Romi Bhatia, and eventually we became friends. Once, when County Sports approached me for selecting eminent players who could endorse their sports equipment, I got both Imran Khan and Kapil Dev signed to use their bats and gear. When Kapil was part of Indian cricket team, and if they had any tour to England, Kapil and other Indian cricketers would come over to my house for dinner; our regular exchanges had only strengthened our friendship. The last time I met Kapil was at the IIFA Awards celebrity cricket match at Headingly in 2007, and we had a great time together. I hold great respect for Kapil Dev, as he was a serious player, and I consider him as one of the best all-rounders known for leading the Indian team towards winning the 1983 World Cup.

Dhiraj Parsana

I knew Dhiraj Parsana through Rahul Mankad when Dhiraj was playing for Cleckheaton and residing in Batley. Dhiraj would visit Rahul frequently, and I also would join them. Dhiraj, much like Karsan Ghavri, was a skilled all-rounder in those days, and he would generously share his knowledge and experience of cricket with all those who are known to him. At the same time, his calm and composed demeanor was pleasant to everyone around him. We played together in a couple of benefit matches, which was also a learning experience for me, particularly the knowledge he had shared about left-arm spin bowling has helped me a lot to improve my bowling skills as I was a left-arm-spin bowler.

Dilip Doshi

My friendship with Dilip Doshi goes far beyond the realm of cricket; he is a very intimate friend to all my family members. Our friendship grew when he was playing for Meltham CC in the Huddersfield League. During weekdays, he would drop his wife in my house before he leaves for his match, and his wife would stay in my house, all through the day, in the company of my wife and children, and then the couple would go back to their residence only after he comes back from the match. They were integral to my family, and eventually, his extended family including his mother, wife's sister, and of course his children also joined us.

Dilip and his family would often visit us even after he moved to Nottingham, owing to his joining the Nottingham County team; my wife and I would also visit his house often, and we lived a life of brotherhood. We played a few benefit-matches together in Yorkshire. Both of us being slow left-arm spin bowlers, Dilip has been a great help in improving my bowling skills. During his stint in the County, Dilip went out of his way, and tried booking the Lord's indoor facility for me, only to assist me to improve my bowling.

When I was on a holiday trip with my family in India, Dilip threw us a huge party in the Taj Hotel in Bombay and showered his love for our children. Dilip's memory is truly outstanding; he remembers every detail of every match, wickets, players, and their names, people he played with, and their opposite teams and their details; he even remembers the intricate details of who dropped catches in his bowling and when, and its resultant score. Whenever I need any information of that sort, he would always be there, ready with it on his fingertips. Dilip's son, Nayan

Doshi (Babu) also pursued his career in cricket; he has played for various county teams in England.

Shivlal Yadav

I met Shivlal Yadav through the Indian team during their tour of England in 1982, and since then, we developed a strong friendship; his younger brother, Rajesh Yadav, was also a professional cricketer. One day, Shivlal Yadav asked me if I could assist Rajesh in signing for a club in England, which I could manage with a local club in Yorkshire. Although I did not play any matches with Shivlal, his brother Rajesh played many friendly and benefit matches for me. Shivlal is known for being a very helpful person, and recently, he called me to check up on my well-being.

Roger Binny

Like several Indian cricketers, I met Roger Binny for the first time when he was on a tour to England as part of the Indian team. Roger is known for his simplicity and soft-spoken nature, and in those days, he would speak primarily in English. One day, I went to Bangalore on some work, where Brijesh Patel organized a get together with our cricket friends, who were present at that time in the city. I remember that Roger was also there in that gathering, along with Syed Kirmani, Gundappa Vishwanath, and many others; it was a great moment for all of us. Roger has an extensive knowledge about cricket, and he is a true professional in the strictest sense of the word.

Sandeep Patil

When I went to India to watch England vs. India Test series in 1981, Sunil introduced me to Sandeep, whom everyone affectionately calls

'Sandy.' Sandy was part of the Indian team, and whenever he visits England with the Indian team, or for his personal reasons, we would try to meet; Sandy also visited my house with his wife. One admirable quality I noticed about Sandeep is that I have never seen him criticize any other cricketer or speak any ill about others. Sandy is consistently cheerful, humble, and a simple person with a great sense of humour. We shared so many cheerful moments in India during Rohan Gavaskar's wedding, and whenever I travel to India, we make it a point to catch up and go out for dinner. I recall that he also worked in Bollywood movies, and so he presents us with first-hand knowledge of the films, and the world of films; his presence is not only enlightening but cheers up the entire surrounding atmosphere.

Ravi Shastri

During my trip to India to watch England vs. India test series in 1981, Ravi Shastri came to me and introduced himself, "Solly Bhai! This is Ravi Shastri, and I called you several times. But unfortunately, I did not get a chance to talk to you." He then pulled out a piece of paper from his pocket, and read out a number, 461138, which indeed was my phone number. Ravi explained that he took my contact number from Bombay cricketers, and he called me to know if there were any opportunities for him to play league cricket in England. Ever since then, we became friends, and whenever he visited England, we would meet for dinners.

I did not get a chance to sign Ravi for any league then, but he eventually evolved himself into a high rated international all-rounder, and then began to play for Glamorgan County in England. During his time with the county, he introduced us to Amrita Singh, who was a popular Bollywood actress. Ravi would often drop Amrita off at our place, and then he would go to play his county matches. Over time, Amrita and my wife developed a close friendship, a deep bonding, that was akin to sisters. Amrita was known for her friendly nature and humility. During one of my visits to India with my family, Amrita cordially invited us all to stay at her place in Lokhandwala Complex. We had a wonderful time, and she even took us to film studios where we had an opportunity to meet several Bollywood actors, including popular Bollywood comedian, Kader Khan. After retiring as cricket player, Ravi Shastri found his fortunes as coach and commentator. While his busy schedule keeps him occupied, whenever we get a chance to talk or meet, we do not pass up any opportunity.

Krishnamachari Srikanth

As Srikanth has been a close friend of Sunil Gavaskar for a long time, I met him when they both visited England. One amazing thing about Srikanth is that once you meet him, he becomes your friend in no time. His jovial nature makes him a favourite of all in the Indian team. We met on several occasions at my home, particularly during his tours in England. In 1998, I, along with my wife, happened to visit my sister-in -law in Karachi. At that time, India-A team was on its tour in Pakistan, and Srikanth was the team manager. From that team, more than 10 cricketers knew me, as I had previously signed them to various clubs in England; the India-A team included, as I remember, Rohan Gavaskar, Wasim Jaffer, Jatin Paranjape, Murali Karthik, Sairaj Bahuthule, Noel David, MSK Prasad, Nekkanti Madhukar, and Ajith Agarkar, etc. Knowing that I was in Karachi, they all wanted to see me, and so they sought the permission of Srikant. Upon hearing my name, Srikant graciously gave them the permission to see me. I too was very happy to see them all together in Pakistan and invited them to my sister-in-law's house. It was a wonderful moment, where we all had biryani together, prepared by wife and sister-in-law, as I knew that they were all fond of biryani prepared by my wife.

Ghulam Parkar

My friendship with Ghulam Bhai goes beyond cricket. I first met him when he came with the Indian team to England in 1982, and ever since then, we developed profound respect for each other. After the tour, he stayed back in England for a few months, and during this period, I suggested him to play league cricket, and make good use of his time. Ghulam Bhai loved my suggestion, and I signed him for Mirfield CC. He worked for the season so well that, the club still talks about his incredible fielding adventures. When he was busy with his matches, his wife, Lubna, would stay with us, and eventually she became a good friend of my wife.

Whenever I visit India, Ghulam Bhai makes sure of meeting me; he even came to Simlak village in Gujarat to meet us and had stayed there for a day. Ghulam Bhai and Lubna have a daughter, and she lives in England. So, their frequent visits to England to meet their daughter assures their frequent visits to my house; he just visited us recently.

Suru Nayak

When Rahul Mankad introduced me to Suru Nayak in 1979, Suru was playing for Cleckheaton. Over time, Suru has become my close friend. In those days in 70's, it was common to have evening matches in the league, with a 20-over game, which resembles IPL and T20 matches that are popular today. In 1982, Suru had an opportunity to represent India during their tour to England. I must say that no one gets bored in Suru's presence, as his art of evoking original humour and his jovial nature impresses everyone. I signed Suru to endorse County Sports, to use their equipment in the matches. In recognition of his commitment to the sport we organized a benefit match for him while he was playing in the Airedale-Wharfedale league. In that benefit match, Suru was the captain of his club team, Bilton CC, and I captained the other team comprising star players such as Sachin Tendulkar, Vinod Kambli, Sanjay Manjrekar, Sameer Dighe, and Atul Wassan. During his initial days in England, Suru also worked in my business for a short while; I have a deep respect for him as a friend.

Navjot Singh Sidhu

Sidhu was first introduced to me by Sunil Gavaskar. However, it was only after he visited my house for dinner in 1990, as part of the Indian team, that we became friends. During the tour of Indian cricket team to England in 1996, Slazengers marketing team gave me a sum of £10,000, and requested me to sign three Indian players to endorse their brand. With that money, I signed Ajay Jadeja, Sourav Ganguly, and Rahul Dravid for the contract, which I did based on recommendations from Sunil. Sidhu, who was also with the Indian team for the tour, rang me one day and asked me if I could get him any contract from Slazengers. I spoke to the management of Slazengers, and found that, unfortunately, there was no budget left to sign him. One day, Sunil visited my house, accompanied by Sidhu and Harsha Bhogle, who was a popular cricket commentator from Hyderabad. All the three of them were vegetarians, and so, my wife had prepared a special veg biryani for them. As far as I remember, that was the last time I met Sidhu, and I have not seen him thereafter.

Mohammad Azharuddin

Abdul Azeem from Hyderabad who is my close friend, and the one who played for Batley CC under my captaincy in the early 80s, had once made his prediction about Azharuddin: "Solly Bhai, there is a young fellow named Azharuddin in Hyderabad, and I foresee him to represent Indian national team soon." True to his foresight, Azharuddin made a sensational debut for India within a year, creating the world record of scoring three consecutive centuries on his debut; the record he created is still unsurpassed. Azhar and Abdul developed a strong friendship, and whenever Azhar visited England, he would come to see Abdul Azeem, who was residing in my house at that time. Eventually, Azhar also became dear to me, as well as to my family. During Azhar's tenure with Derbyshire County, we would meet up frequently, and discuss about cricket and family matters.

During his peak days, Azhar's grace and artistry in batting were truly unparalleled, as he had showcased exceptional cricketing potentials, and I would always relish watching him play live. Azhar had the extraordinary ability to gauge the situation and play shots with great precision; his mastery over shot-placement and his exceptional wristwork were unparalleled. Surprisingly, Azharuddin's bat was undoubtedly one of the lightest ones I had ever come across in professional cricket. It weighs around merely 2.4 lb, like the one used at junior level. We used to playfully tease Azhar about his bat, comparing it to a 'poppadum,' and he would take it sportingly and smile in response. However, despite its lightweight, Azhar managed to amass thousands of runs with that bat. His impeccable timing and placement stood out to be some of the best and unique qualities that I had ever witnessed in the game of cricket, as he had an amazing ability to dictate the direction of his shots between two fielders, whether it be through the covers, extra cover, mid-on, or any other area on the field. This extraordinary skill and control in Azhar, set him apart from the rest of the players; he is one of the all-time greats in the cricketing world. I had a privilege of playing against him in Sanjay Manjrekar's benefit match in 1995, and his batting during that match was a visual delight for all of us.

During one of his tours to England, Azhar was accompanied by Sangeetha Bijlani, (popular Bollywood actress); they both joined us in a family gathering at my residence, where we all shared a dinner together. Azhar also played in the Celebrity Cricket Match that was held as part of the IIFA 2007 awards in England. Since I was one of the main sponsors for the event, he used my company's (Solly Sports) gear for the match. We have mutual respect, as I call him Azhar Bhai, and he, in turn, calls me Solly Bhai. In 2018, when my wife faced a major health issue, Azhar promptly called me from Hyderabad, expressing his heartfelt sympathies for us.

Kiran More

In Saville Town, Dewsbury, where I reside, there was a person named Adam Patel who was a close friend of Kiran More. So, first I knew Kiran as a friend of Adam. However, during the tour of Indian cricket team to England in 1986, the team came to my home for dinner, in which Kiran was also a member of the team; he was also part of the Indian team which made its visit to my residence during the England tour of 1990. Over time, Kiran and I developed a friendship, and we had regular correspondence with each other. Whenever he visits England, he would meet me at my residence, or if not, would inform me at least of his visit to England, and then we would meet elsewhere. Kiran is not only a cool-headed person, but he possesses a kind and generous heart, always willing to go an extra mile to assist others. Kiran's nephew, Viraj Bhosale, is also a cricket professional. Of late, when Viraj moved to England, Kiran asked me if I can help his nephew to find a cricket club. Then, I facilitated him in signing for Treeton Cricket Club. Kiran More is still cordial with me, and calls me often to check about my well-being.

Chandrakanth Pandit

Chandrakanth, whom we all affectionately call Chandu, is truly a nice human being. In 1981, when I visited Bombay during the India vs. England test series, Ashok Mankad (Kaka) took me to a practice session where I was introduced to Nari Contractor and Hemanth Waingankar. Then, they urged me to observe four young cricketers who had potential to thrive in future, among whom Chandu was one, the other three being Lalu Rajput, Ravi Thakkar, and Raju Kulkarni. They also asked me, if I could help signing them to the clubs in English league cricket. Impressed by their talents, I signed them to various clubs for the 1982 season and had accommodated them in one of my houses on Warwick Road. Chandu played for Batley for several seasons under my captaincy and had emerged as one of the best in the Bradford league. Subsequently, Chandu played for India in 1986, and then, he had emerged as one of the most successful coaches in India, after retiring as a player. Currently, he serves as the head coach of the Kolkata Knight Riders in the IPL. I witnessed Chandu sharpening his sporting talents during his time in the Leagues, and he often acknowledged this fact that he had learnt a lot from Batley. He is not only an affectionate person, but he possesses extensive knowledge of the game as well. I have witnessed him growing from a young boy into one of the most successful coaches in India. During his recent visit to England, Chandu came to my house, along with Sean Twohig, who was our long-time friend, and a colleague in Batley CC. Together, we reminisced about our fun-filled old days at Batley.

Sanjay Manjrekar

I knew Sanjay through the Indian cricket team, and it was evident from beginning that he had a sound knowledge of cricket. During my visits to India, we had the opportunity to meet for a meal on several occasions. Sanjay once expressed his interest to playing League cricket, and then, I signed him to Stockton CC in Durham. Initially, I thought of signing Vinod Kambli to the club. But, when Vinod could not make it due to some personal reasons, I promptly signed Sanjay Manjrekar in his place. Sanjay performed very well for the club, where I recall him breaking the highest batting score record. We also played a couple of benefit-matches together, and as I recall, Sanjay played under my captaincy for a benefit match which was meant for Suru Naik. Sanjay is a kind person with a fantastic sense of humour, and he consistently lends a helping hand to the younger players. In fact, it was Sanjay who initially suggested me to take Wasim Jaffer to England. It has been a while since I last met Sanjay, but I hope to see him again in the future.

Rashid Patel

The story of Rashid Patel is quite interesting; he was introduced to me by my good old friend, Mehndi Shaikh, from Bombay in 1988. Rashid, though hailing from an economically humble family, was a talented fast bowler and a very nice gentleman. Mehndi asked me, if I could take Rashid to England to sign him for any club. Rasheed, by then, had already played one Test match and one ODI for India, and had expressed his interest to play for the leagues in England. But, owing to his language constraint in English, Rasheed was a bit hesitant about coming to England. Anyway, I signed Rashid to play for Hanging Heaton, where he had his best performance. Over time, he made England his home, and had settled down with his family. Later, his son, Zafir Patel, also emerged as First-class cricketer in England. Rashid often expressed his gratitude for the help I gave him; he visits my house in Dewsbury even to this day. Rashid Patel is a Gujarati, and when we meet, we fondly talk in Gujarati language about the life we together cherished; we often reminisce our initial struggles in England.

Salil Ankola

Salil Ankola is a true gentleman with the generosity to extend his support to those who are in need, and mentors the young enthusiasts among cricketing community. We met many times in Bombay, where he graciously picked me from the airport on several occasions. Salil shares a close friendship with Abey Kuruvilla, whom I consider akin to my own son. Whenever I connect with Abey and other cricketers, Salil is always expected. Even during his visits to England, Salil always makes it a point to come and see me. His amiable nature and kind heart makes him a truly affectionate person.

Venkatapathy Raju

My initial interaction with Venkatapathy Raju took place, when Man Singh and my friend, Vijay Mohan Raj (Tony), brought a team named Hyderabad Blues to England, to play against a few English local teams. Subsequently, Raju rose to represent the Indian cricket team, which made its visit to England in 1990. As usual, I organised dinner for the team at my residence, where I had an extended discussion with Raju, and other members of the team. We together played in a few friendly matches, and one of the memorable ones was the benefit match that was meant for Jatin Paranjape at Thornhill CC. My impression of Raju is that he is a soft-spoken guy with a great sense of humour.

Praveen Amre

Praveen is a talented player, and he once expressed his interest to play League cricket in England. I signed him for both East Bierley and Liversedge clubs on two different occasions. However, Praveen could not avail any of those opportunities, owing to some personal reasons. Had he joined any of those clubs I signed him for, it could have been beneficial for him in both his personal and professional endeavours; the English conditions, particularly, the experience of playing in Yorkshire, could have been an added advantage for him to refine his sporting talents. Unfortunately, circumstances did not favour him.

Ajay Jadeja

Ajay Jadeja was a young boy when I first met him playing for Brighouse CC, near Dewsbury. Aged around 16 or 17, he was already displaying amazing talents, and had attained very good knowledge of the game. Our friendship grew, and we even played a few friendly matches together. In 1996, shortly after the World Cup, when Slazengers company gave me a sum of £10,000 to spend it for sponsorship, I approached my dear friend Sunil for his advice. Based on Sunil's recommendation, I signed three Indian players to endorse Slazengers' bat. Among those three, the first one was Ajay, whom I signed for £6000, and the other two were, Sourav Ganguly and Rahul Dravid, whom I signed for £2000 each. Jadeja was then a promising cricketer who outshone the cricket community as a young man.

Paras Mhambray

When I first met Paras, he was playing for Skelmanthorpe CC in the Huddersfield League, and was living with other cricketers in Dewsbury. During this period, Paras was a frequent visitor to my house, and had become my family friend. Paras and I played many friendly matches together, and I have one fond memory to share about Paras. One day, he just came to watch our friendly match, and was in his casual attires. Then, there was a shortage of a player in our team, and so I asked him to join us. Since it was unexpected, I gave my spare trousers to him, and another team member had lent his T-shirt. Paras was so tall that my trousers reached just below his knees, while the T-shirt was hardly covering his waist. Paras appeared so funny, and we all laughed loud, only to be reciprocated by his laughter. I have never seen such a casual and sporting person as Paras.

He is now the bowling coach for the Indian cricket team and accompanies the team in all its tours across the continents. Whenever the Indian team is in England, he meets me, and provides us with passes to watch the match. Learning that my wife was suffering from serious illness, he came all the way from India to see her, and had extended his moral support to me, and to my family. I like his kindness, and I always seek his company. Whenever I visit Bombay, I try to meet his family members, and dine with them.

Vikram Rathour

I know Vikram as a player in the Indian cricket team, and I met him for the first time during their tour of England in 1996. But our friendship deepened only after his retirement from cricket, and when he started a shop in Leeds. He played for local teams like Birstall and Hanging Heaton, and I would often watch his games. He had a good reputation in both the clubs, and both the managements often spoke very highly about him; he used to help the youngsters in actively building their cricket careers. After he started his shop, Vikram used to visit my sports store frequently, and we would have great time together. Currently, he is working as the batting coach for the Indian cricket team, and we try to catch up whenever he is in this part of the world.

Sourav Ganguly

Like Vikram, I met Sourav Ganguly also for the first time in 1996, during the tour of Indian cricket team to England, where he too was a part of the team. But our friendship got strengthened after I signed him for Slazengers sponsorship, along with Ajay Jadeja and Rahul Dravid, based on Sunil's recommendation. Among the above three cricketers who were endorsed for Slazengers bat, it was Sourav alone who made a sensational Century at Lords with that bat, while Rahul Dravid scored 95, and interestingly, it was both the debut match in Test cricket. The contract agreement was signed in my house, for which both Sourav and Rahul Dravid visited my house, and we all had dinner afterward. Now that they together had £4000 in cash, which was a substantial amount in 1996, I asked my youngest son, Sohail, to drop them off at their hotel in Nottingham by car; it was also a safety concern to carry such a huge amount at night. It is gratifying to see how they both evolved into cricket legends in later years.

Sourav evolved himself as the captain of the Indian cricket team, and during his tenure as the captain, I met him and his team, just before their third Test match against England at Headingly (in August 2002). I remember Sourav asking me, "Solly, you've been playing in the York-shire region for many decades; do you have any suggestions that could help us?" I told Sourav that if I were in his position, I might consider playing with two spinners, having Sanjay Bangar as an opener, so that Sanjay could also contribute as a bowler. The reasons, as I explained to him, were that the Headingly pitch would generally offer support to swing bowling after a few days of play. Somehow, Sourav followed my suggestion, as he chose Sanjay Bangar as an opener. For Sanjay, it was his first Test match, and yet, it turned out to be a fantastic match. Sanjay performed admirably well, scoring 68 runs, followed by other players of the team who also displayed equally exceptional performances, leading to a flamboyant victory at Headingly, in which India had won by an innings and 46 runs. Sourav fondly recalls this victory still, whenever we get to meet.

Abey Kuruvilla

My affinity with Abey Kuruvilla moves beyond the realm of cricket; he is like a son and has been an integral part of my family. He is a gentle-man in a true sense of the term, both in and off the field of cricket. As a cricketer, he gave 110% attention to the game. I signed him to play for Cleckheaton in the 1994 season, and then we both played together for the same club in the 1995 season. During this period, Abey used to work part-time in my business, making use of his free time between Monday and Friday. Abey went on to play for Indian cricket team in 1997, and then he became a cricket administrator, after his retirement. Recently, he, along with his family, visited me to spend some time with me, and my wife; he is our true child. Whenever I go to Mumbai, Abey will not let me leave Mumbai, without visiting his home; Abey is truly a fantas-tic person, always friendly and welcoming.

Wasim Jaffer

While watching a match in Bombay, Sanjay Manjrekar pointed at a boy, and said, "Solly Bhai! look at that boy; he is going to go far (Lambi race ka ghoda); he will play test cricket for sure." It was Wasim, whom Sanjay praised him for his hard work and exceptional batting skills, and then suggested that I should take him to England. This was my first introduction to Wasim Jaffer, who, despite financial difficulties, had passionately dedicated himself to becoming a skilled cricketer. Then, I signed Wasim to Spen Victoria for the 1998 season to play in the Bradford League, and Wasim was thrilled with this opportunity.

Upon his arrival in England, Wasim stayed in my house for some time, and then he moved to a house of Malcom Hirst, the chairman of Spen Victoria. However, after staying there for a couple of days, Wasim started pleading me to take him back to my house, as he feared a pet-dog that his landlord had, and then, he stayed with us afterward. He works very hard, and his commitment and hard work was evident in his hours of practice in the nets; he even worked part-time in the local mills during weekdays. After playing for a season in Spen Victoria, I signed Wasim with Scholes CC in the Huddersfield League. It was in this League that he broke several batting records. I regard Wasim to be not only a fantastic cricketer, but a wonderful person; I was incredibly happy when he got selected for the Indian team.

Mohammad Kaif

In the early 1999, I heard Wasim Jaffer speaking words of praise about Kaif's brothers and their cricketing talents. Mohammad Kaif was a friend of Wasim, and Wasim once asked me, if I could help Kaif in finding a club to play in Yorkshire. In this regard, Wasim, by then, had already consulted a professional agent, who works for signing overseas cricketers to the clubs in England. The agent started his process of signing Kaif to Hartshead Moore club, where I had already signed another player for the 1999 season. So, owing to the rule that does not permit a club signing two overseas players at once in a season, Kaif had to unfortunately land up in England without having a club to play for; he was misled by the agent, who had no clue about the new rules of club signings.

Understanding his predicament, I immediately contacted several clubs in the Bradford League, and secured a deal for Mohammad Kaif with Lightcliffe Club for the 1999 season. Interestingly, however, the club came forward to offer him with £30 per match, surpassing all their budgetary constraints for signing a professional cricketer. And for that to happen, some players even stepped in to contribute £5 each to make it to £30 for Kaif. As it was the best offer available at that moment, I suggested Kaif to accept it, and Kaif too had no other way than accepting it, as he had already landed in England. Kaif had a fantastic season with Lightcliffe CC, where he scored total of 1,139 runs for the season, with an average of 81.35 runs per match.

Kaif is a hardworking and intelligent cricketer; he would also work at my Pick N Pay supermarket, and local Pizza takeaway shop during his free time. He, then, captained the India U-19 team, and then went on to play for Indian National team. The club management still remembers his contributions to the club and appreciates his commitment and talent. In 2009, a charity event was organised by the Lightcliffe club. Then, this issue of Kaif signing contract with Lightcliffe club had once again resurfaced in the media. A popular daily from Bradford, 'The Telegraph and Argus,' recalled this incident, where six members had chipped in £5 each to pay £30 per match for Kaif. In this regard, the media lauded the benevolence of the club, and the integrity of its members; the media, then, had stated in a light-hearted manner that, the contract kept Kaif "above the poverty line" for that season. I met him a couple of years ago, and he was pleased to see me after a long time.

Sairaj Bahuthule

In my view, Sairaj emerged as one of the most gifted all-rounders and an outstanding fielder during the mid-90s. When I signed him for the 1994 season at Spen Victoria in Bradford League, I publicly hailed him as 'Young Gary Sobers' in multiple media interviews in Yorkshire. His stellar performances with both bat and ball for that season only reinforced my admiration for his talent. This period coincided with the presence of many Bombay cricketers such as Abey Kuruvilla, Jatin Paranjape, Paras Mhambray, Amol Mazumdar, and Nilesh Kulkarni in the Bradford League. They were regular guests at my house for dinners, and during this time, Sairaj became my close associate. He formed strong bonds with many of my family members, including my younger brother Younus and his wife, Rukhsana. We both played for Spen Victoria for 1994 season, and we also played a few benefit-matches together. Despite incurring a tragic car accident during his early days in 1990, Sairaj consistently pursued his cricketing career; he excelled in his game and rose to the greater hights to represent Indian cricket team; after his retirement, he served as the Spin Bowling Coach for the Indian team. His journey, both as a talented cricketer, as well as a successful coach, serves as an inspiration for aspiring young cricketers. Sairaj's passionate commitment to nurturing young talents is an asset to the cricketing fraternity. I feel glad that Sairaj did a lot for the game.

1.B. One Day International (ODI) Cricketers of India:

Below are a few of the ODI cricketers of India with whom I cherished a lasting friendship.

Atul Bedade

Knowing his potential in cricket, I signed Atul for a club. But unfortunately, he could not avail it. Then, again I managed to secure a contract for him in Golcar CC in the Huddersfield League, where he had an impressive performance throughout the season. I recall that during his stint at Golcar, he received wide acclaim for his aggressive batting talents. Sachin Tendulkar also once lauded Atul that he had the capability to send the ball out of the ground.

Prashanth Vaidya

I signed Prashant for Heckmondwike CC to play in the Central Yorkshire League. He proved to be a skilled bowler, with a good ability to bat in the lower order. During his tenure in Yorkshire, we both played in several League and friendly matches together.

Noel David

I signed Noel for Cleckheaton to play in the Bradford League; he hails from Hyderabad. Besides being an adept spin bowler, Noel was also an exceptional fielder. It is noteworthy to mention here that, during their stint in Bradford League, both Noel and VVS Laxman were regular visitors to my house.

Jatin Paranjape

I signed him first for Thornhill, and then for Yorkshire Bank. Jatin is not only a skilful player, but a brilliant strategist who has a potential to be a team leader. He has a profound understanding of pitch conditions, and other relevant factors. I also took part in organizing and playing a benefit match for him at Thornhill; I still cherish this match, because, in that match, my dearest friend Sunil Gavaskar played under my captaincy.

Amay Khurasiya

I recruited Amay to the Broad Okay Cricket Club, which play in the Huddersfield League. In those days, Amay was widely known powerful batsman, having every ideal to play in the One Day format. I also took Amay Khurasiya to Guernsey Island to play in Graham Thorpe's benefit match.

Jacob Martin

I signed Jacob for Hartshead Moor to play in the Bradford League. Jacob was known for his brilliant batting skills and impeccable technique; he did an amazing feat by scoring 11 consecutive half-centuries in his first 11 matches for the club in 1997. This outstanding record remains unconquered still in the Bradford League. It was this exceptional form that he earned in the League cricket that paved a sure way for him to be part of One Day Internationals with the Indian team.

Rohan Gavaskar

Rohan is my personal favourite; he is son of my dearest friend and my brother figure, Sunil Gavaskar. I signed Rohan for Spen Victoria in 1993 to play in Bradford League. Rohan was supremely talented and had the calibre to deliver impressive performances. On one occasion, I had an opportunity to meet his grandfather, Manohar Gavaskar (father of Sunil) in Bombay, and sought his opinion on Rohan's talent. Then he replied, "Rohan possessed even more talent than his son, Sunil; the only distinction is Sunil's superior dedication and focus, which Rohan sometimes lacks, in all his endeavours." I had the pleasure of attending Rohan's wedding in Bombay, and he has been a close friend to all my children and our family.

1. C. First-Class Cricketers of India:

In addition to Test and ODI players, I also managed to sign nearly 100 first-class cricketers from India to various clubs in English leagues. Some of these cricketers have been my close friends, and they include:

Vijay Mohan Raj

Vijay, also known as Tony, originally hails from Bombay. But he has attained Hyderabad nativity, by his volition to be a professional cricketer. He represented Hyderabad Ranji Team for over ten years, and during which, he played more than 50 first-class matches; he then went on to assume the responsibilities in the administration of cricket, later as a coach, and then eventually, he settled in Hyderabad. Following his retirement, he developed a deep passion for identifying young talents in cricket and had nurtured them for their growth.

Our friendship extends far beyond the realm of cricket, as Vijay and his wife Farida have become nothing short of an extended family to us. In fact, my introduction to Vijay happened through Rahul Mankad, when Rahul signed Vijay for Cleckheaton CC in the late '70s. Vijay displays calm and friendly demeanour and has dedicated his life to the cricket field. I used to refer to him as 'Little Geoffrey Boycott,' as his batting prowess, and his exceptional defensive skills were on par with those of Geoff Boycott's renowned excellence. Subsequently, I signed Vijay for several clubs in the Huddersfield and Bradford Leagues. I truly wished that Vijay should have represented Indian team, as his batting skills were on par with those of any Test cricketer of the world.

When Vijay was playing League cricket in England, we would meet almost every day. Vijay's wife, Farida Raj, too would join us in my house, and they were a very good couple. Farida had a genuine respect for my wife, and she would extend her warmth to my wife, by affectionately calling her 'Maryam Bhabi.' Farida is also a renowned writer, having authored a book, *Breaking Through*, in 2010; the book got translated into several Indian languages. Farida authored another book, *Unbreakable Spirit*, which was published recently in February 2024. She is a frequent contributor to journals and newspapers; her articles address the problems concerning, 'the children with differential abilities, and learning difficulties.' The couple also owns a travel business called Sameera Travels & Tours in Secunderabad, India. They are like my family members, and I hold great respect for both. Whenever Vijay visits England, he ensures to come to Dewsbury, to spend time with me and my family.

Shishir Hattangadi

I knew Shishir through our mutual cricket friends in Bombay; I call him Shish. Shishir played 60 first-class matches for the Bombay team, and I sincerely believe that he had the potential to represent Indian team in international cricket. Unfortunately, however, it did not happen. I signed him to play for Hartshead Moor CC, where he performed exceptionally well and scored a lot of runs. During his brief stint in England, it was our daily routine to catch up with Shish, and we often practiced cricket together at Batley. Besides cricketing talents, he is endowed with a wealth of knowledge on various issues in the world, and I would say he is an intellectual and knowledgeable guy. After retiring from playing cricket, Shish served as the Head of Cricket for both the Deccan Chargers, and the Mumbai Indian teams in the IPL.

Ravi Thakkar

Ravi played for Bombay and Assam teams for several years, serving as bowler. In 1982, when Ravi, along with Chandrakanth Pandit, Raju Kulkarni, and Lalchand Rajput, arrived in England to play club cricket, they all used to stay together in the same house. Then, we would frequently gather throughout the week. I believed that Ravi was a highly skilled left-arm spinner with a potential to play for India. I signed Ravi for Hartshead Moor club in the Bradford League, where he showcased an amazing bowling performance. Whenever Ravi visits England, we would ensure to meet up and would have a great time together.

Iqbal (Badruddin) Khan

The journey of Iqbal is undeniably captivating; his life is an inspiration for all. During one of my visits to Bombay, Iqbal, somehow, obtained my contact number, and came on his motor bike to meet me in my hotel room. Thereafter, he continued visiting me every single day, as long as I stayed in Bombay. By then, Iqbal was already playing for Bombay Ranji team, and had expressed his interest to play in English League cricket. Though he hails from a humble family, Iqbal, with his commendable batting skills and diligent work ethic, had left a strong impression on me.

I signed him for Mirfield CC, where he quickly became a significant member of the team and delivered impressive performances. Following his stint at Mirfield, he continued to showcase his talents in successful spells at Liversedge and East Bierley. With this, Iqbal Khan had undoubtedly become a well-known figure in the Bradford League. Besides a brilliant player, he is a responsible person. I also arranged his marriage to a daughter of one of my friends, who was a medical doctor. Iqbal made England his home, and lives happily with his wife and children; Iqbal visits me sometimes and expresses his respect for me for the help he received during his initial struggling days.

Amol Mazumdar

Amol was a brilliant cricketer, with an outstanding bating skill. I genuinely believed that Amol had a potential to play for Indian team. In 1995, I signed Amol for Lidget Green CC, and then for Windhill CC to play in the Bradford League, where he had showcased brilliant performances for both clubs. During that period, I also signed a few cricketers from Bombay to play in the Bradford League. Since all these players were in the same League, we all would often gather when we had free time and would share our thoughts and experiences; we would also share our meals during the matches. I personally admired Amol's style of play, and we played a couple of matches together.

Suresh Shetty

Suresh is truly a gem of a person, a gentleman; he was a former Bombay Ranji player. I brought him on board for Cleckheaton CC, and then for Lidget Green club to play in the Bradford League. Suresh was a bowling all-rounder. He is a humble man with a genteel manner. Even in situations where the batsman is clearly LBW out from his bowling, often he refrains from making an appeal; he leaves it to the rest of his team members to make an appeal. Suresh was not earning good money in cricket those days. So, I suggested he would work at my petrol station during his free time. During his tenure in Yorkshire, we played many matches together. Suresh is genuinely a nice person.

Tushar Arothe

Tushar is a brilliant cricketer, who played under my captaincy at Spen Victoria in the Bradford League. Personally, I believe that Tushar's cricketing skills are no less than any international cricketer, and I truly wished that he had an opportunity to represent Indian team. His abilities make him well-suited for both Test and ODI formats, but regrettably, none of the chances knocked his door. Tushar remains to be an amiable person, and our friendship continues till today. We meet up whenever time permits and have a great time together. I am glad to see his son, Rishi Arothe, is also now making strides in First-class cricket; Rishi represents Baroda team.

Sarfaraz Khan

I knew Sarfaraz's father, Naushad Khan, for a long time, and he too was a first-class cricketer from Bombay. When Sarfaraz was just 15 years old, I first signed him for the Hull CC to play in the Solly Sports Yorkshire

Premier League in 2012; the League was sponsored by my own sports company, Solly Sports. Though he was still young, Sarfaraz exhibited outstanding performance in the Yorkshire Premier League. Later, I signed him to the 'Shenley Village Cricket Club' on the London side. He would also play in Sunday League matches for me in Yorkshire, whenever his schedule allowed.

When I asked about Sarfaraz, the club management praised his batting proficiency; they foresaw him to be a future star for India. Though I have not got a chance to see him play much, I know for the fact that, Sarfaraz always managed to score century in every match he played except in a few matches. His consistent score aggregate showcases not only his massive talent, but his unsatiable urge for runs. Naushad Khan, his father, frequently calls me from India, and we discuss about Sarfaraz's performances. Sarfaraz's younger brother, Musheer Khan, also played a few matches in England when he was just 14 years; he then stepped into first-class cricket, representing Mumbai. Despite his young age, Musheer earned respect of everyone for his impressive bowling and batting skills.

2. My Memories of Cricketers from Pakistan

As if it was a basic human impulse, cricket was deeply entrenched into my body and soul; I began craving for cricket the way one does for basic needs like food and water. Unaware of its reasons, I have always been an ardent cricket enthusiast since my childhood. We would wake up along with the waking sun, and plunge into plains in the empty places of our locality to begin playing; we would be lost in cricket, playing endlessly for hours, not even realising our thirst and hunger; I would come to my senses, only when I hear a shout from my mother calling me loud, "Solly! Come home and eat." Hearing my mother's call, I would run home, and unmindfully gulp some food, only to rush back to play; we would go on playing till the dusk, when we could not even see the ball.

Though it started at my ancestral home in a tiny village of Simlak, which is in the state of Gujarat in India, I cricketing talents got nurtured only at the Natal Colony of Karachi in Pakistan. Eventually, I became part of the youth team of Natal colony, while I was still a schoolboy. In Natal colony, I played with several youth, and passionate cricketers like Mahmood Darsot, who later married my mother's own sister Rukiya aunty, whom we affectionately call Poppy Khala (aunty). Our cricketing interest intensified, with the tour of West-Indies team to Pakistan in 1959, where I had an opportunity to watch the Test match between the teams of Pakistan and West-Indies at the National Stadium in Karachi. Ever since then, I continued playing cricket with ever increased vigour, till I had to leave for England in October 1963.

After an initial attempt to make my living in England for a couple of years, I again began to rekindle my cricketing spirit, and in 1965, I joined Batley Muslim CC. And in 1967, when the Pakistan cricket team toured in England, I had already started playing League cricket in Yorkshire. So, I watched the Test series between the teams of England and Pakistan with great enthusiasm, and with an intent to study high standard cricket. During this match, I met and spoke to some of the cricketers of Pakistan, though it had not paved any foundation for my friendship with any of the cricketers I met there.

However, my profound connection with the cricketers of Pakistan truly commenced in 1971, when I fortunately met Imran Khan during a test match at Headingly; the team, including Asif Masood, Sadiq Mohammad, Mushtaq Mohammad, Majid Khan, etc., along with Imran, graced my house for dinner. And by late'70s when I began assisting Asian cricketers secure club contracts in England, I was widely known in the cricket circles of India and Pakistan. Ever since then, I have had a strong friendship with many of the Pakistani cricketers, and my home became a haven for cricketers from Pakistan and India; they would visit my home regularly, and many of whom went onto become my family friends.

I have had the privilege of acquainting myself with most Pakistani cricketers who graced the field from 1960s to 2015. I either have a personal connection with these cricketers or had aided them in signing club contracts in England. There are some cricketers whom I helped in securing employment in England, and yet others were facilitated by me in procuring sponsorships from various sports companies to endorse their brand. I also organised and played benefit matches for some cricketers, and some were my colleagues in different Leagues.

They include, Test cricketers like, Hanif Mohammad, Shujauddin, Saeed Ahmad, Nasim-ul-Ghani, Mushtaq Mohammad, Shafqat Rana, Asif Iqbal, Majid Jahangir Khan, Salahuddin, Wasim Bari, Aftab Gul, Asif Masood, Sadiq Mohammad, Sarfaraz Nawaz, Zaheer Abbas, Aftab Baloch, Imran Khan, Talat Ali, Waseem Raja, Shafiq Ahmad, Agha Zahid, Sikander Bakht, Iqbal Qasim, Mudassar Nazar, Javed Miandad, Haroon Rasheed, Abdul Qadir, Mohsin Khan, Ehteshamuddin, Anwar Khan, Taslim Arif, Ijaz Faqih, Mansoor Akhtar, Tauseef Ahmed, Rizwan-uz-Zaman, Tahir Naqqash, Jalal-ud-din, Rashid Khan, Saleem Yousuf, Saleem Malik, Azeem Hafeez, Qasim Umar, Shoaib Mohammad, Anil Dalpat, Manzoor Elahi, Rameez Raja, Wasim Akram, Zulqarnain, Zakir Khan, Saleem Jaffar, Asif Mujtaba, Ijaz Ahmed, Aqib Javed, Waqar Younis, Naved Anjum, Akram Raza, Shahid Mahboob, Saeed Anwar, Mushtaq Ahmed, Moin Khan, Nadeem Ghauri, Masood Anwar, Ata-Ur-Rehman, Rashid Latif, Inzamam-ul-Haq, Basit Ali, Nadeem Khan, Saleem Elahi, Saqlain Mushtaq, Azam Khan, Hasan Raza, Zahoor Elahi, Azhar Mahmood, , Shahid Afridi, Mohammad Yousuf, Imran Nazir, Abdul Razzaq, Younis Khan, Faisal Iqbal, Taufeeq Umar, Kamran Akmal, Shabbir Ahmed, Umar Gul, Naved-ul-Hasan, Umar Akmal, Saeed Ajmal, Khurram Manzoor, Sarfaraz Ahmed, Zulqarnain Haider, Yasir Shah, Imran Khan Junior and many more.

The list of the cricketers I know, in fact, is so exhaustive, and given my aging conditions, it is difficult for me to recall all those whom I met in my life; hope they will forgive me, if there is any lapse in my memory. Here, I will try to recollect the best of my experiences with some of these cricketers from Pakistan.

2. A. Test Cricketers of Pakistan:

Hanif Mohammad

What an iconic cricketer Hanif Bhai was! As per the note of obituary on him, published in a website, ESPNcricinfo, which has been exclusive to covering cricket news, Hanif Bhai was rightly and originally hailed as the 'Little Master,' a title which was popularised when it was referred to later day luminaries like, Sunil Gavaskar, and then again to Sachin Tendulkar. My admiration for Hanif Bhai dates to my childhood; I regarded him as one of the greatest batsmen who had represented Pakistan, and he remains to be my hero in cricketing world.

When I first met Hanif Bhai, I was immediately awe struck, and then hearing his pleasing words in Gujarati language, I slowly came to my senses. Eventually, Hanif Bhai began to transform from being my dream hero to a dear friend; our mutual Gujarati heritage helped solidifying our bond. The cricketing spirits runs deep into Hanif Bhai's family, as all his brothers, Wazir, Mushtaq, Sadiq, and Raees, had made their marks of distinction in professional cricket. I also have had the pleasure of meeting his son, Shoaib Mohammad, on several occasions, both in Pakistan and England, and had the privilege of getting to know most of his family members in person; I hold a special attachment to Hanif Bhai, and his family.

Saeed Ahmad

Saeed Bhai was undoubtedly an extraordinary cricketer. He stood out as one of the finest Pakistani batsmen who graced the game with his elegant batting talents. However, our genuine friendship bloomed only after his retirement from cricket, and when he turned towards the path of religion and spirituality. Saeed Bhai would make regular visits to the Markaz in Dewsbury, and I had a distinct honour to sit with him during his visits. Eventually, he came to be a regular presence in my home, where we would share many happy moments together; we would relish meals and would engage in so many insightful discussions on various topics, including cricket. I was always fond of seeing him play, and so, whenever he would visit my home, I would give him a bat and take him to our backyard to play few of my balls. During my trip to Lahore in 1984, Saeed Bhai extended a warm invitation to his residence. I feel that every moment I spent with him was a genuine honour, and an invaluable lesson of my life, as our conversations spanned across a wide array of topics.

Mushtaq Mohammad

Mushtaq Bhai is the younger brother of legendary cricketer, Hanif Mohammad, and the youngest Test cricketer ever in international cricket history, as he was hardly 15 years when he was selected for Pakistan team. I first saw him at the National Stadium, Karachi, which was his debut series against West Indies team in 1959. However, our friendship began to take its roots when Mushtaq Bhai, along with his team, visited my residence in England for dinner in 1971, and eventually, we became good friends. Mushtaq also played for 'Northamptonshire' in England, and during that period, Bishan Singh Bedi from India, and Sarfraz Nawaz from Pakistan were also part of the same county team. When they had any matches in Yorkshire, all the three of them would come to my home, and then, we would have a great time talking and dining together. Mushtaq Bhai was a frequent visitor to my home, and our friendship lasts even to this day. Whenever I travel to Karachi, I also would meet him without fail.

Majid Jahangir Khan

Majid Bhai was formerly a brilliant cricketer, and the captain of the Pakistan national team. During his cricketing career, that spanned across 18 years, he had amassed over 27,000 runs in First-class cricket. What sets him apart is not just his cricketing talents, but his extraordinary humility, intellect, and down-to-earth nature. Majid Bhai is a repository of knowledge with impressive educational credentials, as he is a graduate from Cambridge University; he also captained his university cricket team. Added to his cricketing charisma, he also had a striking physical appearance, for which the British press had awarded him the moniker of 'Majestic Khan.'

Majid Bhai is a cousin of another cricket legend, Imran Khan. In fact, I knew Majid Bhai through Imran Bhai, when the Pakistan team visited my home during its tour to England in 1971. However, my friendship with Majid Bhai grew stronger over years, as he is a close friend of Iqbal Qasim, who is more of a younger brother to me, than a friend. I feel honoured to have Majid Bhai as my friend, and it would be a learning experience to just be with him and converse with him.

Asif Masood

Asif Masood has been my dear friend since our first meeting at my home in 1971; he too was part of the Pakistani team which visited my home for dinner, along with his other colleagues, Imran Khan, Sadiq Mohammad, Mushtaq Mohammad and Majid Khan, etc. However, we became intimate only after he retired from cricket and began working with PIA (Pakistan International Airlines). When he joined PIA, he moved to England, making his residence at Lancashire, which is near my home in Dewsbury. This shifting of his residence brought us much closer to each other, and we are in a regular contact.

Sadiq Mohammad

Sadiq Bhai is the younger brother of Hanif Mohammad and Mushtaq Mohammad. He too was part of the Pakistani team which visited my home during their tour to England in 1971. Sadiq Bhai was also associated with county cricket in England for some time; he played for Gloucestershire and Essex counties. Whenever he had any matches in Yorkshire, we would meet up at my house, and would have a nice time together; he speaks Gujarati language, and our common Gujarati descent also might have helped us strengthen our bond.

Sarfraz Nawaz

Sarfraz was an outstanding bowler known for his ability of reverse-swinging the ball. I knew Sarfraz through our common friend, Malik Rab Nawaz, who is also a cricket enthusiast and a businessman who owned the famous 'Sangeet & Naz' cinema in Bradford. During the 1970s, when I was the captain of the Cross-Bank Muslim team, Sarfraz and Malik would come to watch our matches in the Dewsbury District League. Then, Malik Rab Nawaz would often invite me for a match against their team, when Sarfraz was in Bradford. Sarfraz, by then, had already made his debut into international cricket. Then I would gladly form a team with the top players of our league and would play. In those matches, Sarfraz would lead a team that Malik Nawaz represented, while I would captain the Dewsbury and District League Team. However, our League cricket is quite different from Test cricket; having a huge swing in his bowling, Sarfraz would often be a challenge to the wicketkeeper, rather than to the batsman. Sarfraz would usually bowl only 5-6 overs in a match, and then our strategy was to protect our wickets during his bowling, so that we can hit the other bowlers. In this way, we played five matches against their team in total, and I did not remember us losing even a single match against them.

During these matches, I had cherished a few cheerful moments with Sarfraz. Sarfraz is very tall, and I am short. During tossing, he could not bend down to verify whether it was a head or tail, and he would depend entirely on me for the results. I, on the other hand, would lie to him to pull his legs, and only later would I tell him the truth; we would both laugh and move forward to play the match. However, that never hindered our sporting spirit, and we played the game with utmost seriousness. Meanwhile, we became very close friends; he would visit my house often, and we would discuss cricket, and dine together. Sarfraz was a committed cricketer who was an asset to his team.

Zaheer Abbas

Zaheer Bhai was one of the finest batsmen known for his elegance in his style of batting. He played for Gloucestershire County from 1972 to 1985, and during his tenure, Sadiq Mohammad was also part of the same team. I was already acquainted with Sadiq Bhai through his brother Mushtaq Mohammad. Whenever their team had any matches in the in the Yorkshire region, Zaheer Bhai would visit my house, along with Sadiq Bhai, and the three of us would have a great time talking till late night. I would also watch their matches and would not miss Zaheer Bhai's batting. Our friendship grew over time, and whenever I visited Karachi, he would meet me up there. He is very kind and is always ready to extend his helping hand in need. I recall a moment when there was some issue in the Karachi airport, on my way back to England. It was some formal issue, and Zaheer Bhai knows some authorities in the airport. Then, he took all the burden of waking up early the next morning, picked me up from the hotel, and had settled all the formalities concerned to help me take me off safely to England.

Waseem Raja

Waseem Raja was one of the most stylish and energetic cricketers ever played for the Pakistani team. While describing Waseem's exceptional talents, Imran Khan once praised him as a player with maturity beyond his age. True to his words, everyone who had watched his graceful batting echoed this feeling. Our friendship began in 1974 at Leeds, during the tour of the Pakistani team to England. Then one day (in 1975), Waseem Raja asked me if I could help him finding a club in England, and coincidentally, the Chairman of Ramsbottom's cricket club had also contacted me around the same time for an all-rounder for their team. So, I immediately signed Waseem Raja to Ramsbottom, where he performed very well, and had earned a good name in the Lancashire League. I used to watch his matches, and he would visit me at my residence in Dewsbury. Wasim was not just a great cricketer, but a compassionate person.

Shafiq Ahmed

Known as Shafiq Papa among our friends, Shafiq Ahmed was a prolific opening batsman for Pakistan team, with a track record of amassing 20,000 runs to his credit in domestic cricket. I remember him playing for Saaki League in the Lancashire region on Sundays, in addition to his regular Saturday matches in the Lancashire Cricket League; Saaki is the first Asian cricket League in England, as far as I remember. When I was playing in the Dewsbury District League, once we played against Saaki League team which Shafiq Papa represented. We also played together in several friendly matches, and eventually we got to know each other well. Shafiq Papa was not only a talented batsman, but the one who give a great value to friendship. Interestingly, it was through Shafiq Papa I got to know Iqbal Qasim. I used to visit Manchester to see Shafiq Papa, who then was living with other Pakistani cricketers like Taslim Arif, Abdul Rakib, including Iqbal Qasim. Subsequently, our friendship bloomed.

Mudassar Nazar

I first met Mudassar at Headingly in Leeds during the tour of the Pakistani team to England in 1978. However, our friendship blossomed, only after he began actively engaged in playing club cricket in the Lancashire League. During his stint in the League, we would often meet up, mostly at my home, and would have a great time together. I signed Mudassar for County Sports, which would deliver its cricket equipment at my house from where Mudassar would often collect his kit. Mudassar shares a close bond with his batting partner, Mohsin Khan. Mohsin Khan invited me to play for his benefit match in Lancashire, that had various international cricket stars, including Mudassar.

Haroon Rasheed

Along with other members of the Pakistani cricket team, I met Haroon at Headingly in Leeds, during the tour of their team to England in 1978. Since Haroon and Iqbal Qasim were already good friends by then, it became natural for me to be friends with Haroon. Then, Haroon played in the Bradford League for Queensbury in 1978, and thereafter for Undercliffe Cricket Club. When he was in Undercliffe, I would often visit him to watch him play. Eventually, we also played in several benefit matches together, which had strengthened our friendship further. After retiring from active cricket, Haroon had settled down as a coach and cricket administrator in Pakistan. Whenever I visit Pakistan, we would meet up and recall our good old days.

Mohsin Khan

Mohsin Khan was a former opening batsman for the Pakistan team; he had very handsome looks, which had opened ways for him to make his appearance in Bollywood movies as well. During 1980s, I learnt that Mohsin was playing for Todmorden CC in the Lancashire league and went to watch his match. Then one day, I asked Mohsin if he would be willing to be part of a friendly match in Dewsbury, featuring Asian XI vs League XI. Mohsin agreed to play and had joined us for the match. Since then, our friendship grew, and whenever we had a match scheduled on Sundays, the presence of Mohsin was certain and he would play for my team. Mohsin also invited me to play in his benefit match at Todmorden, involving star cricketers like Clive Lloyd, David Hookes, Mudassar Nassar, Salim Malik, Ramiz Raja, and Martin Crowe.

Friendship means a lot to Mohsin; whenever he travels to Pakistan, he would carry all the things which I wanted delivered to my father-in-law in Karachi. One day, Mohsin informed me over phone that he wanted to meet me at my home, to introduce his friend to me. To our astonishment, it was none other than a renowned Bollywood actress, Reena Roy. All my family members were delighted to see a famous actress visiting our home, and we gave warm welcome to Reena. Despite being a celebrity, Reena was very friendly with us, and quickly became close to all our family members. We also had a pleasant dinner together, and during dinner, Mohsin left us all in another surprise that they were planning to get married. As intended, they got married on August 2, 1983, and took a house in Todmorden which is just an hour drive from our home. The couple would visit us regularly, and eventually they became integral to my family.

Mohsin often would drop Reena Roy at our house in the morning, and my wife and I would take her back to their place in the evening. Reena would spend the entire day chatting with my mom and wife; her mother and siblings also visited our house several times. Reena used to love Mohsin so much, and she would do everything that Mohsin likes. One day, Reena informed me that they bought a house in Todmorden and sought for my assistance in finding a Muslim Imam who can perform a proper ritual for the house warming ceremony. I then took a Hafiz and Imams from Markaz in Dewsbury to conduct a "Quran Khani" in their new house, and to perform necessary rituals. Reena was delighted the way everything went, and they happily moved into their new home. I also extended my assistance to Mohsin and Reena for a special Music Concert that they organised in Bradford. The event featured many Bollywood stars from India, including Barkha Roy, Anju Roy (Reena's sisters), Raja Roy (her brother), Shailendra Singh (a renowned Bollywood singer), Jayshree Talpade (a popular dancer), and many others; of course, all my family members also attended the event, and they all loved it so much.

Regrettably, Mohsin and Reena got divorced later. However, our friendship with them remains unchanged to this day; we still have a regular correspondence and visit each other. In 2018, during our holiday to India, Reena welcomed us with the same warmth that she had shown us when she was in Todmorden; we had a great time talking to Reena.

Ehteshamuddin

Ehteshamuddin was selected for the Pakistani national team, while he was playing League cricket in England in 1979. I met him through Iqbal Qasim, and eventually we became friends. Ehteshamuddin was regarded as one of the best swing bowlers from Pakistan. He also represented a local team, National Bank of Pakistan (NBP), and then was recruited to be an employee of the bank. Whenever I go to Lahore to procure cricket equipment for my company, Solly Sports, Ehteshamuddin would join me in the airport to pick me up and would spend his valuable time for me. From Lahore, Dr. Jameel would accompany me to Sialkot, from where, I would procure the equipment for my business. Both Ehteshamuddin and Dr. Jameel are good friends of Iqbal, and they both were employees in the same bank, National Bank of Pakistan. They extend all this assistance to me not merely as a sign of respect for me, but mainly due to Iqbal and his love for me. Ehteshamuddin has a very kind heart and helps people in need. I regret to hear that his health condition has been deteriorating recently and I wish him a speedy recovery.

Anwar Khan

Anwar Khan played only one test match for Pakistan national team in his career which was against New Zealand in 1979; he is a talented cricketer. I got to know him through Iqbal Qasim, during my visit to Pakistan, as he was a colleague of Iqbal in the National Bank of Pakistan. A little later, he also played club cricket in the Lancashire League, and during the time, we even played a few friendly matches together in Yorkshire.

Anwar Khan is a fun-loving person, who always likes to create a happy and cheerful atmosphere around him; he even evokes fun in difficult times. One day he called me up and asked me if I can help secure a club for him to play, and accordingly I signed him with Staincliffe CC for £40 per match to play in the Central Yorkshire League (CYL). Though he could not get his expected honorarium of £70 per match, he gave his consent to play, by mocking at his own self, and said light heartedly, 'beggars can't be choosers.' During his free time, Anwar would join me at my home, would spend his moments with my family. Later, Anwar settled down in America, though we continue keeping regular contact.

Taslim Arif

In Manchester, there was a house owned by a passionate cricket fan who used to host many cricketers from Pakistan. I knew the owner of the house well, and it was in that house that I met several cricketers including, Taslim Arif. Taslim Bhai, at that moment, was staying along with Shafiq Papa and Iqbal Qasim. Though his international career was relatively short-lived, Taslim Bhai was a talented wicketkeeper and a brilliant batsman with a Test average of 62 runs; he was also known for his remarkable double century against Australia in 1980. I wish he should have played many more matches.

Taslim Bhai was a true gentleman with integrity in his thoughts and deeds; he played a few matches with me in Yorkshire, and whenever I invited him for any friendly matches, he would be certain to join. Unfortunately, he lived a short life and died of lung infection in 2008 at the age of 53.

Mansoor Akhtar

Mansoor was a quiet player, but brilliant in his performances. I met him for the first time in Karachi, and then in England. By then, Mansoor was already a Test player with a strong ability to read English wickets. When he came to England, he asked me to help him find a club to play. Then I was associated with Chickenley Cricket Club, and so I signed him up there. In 1988, I also signed him for Spen Victoria when Chris Pickles was the captain. The following year, when I assumed the captaincy for Spen, I again signed him to play in the Bradford League. During this entire period when he was playing for different clubs in England, along with me, I never saw Mansoor joining us in our practice sessions. However, it has always been a huge surprise for us that, he would maintain a consistency in his scoring of runs in all the matches he played in, having a very good average in total.

After every match, he would visit my house, where we would have dinners together, and discuss various issues, primarily cricket. Mansoor was friendly with all his teammates, irrespective of their age, and was always ready to extend his assistance to all the members of his team, particularly, to his junior players. He was not only a great help for me, to improve my bowling, but was also important in our team's success. He dislikes losing any match, and always works very hard to win the match till its last minute; he keeps alive his competitive spirit, and that would help the team in winning the matches.

Rizwan-uz-Zaman

Rizwan was an opening batsman for the Pakistan team, and was a highly successful cricketer, who had amassed more than 14,000 runs in first-class cricket. When I first met him in Pakistan, he told me that he was aware of my assistance to the Pakistani cricketers to secure club contracts in England. And then, Rizwan called me one day, and sought for my help to find a club for him, and accordingly, I signed him for the Yorkshire Bank team. But the club did not provide any accommodation for him. So, Rizwan stayed in one of my houses in Dewsbury, along with another Pakistani cricketer, Rashid Khan. During the time, we three would meet up frequently, and practice and discuss cricket. Rizwan played very well for the Yorkshire Bank team and was credited for scoring loads of runs.

Rashid Khan

When Rashid Khan was introduced to me by Iqbal Qasim, Rashid had already signed up, through an agent, to play in Lancashire League. Rashid is a talented bowler, and his style of bowling was characterized by an unusually 'wrong foot' approach, which had a resemblance to that of Mike Procter from South Africa.

When I was the captain of the Batley Cricket Club, Rashid once visited our club. Upon seeing the friendly atmosphere there, he expressed his interest to join us. By then, he was already an international player, and was also playing in the Lancashire League with a very good honorarium. However, Rashid chose to play for Batley CC, even though the honorarium that Batley CC offers was relatively lesser than that of Lancashire club; he joined Batley CC and began to reside in one of my houses in Dewsbury along with other cricketers. But he left us in the middle of the season, as Rashid was selected for the Pakistan team to play in the 1983 World Cup under the captaincy of Imran Khan. He successfully played in the world-cup and re-joined us for the next season to continue playing for Batley. During this period, we played many matches together, including benefit/friendly matches.

Qasim Umar

Qasim Bhai is a brilliant cricketer and a very nice person; he is a spiritualist, and practices religion. When Qasim Bhai was residing at Oldham, or Rochdale (Lancashire), I invited him for a cricket function at Mount Cricket Club in Dewsbury, which he gladly attended. Since then, Qasim Bhai would visit my house frequently. Over time, we developed a good friendship; he would speak Gujarati language, and that brought him close to my parents also. I remember that Qasim Umar once had a dispute with the cricket board of Pakistan, and since then he grew distance with Pakistani cricket team. When I met him in Manchester, he explained the whole story of his dispute with the cricket board. Unfortunately, thereafter, we lost touch with each other, and I have not seen him since.

Manzoor Elahi

I first met Manzoor Elahi through Mohammad Asif, a cricket umpire of Pakistan. Manzoor and his brothers, Saleem Elahi and Zahoor Elahi, would often visit Asif's house in Dewsbury area. When we were playing a friendly match at Scholes, Manzoor also joined us; he liked our cricket and our sporting spirit, so he had continued visiting us, and we played several matches together. Over time, we got to know each other well.

Ramiz Raja

Ramiz Raja is the younger brother of Waseem Raja, whom I signed for Ramsbottom Cricket Club. Wasim is my family friend, so Ramiz have been naturally my friend. However, I knew Ramiz only because of his association with cricket. To the best of my memory, I first met Ramiz in England, when he was on his tour, along with his Pakistani team, to

England, to play Under-19 cricket series. Then, the entire cricket team of Pakistan visited my house for dinner, and I had a pleasant time with the young cricketers. Later, Ramiz went on to play for Pakistan, and whenever they had any cricket tour in England, Ramiz and the entire Pakistani team would certainly meet me. Ramiz is a true gentleman, with a deep knowledge of the game. Eventually, he served as the Chairman of the Cricket Board of Pakistan.

Wasim Akram

Wasim Akram, undoubtedly, is one of the greatest fast bowlers in cricket history and one of the finest left-arm bowlers the game has ever witnessed. In 1983, when I was the captain of Batley CC, Imran Khan called me one day, and told me about this young prospective player; he prophesied that, one day, Wasim would write a page for himself in the annals of the cricketing world. Imran advised me to sign Wasim to Batley CC and had commended Wasim's exceptional talent as a fast bowler. Since, we had already signed Chandrakanth Pandit from India for that season, I expressed my inability to sign him. I could sense that Imran was a bit upset about it, but I am sure that, he might have understood the club's commitments and policies. However, as anticipated by Imran, Wasim Akram got selected for the Pakistani Test team the following year. Popularised as the 'Sultan of the Swing,' he had emerged as one of the best bowlers in the cricketing history. It makes me feel great that I too had an opportunity to play two matches against Wasim; the first match was Imran Khan's benefit match at Batley in 1987, and the second was of a benefit match for Mansoor Rana in 1998, where I captained India XI, as against Pakistan XI, which was captained by Wasim Akram.

Ijaz Ahmad

I remember Ijaz Bhai playing in the "North Yorkshire & South Durham Cricket League," and often I would visit him to watch his matches.

Later, he also played for Durham County cricket, and during which, we would regularly catch up to discuss cricket. Through our regular interactions, we got to know each other well, though we together did not get a chance to play many cricket matches. However, once I had chance to play against Ijaz, when he played for Imran Khan's benefit match in 1987 against our Batley team, where I was its captain.

Waqar Younis

Waqar Bhai was one of the finest fast bowlers to grace the game of cricket and was known for his ability to deliver reverse swing at will. I met Waqar on few occasions when he came to England, as part of the cricket team of Pakistan. Though I did not get a chance to play with him, there was an interesting episode involving Waqar. In 2004, a socio-religious Ashram named Dera Sacha Sauda, had constructed a cricket stadium at Sirsa in India; as part of inaugurating the stadium, they approached me, to organize a match between veteran cricketers of India and Pakistan. I contacted some of my cricket friends from both countries to check their will and availability, and Waqar was one among them, who happily came forward to play the match as part of the Pakistan team. It was joyful to see several veteran players together, playing after a long while.

Shahid Mahboob

The story of Shahid is inspiring to everyone. In the early 1980s, during one of my trips to Karachi, Shahid managed to track down my address in the house of my parents-in-law at Natal Colony and had met me there. He introduced himself as someone who was playing competitive cricket in Pakistan, with very limited support, hailing from a financially disadvantaged family. He also told me that someone had suggested him to seek my help in getting contract with some cricket club in English Leagues. Upon my return to England, I spoke to Hartshead Moor Cricket Club, and signed Shahid for the club. Shahid was very happy to find an opportunity to play in the English League; he spent several years playing for Hartshead Moore club and made significant contributions to the club. Following this, he went on to play for Birstall CC in the Central Yorkshire League (CYL), and then for the Skelmanthorpe CC in the Huddersfield League. Shahid is a nice person, and we played several matches together in Yorkshire. During his stay in England, he would visit us regularly, and had emerged as a close associate of my family. Whenever he would come towards Dewsbury, Shahid would also visit me at my sports store.

With the gaining of experience and knowledge of cricket from the English Leagues, Shahid was selected for the national team of Pakistan to play international Test cricket. Subsequently, he made England his home, and lived here with his wife, and children. In England, he also served as coach, assisting young cricketers in the Lancashire and Bolton cricket clubs. Of late, he went to Qatar to serve as a coach of their national team, and when I went to Doha on my family holiday, I had the pleasure of meeting him there; he took me around Doha, and we did a lot of shopping there.

It fills me with great joy even to think of Shahid's personal and professional growth. Shahid always expresses his gratitude and respect towards me for a little support he received from me. I sincerely believe that it was his personal endeavours and commitment to cricket that brought him all those successes that he attained.

Saeed Anwar

I met Saeed Bhai a few times, along with the Pakistan test cricket team, as he was part of the team. Despite his star status, I found him to be to be humble and friendly.

He is very principled man, and never breaks his principles. I recall an incident, when he played India vs. Pakistan Veteran cricket match in 2004 at Sirsa, upon my request. Since the match was organised by a religious Ashram, the authorities of the Ashram asked us to perform pledge that signifies their head, Baba, as the deity, to which the Indian team conceded. But, when it came to the Pakistani team, Saeed Bhai gently opposed it; he stated that he can respect Baba as a Guru, a learned person, but he cannot regard Baba as God. Because, according to his religion, there was only one GOD, and so, all the team members of Pakistan followed Saeed Bhai, and they did not participate in the pledge. Baba heard his views and smiled gently.

True to his faith, Saeed Bhai turned to spiritual life after retiring from professional cricket; other cricketers such as Inzamam-ul-Haq, Mohammad Yousuf, and Mushtaq Ahmed also turned to spirituality after retiring from cricket. Since I know all these cricketers for a long time, whenever they visited Yorkshire on any religious event, they all would visit my house. It was my pleasure to sit with them, and to have conversations with them on religion and spirituality; we would have lunch and dinner together and would also visit mosque together. On one occasion, Saeed Bhai visited my house with Junaid Jamshed, a famous singer of Pakistan, and a religious preacher; we together had lunch at my home and visited Markaz.

Moin Khan & Nadeem Khan

I know Moin Khan well through Pakistan cricket team members. I helped his brother, Nadeem Khan, to sign with a club in Yorkshire. When I spoke to the club about signing Nadeem Khan, they asked me if I too could play a few matches for them. Since our season started a bit later than theirs, I agreed to play for them, and as a result, both Nadeem and I played a couple of matches together for the club.

Masood Anwar

Masood Anwar is one of the most passionate cricketers I have come across. I remember Masood was not receiving any honorarium when he was playing for the Thornhill CC, as his association with the team was performance based, and as per that he was paid 50p for a run, and 20p for a catch, which would not even cover his travel expenses. Nonetheless, he continued to play for Thornhill out of sheer passion for the game, and he had performed exceptionally well during his time at Thornhill CC.

However, he sought for more challenges in cricket. So, one day, he asked me if I can find a place in Batley CC for the coming season. I then signed him for Batley team for £25 per match, which was much lower than the amount paid to an average club cricketer of the time. However, he accepted the offer, to play for Batley team under my captaincy. Masood performed exceptionally well for the season and had scored loads of runs for the club; he was amicable with all the team members and had also devoted his time to helping the young cricketers during practice sessions. With all our individual hard work and coordinated efforts of the team members, we managed to win the championship for the season. Masood Anwar is a passionate cricketer, and he never surrendered his principle for financial gains.

Saqlain Mushtaq

Saqlain is a kind and compassionate person, and we have great mutual respect. We together played a benefit match for Mansoor Rana in 1998, and upon my request, he also played in the India vs. Pakistan veteran match at Shirsha, India. After retiring from cricket, Saqlain grew religious, and would often visit Markaz in Dewsbury. We were very good friends, and during my family gatherings, Saqlain would visit my house, along with his wife and children. I also invited him for a few dinner parties at League and Mount Cricket Clubs, and he was pleased to attend those events. He also worked as a coach for the Pakistan team for some time, and during which, he used to provide me with several tickets for international matches, and I would circulate them among our friends and relatives. Saqlain is now settled in Leicester, and I meet him sometimes, whenever I go there.

Azam Khan

In Karachi, during our conversation, Anwar Khan, a former Pakistani test cricketer, told me about Azam and his cricketing talents. Anwar also asked me if I could help facilitate Azam get a spot in the League cricket in England. After I returned to England, I signed Azam for Hartshead Moor Club. Azam Khan came to England, along with his wife and mother, thinking that the club would arrange an accommodation. But for some reason, they could not. So, I managed to secure a place for him in Manchester, where he stayed with his family; we also provided him with a car.

I recall a funny incident about Azam Khan on the very first day of his debut in English League cricket. The day before the match, I briefed him about the match schedule, venue, and its timings, and advised him to reach the ground before 12pm. Azam strictly followed my instructions, and reached the grounds on time only to find that there were no one in the ground. Azam grew suspicious and called me up to check about the reason. Now it was my turn to get surprised, as it was not even 8 am, and I began to think why the hell would he go this early to the grounds. After some thought, it suddenly dawned on me that he might not have adjusted his watch to the UK time and so it must be this difference in time. True to my suspicion, he did not adjust his watch to the changed time zone, after his landing, and continue to follow the timings of Pakistan time zone, which would be 5 hours ahead of the UK time. We both took to laughter, upon realising this common experience of many Asians who land in UK, and it was a fun-filled moment for us that we cherish it even

261

to this day, whenever we meet. He is a very good friend of mine, and I love his company.

Shahid Afridi

Shahid Afridi is undoubtedly one of the most exciting cricketers that graced the Pakistan team. I knew Afridi for quite some time as an international cricketer of Pakistan, and not as someone who was associated with League cricket in England.

However, to recall a moment of Afridi in England, my memory takes me back to a single-wicket competition conducted by Scholes Cricket Club in Huddersfield. The club approached me, if I could get Shahid Afridi to play a match for them in that competition. Given Afridi's significant fan base among British-Asians, the club thought that his presence would be a great asset to the event; the club was also ready to offer him a prize money that amounts to £1000. I proposed the same to Afridi, and he expressed his happy consent to the offer and readily agreed to be part of the competition.

In the match, Afridi was already leading by 8 runs, which means he had already won the match, and on the final ball, all he had to do was just to defend the ball, only to protect his wicket. But in a surprising turn of events, he attempted to hit the ball out of the ground, and a fielder took a brilliant catch right on the boundary line. The rule of the game was that if a batsman gets out, he will lose 10 runs, and in that case, it amounted to losing the match. Unfortunately, with this sudden fall of his wicket, Afridi had to miss out on the prize money by just 2 runs.

In another instance, we organized a customary competition, with a fee of £1 per participant, where the participants were asked to throw the ball, and the one who throws it to a farthest distance would be the winner. Many of us gave it a shot, and for fun, I asked Afridi to join in. But when Afridi took his turn, to everyone's astonishment, he threw the ball completely out of the ground; his arm power left us all in disbelief.

In yet another instance, the Holland Cricket Association requested me to bring in a few international players for their centenary cricket celebration match, featuring International XI against a Netherlands XI. I managed to get Shahid Afridi, Dinesh Mongia, and Sameer Dighe for this special event. My wife and I travelled to Holland, along with these cricketers, and the event turned out to be a resounding success, as several international cricket stars played, and several others attended. For this match, Afridi used the cricket gear produced by my own sports company, Solly Sports. As a thoughtful gesture, Afridi gifted me the bat he used for the match, which is my proud possession to this day. We all had an incredible time in the entire trip together, that include our sightseeing in Holland.

Imran Nazir

In one of the benefit-matches we played at Mirfield, I was the captain of the team, and we took to fielding against the team that Imran Nazir represented. Imran Nazir, then, was a young opening batsman, against whom Abey Kuruvilla was an experienced opening bowler. As the captain, I gave a brand-new ball to Abey for his first over. Despite Abey's international status, Imran astonishingly smashed the first ball for a six, sending it out of the ground; the ball disappeared, and it left everyone in disbelief. I asked Imran with a smile whether he had planned it at his home to hit the first ball for a six. Usually, most batsmen take some time to get used to the pitch and ball. But this young man, did not take any such measures; he was bold enough to hit an international bowler for six on the very first ball. He continued mercilessly attacking all the fast bowlers, leaving everyone in shock. Having no option left with me, I took my turn to switch to spin bowling, and Imran tried my ball with same aggression. Unfortunately for him, I managed to dismiss him in just a few balls. What an energetic and aggressive batsman he was in his day!

Abdul Razzaq

I got to know Abdul Razzaq, through Anwar Khan. Anwar had a lot of hopes on Abdul Razzaq and his cricketing potentials, and had predicted that Razzaq would, one day, be sure of representing Pakistan national team. When I was in Karachi, Anwar took me all the way to the National Stadium just to watch Abdul playing. Upon witnessing Abdul's impressive talent as an all-rounder, I asked him if he was interested to play for the League cricket in England. Then, Abdul responded in Urdu that he would love to be in England, but was not sure of his survival there, as he could not speak English. However, as anticipated by Anwar, Abdul went on to represent Pakistan, and had also played multiple county teams in England. I strongly feel that Abdul is a highly talented and gifted all-rounder from Pakistan in recent times.

Younis Khan

I met Younis Khan a few times while he was with the Pakistani Test team. But we would frequently catch up each other only after he began playing for the Yorkshire County team. Once, Younis Khan expressed his interest to use Solly Sports cricket gear, as a way of endorsing my sports brand, and I was very happy about it. But unfortunately, it did not happen, as I could not afford his amount. Nevertheless, we remain friends, and whenever Younus visits northern part of England, we try to meet up.

Kamran Akmal

Many Pakistani players, including Kamran Akmal, used cricket gear of my brand, Solly Sports, in their matches. Kamran was a frequent visitor to my store, often accompanied by other Pakistani cricketers like Umar

Gul and Taufeeq Umar. Kamran, who worked for the National Bank of Pakistan (NBP), was introduced to me by Iqbal Qasim; he also played with Iqbal. And through Kamran, I met his younger brother, Umar Akmal, who also played for Pakistan national team for many years.

Shabbir Ahmed

Shabbir is a talented cricketer, and a very good person who is friendly with everyone. I have a distinct memory of signing Shabbir Ahmed to League cricket in South Yorkshire, and that was when I first met him. Shabbir was a tall and highly skilled right-arm fast bowler. He played very well for the club, but he used to have a difficulty to communicate with the club management in English. So, I would extend my assistance to him in all his important communications with the club management.

Saeed Ajmal

Saeed Ajmal is a brilliant spinner, and a humble human-being. He signed a 1-year contract to use the cricket gear of my sports brand, Solly Sports, and eventually our friendship grew. He also played 2011 World Cup, which was held in India, using the cricket gear of my brand. As he shared with me, he still preserves the cricket gear (equipment & dress) that he wore during the World Cup, as his most cherished memories. I also remember Saeed scoring 50 runs, which was his best in the Test matches, where he used Solly Sports bat, and in another test match, he took 5 wickets, wearing our brand of trousers, which he still preserves. Our friendship remains strong to this day, and we continue to meet whenever he visits England.

Yasir Shah

Yasir Shah is a very nice person, and I met him many times when the Pakistan cricket team toured England. I also met him during my family vacation in New Zealand which coincided with the test match, that was held between the teams of Pakistan and New Zealand. In New Zeeland, we had an opportunity to spend a couple of days with Yasir. Moreover, Yasir was a regular visitor to Batley CC, when he was playing for the Huddersfield League, and at Batley, he would practice cricket.

2. B. One-Day International (ODI) and First-class Cricketers of Pakistan

Besides test cricketers, I also have an affinity with several Pakistani cricketers who played ODI and First-class cricket. I signed them for various clubs to play in different Leagues in England. Some of these talented cricketers include, Amin Lakhani, Sajid Ali, Suleman Huda, Kashif Ahmad, Ali Reza, Faizal, Mohyuddin Ahmed Khan (Puppy), and many others.

Amin Lakhani

Amin Lakhani has been a great friend of mine, and he had close affinity with all the members of my family. Ever since I signed him for the Bradley Mills CC in the Huddersfield League, he began to be a regular visitor to my house. Amin was an exceptional left-arm spinner. I remember, he was the first bowler ever to achieve hat-trick in both innings of the same first-class match in 1978; he did this twin hat-tricks against the touring Indian Test team, while he was playing for Universities & Young Pakistan team. Given his exceptional abilities and talent in cricket, it was my strongest belief that Amin would enjoy a long and successful career in Test cricket. However, it is unfortunate that he never had an opportunity to play any matches in Test cricket. Whenever I visit Pakistan, I do not miss meeting Amin, and we spend good time together; he also visits me in England. I am fortunate to have him, and our friendship remains as strong as ever.

Sajid Ali

Sajid Ali was a former ODI player of Pakistan. I signed Sajid to play for Bradley Mills CC in the Huddersfield League. He had an impressive track of scoring tons of runs in Pakistan's domestic cricket. But unfortunately, he did not get the opportunity to play Test matches in his career. Sajid Ali was a colleague of Amin Lakhani in Bradley Mills CC, as they played for the club for the same season. A couple of years ago, I also signed Sajid Ali's son to Mount Cricket Club.

Suleman Huda

I was impressed by the talents of Suleman Huda as an under-19 cricket player in the Pakistan team. I first saw him in Karachi while he was playing, and asked him, if he would be interested in playing League cricket in England, to which he joyfully agreed. When I returned to England, I signed Suleman to play for Hanging Heaton. During his season with the club, Suleman used to share his flat with other cricketers like Ali Raza, Kashif Ahmed (Tauseef Ahmed's nephew), etc. Suleman Huda is a true gentleman with an exceptional knowledge of cricket, and other issues of socio-political concern. In some of my media interviews, I expressed my admiration for Suleman, and his talents in cricket, and had anticipated him to be a star cricketer from Pakistan. However, he prioritized education to cricket, and has emerged as a well-known lawyer in Karachi; he is now a practicing advocate in the higher courts of Pakistan.

To sum up

Over the years, many of these cricketers from Pakistan have gone beyond the realm of their professional relationship with me, and have come to become one with me, and with my family. Even to this day, many of these cricketers are in regular contact with me, and whenever they make their way to the northern part of England, they often visit us to reaffirm the enduring friendship we cherish. It has been an incredibly gratifying experience to have all these players as my friends.

My Memories of English Cricketers, and the League Cricketers

My journey of cricket in England commenced in 1964 as a player in the Dewsbury and District League. Ever since, I had a brilliant cricketing career, having played for several cricket clubs in different Leagues, both as a player and captain, till I finally hung up my boots in 2002. In this cricketing journey which lasted a little less than four decades, I could churn out the best of my sporting potentials, as well as try to nurture the young talents, among whom many had even emerged as international cricket stars and star legends. I ascended as the captain at Batley CC in the Central Yorkshire League (CYL) in 1983, and then moved to the Spen Victoria CC in the Bradford League in 1989 to assume its captaincy. Subsequently I also played for a Minor County team 'Cumberland,' only to come back to the League cricket after a brief stint there; I have also been a successful businessman, and had ventured to set up multiple business firms, beginning with petrol stations. Now, having been left with my wife, children, grand-children, and great-grand-children, it has been my avocation to spend my time and energies in my favourite sport store, Solly Sports; I am still active in my sports business.

In this journey of my life, I got an opportunity to meet numerous English cricketers, besides being a key figure in recruiting hundreds of Asian cricketers to various cricket Leagues in England. It is during my association with League cricket that I befriended many English cricketers, and eventually some of them became my very intimate friends, with whom I cherish the most enduring relationship to this day; some of them even played a crucial role in my making as League cricketer in England. I have wonderful memories to cherish with most English cricketers, though I also had some bitter experiences with some of them. However, in the end, everything turned out to be harmonious, and we have become one with each other as a cricket fraternity of Yorkshire. I feel it is necessary to lay down some of those memories, and experiences, that have touched the bottom of my heart, during my active life as a cricketer, and my affinity with the following English League and County cricketers in England.

Barry Wood

Barry Wood has been the first, among several English cricketers, that I have come across in my life. One day, when I was serving petrol in my Dewsbury petrol station, Barry Wood, visited our station to fuel his vehicle. It was probably in 1976, and Barry Wood, by then, was already a renowned Test cricketer of England. I was so happy to see him visiting my petrol station, and swiftly introduced myself to Barry, who too was pleased, and in turn, he asked about my affinity with League cricket. Eventually, Barry turned out to be our regular customer, and we became familiar to each other.

Knowing of my familiarity with Barry Wood, Batley Muslim CC asked me whether I can help them in inviting Barry to their club, as they want to honour him, and through him, they wanted to distribute trophies to their team members. It was just around the same time that the Batley Muslim CC had offered me the captaincy for their team, and we still were on talks about it. I was so glad, and one day, I went to his home with a friend, Shabbir Aswat, to invite Barry as a guest for the occasion. Barry was pleased to accept my invitation, and had joined us along with his wife at Batley Muslim CC.

I was sitting beside Barry and on his other side was his wife, while the chairman of the club and the captain of the team were also present, and the trophies were presented to the players; I had also arranged dinner for them in Shama restaurant in Dewsbury. The local media took photographs, and the Dewsbury news reporter also showed me the photograph that was going to appear in their newspaper in which the heads of the club like Captain and chairman of the club, including me, were present beside Barry and his wife. But unfortunately, our secretary was not covered in the picture. My happiness knows no bounds, as it was first time in my life that my photograph was going to appear in a famous newspaper, Dewsbury Report. I was looking forward to the day to buy about a dozen newspapers to distribute them among my friends across and to preserve it forever.

But when the actual news got published, to my shock, there were all others, but not me. I did not know the exact reason. But a little later, I learnt that the club management asked the reporter to remove my photograph from the scene, as I think I was the only non-member of the club with a strong visible presence, while one of the important members of the club himself could not find his presence in it. I was so upset about this unexpected turn, as I did everything for making this event success.

Sensing my excruciating disappointment, my mother had consoled me with her prophetic words: "Don't worry Solly! There will be a day when people will be asking for your autographs and your pictures." True to my mom's words, I hosted dozens of the world-renowned cricket stars and legends, and hundreds of international cricketers; they dined with me and have played with me for several decades; I cherished some of the finest moments with them and have hundreds of photographs with them.

Geoffrey Boycott

My encounter with Geoffrey Boycott is one of the most unpleasant incidences in my life, though in the end, we emerged as friends. For the reasons unknown, and with no mistake of mine, once, I was an object of humiliation in the hands of Geoffrey.

This unfortunate incidence had unfolded on my visit to India in 1981; it was during a Test series between England and India, where Keith Fletcher was the captain of England team, and Sunil Gavaskar was leading the Indian team. Sunil arranged complimentary tickets for my family, and I, along with my family, reached Bombay a few days before commencement of the match. During practice session on one morning at Wankhede Stadium, Sunil asked me to observe the net-practice of cricketers of both the teams, and I had gladly joined them. As I stood there, I noticed Geoffrey Boycott behind the nets, who was attentively watching his team players taking their turns to bat. I was excited to see Geoffrey, as I was his ardent fan, and had always held him in high regard, as he, by then, was already one of the all-time English greats. My admiration for him also had heightened because he hails from Yorkshire, as I had developed a deep affection for the land and its people, ever since I made Yorkshire my home in 1963. Though I was not familiar to him, I approached Geoffrey, out of my sheer excitement to meet him in person, to admire his sporting talents as being his fan, and greeted him pleasingly, "Hello Sir, I'm Solly Adam from Yorkshire, and I am glad to meet you." But, to my shock, he looked at me and hurled his swearing remarks, "F*** off."

I was taken aback by this unexpected reaction from Geoffrey, and quietly moved away from him, as I felt deeply hurt and humiliated. Badly disturbed by this act of Geoffrey, I sat down to keep my cool, while different thoughts were overriding my mind, and I exerted all my energies to focus my attention on the players in the net practice. But all my efforts went in vain, and yet, with a great difficulty, I managed somehow, to stay in the stadium till the end of the practising session. I did not share this issue with anyone, including Sunil, even to this day.

Upon my return to England, I contacted the Yorkshire Cricket Board, and lodged a detailed complaint against Geoffrey Boycott. The office bearer expressed his helplessness about it, though his reply was sympathetic: "Solly, I feel sorry for whatever happened to you in Bombay. But I suggest you to just please ignore him. If we note down all the complaints against him, we will probably need a separate book to do so." Then, I left the office without any further pursuit of the case. But the incident left a deep scar on my conscience, and even to this day, when I happened to see Geoffrey, it flashes just before my eyes.

By early 80's, I emerged as a single most contact for organizing benefit/testimonial matches for all the popular cricketers and cricket legends at Batley; players from the Yorkshire County cricket team also began approaching me for their testimonial matches. Consequently, I organized and played in testimonial matches for several players, that include David Bairstow in 1982, and for Richard Lumb in 1983, from Yorkshire. And then one day, in 1984, I received a call from a person, who greeted me, "Hi Solly! how are you?" It was a familiar voice but was indistinct. When I inquired, to my surprise, it was none other than Geoffrey Boycott himself, one of the all-time greats of England; the same person who had badly offended me; the one who had ripped my conscience apart.

Geoffrey, then, asked me, if I can help him in organizing a testimonial match for him at Batley. For a moment, I dazed off, as all that had buried down for three years in my consciousness, at once flashed before me for a fraction of a second. Then, I came back to my senses, while trying to be poised and respectful to him, and only then, I expressed my willingness to organise the match for him.

I spoke about the same to the committee, which was glad to honour such a prestigious cricketer, and the match was scheduled on May 29, 1984, at Batley, involving several prominent cricketers. Meanwhile, Geoffrey called me again, to verify the status. The match was tremendously successful, and in the end, Geoffrey admired me, in recognition of my role in organizing the match for him, and for playing the match.

Since then, Geoffrey appeared sensitive and friendly towards me.

One day, Geoffrey invited Sunil Gavaskar to his house for dinner. Upon learning that Sunil was staying with me in my house, Geoffrey insisted that both of us join him for dinner. Sunil and I visited Geoffrey's house in Wakefield (Woolley Village, if I recall correctly), and we three dined together. I met Geoffrey once again with Sunil, when Sunil was looking for a good designer for his suits. Being acquainted with renowned costume designers in Manchester, Geoffrey accompanied us all the way to the Manchester to introduce us to the suit designer; three of us did some shopping there and had coffee together.

With this experience of mine with Geoffrey, I have learnt an important lesson of the need for moving on, rather than dwelling on the past. I believe that *life is just a few heartbeats away,* and so, one can exert one's energies on doing something that we deem to be good, and humane, rather than holding on to petty and unpleasant issues. I have also learnt a truth of life that, we get buried under the dead weight of history, when we keep digging and harping on the past. Instead, we should keep surging in the living present, only to keep rejuvenating ourselves, and then move forward anticipating a glorious future.

Chris Pickles

Chris Pickles is an important person among a few of Yorkshire cricketers, who had played a significant role in my cricketing journey. Having played for Yorkshire County for several years, Chris' knowledge and experience of cricket have been invaluable for us; he was a professional player in a true sense of the term and would extend his helping hand to all those who were interested in cricket. After I had achieved considerable success as the captain of Batley CC in the Central Yorkshire League, Chris suggested me to move into the Bradford League, as it was one of the best Leagues in England. In 1988, he facilitated my entry into Spen Victoria, to play in the Bradford League, under his captaincy. A little later, he also recommended me to be the captain of the same club, when

Chris was occupied with his responsibilities in Yorkshire County.

My association with Spen Victoria undeniably honed my skills as a player and a captain and had immensely contributed to my growth as a cricketer. At Spen Victoria, I signed several local cricketers, including John Wood, Mike Smith, Bethel Brothers, Tim Walton, John Carruthers (JC), Steve Foster, Gary Brook, and several others with whom I developed a good friendship over time. Some of them went on to play for counties as well, and many of them remained my close friends. I consider that winning of the Priestley Cup for Spen Victoria in 1990, under my captaincy, is one of the major achievements of my cricketing career. I remain deeply indebted to Chris Pickles for his unwavering support, and friendship.

Paul Jarvis

Paul Jarvis is a very interesting cricketer, among several other notable players who played for Batley CC; they include players like Barry Petty, Paul Blakely, Neil Haynes, etc., and my memories of Paul are worth mentioning here.

Paul Jarvis was a popular player in Yorkshire County, when I took the captaincy of Batley CC in the Central Yorkshire League (CYL); he later represented the national team of England. He was a dedicated cricketer, his only focus was to play cricket without expecting anything in return, and he would land up in our grounds as and when he found time to play with us. Since he had to play for the Yorkshire County during weekdays, he would spare the weekends to play with us. But he never sought any remuneration for the matches he played for Batley CC. Paul was fond of our home curries, and so, after every match he played with us, he would visit our home to dine with us, only to have the food of his choice at my home. Seeing his dedication for the game, and his love for our home curries, we would jokingly say that the curry he enjoys during the weekend at my home would be his match fee. That was how most players in Batley also played, laughed and accordingly our friendship also bloomed.

During my five-years stint with Batley CC as its captain, we not only registered significant successes, but also nurtured enduring friendship among all those who played with us. In due course, Paul became one of my dearest friends in England; he sometimes visits me still, as does many other friends from Batley CC, and whenever we meet up, we recall the wonderful times we had lived through.

David Byrne

Another key figure whose enduring friendship I cherish is David Byrne; he was the vice-captain of the Batley CC team when I joined their team and was an intimate friend of Chandrakanth Pandit. Chandu would visit David Byrne, whenever he comes to England, and so, they together would certainly meet me, as I had a lasting friendship with Chandu. David has profound knowledge of the game, and his advice on bowling changes and fielding settings were invaluable to the success of the team. Having been a sound batsman, David always gave his all for the team.

Sean Twohig

Sean is a very nice person with an excellent knowledge of cricket. His intense focus on the game, and his perseverance in bringing the team to its successes were evident to all those who played with him; his focus enhances further, particularly, when he takes to the batting crease, as he is mainly a batsman. Having been an opening batsman for Batley CC, alongside Chandu, Sean would deliver consistent score of runs, and their partnership had a significant contribution in the success of the team. Sean resides in Dewsbury, and we have regular contact with each other. While writing this book, Sean was kind to invite Vara to his home, shared his experiences and information about our matches and players at Batley, and had helped us collecting necessary data for the book. I owe my heartfelt thanks to Sean Twohig for his generosity and support.

David Peel

A special mention must be made about my memories of David Peel, and his dedication to cricket. David shared a lasting friendship with me that spans over 50 years. I had a pleasure of playing with him at Whitley Lower CC (now Hopton Mills CC), where attained several successes for the team, including having an opportunity to win the prestigious *Sheard Cup* in 1970. David has an incredible memory, and whenever we meet up, he vividly recalls all the finest moments that we had cherished together during our cricketing days. He is always special, and all our nostalgia floods in, the moment we catch up; it's great seeing him and being with him.

Frank Tyson

Frank was born in Lancashire, and I hold a special memory with him though I did not share much personal affinity with him. Popularised as Typhoon Tyson for his incredible bowling speed that often would scare batsmen of his time, Frank was one of the most famous fast bowlers who went on to play for the national team of England. Later, he became a bowling coach, after retiring from cricket. One day, Frank happened to visit our net practise sessions when I was bowling in the nets. Then, he noticed something unusual in my bowling action and had suggested me to correct it. As he observed, I block my view with my right hand while delivering the ball through my left hand which hinders my ability to see precisely where the ball would be landing. With this keen insight from Frank, I subsequently began to experience great successes in my left-arm bowling. I am deeply indebted to Frank for this great help, that had hugely contributed to sharpening my bowling skills.

Phil Carrick

I endured a special affinity with Phil Carrick, who was the captain of the Yorkshire County team. Phil had been more than my cricket companion, as Phil and I played for two different clubs, however, under the same Bradford League. Therefore, we played against each other in several matches. While I played for Spen Victoria, Phil represented Pudsey Congs; we also played in several friendly matches together. Phil and I are left-arm spinners, and we would play Sunday matches together. Like Frank Tyson, Phil also had a significance in refining my bowling.

Following a match one Sunday, Phil detected an anomaly in my bowling action, and he remarked, "Solly, you exhibit a nice dip and zip in your bowling, but somehow the bounce seems to have diminished." With this observation from Phil, I began pondering the reason behind this decline in the bounce of my ball, and then I realised that this change was of recent times. But I could not figure out the reasons for such a decline. Then, Phil called me to the Pudsey Congs ground the very next day, which was Monday, and asked me to bowl, only to detect the reasons for its decline. After bowling a few overs, he promptly pointed out the problem in my bowling, as he remarked, "Solly, everything looks fine, but your 'follow-through' after delivering the ball is shorter than before." I continued bowling, based on his instructions, and after a few overs, I could do the complete 'follow-through.' Suddenly, there was a very good bounce, with a joyful revival of a bounce in my bowling. I was very happy, and Phil held me with great joy. Phil had been a very generous person and was always ready to extend his helping hand to all his cricketing friends; his extensive knowledge and experience of cricket has been an immense help to us all. Unfortunately, however, such a noble soul is no more, as Phil Carrick (1952-2000) left us all in tears in his very young age of 48; I shall always be indebted to him.

Summing Up:

The above-mentioned cricketers are a few among several English cricketers with whom I had shared an enduring friendship. I recall around half-a-dozen League cricketers as my friends in different clubs, beginning with Cross Bank Muslim CC, Thornhill CC, Batley CC, Spen Victoria CC, and Slazengers CC, besides my friendship with several English cricketers in Yorkshire County Team. In the Yorkshire County alone, I am fortunate to have acquaintances with David Bairstow, Richard Lumb, Arnie Sidebottom, Andrew Townsley, Martyn Moxon, Peter Hartley, Darren Gough, Chris Silverwood, Michael Vaughan, Anthony McGrath, Richard Kettleborough, Matthew Hoggard and Ryan Sidebottom. I am blessed to have all these great stalwarts as my friends, and in whose company, I believe, I could also contribute my bit to League cricket in Yorkshire.

KEY EVENTS OF MY LIFE

In this long life of over seven decades, I have lived through experiences in varied forms and magnitudes; I have had the share of both darker and lighter moments, involving a sense of joy resulting from each of my successes, and that of disappointment in every failure, as it would be natural to every human. But soon I would come to my rational senses to keep my cool and to keep my feet firm on the ground, so that I would not fall into an illusion that neither elevates me to the status of superhuman, nor reduces to be a sub-human. Of all my experiences, ideas, actions and achievements, the following few events, I feel worth mentioning here:

1) The earliest among the best of these events was the one when I bought a Mercedes-Benz car in 1971. Though it might be considered insignificant by many but owning a car was a huge thing for someone like me who was uprooted from one's own land and home. I had been ridiculed just for being curious to see a car for the first time in my life when a Ford car was owned by someone in our locality in Karachi (whose name I do not want to mention here) but my dream of owning my car was finally realized under the new circumstances in England, when the doors of fortune began to open one after another. Across my career as a worker in a factory, then as a car driver and motor mechanic, and then finally, as one of the earliest Asians to have attained success as a businessman in England, I have owned several cars. However, it was owing to increasing profits in my businesses that I finally bought one of the world class pre-

mium cars, Mercedes-Benz. In those days, the Mercedes motor company would not deliver its car immediately upon our order, and one had to wait for at least two years after placing an order for the car. Accordingly, I ordered for the car in 1969 and gifted it to my parents at last in 1971; it is in fact lovely to see our loved ones happy, and their happiness cannot be equated with any amount of material gain and physical comforts. At the same time, would there be any bounds to the happiness of parents, who had been deprived of even basic needs like food, when one of their children had grown to riches, yet retains his love for them? My parents were very happy that I was in good health, and was growing prosperous, and so was I for keeping them so happy and healthy till their last breath.

2) The second best of my experiences was when I bought a bungalow in Karachi in 1980. Just when I think of Pakistan even to this day, like sitting in a mysterious time machine, I take voyage to my childhood days in 1954 at Natal Colony in Karachi of Pakistan. Subsequently, like an ice-block upon a furnace, my heart gets fumed irresistibly to drip out tides of hot tears over my cheek, when I recount the difficult times, often horrific circumstances, that our family went through in Karachi. The dark clouds still pass by right in front of my eyes, as I commemorate the infantile deaths of my two young brothers who were the victims to the circumstance of my family's poverty. In Karachi, we lived in a small dark room under the staircase of a building, without any ventilation; there was no bathroom, nor a toilet. It was, in fact, owing to our circumstances whereby we had to live in such a dark, dampened, unhygienic and unventilated condition that I unfortunately had to lose both my brothers, in a difference of a week; they died young of jaundice, a disease that proved fatal all because we did not even have money to see a doctor. These were, however, the same circumstances that have shaped me to stand still against every adverse situation, which have instilled courage in me to dream and to actualize my dreams with dedication, determination, and discipline.

The fruits of my hard work began to shower and by God's grace, I bought a bungalow at the same place and in same country, Karachi, city of Pakistan, where I lost my two brothers. I was extremely elated, and greatly satisfied, to place the keys of that newly bought house in the hands of my parents, as they were the ones who always prayed Allah, the Almighty, that someday I would build a decent house there. To fulfil the wishes of my parents, I finally bought a huge, new, beautiful bungalow of five-bedrooms, with a spacious garden in 500 square yards in a prime locality, Phase Five Khayaban-e-Shujaat, in the defence area of Karachi. The happiness of my parents knew no bounds; though they did not express it in words, the tears that filled in their eyes made me realize how deeply they had been moved when their child owned a huge mansion-like bungalow in a place where they themselves began looking for fortunes, without even having a small shelter of their own.

3) The third event of my life that occupies a historic significance was regarding my role in organizing Indo-Pakistan veteran cricket match in December 2004 at Shah Satnam Singh Ji Cricket Stadium, Sirsa, Haryana of India. This was the first of its kind ever organized by any non-Governmental, non-sport voluntary organization, other than a sport board or an association; similar such efforts were also made in the same year for the month of February at Patiala stadium in Punjab of India, just a few months before this match, in which Panjab Cricket Association organized a competitive cricket match with the teams, Punjab Chief Minister's XI Vs Pakistan Invitation XI. Though the initial idea of the match was mooted to me by a socio-religious Ashram, Dera Sacha Sauda, headed by its guru, Gurmeet Ram Rahim Singh Insan, popularly known as Dera Baba, and was intended to raise funds for an orphanage of their Ashram, this match eventually turned out to be a peace match that establishes a harmonious relationship in the national lives of both India and Pakistan; it instilled an immense joy in me of shouldering this greatest responsibility to organize such an historic match, with

the veteran cricketing professionals of both the nations of my origin. It was a post war period and the agonies of Kargil war (1999) had not yet been wiped out from the memories of both these nations; every activity across their national borders had been stalled and bilateral relations between them were yet to be reestablished. On the other hand, I had just retired from cricket in 2002, leaving aside my long passionate cricketing career, and began to confine myself to my familial and business worlds.

It was at that moment on one day, that I received a phone call, when I was in my sports office, Solly Sports; the person who called me, introduced himself as Jasbir Singh from India and it was on behalf of Dera Sacha Sauda and its guru Dera Baba. I learnt from Jasbir that the *Ashram* of Dera Baba had just completed building a beautiful cricket stadium with a huge ground at Sirsa, Haryana in India, and they sought my help in organizing a cricket match with veteran players from India and Pakistan, as part of inaugurating the stadium and its allied sports academy, Shah Satnamji Cricket Academy. I was so glad that I immediately accepted the offer with great enthusiasm, and in a few days, I could form both the teams with the players from both the nations. Having scheduled to be held in Sirsa on December 9, 2004, Pakistan veteran team comprised of great and veteran players as Waqar Younis, Ijaz Ahmad, Mushtaq Ahmad, Shoaib Mohammed (Man of the Match), Masood Anwar, Zaheer Abbas, etc., with Sayeed Anwar as its captain; on the other hand, Indian veteran team also had equally competent and veteran players like Saeed Kirmani, Praveen Amre, Sameer Dighe, Atul Wassan, etc. In forming the Pakistan team, Iqbal Qasim, though was not part of the team owing to his professional commitments as an employee of a bank, was of immense help, besides our common friend, Rana, who acted as manager of the team. The match was inaugurated by Dera Baba whom both his volunteers and match audience treated with utmost reverence, while the match was attended by several dignitaries and politicians; I felt delighted that I was the guest of honour of the event, and so my wife and I had watched the match alongside Dera Baba, his wife and children, and other dignitaries.

In this match, Sayeed Anwar had won the toss and had opted to bat first in which the Pakistan team did the best score with a total of 210 runs in 40 overs, besides being credited with the Man of the Match for their team member, Shoaib Mohammed, for his fine record of unbeaten 110 runs in 137 balls, beside a second best, Ejaz Ahmad, with his half-century (52 runs). However, with a fine knock of 48 runs by Praveen Amre in 66 balls, and its opener Sameer Dighe with 41 runs, with the rest of the team members playing moderate scores, the Indian team could defeat team Pakistan in the end. The match was a huge success that had attracted as many as 35000 cricket enthusiasts and religious followers. DD Television India relayed the entire event on live, while all important newspapers and visual media commended the good intent and success of the match; some print media had even recognized my efforts in its organization and success, and published it with a title, "Dewsbury man makes history." I was also admired and congratulated by none other than the then Prime Minister of the India, Manmohan Singh, himself for all my efforts in its success; it was a great honour for me to receive such applauses from such high dignitaries.

4) My dedication to a range of fields such as business, sports, and social welfare activities for decades, began to be recognized both at home and in abroad, by public as well as private agencies. One day in 2012, a gentle man from Kirklees Council in West Yorkshire of England, called me up to know if they can see me to talk to me about nominating me for my statue to be installed in Yorkshire, which I warmly welcomed. The next morning, some people of Kirklees visited my home and said that they had shortlisted the names of ten persons, including me, who had dedicated their lives in different fields; out of them three persons would be selected, and then the thence selected persons' statues would later be erected in some public space. They also took my formal approval for my

nomination, and as per its terms and conditions, I could withdraw my nomination within six weeks, if for any reason I changed my mind, and for which, they also did all the required paperwork. It was in fact a great honour and I was delighted for the fact that I, a man who came here from nowhere a few decades ago, was now a name to be nominated for a statue in this land of England, which I had made my home.

But something was troubling my mind, and I was not sure whether it was fine to go about with this offer. I discussed with all my children, and of course my brother-figure Iqbal Qasim, about it. To my surprise, it was a unified, straight, and probably a correct response from all. They said that they won't mind my statue, and in fact it would be a great honour for them too. But at the same time, they also expressed their concern for the actual situation that my statue would be falling into, and they said: "Imagine Papa! the birds whose droppings might defile your image, which would be a huge dishonour not only for you, but also to all of us; animals and some humans also might taint your image." This aspect, my children were not happy about, which they found hard even to imagine; I totally agreed with them. With this, I immediately withdrew my nomination papers and stood away from that contest. However, by then, they had already developed my photograph in which I was posing in cricket gear at some sports field in Dewsbury and had displayed it at *Dewsbury Museum*. It is unbelievable, and I thank God for all my good deeds, my mom and dad for they always prayed to God for my prosperity and well-being, and I do pray the same God for my children who extend their care for me and had been looking out for my health and dignity.

It was in this context that, I received the honour of being invited to be part of the Royal Garden Party at the *Buckingham Palace*, the royal residence of England, by none other than the office of Her Highness, The Late Queen Elizabeth II, herself. This was the greatest honour that any citizen of England could achieve, and I was fortunate to have such a noble opportunity. I consider it as the last and most significant event in my life, and the details of which I will try to put down in the subsequent chapter.

5) Acting as a Coach cum Mentor for the team of Mount Cricket Club, in their Vatican tour to play a match against a team that represented St. Peter's Cricket Club of Rome, was the fifth most important event in my life. It assumes historical significance in my life, because, the Vatican team, against which our team had played this match, was known for its play of cricket against the teams that held on to various religious faiths; this they did as means of communal harmony across the globe, and I feel glad to be a part of such a noble mission. While Mount Cricket Club consists of players hailing from Muslim community in England, the team of St Peter's Cricket Club consisted of seminarians, or trainee priests, from different countries of the world who were seeking to attain priesthood under the Papal Basilica of St. Peter in the Vatican City of Rome. As I have been associated with Mount Cricket Club since its inception and have been their well-wisher and motivator for years in their successes as a senior and experienced cricketer in English League cricket, I received this great honour to be the mentor for the team in this prestigious tour. I joyfully accepted the offer, when Hanif Mayat, also known as Mr. Mount for his identification with the club, and Sadiq Patel (lawyer) pleasingly invited me to assume such a noble responsibility, and so I joined them, along with my wife; some other guests like Nazir Mangali, Dr Rajpura and his wife Dr Abida also joined us in our tour to Rome, and it was a pleasurable trip. The team of the Mount Club was already in its high spirits as they had just won the Halifax League finals, and this invitation from Vatican team doubled their happiness.

The match was scheduled on October 17, 2015, at Vatican grounds in Rome. We received tremendous hospitality in a serene atmosphere of the church, amidst priests and priest of tomorrow, at a place none other than the headquarters of Christendom, the Vatican City of Rome in Italy. It was a friendly atmosphere where Vatican team also invited me to share my experiences and knowledge as a veteran cricketer, and I was pleased to do so. As intended by the noble hearts, this match and its significance was that "the fixture against the Yorkshire team will gather together players and spectators in friendship, energy, good competition and a desire to win," as Father Robert McCulloch, an Australian priest and a founding member of the Vatican team said while announcing the match. I observed tossing between the captains of both the teams, and the match was for one of the noble causes for human good. As representative of the Mount team, Hanif also addressed the gathering.

It was a great opportunity to sit in the closest proximity of the Pope, Father Francis, and to listen to the public lecture of Pope where he delivered the message of peace and harmonious fraternity among the global humanity, and about the role that sports play in achieving such noble objective; in the end we all received blessings from the Pope. After the match, we had a special dinner, as we were the guest for the occasion. Following this, my wife and I, along with our friends (Nazir Mangali, Dr. Rajpura and his wife Dr. Abida Rajpura) visited places around— Pisa Tower, Milan, Venice, etc., —and it was a great honour for us that the travel arrangements for all that had been done by Vatican authorities themselves; they did it as a mark of their friendship and universal brotherhood.

Ever since, the Vatican team frequented its visits to England to play matches with the teams of various other faith, and they named this mission as Light of Faith. I was fascinated by this idea, as I have always been imbued with this spirit of universal brotherhood and communal harmony, and have always believed that the fundamental motto of sport is to unite the people regardless of their faiths and backgrounds. It was a great pleasure to be part of such a noble cause.

MY FAMILY! MY FORTUNES!!

If, as proverb goes, *there is a woman behind every successful man*, I am fortunate to have two women in my life who laid a firm foundation, for all my successful endeavours, with the bricks that others had hurled at me. The first was my mother, and the other is my wife; they are two angels of my life.

My Mother, Ayesha Saeed Adam

Like every child of every mother, I too am an offshoot of my mother, being born out of churning her blood and flesh. But unlike most children whose emotions with their mothers correspond with the amount of pampering that they receive from them during their formative years, I cherished an altogether different, yet an inalienable bonding with my mother, right from my birth, till her final departure. In fact, my bond with my mother grew stronger as I was growing up, and I had mystically embraced her extended being and her own self in all her life and struggles.

I grew up listening to the heart wrenching stories of my mother; she was born on April 5, 1930, in Simlak; her poverty ridden childhood; migration of her family to Lourenco Marques (Mozambique); her return to India at the age of six, along with her maternal grand-father, and sister, Khatija (elder to her), to live under the mercy of her uncle; and her eventual growing up into adolescence as a semi-slave in her maternal uncle's house, right till her marriage with my father, followed by my

287

birth and upbringing, altogether made me integral to her life; I would feel my heart melt listening to those stories and became one with her, only to wage her battles.

Under these circumstances, my life and emotions as a child were unusually different from other children of my age. I grew up in being part of my mother's expression of love and care for my younger siblings, as I was her first child and so eldest among my siblings. While my father was out all day and night, toiling to earn bread for us, I joined my mother in her efforts to patiently look after the house. I walked with my mother in all her hardships; I held her hand, walking across the *Thar Desert* as a young boy of hardly six, when we had to flee our home and country, and to take shelter in Pakistan as refugees from India; I spent countless sleepless nights with her as a boy of eight or nine, attending to all my four ailing siblings who were younger to me, and when all her efforts to save the lives of my two brothers and two sisters failed, leading to the loss of all their lives, one after another, to a deadly disease, I also walked with her in a vale of tears to burial grounds, to pay our last homage to my lost baby-siblings.

The trauma of my four deceased siblings had such an irrevocable shock-effect on my mother that she would undergo panic attacks about the anxiety for the future of her surviving children, particularly about my brother, Younus and sister, Haseena; I was there with her all along to ease all her anxieties. I treated my siblings as my own children, and my mother had been the care giver for all of us, including my own children. In due course, I cherished all the moral and emotional sensibilities of my mother, and it was these sensibilities, that later became my strength of character, helping me to do whatever little I could do so far in life. Now, I feel so glad to acknowledge the underlying greatest contributions of this simple, yet noble soul, my mother, in my making.

My mother was so compassionate towards us that, in our poverty ridden childhood, she would starve, only to feed us; she would look for our comforts, at the cost of losing her own; and when my father's earnings were insufficient to run the family, she would borrow money from our near and dear ones in Natal colony, Karachi to feed us, and then she would pay back all the debts later. I was her great companion. But I was also a very naughty child, and as and when I had any fight with any child of our locality, as I would fight so often, my mother would beat me up. She would lose all her temper at once, and shout and beat me, and quickly come back to her senses to hug me and cry. In my childhood, I do not remember a day passing without, at least, a single beating from my mother, followed by her hug and cry. I miss her beatings, shouts, hugs, and cries so much now.

When I was working as a taxi-driver in England, where I had to stay out late at night, my mother would not miss a single day to warn me to be careful about my driving, and she would stay awake wating for me, without even eating her dinner, till I came back; she would join me in eating, only after confirming that I had reached home safely, and only then she would retire to her bed. She would also make sure that I leave the house in the morning, only after eating some good food. She did this all through her life, even after my marriage and my children.

Ever since she left her parents in Maputo, my mother could not once see her parents and siblings. We were her only world, and her only happiness was seeing us happy, and so she made her living around us. It was only after we came to England, and made a decent living here, that I made all the arrangements for my mother to go to Maputo in 1967. There at last in her late 30s, she could see her father and siblings. But unfortunately, her mother had already passed away. I was glad to have been able to do this for my mother.

I did everything, be it my personal or professional work, only after taking consent from my parents, and never did anything against their will, as I always believed that the length and breadth of their experience can teach us more than what we could learn from being tutored

289

in the hands of learned scholars; moreover, my parental blessings also mattered a lot for my well-being. I never kept my earnings with me, and I would always give all my earnings to my mother till her last breath, and she would plan all my savings with the help of my father. Every business venture I started, and every property I bought, I always made sure that both my parents would be present, and I had inaugurated everything in the hands of my mother with her prayer to the God and took the blessings of God through my mother. I preferred the blessings of my parents to be more pious than anyone; my mother was next only to GOD for me.

And then, one day in her late seventies, in May 2008, she fell sick, and was admitted to Wakefield Hospital. In the hospital, while she was still under examination, and doctors had not yet diagnosed the disease, she cryingly held my hand and said, "why did you take me here, Solly? I am contracted with cancer, and I will not live anymore." I tried to console her, but she resorted to weeping, with her repeated apologies, "forgive me Solly! forgive me for beating you so often in your childhood." With this, I too lost my control and fell on her body and cried out loud. Then, she also held my wife's hands, and pleaded her for apologies.

After sustaining in the hospital for five days, she passed away on June 4, 2008, leaving all of us in a vale of tears. Just before she took her last beath, she called all her children and grand-children, and then she peacefully set to rest in the lap of God for ever. I thank GOD for bringing me into this world through my mother. I love my mother for her great sacrifices, and her blessings will always be there for me and my wife, and on all our children, grand-children, and great-grand-children. My mother was everything for me, and I miss her forever; miss her food, her shouts, her warmth love, and her presence itself; I wish I should see her in another world too, to be her son there too, when I go there, leaving this world forever.

My Wife, Maryam Adam

The credit of my success and well-being also goes, without saying, to my wife, Maryam. She is so capable and decent a woman that, I am fortunate to have her as my wife, and without whom I would not have been what I have been to this day. Being a daughter of my own uncle, she is my cousin, and she grew up along with me, as part of our extended family. Ever since she married me, Maryam has been my devout wife, and shared her affectionate partnership with me in all my ways and views, and in all my actions and commitments towards our family, friends, and society. She has been a good daughter-in-law to my parents, and had treated them like her own parents, while extending her love to other members of our family. She also hosted all my friends and relatives for decades, particularly hundreds of cricketing friends whom I came across in my life, and in turn she won the respect of all as a Bhabhi (elder brother's wife). She was Bhabhi to all my peers, and a motherly figure to those who are of my children's age. While so doing, she immensely contributed for both my personal and professional career, as well as for the harmony in our familial lives; she has been the centre of attention for all of us, the soul of my entire family.

When I began to think of marrying Maryam, we both were still in school at Natal Colony, and had not even hit our adolescence yet. However, our marriage took place a little later, on April 14, 1968, in England, only after we bought a house there, and when I began to earn my livelihood as a mechanic and taxi-driver. Ever since, Maryam dedicated all her life for the family. She began initially assisting my mother in the kitchen and for other household activities, and eventually rose to become the focal point of the family. As I was a taxi-driver then, my timings were very odd; I would leave the house in the evening, and then would return home only sometime between 1:00 and 2:00 in the morning. However, Maryam would never sleep before I reached home, and would join my mother in waiting for my return; they both would retire to bed only after serving me food, wait till I finish my eating, and then see me off to bed.

Maryam was so committed to the family that, she never sought my presence, even in the most crucial moments, like pregnancy and childbirth. Instead, she selflessly supported my interests, prioritising the well-being of our family, over and above her own. For instance, when I wanted to go to Mecca for better opportunities, she readily gave her approval, despite being in a critical stage of her first pregnancy. She never sought any material comforts, and had always found her happiness in my happiness, and that of our family. My parents admired her modesty; they always expressed their fondness for her; to recount my mother's words, she has been the angel of our house.

After returning from Mecca in 1969, I ventured into multiple petrol and other businesses, that resulted in significant increase in my income. Maryam took on various responsibilities; apart from her household chores and childcare, she would also accompany me to oversee our businesses in the evenings. I provided her with a MINI car to pick and drop our kids in school, and for other works. With her takeover of household duties, besides my mother, and my father's dedication to petrol business, I could focus on business and cricket. They played a crucial role in all my achievements, enabling me to become a key figure in signing Asian cricketers for English Leagues, allowing me time to organize various benefit matches. Without these three important persons in my life, I would not have attained any of these successes.

Eventually, hundreds of cricketers from Asia came to become my friends, and most of whom would dine and reside in my house. Then, Maryam would pleasingly greet every single guest, and prepare their choicest Asian cuisines for them; she would cook so well that, everyone would express their love for her food. Every single cricketer from India, and Pakistan, who played in England, you name it, be it Sunil Gavaskar, Sachin Tendulkar, Imran Khan, Javed Miandad, Mohinder Amarnath, or Sandip Patil, Ravi Shastri, Iqbal Qasim, they all unanimously admire the food prepared by Maryam, and they affectionately call her Bhabhi.

Despite greeting a host of cricket stars and legends in her own home, and then hosting them with great Asian delicacies, my wife had absolutely no idea of who is who, and of their what and whereabouts; she never looked up to legends, nor others down; she never even cared to know about their popularity, and high esteems in society. For her, it was just simple: they were simply her family friends, and she was their beloved Bhabhi or Aunt, and no other parameters were really of any concern for her.

I recollect an incident that explains my wife's innocence of stardom, and her plain reception of everyone and everything in equal terms. It was an occasion when Sunil Gavaskar made a century of 188 runs at Lords in 1987, while he was playing for the 'Rest of the World' team against 'MCC'; it was also his first century at Lords. So, it was a huge news for the media and the cricket fans, and every media was desperate trying to contact Sunil for his interview. My house was his official contact in England in those days, and Sunil and I were out on some important work. Upon our returning home, my wife expressed her wonder, of why so many people were making calls for Sunil? When I explained her in great excitement, of the glorious achievement of Sunil, and the media's intent to interview him in that regard, my wife plainly expressed her wonder again, "Sunil is a cricketer by profession and he travelled more than 5000 miles from India to England to play cricket, and he scored a century as part of his work, so what's so great about it?" With this, Sunil laughed out loud, and I was awestruck. For her, Sunil is just a family member, who loves and cares for her, and his occupation is something called cricket, and nothing more; how blissful she is, and so I love her so much.

We were very happy and grew prosperous with four children. Then one day, my whole family, including children, went on a pilgrimage to

Mecca in December 2017, and it was a lovely time for all of us, to be together; we then returned home on January 9, 2018. A few days after, on January 18 at around 08:30pm, Maryam expressed some pain in her left leg, besides a rise in her body temperature, cough and cold. In the next morning, by the time we took her to the hospital, her leg got swollen quite a bit. Doctor tested her, and prescribed some basic medicine, saying, 'nothing to be serious about it.'

But the swelling did not go down. Instead, it got aggravated, worsening the pain, and swelling every hour. Then, we visited Pinderfields Hospital in Wakefield. As we reached hospital, Maryam fell unconscious, and the duty doctor announced that she was no more. For a moment, I grew stony; my mind went blank, and everything around me turned grey. When I came to senses, it was terrible; I felt like jumping through the windows and killing myself. Then emptiness paraded, and I was standing in the hospital all alone, and began to cry; all my children also came and joined my cry. But fortunately, soon we learnt that she was breathing still. Dr Muzumdar examined the patient, diagnosed it as Necrotizing Fasciitis, which is a rare bacterial infection that rapidly spreads along skin and eats away the muscles; he also suggested that the only remedy for this problem at that moment was to amputate the leg, and remove its infected portion, though he was not sure of the chances of her survival; as per the records, just 4 in 1 million people would be affected with this disease, and its chances of survival was almost none.

On January 20, 2018, doctor conducted a surgery, in which her leg got amputated just above the knee. But she did not come back to her senses immediately, though her heart and lungs were in function; it took 10 long weeks for her to come out of coma, and then one morning she miraculously opened her eyes slowly. The doctor congratulated me for her miraculous survival and admired my wife for her tough fight against death. But we continued to keep her in the hospital, and it took a total of 6 months and 2 days for her to see the light of day, and finally to came back to our home. All these days, our entire family were around the hospital, doing nothing, but praying to God all through. I am grateful to Dr. Mazumdar, forever, for extending my wife's life to stay with me further; Sunil Gavaskar also thanked the doctor, through his recorded video message, for saving the life of his Bhabhi who was so dear to him.

Later, she also had to undergo 20 or 22 surgeries to graft skin on her amputated leg, and now she is on her wheelchair, being able to do small chores on her own. To give her better comforts, a friend of mine, Moosa Akudi, designed a special electrical bed for her, and gifted us. During this period, all my three daughters-in-law had done amazing services for my wife, whom they treated like a small baby. Many cricketers from India and Pakistan visited her in the hospital, expressed their regards for her, and wished for her recovery; seeing my wife's situation, some of my friend-cricketers could not control themselves; tears welled out of their eyes. I am fortunate to have all these loving friends who had genuine concern for me, my wife, and our children.

Now, I spend most of my time, talking to my wife, and attending to her, though we two are now looked after by my children, daughters-in-law, and grandchildren. Though left with only one leg, she never expressed any displeasure about it; she pleasingly accepted whatever God had given her and did the part that God had assigned to her. People say that, life will be happy, if you can get money, things, and position. But I believe that if you have a good wife and can share the best of your life with her, you can experience a heaven on earth, and I find such heavenly life on earth, in the divine presence of my wife. Except few years, we (Maryam and me) grew together, and lived fifty-five odd years of our married life; I feel blessed to have such a wonderful wife in my life, upon whose protective wings my family still thrives on.

My Father, Saeed Adam

My father was no less in his significance to me and to my family, yet he was different in his approach than my mother. I call my father Baji. Unlike my mother who left her mark on me, with her active intervention in the form of her emotional outbursts of love and anger, to instil discipline and morals in me, the influence of my father on me was through an indirect means, yet it was deep and concrete; he never taught me anything in words, nor expressed his love openly, but he continues to be a latent influence on me, as he was quiet and composed being. Like most fathers to most of the children, my father too was a great attraction for me; his love and respect for my mother, his devotion to God and dedication to family, his keen observation and grasp over the situation, his firmness in the matters of decision making, and his industrious temperament and unwavering attitude to stand against any difficulty, are some of the noble character traits that were naturally induced into my life.

My father was a man of supreme self-respect; he believed that all are equal before God; he dissented quietly the practice of high and low among humans, as he considered it not only inhuman, but a great disservice to God. Having believed in the principle of work as worship, he detested roaming idly, in dependence on others, and tirelessly exerted all his energies for the cause of our family. As a young boy, in Karachi, when I was doing part-time work in a shoe shop, where I would colour shoe, to extend my support to the family, I would notice my father admiring my efforts silently, without even uttering a word.

My father loved independence and freedom, and he worked all his life for attaining those ideals to live with self-respect and dignity. It was only for his self-respect that, he left the job offered by my aunt Ayesha Gardee at their own factory in Lahore, and moved along with his family to Karachi, to build his life independently. In Karachi, we experienced hardest times ever, and went through tragic consequences of losing the lives of my two siblings in a short period of time, when I was still very young. However, the invincible spirit in him did not die; instead, he stood firm, continued working hard, and had resolved to face any adversity; his resolute to work hard has not only paved paths for the fortunes that we enjoy today, but had also shaped my moral character, which subscribes to the philosophical view that to believe in God, is to believe in the self; I nurtured this moral spirit also among my children, and it served as a potent force for my individual progress and for the harmony in my family.

When we moved to England, my father continued his hard work, both as a worker in a factory, and would also hire out his vehicle to his fellow workers who worked in the same factory. In this way, he evolved multiple possibilities to channel out his energies for a productive cause. He was extremely disciplined and would make good financial planning for the house. In fact, it was my father who took care of my financial administration; whatever the money I earned I would give it to my mother, who in turn handed over the same to my father. I had full freedom to cherish and nurture my interests. But I always sought my father's advice in everything I did, and I never invested even a penny on my own without discussing it with my father. I think his advice and support immensely helped me in doing my best in everything that I took up in my life.

My father has always been my silent support, and the strength of my life. When I thought of investing in Petrol business in 1972, the whole family went against my plans, except my father; he extended his outright support and heightened my confidence to carry forth my very first business venture. In fact, he went further to take out all his savings, sold out his car, and contributed a huge lot for my investment. But my father continued working in the factory, and only when he sensed that my business had a greater prospect to reap more profits than the income that he was getting as worker in the factory, he resigned his job, and took over the responsibility of my business. Ever since, he devoted his entire life for the cause of our business and played a significant role in ushering our business towards profits. If not by my father, it would not have been possible for me to do it all alone, the success that I have attained today. Particularly when I was busy being involved in cricket, alongside my business, attaining success in both the fields would have been just impossible but my father was my foundational pillar for whatever I have attained today, though my other family members and friends have also played their parts.

My father was a punctual and hard-working person; he was humble with great confidence on his self. He often would tell us, "Always keep our feet firm on ground like a tree, and never get floated like clouds; don't be a miser, but do not be a spend thrift either." I never remember my father taking even one day off from his work, ever since he took over our petrol business, and he served all the seven days of every week throughout his active life. In addition to it, he would also adjust his lunch time according to my changing schedules, owing to my cricket matches. The usual lunch timings of my father were between 1 and 2 pm, and during this one hour break I would relieve him, till he took back his charge at 2 pm, and then we would both proceed on our respective works. However, on the days when I had a cricket match, particularly on Saturdays when our match would usually start at 2:30 pm, my father would have to quickly finish his lunch in half-an-hour and would reach the office by 01: 30 so that I can reach the grounds at a scheduled time. He made sure that I should not miss the match, and only because of his support I dedicated my time for cricket, and never missed a single opportunity to play cricket in my career; I am indebted to my father, for everything that I am.

The death of my mother in 2008 took a huge toll on my father, though, as usual, he did not exhibit it openly; he underwent a massive stroke of paralysis in 2011 and was hospitalised. He recovered a bit and was given a regular massage at physiotherapy clinic; I would also give him bath regularly, and all my family members were serving him well. And then one day, I was sitting with my father and was talking to him after his dinner; he was trying to say something, but for some reason words did not come out of his mouth; he then said, "Solly, I am really tired, can you take me upstairs?" I could not control my tears, as I had never got to hear the word 'tired' uttered by my father, ever in his life; I spent all my life with my father, and he had been an untiring soul, always filled with zeal to work. Now he is seeking rest; my heart sensed something wrong. I quietly helped him to slowly climb the stairs, and then I put him to sleep. I was terribly sad; I alerted my brother and his wife with whom my father was staying then, and slowly walked up to my house. While having dinner, I shared the same with my wife, who got worried and asked whether we should go and sleep there with my father. But for some reason, we did not go. And on the bed, I began to ponder silently about my father, intermittently talking to my wife, and finally took a nap. Early the next morning, that was March 8, 2011, I woke up to the ring of the telephone. It was from my brother (Younus). 'Father is no more,' he said. My father had struggled for seven weeks with his paralysed body, and then departed from us. I felt that the main tree of my family has collapsed; silence paraded in my life; numbness stuck in my body. I could not even walk fast; I slowly went to my father, and paid homage to him, while tears dripping down my cheek. I was half dead with my mother, and now with my father, I felt I was no more.

My Siblings, and their Families

Being the eldest, I have two younger siblings—one is my sister, Haseena, and the other was my brother, Younus, who was the youngest of all, and was 12 years younger to me. Haseena was married off to Masood Khurshid, and has got three sons (Ehtesham, Bilal and Umar) and three daughters (Attiya, Saima, and Safiya). She lives in our nearby locality of Dewsbury, and I make frequent visits to her, and she too makes her presence at all the important events of our family. Younus Adam, on the other hand, was born at a time when we had not yet recovered from the trauma of my four deceased siblings, and so, he was the most pampered child of all; I too considered Younus as my own child and had always treated him with utmost love and care. When Younus fell severely ill, he was just two years old, and my mother and I panicked; we rushed to Natal Muslim Welfare Society Hospital. My mother would also ask me to take my brother to Mosque for Maghrib (sunset prayer), as she believed that Maghrib was very significant to communicate our message to God. Accordingly, I would take my brother to the Mosque every single day and would request all the devotees there to pray for my brother; fortunately, he recovered from illness.

When I started working in a factory in England, Younus was just 7 years old attending primary school. Unlike me, he never had to face any hardships, and had a life of freedom and joy. I wished to see him grow without difficulties, and so I would give him ample pocket money. Having faced poverty in my own childhood, I wanted him to have everything that I had missed; I would find my happiness in his joy. I also wanted him to study well and get educated. But unfortunately, he could not even attend college, though he completed his schooling with great difficulty.

Then we got him married to our cousin, Rukhsana, who was also a younger sister of my wife, Maryam. So, both my brother and Rukhsana were treated affectionately by my wife and I, and the couple were given full freedom and care. Rukhsana too was joyous to extend her helping hand to her sister (my wife) at home, while my brother was helping me in business; they were a happy couple, always lived happily under our protective guidance and care. With that affection, I registered my firm as Adam Brothers, and had made him entitled to have equal rights over our business.

They got three children (first two daughters, Ashiya and Alia, and then a son, Amir who was the youngest). We would pamper these children a lot as our own when they were kids; my wife would give bath to the children, feed them food, and play and sing lullabies for them, while my own children, who by then had already grown up, would also join them to play with them. The happiness of my parents knew no bounds, as we were all living together as one united family under the same roof. Eventually, when my children had grown up to be adults and of marriageable age, we moved to another house of ours, which was just adjacent to it, keeping my parents in that house with my brother. However, we never got separated, and had always lived together.

But my happiness did not last long. Younus had succumbed to Covid in 2020; after sustaining through the pandemic for two years, he unfortunately left us forever on November 5, 2022. I feel terrible to lose my dearest brother, who was most loving kid of my life. Rukhsana still lives with her children in the same house, adjacent to us. We all still live together as one united family.

My Children, and my Grandchildren

In the most formative years of my career, while I was establishing myself both as a businessman and a local club cricketer in England, I got four children (three sons, Ebrahim, Afzal and Sohail and a daughter, Asma). As I was busy building my career, I could not spare much time for my children in their childhood; except my daughter, unfortunately, the rest of my children did not feel much of my presence. Particularly, when my first son, Ebrahim, was born, I was not even at home; as I was in Mecca in search of my fortunes then, I had to miss the greatest moment of my life to be with my wife, and to extend my helping hand to relieve my wife from her excruciating labour pains; nor was I with her, to share the happy moments of seeing, holding, and kissing my new born first child; I was not even there to name him.

I feel sorry for not being able to be with my wife in that most crucial and memorable moment of her life, and for not sparing time for my children, to extend my parental love for them in their age of playfulness. However, they had no dearth of love and care, as they were apples of the eyes of my entire family members, both my parents and my wife, and to my brother and his wife. But I thought a lot about my children's careers and strived every single minute to establish necessary conditions for them to lead their flourishing lives. I wanted all my four children to be well educated and disciplined, and fortunately every single one of them did well in their studies and set their moral high grounds, though the care, well-being, and disciplined lives of all my children should be entirely credited to my parents and to my wife.

To begin with, my first child, Ebrahim Adam (born in May 1969) is a brilliant accountant, who runs his own accounting firm called 'Adam Accountants' in Saville Town; he is very humble, kind, and soft spoken. Ebrahim is always ready to address all our concerns, and so everyone in our family approach him for any problem they encounter. Ebrahim married Fatima who is a daughter of Bashir Ahmed; Bashir Bhai was one of my father's close friends. They got three lovely children, two sons and a daughter. His first child is Mohammed Saeed, whom I call Sunny, after Sunil Gavaskar whose nick name is Sunny. Sunny is a practicing lawyer who is working for a solicitor company and is doing his work so well. Sunny married Fatima and they have a child, named Eesa. The second son of Ebrahim is Bilal whom I call Abu Bilal. Abu has just finished his masters in physiotherapy, and has, somehow, turned out to be closer to my heart, though I love all my grandchildren equally. Then the last and the youngest child of Ebrahim is a daughter named Maleehah; she is lovely and talented; her business knowledge is unparalleled with anyone, and she almost single handedly runs our business. She is one of the sweetest girls I have ever come across.

My second son, Afzal Adam (born in November 1970), is a brilliant businessman with a great sense of humour. Like me, Afzal has hands on multiple interests, and now he looks after our family businesses. Afzal's heart is like gold, he is a compassionate person who extends his helping hand to anyone in need. He is quick at making decisions which are mostly accurate and moves forward. He married his cousin, whose name is also Fatima. She is very nice and looks after the house and children with great commitment. Like Ebrahim, Afzal too has got two sons and a daughter. Afzal's first child is a son, Anas, who married a very nice girl, Kolsuma (we call her Kully); Kully has given birth to two children, a daughter, Nusaybah and then recently a son, Yousuf. The second son of Afzal is Usaamah, who is a qualified optician; he talks very less, but whenever he talks, we jokingly say, he makes a hole in the sky. Usaamah has recently got married to Faiza, daughter of an Imam; they are a cute and very happy couple. And then, the last and youngest child of Afzal is Zahra; she is very reserved, and a quiet person. She is a teacher, and has got married recently to Usama Patel, an optician; they are a lovely couple.

Sohail Adam (born in September 1977) is my youngest son; he is his mom's child and was so intimate to Maryam. Being the youngest, he was fortunate to have received my pampering as well in his childhood, as by then, I had established myself both in business as well as in cricket. He is a business graduate and has set up a firm named Adam Estates; he is intelligent and is amicable to all. Sohail married a girl named Maryam, who is sociable and friendly. They got a child and named him Muhammad. Like his parents, he is always at hand, and quickly attends to us at beck and call; he also looks after his father's business.

The last, but the most important part of my life is my darling child, Asma (born in March 1972). Being my only girl child, she has naturally received maximum pampering from all of us, including my parents. My mother often considered Asma a blessing who had brought luck to our house, as my mother always believed that our fortunes grew only after Asma's birth. She is well educated and has a sound business mind; she is very sociable and friendly, and my friends would often say, she is my carbon copy. Asma started her own travel business, Travel Tonight, and stays within our proximity. Fortunately, she got a very nice and caring husband, Omar Aiobo; he also cares for us a lot and loves all our family members. We are blessed to have such as loving and caring son-in-law whom my wife considers as my fourth son. Asma and Omar got three lovely children—two daughters (Sumaiyah and Aatikha) and a son, Muhammad; they are all well-educated. Asma's eldest daughter is Sumaiyah; she has done her master's degree in architecture and got recently married to Zubair; Sumaiyah has been deeply spiritual, and now she is an Alima. The second child of Asma is a son, Mohammad. He is very humble and helpful to his mother; he works with Sohail in real estate and is also in travel business. The last child of Asma is again a daughter, Aatikha, whom I call Muskaan, meaning smile, as she has had a beautiful smile on her face.

I am lucky to have such a sweet and beautiful family, where each one of us is working for the happiness and wellbeing of the other. All my sons and daughters-in-law, and my daughter and son-in-law, along with my 10 grandchildren and 3 great-grand-children, all affectionately live for one another as one unified family. Maryam and I are really blessed to have such great daughters-like daughters-in-law, and a son-like son-in-law. They are all very kind, humble, and affectionate towards us; they all showered immense respect and love for me and Maryam and had extended great services to us and to our family. I am fortunate to have them as life partners for my children, and they have now become my own children.

I thank GOD for being so kind to keep our family together and affectionately. I firmly believe that happiness does not lie in wealth, nor power and position, but in the unity and integrity, and in love and compassion for each other. I think, I am fortunate to have all that in all my family members; we live together as one unified family, and its lovely to be one with each other.

QUEEN'S INVITATION

It was in the wee hour of a Monday in 2015, I had not yet finished even my morning routine, that I was stuck with a surprise of an HR envelope landing at my table. Unsure of the letter, I just took it into my hands intending to see through it, when my mobile phone rang; it was my friend, Iqbal Bhana (OBE.DL), who worked in the office of Her Majesty, the late Queen of England Elizabeth II. Iqbal called me up to check about the letter which had just reached me and informed me that the letter was nothing but a letter of invitation from the Queen; he congratulated me and my wife Maryam upon receiving an invitation to have the rarest opportunity to participate in Garden Tea Party at Buckingham Palace. It was unbelievable; for a moment, I was shocked, and then, slowly by the time I came to my senses to find my name, Mr., and Mrs. Suleman Adam, being printed in the royal letter of invitation, tears started rolling down my eyes involuntarily. The card with the logo, having the royal symbol on it, reads: "The Lord Chamberlain is commanded by Her Majesty to invite Mr. Suleman Saeed Adam and Mrs. Maryam Adam to a Garden Party at Buckingham on Wednesday, May 20, 2015 from 4 to 6 pm. With this, I began to ponder over my humble beginnings:

Was that the same boy of six years old!

Who bit the bitterness of destiny as a refugee;

A boy, who was deported from India to Pakistan, along with his parents;

A boy, who had to walk incessantly through deadly desert's sands of midsummer for four long hot days and three long, dark and cold nights;

A boy, who was starved of food, water and shelter and had survived on the benevolence of some unknown on the way, during his long sojourn to find one's own home;

A boy, who had survived the temperature of 50 degrees during summers in Lahore, without even a fan, but merely upon the protective wings of his mother who would pour water on the walls of a small shed in which they took shelter;

A boy, who had to lose his two young loving brothers to deadly disease, Jaundice, and two young loving sisters to its equally deadly chicken pox, in a circumstance that incurs us to a dearth of proper food, shelter and medical care;

A boy, who lived his worst, difficult times during his most formative years at Natal colony of Karachi in Pakistan;

A boy, who could not afford paying fee to attend his school;

A boy, who could not afford buying a ball for his cricketing practice;

A boy, who had no shoes to wear;

A boy, who could not afford buying eye-glasses;

A boy, who toiled hard against the fuming heat of the factory in England, in his late teens;

A boy, who spent his sleepless nights as a car-driver and as a mechanic, against the cold winds of winter in the open yards of England in his early twenties;

A boy, who missed an opportunity to play for a club, in an unfortunate circumstance of not being able to pay a match fee of 20 pence;

A boy, whose photograph had been cunningly removed from its publication in a newspaper by unknown forces;

A boy, who paid several visits, like millions of other commoners and tourists from abroad, to Queen's palace, only to see it from outside of the palace gates, and had never even dared to dream of entering its gates one day;

A boy, who rose to be one of the earliest Asians to embark himself to be a businessman;

Was that the same boy! Was that the same boy!!

Yes, yes, the very same boy!

He has now been nominated as an invitee by the office of the Lord Lieutenant of West Yorkshire, Dr Ingrid Roscoe, to have a tea-time in the Garden Party at Buckingham Palace, convened by the office of Her Majesty, the Queen of England, and of course upon the royal beckons of the Queen herself.

I cherished this news with all my family members and friends, and we were all happy for the royal honours. I acknowledged the invite in my reply to the royal office on the same day of receiving the letter and expressed my consent and my pleasure at being part of the event. The news of my invite had spread far beyond the Savile Town, the town of my domicile, and was also celebrated in and around my ancestral home-town, Surat in Gujarat state of India. A fashion designer from Surat named Sonica, came forward to design and make a special dress for me and Maryam to wear on that special occasion, however, our long-time friend, Munaf, was finally assigned to design the dress for us. The news-papers in England lauded the occasion as a mark of royal recognition to the cause of my passion for cricket, that got manifested into me be-coming a community champion in my own right. I played cricket for around 40 years and it had always been my ambition to get more people involved in the sport. During this period, particularly the last 15 years which were crucial, I sponsored various cricket leagues, besides help-ing innumerable young, enthusiastic minds to gain access to the game, including the likes of legendary cricketer Sachin Tendulkar during his formative times whom I recommended to sign for Yorkshire County. As one newspaper remarked, "Solly Sports has sponsored virtually every league and cup competition across West Yorkshire." Now, I have got one of the biggest honours with this invite to see the Queen. Maryam was pleased with this honour of great prestige, and I cheered with her.

Having gone through the etiquettes guide to meet Her Majesty, finally, Maryam and I set our travel to the Capital on Wednesday morning, May 20, 2015, and reached the Royal residence before the appointed time at 4 pm. The palace was as beautiful inside with several spacious rooms as its courtyard with huge lush-green lawns, a lake, and trees in it. Tea, Coffee, biscuits, fruits, water, etc. were arranged on the tables. We were not the only couple present, as there were also quite a few people who graced the occasion. We all greeted each other and sat across the table to join the interaction; The Queen had not graced in yet, as it was not yet the appointed time. As appointed, it was sharp at 4:00 that the door opened, and the late Queen Elizabeth II and her husband Prince Philip, along with their royal family, made their entry into the meeting hall. As they entered, the Royal couple reached out to every one of us in person, while the Queen graciously greeted us all in her mellowed voice and went forth making casual inquiries after us. The Queen finished meeting us all in one hour, and was still going to be with us, since as per the schedule she would leave by 6 pm. At around 5: 40 pm I grew a bit anxious of the waning time, then I slowly went to one of the members of the royal family to enquire about when I could get a chance to talk to the Queen. To my surprise, I learnt from him that the first one hour in which the Queen met us was the actual time that was allocated for us to talk to the Queen. The later one hour, on the other hand, was the Queen's time during which, it would be our free will and liberty, whether we would talk to the Queen or leave the space at any given moment; her majesty did not like to waste even a minute out of our productive, valuable time. It was a big lesson for me to begin considering the value of time as more valuable than the value of any great material worth; it was more so in the case of the time of other's than that of one's own. From that moment, I tried my best to value time, and had not let others wait for me, beyond an appointed time.

Following this prestigious moment, I again had the fortunate to meet the then Prince Charles, who is now the King of England, however, at Al-Hikmah Centre at Mount Pleasant Road in Batley Carr, when the prince was invited to be the Guest of honour to pay his visit to the Centre. This was the second time, and again it was Iqbal Bhana who provided me with the opportunity to meet the prince. I am so lucky that I could meet the prince in person, shook his hands and had a short interaction. I feel privileged to see both the prince and the Queen of UK. Since the day I had laid my foot on English soil with empty hands and had joined my labouring father in factory, it was Yorkshire that was my country, and Dewsbury that was my home. Today, I am a successful businessman, a long-time cricketer in various leagues, and I have lived on this soil for over 50 long years, having children and grandchildren; I am a proud citizen of England who always believes that well-being of citizens is integral to the well-being of the nation, and continue working towards harmonious global humanity.

CONCLUSION

As an eminent American writer and philosopher, Ralph Waldo Emerson, once said, 'life is a journey, not a destination.' In this incredible journey of my life that spans over 78 years, I reckon every moment of my life as valuable as every other moment that I have experienced. It was owing to this view that I 'never counted my chicken, before they hatched,' and had always lived in the moment, without presuming the end results. With this, I feel that I did whatever the little I could, be it familial, or social, particularly in the realm of cricket and business. During my journey, I received help from several people, and had made friends with them, while extending my helping hand to several others whom I have come across.

To that effect, my life echoes the famous words of a world-renowned American astronaut, Neil Armstrong, when he said as he set his foot on moon, 'one giant leap for mankind.' Though it was a little help that I received from my friends during initial stages of my business establishments, it had a profound significance in my emergence as an entrepreneur in England. I witnessed ups and downs in my business career, and yet was resolute in making my foray into several businesses. While doing so, I made sure of not being greedy beyond a point and had extended my assistance to several individuals to emerge as businessmen. For instance, Younus Patel used to work initially at my mechanic garage, as my help in handling mechanic tools, including cleaning my garage floor and the workspace, before his emergence as multi-millionaire. It was I who recommended Younus to take over AMOCO petrol station, when I got the opportunity for myself. Then Younus, eventually, with all his hard work emerged as one of the wealthiest Asians in England; he is now a popular figure in northern England with his own company, AY & Y Patel.

Likewise, Suleman (Adam) Patel, son of Mohammad Adam Patel, also used to work as a mechanic in my garage. Seeing his honesty and hard work, I guided Suleman to take over a petrol station in Birstall with which he carved his niche in business; from him being a mere mechanic, his sons, today, own multiple petrol stations in England. Witnessing the assistance that I provided several people in making their mark as businessmen, Yakub Valli, a close friend of mine, expressed his desire for a petrol station site. When AMOCO gave me an offer to take over one of their sites, I recommended Yakub Valli to them, and assisted him in establishing his petrol business; he now possesses multiple petrol stations in Yorkshire. These are some of a famous few, who have risen from rags to riches in my association and with my assistance; there are several others too, who rose to be successful businessmen in England, under my guidance and assistance. I feel pleased to see them rise in their businesses, and most of them are still my good friends. I am blessed to have had this opportunity to help them, and therefore, when the media refers to me as a 'successful businessman,' I humbly disagree with them. Instead, I deem myself to be a 'satisfied businessman,' rather than a successful one, as 'success' is a physical measure by others, while 'satisfaction' refers to the contentment of one's own self.

Therefore, despite lucrative opportunities in business to get richer and richer every day, I chose to channel out some of my opportunities to my friends and known people, while carving out a good part of my time for cricket, rather than exerting my energies for mere financial gains. In fact, I dedicated a great deal of my time, particularly weekends, for cricket, and shaped myself to be a cricketer in English leagues, while nurturing the young talents around me. Seeing my 'mad love for cricket,' for which I would give up opportunities in business, some of my friends and well-wishers would even express their wonder.

Right from my childhood, I believed that 'play is the highest form of learning,' and had passionately nurtured cricketing interest in me, as well as among those who embody potentials in cricket. Therefore, in a little over 50 years of my involvement in business, I hardly found 10 businessmen as my friends. However, in the four decades of my life as a cricketer, I met hundreds of star-cricketers, nourished some budding cricketers into cricket-stars, made friends with them, and had cherished some of my best moments with them; several of them became my family friends also. And from the lives and world views of my legendary cricket friends, I also learnt invaluable lessons for my life, like how to be a good cricketer, businessman, and moreover, a good human being. I believe that sports possess the spirit of integrity and help uniting the people of the world. Furthermore, it leaves enduring memories that can be treasured for times eternal.

In recognition of my contributions to cricket, particularly my assistance to the young cricketers in finding their careers, several cricketers from India and Pakistan expressed their gratitude both in person as well as through various media channels. I recall an Indian test cricketer once telling me, "Solly Bhai, if you hadn't invited me to England, I might never have had the opportunity to play even first-class cricket," while yet another cricketer would share his joy to tell me that, he would not even have known about the location of England on the world map, had I not signed him for English league. Several players also attest to the fact that their cricketing skills and standards substantially improved, after playing in league cricket in England, which had helped them later to represent their respective countries; many of them still acknowledge my assistance and support in this process.

However, life is uncertain, and it takes its own course, as its history unveils unknown paths in varied dispositions. Some people may be born with a golden spoon in their mouths, and yet might end up in turning out to be paupers. And for others, life may be a testament of hell, until from out of such a hellish life, they might become rich and have the whole world surrender before their feet. The memories of each of the cricketers I have shared here, presents this fact that, life miraculously takes its own turns, and yet, it also demands human efforts in taking its own course. I feel that I am fortunate to meet these many people in my life, with whom I cherished various dimensions of life, having mutually benefitted from each other. Moreover, I have got the rarest opportunity to meet several legendary cricketers, and I feel that the life of each of these cricket legends, and world-renowned star cricketers of Asia, is larger than the life of the sub-continent. It was nothing but my fortune to experience this huge a life, that sometimes I wonder about my own self.

At this moment, I would like to recount the life experiences of three legendary cricketers, whose fate had turned bleak, after enjoying fame and privilege as cricketers during their active phase.

The first one among them was a legendary cricketer of England once known for his world record of taking highest wickets in Test matches. He had such a huge fanbase in the Yorkshire cricket circles that I, as a young cricket lover in 1960s, had to stand in the queue for over an hour at Headingly stadium just to secure his autograph. Several years later, when Sunil took me into the VIP lounge, it was astounding for me to witness the same retired cricketer, sitting right beside me, unnoticed by all. Subsequently, his identity turned far bleaker, and during a test match at Headingly stadium, the same cricket legend was barred from making his entry; the gate keeper at the stadium blocked his entry, for not producing a gate pass. What a pathetic circumstance it was to someone who contributed immensely to the game.

The second cricketer in this line was a Caribbean Cricket Star, known for his role in winning World Cup twice for their country. It would be no exaggeration to say that he was adored by every Caribbean cricket fan. After his retirement from cricket, when he settled in England, we developed a strong friendship; he would frequent my residence, and we together shared the joy of endlessly discussing cricket. Unfortunately, however, he lost everything, owing to his personal and familial reasons, and now he is in a sad state, having to endure a hand to mouth existence. I am deeply empathetic to him.

The third cricketer to mention here in this regard was a celebrated test player from India known for his handsome looks, his brilliant batting skills; he was gifted with a bundle of talents and would hit sixes on demand. During his peak as a test cricketer, cricket fans were madly in love with him, thronging him wherever he went to secure his autograph. However, his personal and social circumstances seemed to have badly affected him. Eventually, he turned towards alcoholism, and unfortunately, all his fans who had once adored him so much, now began drifting away. There was a palpable fear among all that he might ask them for a drink.

These stark and saddening realities should be life lessons for all of us, particularly to those who enjoy the glories of name and fame, as they expose the transient nature of the worldly glories, as popularity dissipates along with one's dissociation from the game. However, having had the privilege of personal acquaintance with them, I attest to their exceptional humanity and unwavering dedication to the sport; they remain to be my champions of the game.

Though my active engagement in various public activities, particularly cricket and business, has left me with loads of pleasant memories to hoard and cherish, it is worth noting here that I have also been the victim of some unfortunate incidents in my life. They include life threatening experiences as result of blatant racism in South Africa. We settled in England and were doing well in business. In 1978, I, along with my wife, and our 2 sons, Ebrahim and Afzal, visited Maputo (Mozambique) to see my maternal family, and relatives there. On our way back home in England, we set our travel plan from Maputo to Johannesburg in South Africa by trains, and from there to England by flight. Despite booking first-class train tickets for the journey, we encountered a setback, unfortunately when we had to miss the daily train to Johannesburg. It was a moment of panic for us, and we were in an utter confusion. The station master, who was empathetic to our predicament, suggested that we go by a cargo train, as there were no other trains than a cargo train. Not knowing what to do, we got into a cargo train, else we would be missing our flight. The last bogie of the cargo trains had a small room-like compartment, which was meant for the guard, and yet could accommodate about four or five people to sit in; it also had a door which could be latched.

We got into the guard's compartment, and a young man in guard's duty allowed us to get in, though he was unease, as was apparent on his face. Unfortunately, it was a time imbued with pervasive racism in South Africa. We, the four of us, sat in that small room with a door and latch, while the guard sat out in a place attached to the room. As the train started, I checked with the guard about the nearest station where we can get some food to eat, as we had not eaten anything from the morning in that fiasco. Then the guard told me that there would be 20-30 minutes halt in the next station. So, when the train halted in the next station, I, along with my elder son, Ebrahim, got down from the train to find a food-store, which was just adjacent, and yet, outside the platform. I quickly purchased some food and water, and returned within five minutes to the train, only to see that it had just left the platform, leaving me in yet another shock.

Except for a coloured man who observed the situation, the station was almost empty, without any passengers on the platform. I turned stony for a moment and repented for our sorry state. It was quite evident that the guard had deliberately misled us and had created a situation where my wife and I was made to be stranded in separate places, each accompanied by one of our two sons. I reproached myself for being tricked by the train guard. Seeing my predicament, that coloured man on platform approached me to console me; he told me that such incidents were common, where racists in general would take advantage of the situation to harass, or even to molest coloured women. The man even came forward to extend his solidarity to me and offered me a transport by his car for 60 rands, to catch the train in the next station.

Without any second thought, we just got into the car, and the driver hurried us to the next station. During his drive, the driver warned me against raising my voice against the guard, as it would, in turn, entails false police charges against me. I might even have had to undergo detention, if I dared to complain against that Guard, and I was warned by him, in his words, 'you may never see a sun again.' It took almost two hours, and fortunately, we had finally reached the next station, a few minutes before the train was to reach there. I thanked the man for his greatest help, and without whom, I just cannot imagine, what could have been our fate.

My wife burst into tears, the moment she spotted us at the station. Till then, she latched herself inside, clinging tightly to our 8-year-old son, Afzal, and had not even opened the door at once. When I got into the chamber, she held me, and wept ceaselessly; she told me that, the guard banged the door persistently to open it, leaving her and the child to tremble in the grip of fear for hours. However, I maintained my cool, and as instructed by the man who helped me, I cried silently without uttering even a word of complaint. This traumatic incident has left a deep scar on us and continued to haunt us for years.

In fact, we witnessed several distressing incidents in South Africa during our short visit, as racism was still pervasive in that part of the globe. One such detestable incident was of an act and remark from a waiter in an ice-cream parlour. One evening, we all went to an ice cream parlour in Durban. Our children were all excited, and we wanted to place an order for our choicest ice-creams. But no one paid any attention to us. I thought they were busy, and after waiting for some time, I reminded the staff again. To my shock, the lady at the counter bluntly told me that they would not serve the coloured people. All our faces turned pale, and we left the shop silently. In an yet another incident of disgrace, we were not allowed into a beach in Durban, and were directed to a separate beach carved out for coloured people. These instances of blatant racism have deeply wounded me, and I always seek for harmonious coexistence of all the people of the world and extend my solidarity to all those who work towards establishing peace and harmony. So, when Nelson Mandela was released from jail, and subsequently became the President of South Africa in 1994, I made all my deliberations of meeting him, as a mark of my respect for his dedication to the cause of annihilating racism in South Africa, and other parts of the world.

For the well-being of the people at my reach, I have also been trying to make a modest contribution in a variety of means for the welfare of the societies both in England as well as in India and Pakistan. I engage in these activities irrespective of languages, ethnicities, and religion, and have been associated with community building, and other philanthropic activities for over 45 odd years. I keep myself approachable to all, and for which I have been popular in the Dewsbury region. All my endeavours in cricket, business, and other welfare activities, began to find recognition of all, leading me to have the honour of being felicitated on several occasions. The prominent among them all, was to receive the greatest honour of being part of the most celebrated garden party on May 20, 2015, at Buckingham Palace, hosted by Her Majesty Queen Elizabeth herself.

I also have had the privilege to receive an invitation to be part of an event hosted by the Savayra Foundation, UK, at Dewsbury Town Hall, on

August 16, 2003. Savayra Foundation is a charitable organization, which was founded by a Dewsbury solicitor, Sayeeda Hussain Warsi. The chief guest for the occasion was the then Prime Minister of Pakistan, Mohtarma Benazir Bhutto, and in whose hands, I was felicitated with a sports award for my lifetime contributions to cricket. Subsequently, I also had the honour of joining the dinner party with the Prime Minister Mrs. Bhutto, and during dinner, I had a great time conversing with her on various issues of socio-cultural concern, including cricket in Yorkshire. She undoubtedly has a profound knowledge on wide range of subjects, including cricket, world history, cultures, economy, law, and of course politics, and the event is still etched in my memory.

Finally, I also have had the privilege of being a biographic interest for a young man, Vara Vantapati. A couple of years ago, when I was in my sport's shop, Solly Sports, a young man walked into our shop to buy a cricket bat. Impressed by the quality of our bat, he plunged into a conversation with me, and introduced himself as Vara from Bradford. After a few days, he again visited our shop, along with his other friends from Manchester, to buy some more bats and other equipment. Over time, Vara grew curious to know about me, and upon learning about my long association with league cricket, and my friendship with several cricket legends, he approached me with this project of writing my biography. Later I learnt that he had already read about me in Sachin's autobiography! It was unbelievable for me, as I had never even thought about it, nor did I know of its worth and possibility. In a few days, he left a new phone, a digital voice recorder, and other electronic gadgets with me, and asked me to speak about my life, beginning with my childhood to the present, probing in depth into my cricket life, and the cricketers around me.

Ever since then, he took up this untiring journey between his home in Bradford, to my home and shop in Dewsbury, which is about 13 miles away. During this period of a little less than two years, Vara dedicat-

318

ed his valuable time and resources for documenting my life history, through our regular correspondences, and exchange of ideas; he also did archival research at length and had extracted great deal of information from newspaper archives, and other on-line sources for writing this book. While doing so, I have learnt that he took the assistance of some of his friends in Hyderabad, India. I also learnt that his wife too would join him for the cause and had assisted him in reading and appreciating the book content. Meanwhile, he visited India a couple of times, once to discuss with a publisher, and then in February 2024, to look after the job of printing and binding of the book. All this he did without expecting anything in return, and merely for his love for the game, and its history in England; he never at once sought a penny from me, and all the expenses incurred in due course were all borne by him. I feel amazed to see his selfless endeavours to make this book a reality. Had it not been for Vara, both the idea and execution of this herculean task of documenting the history of my life as a businessman, league cricketer and leader-organiser of cricket would not have been possible, and these huge bundles of relics underneath the darkest layers of the earth would not have seen the light of day. Therefore, the words of thanks are insufficient to express my gratefulness to Vara, and his family.

I feel that, if not blessed by God, it would have not been possible for a common man like me to have come across this range of people of varied nationalities, and to endure lasting friendship with some of the all-time greats in cricketing history. I also humbly acknowledge the fact that I got immensely benefitted from each one of them, without whom my life could have been incomplete. Now that the book has come into being, with all the depiction of my life and times around the world of cricket and cricketers, it feels my life is so complete and satisfied. I thank each one of them for coming into my life, and for making my life so happy. I thank God, the Almighty for making them part of my life, and making my life so happy and satisfied. I thank my parents, who are next only to God, as their only happiness was the happiness and well-being of me and my siblings, and our children and grand-children, and so on. I cherish the same spirit of devotion towards my family, and love for my friends and society at large.

Signing Off,

Solly Adam

TESTIMONIALS

Testimonials from Cricketers and Other Friends

Farokh Engineer
(Former Indian Cricketer)
September 16, 2022

Solly bhaiya is a legend, and has been an inspiration for several later day legends, Including Indian cricketing legend Sachin Tendulkar, and many other cricket stars from India and Pakistan who are too numerous to mention. I thank him for his motivational presence for young cricketers in aiding and nurturing their fullest potentials, and I feel fortunate to be his friend. Though I stay in Lancashire, and he in Dewsbury, we would often meet whenever we cross our ways. I wish him all the success for his forthcoming book, and he is so richly deserving a biography.

========

Sachin Tendulkar
(Former Indian Cricketer)
October 17, 2022

During my initial days in professional cricket, every cricketer from Mumbai who had played league cricket in England would always speak very highly about Solly Bhai's hospitality. I had heard so much about him that I was also looking forward to meeting him and his family. I finally met him and his wife, Maryam, in the company of

Dilip Vengsarkar in 1990 and my experience was no different. Solly Bhai and his family were so welcoming that I immediately became close to them.

My three-and-a-half-month stint with Yorkshire in 1992 helped me mature as a cricketer. It also taught me some important life lessons. I was only 19 then, in a new place and had to do everything on my own. While I tried cooking food and doing laundry by myself, I could not do it as well and Solly Bhai's family helped me with it. I would visit them at least three times a week during that period, and I remember the delicious food that I would have at their place. My stay at Yorkshire was a memorable one, thanks to Solly Bhai and his family's warm and welcoming nature.

Solly Bhai's house was a go-to place for many cricketers and I am sure that in this biography, there would be plenty of memorable stories that cricket lovers across the world can look forward to. I'd like to take this opportunity to extend my best wishes to Vara Vantapati and the team for the success of this book.

Dear Solly Bhai, wishing you the best of health and prosperity, always!

========

Iqbal Qasim
(Former Pakistani Cricketer)
January 18, 2023

Like most professional cricketers of Asia, I too landed in England in 1976 in search of a club contract to play league cricket, as it was a means to gain experience to play in English conditions. By then, I was already a test player for Pakistan team, and had just finished our tour to Australia against West-Indies. In my desperation to get rid of my loneliness, when all my friends were busy playing for different clubs, I was introduced to Solly over phone by my dear friend and team mate Shafiq Ahmed who then was playing for Blackburn Club. Then, Solly took me to his house by car, and I had a warm welcoming of all his family members. Later, Solly signed me a contract to play for Spen Victoria for two seasons, followed by signing me for Hanging Heaton (2yrs) and Esh- Winning (1yr).

Ever since then, I became integral to his family, and began to live in the caring company of his mother whom I would call 'Mata ji.' During my stay there, I had a special moment to cherish. Mata Ji used to make a special Mix tea at night 11.00 for me, while Solly's father would do his business accounts, and I would pass my favourite time, listening to her ancestral stories, and sharing my own family stories to her. I had a very safe and joyful days in England in the house of Solly, except one season when Solly signed me for Esh- Winning club which is outside the Dewsbury /Bradford Area where I had to face the worst times of staying alone.

Solly has been more of my brother, than a friend, and I used to take part in all the daily chores of his family, including his businesses. I also used to involve in the issues of his family members, and Solly too would consider my involvement with great respect and take my advices to deal with all his problems. I also saw him assisting many Asian cricketers in various ways in England, and his house in England has been a home for several others.

I am glad that Solly Bhai's biography is finally out, and I am sure it will be an inspirational for the young generation. I also applaud Vara for his dedication in composing this biography and the manner in which he interacted with all the cricketers to gather valuable information.

========

Paul Jarvis

(Former English Cricketer)

January 10, 2023

I had the immense pleasure of playing cricket for a living for over 20 years, and in the early years of my professional career at Yorkshire, I was asked by Solly Adam to join Batley Cricket Club to play for them starting with the 1984 season. At the age of 18 I was not a regular Yorkshire first team player and needed to play on a Saturday in one of the Yorkshire leagues to gain experience and broaden my cricketing knowledge.

Solly's enthusiasm and energy was very infectious and I wanted to play for a captain and club that wanted to win things. He took me under his wings and introduced me to his family and many fantastic people at the club, some are still friends now. To say that this experience at Batley enrichened my life would be an understatement!

Coming from the North East coast, Batley in West Yorkshire was very different. Being involved in a more diverse environment was wholesome, and the welcoming and amazing food I had every time I went to Solly's house was just so special. Seeing how Solly lived with his family always there made me feel that this person, my captain Solly, was someone special.

On the cricket field Solly was always trying different things, changing the field placings here and there, mixing the bowlers up, just a little adjustment to try and get the opposition thinking and hoping to gain the advantage. He did some things and I thought, 'why has he done that?,' or I'd think 'that won't work?' But many times, he was right and that I guess is what Solly is like, always willing to try something and be a bit different, doing things whole heartedly and with lots of energy, which I guess is what makes him special, successful and above all unique.

Thank you Solly in helping me develop as a cricketer and as a person, my life has been richer for the experiences, memories and your friendship.

========

Madan Lal
(Former Indian Cricketer)
October 13, 2022

I met Solly with Brijesh Patel when we were playing cricket in Huddersfield. Ever since then, I frequented his house and came to become his family friend. He is a true lover of cricket, and we together played several matches in Yorkshire. Solly was also a great help for several Indian and Pakistani cricketers in England, to find place for them in English leagues. He had been a great help for me too in England, and it was through his assistance that I got an opportunity to sign for Enfield club in Lancashire. I thank him for all his help, and I wish him and his family to be happy and healthy. I also congratulate Vara Vantapati for conceiving the idea and initiating the writing of the book.

========

Mohinder Amarnath
(Former Indian Cricketer)
February 9, 2023

Solly Adam has been an old friend of mine since 1977. I used to visit him regularly at his residence in Dewsbury during week days, while playing league cricket in Lancashire.

He was a popular cricketer in English leagues, and has always been an enthusiastic cricket lover who had helped numerous promising cricketers from Indian sub-continent in signing contracts to play in different leagues in England. He is still the one to be contacted in England, if you are lost, or in any trouble. Everyone knew Solly in my playing days in Indian team, and he was the one who was a ready welcome into the spaces meant for our team, including dressing room, hotel room, etc., whenever we had toured England.

Solly made his presence when I got married in Dewsbury in 1977, and he had organized the press to break the news of our marriage. My wife and me also enjoyed his warm hospitality, having various tasty dishes cooked by his lovely wife, Maryam. He has also been a great help for me in many ways, including signing bat contract with Crown Sports, whilst playing in league as well as on our tour of Australia in 1977-78.

Wishing him and his family a long happy healthy life with a lot of fun.

Finally, I admire Vara Vantapati for creating this astonishing biography. The dedication to capturing the essence of Solly's life and experiences is genuinely commendable.

========

V.V.S. Laxman
(Former Indian Cricketer)
December 22, 2023

Solly Bhai is like an elder brother for me, or rather my father figure, who nurtured me not only into a mature cricketer, but to be a competent person to face the challenges of the world. I just finished my under-19 cricket with a match against England, and had reached an age 20, when my coach Sandeep Patel introduced me to Solly Bhai in 1994. Then Solly Bhai signed me with Hanging Heaton CC to play in Bradford League for the 1995 season. Since then, I was made to be integral to his family, and during the two years of my stay in England in 1995 and 1996, I had lived amidst the care and concerns of Bhai, Bhabhi, Younus Bhai and Rukhsana Bhabhi.

I played well in the first season, and then when Solly Bhai asked me to move into the Pudsey Congs CC for the second season in 1996 to play under the captaincy of Phil Carrick, I just simply followed his instructions. The team had very experienced and competent players like Matthew Hoggard, Richard Kettleborough, etc., and by playing practice matches in their company headed by Phil, I shaped myself into skilled cricketer, and had got a good grasp over an art of batting. I also played several benefit matches organised by Solly Bhai which were a great learning experience for me.

During these two seasons in England, I just spend most of my time with Solly Bhai, playing practice matches, and talking, working, eating in house, and travelling with him in his car. My other Asian friends Abey Kuruvilla, Jatin Paranjape, Sameer Dighe, Paras Mhambray and Atul Ranade also used to meet up regularly in the house of Solly Bhai, and we all together discuss cricket and eat the tasty food prepared by Bhabhi. We also would drink an amazing chai prepared by Solly, while listening to his anecdotes on stars and cricket legends like Sunil Gavaskar.

In this way, with the training and experience gained in England, I was selected for the Indian test team, in which the role of Solly Bhai was immense. I am hugely indebted to Solly Bhai and his family for their love and caring during my stay there.

Special recognition is also extended to Vara for his efforts in composing this biography.

========

A Note of Love for our Pappa

We feel deeply honoured to pen down a few of our thoughts about our father, whom we lovingly call Pappa. As the light of the stars will not be realised in the day light, being grown up amidst star cricketers and cricket legends, we never knew how big stars they were. During our childhood, hardly a day passed without his cricket companions and business associates visiting our home, and our house was always flooded with cricketers from India and Pakistan, and our Pappa busy interacting with cricketers at home, or going out to play cricket in the club. However, his busy schedule in business and cricket never hampered him from sparing his time for us, as he ensured that he was there for us whenever we needed him.

From our early childhood, our father has been a beacon of inspiration for all of us, and we take great pride in the admirable balance that he maintained between his professional engagement, and his personal and familial life. Mamma has been a great help for Pappa, and their togetherness in their share of equanimity of responsibilities of the home, might have been the secret of their successful parenting. Today when we all became parents, we often began to feel wondered how could our Pappa managed his time amidst his unbelievably busy schedule, surrounded by dozens of people throughout, and how Mamma looked after us, besides being busy in the kitchen all the time attending to the guests.

Despite being a passionate cricketer, Pappa has always maintained his cool and was caring for everyone, be it our family members, local community, or even his cricketing fraternity. But when, when our Mamma fell severely ill to the fatal disease, Pappa had totally collapsed, and had left everything for the care of Mamma. This shows how inalienable our parents are towards each other, and our firm belief is that, it is this togetherness in them has brought us into what we are today. Our Pappa has been a true descendent of his parents, a well-cherished companion to our mom, the best care-giver to all of us, and passionate playmate to his to all his grandchildren, and great grand-children.

This biography of Pappa presents an authentic portrayal of his life as a cricketer, mentor and a businessman. We as his children have the privilege to go through every page of the book, 'Solly Adam – Beyond Boundaries', before it was taken to print, which is a true reflection of his passion for cricket, and committed compassion for his fellow cricketers, and profound love and care for his family and children.

As his children, we feel fortunate to have him as our father, who have been father figure for various cricket stars and legends, and as some-one who have created a good wealth of business firms for our familial well-being.

We pray Almighty for a long and healthy life of togetherness to our parents, and our hearty greetings to Pappa for his biography to see the light of the day. And on behalf of our family, we express our indebt-edness to Vara for his conceiving the idea of writing the book, and his sincere efforts in documenting the life story of our father and bringing it to fruition. Our best wishes to Vara and his family.

Love you Pappa!

Ebrahim Adam
Afzal Adam
Asma Omar Adam &
Sohail Adam

========

Reena Roy
(Bollywood Actress)
January 9, 2024

Salaam Solly Bhai, I feel pleased to cherish my good old days in England. My day long chatting with Maryam, and dining, shopping, and moving between the houses with her, were some of the finest moments to recount with. I remember how greatly you used to treat me and my family as your own family, and how you took care of our safety and security, when I was with Mohsin Saheb. The loving care that you both gave me and my family makes me to feel that I should keep my daughter in your house in the days to come, so that she too will feel the same warmth that I once had, and I am sure she will be better trained, under your care and guidance, to live with compassion for fellow humans. I wish you both to have a good health, and may the God bless you for a happy life together.

========

Rashid Khan
(Former Pakistani Cricketer)
February 7, 2023

Solly Bhai had always been helpful to all the cricketers who would visit England from Pakistan and India. He used to sign contracts for the cricketers with the clubs in England, and would arrange food and accommodation for them. He had a respect of all, and most cricketers used to treat him as an elder brother. After I played in Lancashire League for a season, Solly Bhai signed me for Batley CC to play under his captaincy. During my play in Batley, I used to stay in his house for a season or so, along with other cricketers. Solly Bhai was a passionate cricketer, who used conduct several benefit matches, which we used to play together. This experience was of an immense help for me to sharpening my cricketing talents, and with the knowledge gained from it, I got selected for the Pakistan team to play for world cup in 1983.

I thank Solly Bhai for all his help to me, and to the cricketing community, and I wish him the best. May Almighty bless him and his family with good health.

========

Vijay Mohan Raj
(Former Indian First-class Cricketer)
September 21, 2022

I met Solly through a common friend, Rahul Mankad, when I was playing for a club in the Bradford League in Yorkshire. Solly by then was already popular in Yorkshire as a passionate cricketer, and as someone who was ready extending his helping hand to all those cricketers in need. I used to visit him regularly when I had no matches.

In these more than three decades of my friendship with him, I have graduated from a helpless visitor in England, to a virtual member of his and his extended family. He is friends with several cricketers from India, including star cricketers, all of them would love him, and speak admiring words about his family members.

I always thought that I knew him very well. But, when I read his book, particularly of his formative years, I began to realise his back ground, and the reason for his compassion for his fellow humans. His book would be delight for all the cricket lovers, as it entails a great deal of information about cricket and cricketers, with real time stories.

My best wishes to Solly Adam. My friend for Life.

========

Ameen Lakhani
(Former Pakistani First-Class Cricketer)
March 20, 2023

I met Solly Bhai for the first time during my trip to England as part of my Pakistan Junior Cricket Team. But our friendship grew only after he signed me a club contract to play league cricket in England. During my days in England, I used to visit his house in Dewsbury, and would stay in his house for days. I had a great reception of all his family members, as I never at once felt that I was not part of their family.

He is a passionate cricketer, and he expresses his love for cricket by helping the cricketers. He organized several benefit-matches for the cricketers, and in one of such matches he organized against Asian 11 team, I played under the captaincy of Solly Bhai. After the match, he took the whole team to his home, and it was the holy month of 'Ramadan' where a huge dinner party was arranged at night. Solly Bhai is the favorite of all the cricketers of my time.

May Almighty bless him and give him a very long life.

========

Yajurvindra Singh
(Former Indian Cricketer)
November 16, 2022

Solly Adam is a simple man, a cricket-lover, and a well-known league cricketer from Dewsbury in England. At some time, he was hailed as the Adam of Cricket by the popular media, and it is appropriate to call him as "A Messiah of Cricketers."

I met Solly Adam through my dear friend, Rahul Mankad (Late), during my tour to England as part of Indian team to play a test match against England in 1977. I was an Indian test player, and was just basking in the glory of my two World Records for the catches in test-innings. But, my tour to England brought me down to earth that I began to witness the difficulties that a professional cricketer faces both on and off the field, as the honorarium for the cricketers in those days was not even sufficient to live humble lives.

In my prolonged distress of eating street food for days, along with Rahul, I craved for a nice home food. Then Rahul took me to Solly's home to feed me home made Indian delicacies. We were affectionately greeted us by all his family members, and I felt at home in warmth of their hospitality. Ever since then, I never miss visiting Solly in each of my tour to England, particularly during our test series in 1979, all the players of the Indian team made a special trip to his home, where we were hosted with a great dinner party. I was also an invitee to be part of the charity match organised by Solly in 1980. He drew all the international players from India and Pakistan, and constituted teams into Kathiawar XI and Rest of the World. It was a much-anticipated match, but unfortunately the match got interrupted due to unexpected rain. However, we had yet another opportunity to have a get together in Solly's house, as always, and his home always fills in an atmosphere riveted in cricketing camaraderie and friendly banter. I thank him for everything, and I anticipate reading his book.

========

Iqbal Bhana OBE. DL
(Officer of the Order of the British Empire)
October 8, 2022

I have known Solly Adam for over 45 years, and he has been my most trusted friend who is always ready to offer me guidance and support. In fact, though I was not made for cricket, as I had a very limited abilities and talents, Solly made sure that I enjoyed playing cricket. During this brief period, I had the pleasure of playing cricket under his captaincy. I still have a regular contact with him, and I receive a great reception among all the members of his family.

Over years, Solly has also nurtured and supported many young and inexperienced cricketers, and under his guidance many went onto become major international cricketer stars. He is a dedicated cricketer, and his love for the game, has not only enhanced his cricketing knowledge, but has expanded his connections with the cricketers across the national and ethnic boundaries, and he is truly an international. Many reputed international cricketers have high regards for Solly. I am proud to have been his friend for decades, and I cherish his friendship for ever.

========

Sean Twohig
(Former English League Cricketer)
December 4, 2022

I was twenty years old when I signed for Batley CC in 1984 to play in Central Yorkshire League under the captaincy of Solly. Solly was a left arm spinner, with a very good talent in batting and fielding, though he did not take a chance to bat, as he always chose to bat at 11th position. He used to be composed, and I never really saw him losing his temper. However, as a captain, he was always very keen to encourage all his team members with his quick movements, and would often shout, 'come on lads on your toe'! (singular), to which the whole team used to burst into laughter.

During my first season, my batting performance was not so good, and yet, Solly backed me and had persisted to keep me intact, despite the club management wanted to drop me. I continued to be an opening batsman in partnership with an Indian overseas batting sensation, Chandrakant Pandit, as Solly knew that my role was vital, and Pandit too was happy to share his batting with. Our team did very well under his captaincy, leading to win the prestigious Heavy Woollen Cup in 1986. To celebrate this happy moment, Solly took the whole team and its club members, along their wives and girlfriends, to a local restaurant, and gave us a big treat, for which he paid from his own pocket.

My friendship with Solly lasted for over forty years, and he has also helped my youngest son, Ben, in signing for Worcestershire. Ben grew as a Professional cricketer, and coincidentally, he is also a left arm spinner like Solly.

========

Chris Pickles
(Former Yorkshire County Cricketer)
January 20, 2023

When you think of Solly Adam and cricket, three words come to mind – Passion – Enthusiasm – Confidence. Solly and cricket will continually go together in the same sentence, and one will have a pleasure to play in the same team as that of Solly.

I first met Solly soon after I took over the captaincy of Spen Victoria in the Bradford League. Solly was never deterred from bowling to any style of batsmen, whether a young junior or the overseas player, you just throw the ball to him and know he would give you 100%. It was never dull when Solly was bowling, forever changing the fielder to where the ball went last, with all his ceaseless running commentary. It took the opposition sometime to realise that Solly was not trying to undermine their abilities, but only to show his passion and enthusiasm to take a wicket and to secure a win for his team. You could never criticise or doubt his approach as most times his unorthodox tactics actually worked!! As my opportunities to play league cricket decreased, and Spen Victoria needed a new captain, the whole committee of the Spen was unanimous to opt for one and only one person, that was Solly.

You always knew Solly who would have a talented overseas cricketer in his team, his ability to lead talented cricketers, and to mould them into a solid unit by showing such respect towards each player, brought series of successes to his team. This has further allowed Spen Victoria to rise from being an up and down divisional team, to being one of the most formidable 1st Division teams in the Bradford League.

I was fortunate to play a season with one of the India's most talented batsmen, Vinod Kambli, before he rose to emerge as test cricketer, and Kambli came about through Solly's contacts. I have a lot to thank Solly, and particularly for my joy on a cricket field, as Solly is without doubt one of the most enthusiastic, passionate, and confident club cricketers I was fortunate enough to play alongside.

========

Kiran More
(Former Indian Cricketer)
October 7, 2022

Solly Bhai—truly a man with a heart of gold. He was a left-arm spinner who played league cricket for decades till the age of 60. When I first visited England in 1980-81 to play for Barrow Cricket Club in the Northern Lancashire League, Adam Patel took me to the residence of Solly Bhai in Dewsbury, and introduced me to him. Dewsbury was just 90-minute drive from Barrow. So, whenever I had felt homesick, I would either visit the house of Adam Patel, or of Solly Bhai.

His home was a home for cricketers, and Solly Bhai was always a helping hand for several cricketers from India and Pakistan in every generation from Gavaskar and Kapil Dev who were so dear to Solly Bhai, including Chandrakant Pandit, Lalchand Rajput, Nilesh Kulkarni, Raju Kulkarni, etc., just to name a few. Abey Kuruvilla is an another one in this line who is close to Solly Bhai. When India toured England in 1986, the full squad of India would visit his house for regular lunches and dinners. Solly Bhai was crucial even in signing Sachin for Yorkshire in 1992.

Solly Bhai has been so generous to all those cricketers who approach him, and would help them in signing contracts for various clubs. During their stay in England, several cricketers have largely survived upon the hospitality from Solly Bhai; thanks to Bhabhi for her kind reception. Solly Bhai also helped some cricketers to get jobs, and some of them would even work in his petrol stations, or pop stores, to make their living. He would treat the young cricketers as his own children, and would nurture them to be competent cricketers. I still visit him, whenever I am in London. Thank you very much Solly Bhai for everything, and also special recognition goes to Vara Vantapati for his dedication in crafting this distinctive biography.

========

Sairaj Bahuthule
(Former Indian Cricketer)
February 9, 2023

When I started playing for Mumbai in 1991, Solly Bhai signed me a contract to play for Spen Victoria. I was so young, and was with so many fears and anxieties of living in a foreign country amidst strangers, and against its tough weather conditions. But, Solly Bhai took me off from all those fears, and had opened the gates of his house for all the Asian cricketers who were playing for different leagues in Yorkshire.

Though initially thought of playing for a couple seasons, the time went unnoticed in the guidance and support of Solly Bhai, and I played for 14 long years for different clubs in England. It was amazing experience, as several Indian cricketers would meet up in the house of Solly Bhai, and we used to have fun of talking and dining there. All the family members of Solly Bhai and Maryam Bhabhi, including his brother, Yunus Bhai and Rukhsana Bhabhi, along with their children used to treat us well, and we had a great reception all through our life in England. This experience of playing in English conditions, helped me understanding the game better, and was crucial in shaping me as a professional cricketer in the initial stages of my career. The same was true for several other cricketers of time which include, VVS Lakshman, Abey Kuruvilla, Nilesh Kulkarni, Salil Ankola, Amol Mazumdar, Nilesh Kulkarni and Paras Mhambray.

I genuinely wish good health and happiness to Solly Bhai and his family. Also, I extend my congratulations to Vara for his sincere efforts in narrating Solly Bhai's life story to the cricket enthusiasts across the globe.

========

Sajid Ali
(Former Pakistani Cricketer)
May 17, 2023

I met Solly for the first time on my visit to England in 1984. He is very kind and passionate man, who is always ready to help the people in need, a character very rare to be seen in these days.

In the most distressing times of my life, Solly helped me signing for a club in England, and when I landed in England, he took me to his home and hosted me with great comforts of food and shelter. He also helped my son signing for a club in England in 2018.

I thank Solly for everything that he had done to me, to my son, and to the cricket community, and I pray Almighty to bless him with long life to live amidst the warmth love of his children, and grand-children.

========

Dr Kedar Korde
(MBBS, MD MRCP CCST (UK) Consultant and a Former Club Cricketer)
October 27, 2022

As a kid playing cricket in the streets of Shivaji Park area of Mumbai, India, I used to read about Solly Bhai as a league cricketer in England. His name would often feature in the local sports magazine as a very generous cricket lover in Yorkshire who would help young, budding cricketers from India and Pakistan in the league circuit of Yorkshire. Years later, when I took to my dream of pursuing postgraduate specialist training in the UK, after completing my MBBS from India, I had my first major training job in Yorkshire. Not long after that, I got to know Solly bhai in person, and he had this incredibly captivating friendly personality that had hooked us together forever!!

We met over a number of matches, dinners and festivities, and do meet up still, and our friendship grew day after day. Besides his dedication to cricket and business, he is equally committed to his family. I have seen all the family members of Solly Bhai from close quarters as a medical doctor to attend their health, and his children too have imbibed several great ethics from him to live together as one unified family. I am fortunate to have Solly Bhai as my friend, as I learnt a lot of life lessons from him. I wish him good health, and continue guiding us all as an elder brother.

========

John Wood
(Former Lancashire County Cricketer)
December 4, 2022

I was 17 when I first met Solly. Solly really looked after me as a teenager trying to make my way in the game. He is a pretty infectious character and it's hard not to get carried along with his enthusiasm for the game of cricket. I do not recall many good left arm spinners from my time in the Bradford League, but Solly was certainly one of them.

Solly's contacts in India also paid dividend with the quality of overseas players that he could procure for us at Spen. Tosh Arothe and Vinod Kambli to name, but Kambli, in particular, was a different class to anything I had seen before. These singings elevated Spen to a different level and made us a force to be reckoned with in the Bradford League. I won't dwell on our Priestley Cup Final win against Pudsey St Lawrence, because I imagine it will have been covered elsewhere in this book. However, it is a game and time that I will never forget. I suppose it launched my career into professional cricket, and it was largely due to Solly that I had got my opportunity.

Solly also employed me to work in one of his businesses which was a real help as I was looking to save some money to go away on holiday. Once, I was an invitee to dine at his home with a couple of the other players which was an incredible experience as Sunil Gavaskar was also present.

Even after his retiring from cricket, Solly would occasionally pop down to watch for an hour or so. It was always a pleasure to see and spend some time with him. He has certainly not lost any of his enthusiasm for the game, and is still as positive a character as ever.

I wish you and your family all the best for the future, and thank you for the effort and time you spent with me over our time together at Spen.

========

David Byrn
(Former English League Cricketer)
February 14, 2023

The year 1983 was the start of a golden decade in Solly Adam's cricket career. I first met Solly in the early 1980's, when I was playing for Dewsbury Cricket Club of the Central Yorkshire League. I enjoyed talking to him, as I never saw anyone as passionate cricketers as he is. When Solly took over the captaincy of Batley CC in 1983, he invited me to join his team, and I just jumped on the board.

During this period, he had also been instrumental in bringing over talented players from India and Pakistan to play in the Yorkshire leagues. His boundless enthusiasm and ability to get the best out of people ensured that Batley finished near the top of the 1st Division and won the Jack Hampshire Trophy, a 40 over knockout final by the slender margin of one wicket. It was great to be part of such a team and to be playing alongside of the First-Class players such as Chandrakant Pandit, Rashid Khan, Barun Burman and Mehndi Sheikh.

Solly as a captain is accredited for all these achievement for our team, and I thank him for making me part of this glorious event in the history of the league cricket.

I want to appreciate Vara as well for writing this biography. In our talks, I could feel his passion for the project. He was open to the changes I suggested for one of the chapters. Best wishes to him too!

========

Abey Kuruvilla
(Former Indian Cricketer)
April 7, 2023

I heard the name Solly Adam from my Mumbai teammates a lot. But I got to meet him only in 1993 when I was playing for Darlington in Durham. My contract was not great, and so, Solly Bhai offered me a job in his petrol station to make some extra money. For the following season in 1994, Solly Bhai signed me for Cleckheaton to play in Bradford League. He was a very good left arm Spinner with a sharp cricketing brain, and I enjoyed every bit of my time with him both in, and off the track. During my stay in England, Solly Bhai invited me to play a couple of benefit matches between India and Pakistan. He was very happy when I was selected for the Indian team to play test cricket.

I was part of his family, as Solly Bhai always treated me like one of his own kids. When I miss my home, the home of Solly Bhai in Dewsbury was always open for me, and so all of us Jatin, Sairaj, Paras and myself would frequent him for lunch and dinner. He has helped so many cricketers that you lose count. Maryam Bhabhi is an amazing cook, and the taste of the food still lingers on. I know that in UK, I have a home to go to where I am always welcome.

It was unfortunate that Solly Bhai had to face very big tough times recently with the ill health of Maryam Bhabhi, and with the sudden loss of life of his beloved brother Younus bhai (A Gem). But I know that his zest for life and positive nature caries him further against all odds. I will forever be indebted to Solly bhai and his family (Maryam Bhabhi, Younus bhai, Rukhsana Bhabhi, Sohail, Afzal, Ibrahim).

My good wishes are always for him to be healthy and happy. God bless him always.

========

Wasim Jaffer
(Former Indian Cricketer)
January 21, 2024

The cricketing journey of Solly Bhai was so long and colourful that, it involved several cricketers of varied countries including me. It was Solly bhai who signed me for Spen Victoria CC in 1998 to play in the Bradford League, and then with Scholes CC in the Huddersfield League. During my days in England, I used to live in the house of Solly Bhai, and everyone in his family treated me like their own family member. It was always a learning experience to play with Solly Bhai and even to be with him. He used to tell me several stories about cricket and cricketers. We also used to play cricket in the nets, and the experience thus gaining in England was so crucial in my making as a professional cricketer, and to be selected for Indian cricket team.

I am happy to know that the biography of Solly Bhai is about to be published at last, and I am sure cricket lovers of the world would love reading it. I congratulate Vara Vantapati for writing this biography of a man of historical significance. I anticipate several cricket anecdotes in the book, with full of historical details. Looking forward for the much-awaited book to read.

I thank Solly Bhai for everything, and I wish him all the best.

========

Chandresh Patel
(Family Friend)
February 16, 2024

Suleman Adam is known as Solly Bhai among all his friends. I have had the honour of knowing Solly Bhai for nearly 30 years, and over the years our friendship has turned into a family bond. It has always been a pleasure to visit him and Maryam Bhabhi in Savile Town for a wonderful Biryani.

Like all of us Solly Bhai and his family too have had their ups and downs in life. But that has never hindered them from being generous, as their hospitality to scores of young cricketers from India and Pakistan is widely acknowledged.

Cricket runs in his blood. Solly Bhai! you are a legend.

Chandresh and Purnima.

========

Ravi Thakkar
(Former Indian First-Class Cricketer)
January 2, 2024

Solly Bhai is a man sent by God for all the Indian cricketers who went to play league and county cricket in the north of England. He has been described by many as the pioneer of the Asians to play English leagues, as he not only broke the shell of inducting cricketers from India and Pakistan into the leagues, but had also nurtured several of them into world class cricketers, and even some of them into star legends.

Solly Bhai was also pivotal in signing Sachin Tendulkar to Yorkshire County, and for breaking the county's century-old norm of not signing a foreign player. He had always been in his hunt for talented cricketers, and I was fortunate to catch his eye, when I was in a practicing session in the grounds of Cricket Club of India in Bombay. Then he enquired of me with his friend, and my captain, Ashok Mankad, and then, soon he signed me for Hartshead Moor Cricket Club in the Bradford League.

He was hailed as an unofficial selector for the generations to sign enthusiastic cricketers from India to the leagues in Yorkshire, and then into Indian team, as most cricketers whom he would pick from India

344

used to be selected for the Indian team later. I too am fortunate to catch his sight, and I am grateful to Solly Bhai for his fatherly care and guidance, and Bhabhi for her motherly reception at home all through my playing life in England.

========

Manzoor Elahi
(Former Pakistani Cricketer)
February 13, 2023

I am fortunate to have some of the greatest moments with Solly Bhai. I remember playing several friendly matches with Solly Bhai, and they had been a great learning for me to perform better in my international matches. Our friendship also grew in due course, and whenever I go to England, we used to meet up, and had a great time together. I thank him for all his love and great reception. I wish Solly Bhai having a good health, and happiness, and pray Almighty to bless him and his family.

========

Chandrakanth Pandit
(Former Indian Cricketer)
December 6, 2023

It was Solly Bhai who took the sole responsibility to sign me and my three other colleagues, Mr. Raju Kulkarni, Mr. Ravi Thakkar & Mr. Lalchand Rajput from Mumbai team to play for Batley CC in 1981-82. We never had any personal connection with him till then, and he did this all with a sheer intention to promote potential cricketers. Like a father figure to all of us, he also looked after our accommodation in Yorkshire, and had made sure of making us feel at home in England.

I cannot forget Maryam Bhabhi whom we fondly call Hamari Bhabhi for caring us all like her own kids. We were always welcomed with a smile, and Bhabhi would let us leave the house, only after feeding us nice food; often, she would even pack food for us. There were times, Solly Bhai and Bhabhi would visit us to keep a check on us to ensure that we were comfortable, and not short of any food.

Solly bhai would also pick us all for practice matches regularly, and drop us back by his car. He had a great passion for the game, and I have learnt a lot from him under his captaincy. I am deeply indebted to him for his mentoring me in England as he is always my father figure, and owe my thanks to Bhabhi and other family members.

My visit to England would always be incomplete without meeting Bhai and Bhabhi, and it was wonderful meeting them recently.

Wishing Solly bhai for his much-anticipated book.

========

Tushar Arothe
(Former Indian First-Class Cricketer)
September 19, 2022

I would like to take this opportunity to thank Solly Bhai and his Family for the support and help they had extended to me when I was in England. Solly bhai has been like my elder brother, and a mentor, who always guided me in building my cricketing career. He was very popular among Yorkshire cricket circles, and the managements of various clubs had a great respect for him. So, Solly Bhai was the main contact for all the players from India, Pakistan and other Asian countries who wanted to find opportunities in the league cricket in England.

Solly Bhai signed me to play for Spen Victoria CC in the Bradford league, and I played in the league for two seasons under his captaincy. It was under the leadership of this great man with gifted talents and loving temperament that won the prestigious Priestley Cup Championship for the club. His Contribution as a cricketer and his helping nature to assist numerous cricketers was immense. During my playing days in England, I had a wonderful time with him, and his family was of a great support for me and my family. I owe a lot to him, and we always have a huge respect for Solly Bhai and his family.

Looking forward to reading the biography of this wonderful human being, and I am sure it will be a delightful experience for all the readers, particularly the cricket lovers of the world. He is always in my prayers.

========

Shahid Mahboob

(Former Pakistani Cricketer)

January 27, 2023

I met Solly Bhai in my earliest visit to England in 1981 which I made as part of the Pakistan Junior Team to play against his side Hanging Heaton. Later, he signed me a contract to play for a club named Hartshead Moor in Bradford League, and then with other clubs in Yorkshire. Solly Bhai also helped me in every way that he could, and had guided me to settle down, and to have me a safe and comfortable life in England. He was so generous that he looked after a several lot of players, and has been there to help shaping their careers.

We see each other to this day, whenever I visit England, or he to Pakistan. I am forever grateful to him all his love and support for me in England that, he had been a sort of a backbone for several other cricketers like me. I wish him and his family to have good health and happiness. Allah Hafiz.

========

Farida Raj
(Family Friend and a Writer)
September 21, 2022

I am not a cricket enthusiast, and I have no knowledge of cricket. All my connection to the game is through my husband, Vijay Mohan Raj, affectionately called Tony. Solly Bhai, an intimate friend of Tony, is a very warm and compassionate human being.

I accompanied Tony when he went to play league in Yorkshire. Then, Solly Bhai's very charming wife, whom everyone addresses as Marriam Bhabhi, drove all the way from Dewsbury to Heathrow to fetch us, and we had a warm welcoming from every member of the family.

Solly Bhai's mother whom I called 'Ammi' was a remarkable lady. She was always ready to feed the 'hungry' young cricketers whom Solly bhai brought home for the meal without informing her. What surprises me till date is there was always enough food on the table, no matter how many young men walked in!

Another thing that stayed in my memory when I went to his hometown with our young children. He put us up in one of his apartments and asked us to feel at home. The day we decided to go to Brighton, we drove our car to his petrol station. Then, Solly Bhai not only filled the tank but also asked the children to pick the chocolates and chips of their choices from the counter! All I say is, I feel blessed to be a small part of his family. He is most dependable and a friend for life.

========

David I Peel
(Former English League Cricketer)
October 5, 2022

Solly and I are of a similar age, and we met each other for the first time in the mid 1960's in a match at Hyrstlands Park. At that moment, I was playing for Whitley Lower CC in the Dewsbury & District Cricket League which was a bit lower in standard of its cricket than that of Batley Muslim which Solly represented. I recall, he had ambitions as a left arm pace bowler in those days.

Then, Solly joined us to play for Whitley Lower team in the late 60s, and soon he emerged as a popular member of the team. Solly was a pioneer in this respect, as in those days, very few (if any) cricketers of Asian descent played cricket with the clubs other than those of their own exclusive ones. In this club, we shared the pleasure winning the league's knockout competition, the 'Sheard Cup.'

Solly was also a successful business man, and despite his endeavor in being successful in business, his main passion, however, has always been cricket, and his enthusiasm for cricket has never diminished. I can honestly say that it has been my pleasure knowing him, and we remain firm friends.

========

A. Nanda Kishore
(Former Indian First-Class Cricketer)
September 26, 2022

Solly Bhai has signed me for Woodland CC in Bradford League in 1998. He treated me like his own brother, and soon I became part of their family. I always feel amazed at seeing him, as I never came across a well-organized, calm, and confident person as Solly Bhai was. He is like a calm sea with a tempest in its heart, and tackles every situation of crises, having smile on his face. Nothing seemed to faze him, no matter how frantic the others are.

I was often his host, and Bhabhi Ji was always so kind to feed me and my colleagues with the most delicious and authentic Asian dishes. I never missed my parents in his presence, and I always felt the presence of my own family members, when I make my visit his house.

I really appreciate the author, Vara Vantapati, for his efforts in writing this book and I am sure this book will be a delightful experience for all the readers, particularly to the cricket lovers across the globe, who would relish reading about several cricket legends, through this 'Reservoir of Great Memories.'

========

Steve Foster
(Former Minor County Cricketer)
October 14, 2022

Solly has been a great friend to my father, and I first came across him when my father represented South Yorkshire league against Central Yorkshire league captained by Solly. Our paths again crossed after 10 years, when Solly provided me with an opportunity to play for Spen Victoria in Bradford league. At Spen, Solly assembled a formidable team, and captained us with a great skill to win the prestigious Priestley Cup.

Indeed, making a move from Sheffield to Bradford league was the springboard of my career, as it had opened many doors for me on the cricket pitch, and most importantly, it had allowed me to make many true cricketing friends both in the UK and in India. I will be forever grateful to Solly for providing the opportunity.

This was the start of a great friendship that still blossoms to this day. Whenever I am in Dewsbury, I try to pop in for a cup of tea with Solly, and he always travels an extra mile to watch my play. This is typical of what he does for many of his friends in the English cricketing community.

I am sure this biography will be a great read, particularly the cricket lovers across the globe will love reading about one of the legends of Yorkshire cricket.

All the best Solly and much deserved.

========

Abdul Azeem
(Former Indian First-Class Cricketer)
October 16, 2022

I met Solly bhai in the year 1986 in England, and had played cricket under his captaincy. In fact, it was Solly Bhai who signed me for Batley CC in the Central Yorkshire League where he was the captain. I have immensely benefitted from Batley, as my standards of cricket have been improved so much after playing in English conditions that when I went back to India, I showcased tremendous successes in my career as a cricketer.

Solly Bhai was crucial in building my career in cricket, and he would share his incites derived from his experiences. I remember he started playing league cricket at a very late age, though he knew that he had no chance of playing higher grade cricket further. Such a cricket enthusiast he was!

When I was in England, I often would visit his house, and eventually I became intimate to all his family members. He was also a great businessman, and would always be busy in his work. During his active life as cricketer, several cricketers from India and Pakistan used to visit him, and his family was always well receptive for all the cricketers. Whenever my friend Azharuddin visits England, he would catch me up in Solly Bhai's home, where we used to have a delicious dinner together.

It was pleasant to be in the company of Solly Bhai as his sense of humour always kept us strong and happy.

Wishing him good health and success always!

========

Shahid Tanveer
(Former Pakistani First-Class Cricketer)
September 16, 2022

I know Solly Bhai for a long time from the days I started playing cricket as a pro in Yorkshire area. He is a brilliant cricketer who had been credited for winning several records as an individual, as well as for leading the team towards winning prestigious trophies. I also know him as a great human being who had extended his helping hand to several enthusiastic cricketers, and as man behind the success of several cricket stars. The gates of his home have always been open for all the cricketers, and we would just knock the door at any time, without even informing them in advance, to stay there, and to have food from there. I wish you all the best, Solly Bhai.

========

Amol Muzumdar
(Former Indian First-Class Cricketer)
October 26, 2022

Solly Bhai, the name familiar to all the Mumbai based cricketers during 1980s and 1990s. The reason being that, it was Solly Bhai who would look after every cricketer when they go on for cricket tour in England.

Saville town and Solly Bhai are synonyms for all those cricketers who venture into club cricket in England, as every single one of us would frequent our visits to the town where Solly Bhai made his residence. When I first arrived at Yorkshire in 1994, little did I know about the place, but as I met Solly Bhai, everything turned familiar. He was a sense of safety and security for all of us, and we would treat him father figure.

All the family members of Solly Bhai too were warmth in the reception of the cricketers, and Bhabhi would always be there to serve us with delicious food at any time during lunch and dinner.

Solly Bhai! My Salaam to you and Bhabhi.

========

Suru Nayak
(Former Indian Cricketer)
November 18, 2022

I know Solly Bhai through my dearest friend Rahul Mankad (late) with whom I played Cricket for almost 40 long years. It was Rahul who advised me to play for leagues in England to enhance my cricketing skills, and in his assistance that I got an opportunity to play for Cleckheaton CC in Yorkshire in 1979.

Solly Bhai at that time was very busy, and would hardly have 10 minutes to sit in one place. Like an elder brother, he was the man on run, having an obligation to fulfil the needs of all the cricketers from India, Pakistan, and other countries. He was there to provide us with accommodation to the home-made food, and would create an atmosphere of home in England. I had a very tough time as the money that we get in cricket in those days was insufficient to make our living, and so, I used to work at his petrol station, and other outlets. When I feel home sick, Solly Bhai used to come and pick me up from Batley to Dewsbury, where I would be fed home delicacies. In 1982 when I was part of the Indian team, he also organised a bat contract for me with County Sports.

In this way, Solly Bai was everything for me in England, and the support he extended to me was the stepping stone for my success in the journey of cricket. I thank him from the bottom of my heart all his support, and I wish him and his family a good health and happiness.

========

Mehndi Shaikh
(Former Indian First-Class Cricketer)
January 4, 2023

Solly Bhai has been my friend, philosopher, and a guide, who had treated me like his own brother, and was crucial in my making as a professional cricketer during my early days in England.

I was already into English leagues by 1980. However, I began to feel at home only after Solly Bhai signed me to play under his captaincy. I played with him for a good amount of time, and each moment I spent with him was a learning experience. It was pleasure traveling with him for the matches, sharing food during breaks, and a lot of fun filled moments that made my stay in England so memorable. I always find a mentor in him who guided me in the toughest times to play the game with poise and confidence. This, in many ways helped me to better my career.

He used to host me several times for lunch and dinner, and Bhabhi Ji was always so kind to cook delicious Asian dishes. I can honestly say, going to Solly Bhai's house was like going to my own house.

I thank Solly Bhai for presenting me with the best of my moments in England, and I wish him all the best to live a very long life with good health, love, and care in the rest of his life.

Lastly, I'm so pleased to see someone has taken up this important initiative to pen-down the biography of this wonderful human being, Solly Bhai. I truly appreciate Vara Vantapati for his dedication in writing this book, and I am confident that it will provide a delightful experience for all cricket enthusiasts.

========

Shishir Hattangadi
(Former Indian First-Class Cricketer)
January 18, 2023

During summer when it was off season for cricket in India, many cricketers used to land in England to retain their hands on the game, and then, Batley in the west of Yorkshire was the citadel for most Asian cricketers. Then, the house of Solly Bhai was the home for all these Asian cricketers in Yorkshire, and Solly Bhai would provide them with food, accommodation, etc. I too was one such cricketer from India who landed in England during early eighties in search of opportunities in league cricket. When I checked with my friends for an opportunity in Yorkshire, there was unanimous response from all quarters that the name of Solly Bhai was the single most assurance for all my queries.

When I approached Solly Bhai, with the help of my friends, he quietly signed me for Hartshead Moor CC, and had paved my way into English cricket league. Since then, he has been my friend, guide, mentor and philosopher, and like several cricketers, I too received all kinds of services from Solly Bhai for my growth as a professional cricketer. As the famous writer, Neville Cardus, mentions, "we remember not the results in the after years, it is the men who live on in our minds, in our imagination." Solly Bhai live in my memories forever, and I am indebted to him and his family for everything that is done to me. Solly Bhai, may God bless you and your family with health and happiness.

========

Mohammad Arif
(Former English League Cricketer)
January 25, 2023

It is my privilege witness a passionate cricketer and former captain at Batley CC Solly Adam. Solly Bhai was one of the first Asian Captains, who was instrumental in introducing international professional cricketers to the Yorkshire League. He always had the desire to win, and hence he had played hard, along with his great management skills to motivate and gel players to achieve the winning formula. In his captaincy, the team won the central Yorkshire and Heavy Woollen Cup. It was always a joy to come to nets somehow or the other, to getting to see Solly Bhai with great stars such a Sunil Gavaskar, Dilip Vengsarkar, Chandrakant Pandit, Mohsin Khan, Rashid Khan, Abdul Qadir. A dream come true for any young lad to meet and see these greats having a net session.

All in all, Solly bhai will be remembered as the first Asian pioneer who raised the cricketing standards in the Yorkshire League.

Salute to a legend!!

========

Hoshedar Contractor
(Former Indian First-Class Cricketer)
April 6, 2023

Solly had an important role in my formative years as a cricketer, as it was Solly who inducted me to English leagues. Having a great influence in the Yorkshire cricket circles, Solly helped shaping the lives of several youngsters, including me.

He was a passionate cricketer, and his sound knowledge of the game was of an immense use in my own making as a cricketer, as he used to share his knowledge with us. The experience thus gained in England helped sharpening my bowling skills to my emergence as a first-class cricketer in India. I always had a warm welcoming into his home for a meal, and I feel that it is my extended family.

A big thanks to you, Solly, for everything that you did for me, and I wish you the best in the years ahead.

========

Iqbal Shaikh
(Mumbai Retired Police Officer)
September 16, 2022

It will be a pleasure and pride for me to write few words about your book though it will be bit cumbersome to write few words on multi-faceted personality like you specially known as Messiah specially Cricketers from India and Pakistan.

========

Rohit Sharma
(Former Indian First-Class Cricketer)
September 20, 2022

Solly Bhai is a dedicated cricketer, who played and helped several cricketers. I knew Solly Bhai since 1988 when I was part of Thongsbridge CC. For the following season in 1989, he signed me for Clarkston Cricket club in Bradford league. During the time, Solly Bhai used to organise several benefit-matches in Dewsbury, I would play almost every match along with my other Indian cricketers in England. We would frequent his home whenever we get time, particularly after every match, and would have a great reception from Solly Bhai and his family.

I was like his younger brother, as all my colleagues too were, and we never felt that we are out of India in his care and hospitality. Thank you Solly Bhai.

========

Nilesh Kulkarni
(Former Indian Cricketer)
September 21, 2022

There was a time when every Indian cricketer who landed in Yorkshire will know Solly Bhai as the man who helped numerous young cricketers, welcomed them into his humble abode and had treated everyone like his family member. I was just 16 when he took me under his wings in 1989. He signed contracts for me to play for leagues, and had assisted me in boosting my cricketing career.

Solly Bhai has been an incredible help for me, both on and off the field. During my struggling days, I have literally been nurtured by Solly Bhai, and his continual support and guidance immensely helped me in my emergence to represent Indian team. got to learn so many valuable lessons about cricket because of his constant support and guidance. Several other cricketers like Paras Mhambray, Abey Kuruvilla, Sairaj Bahuthule and many more also grew up under the care and guidance of Solly Bhai.

The India delicacies prepared by Bhabhi, particularly the taste of her home-made mango lassi still lingers in my memories. Solly Bhai will always have a special place in my life, and I am glad that I too am a left-arm spinner like him.

========

Atul Ranade
(Former Indian First-Class Cricketer)
October 5, 2022

If there is a good cricketer in India, he will not miss the sight of Solly Bhai, who has always been in an incessant hunt for the promising young cricketers. The moment he finds any cricketers with any talent, he promptly picks him, and place him in a right place where he could have nourished to highest potential.

The success he attained should also be shared with his wife, without whom, Solly Bhai would not have collected such a huge array of cricket stars and legends as his friends. At any given hour, Maryam Bhabhi would serve us the best possible food with a pleasant smile on her face, which one could only dream of having at such odd hours, that too, in cold unforgiving Yorkshire weather.

Love from Mumbai, and a humble thanks to Solly Bhai and Bhabhi.

========

Raju Kulkarni
(Former Indian Cricketer)
December 7, 2023

Solly Bhai played a pivotal role in shaping my cricketing career. Soon after he spotted me bowling in the nets at the Cricket Club of India, Bombay, he approached my captain, Ashok Mankad, to sign me for Thornhill CC in West Yorkshire, England. This opportunity at my tender age of 19 was a turning point in my life, as its experience was invaluable for my learning that helped me getting selected for Indian team later.

I played with Solly Bhai at Thornhill CC, and his unwavering passion, dedication, and commitment to the game became infectious, leaving an unforgettable mark on me and my other colleagues like Chandu Pandit, Samir Dighe, Lalu Rajput, Vinod Kambli, Ravi Thacker, etc., during my formative years. He literally nurtured us in cricket, besides looking after our survivals by providing accommodation. We would frequent his house, where Maryam Bhabhi would serve us with delicious food; I will still feel her unforgettable mutton biryani and Dal.

I remain forever indebted to Solly bhai for everything that he did to me, and the cricketing fraternity.

========

Ayub Khan
(Former Indian First-class Cricketer)
September 9, 2022

Solly Bhaijaan is a unique person gifted with kindness for fellow humans. His simplicity and down to earth nature to help anyone in need is commendable.

It was Solly Bhaijaan who signed contract for me to play league cricket, provided me with an accommodation to stay in, and fed me with the delicious Asian food, which otherwise would not been possible to find in England. He also provided me with a job to earn my living, as I used to work in his sport show room.

I am indebted a lot to Solly Bhaijaan and Maryam Bhabhi for all their care during my stay in England, and it was out of my respect for Maryam Bhabhi that I named my daughter's name as Ayra Maryam Khan.

I pray GOD to give this great couple with good health and strength.

========

Abdul Moosabhoy Ismail
(Former Indian First-Class Cricketer)
September 7, 2022

Solly is a simple and down to earth person, who is always ready to extend his helping hand to all those in need, and had never say no to anyone. He helped so many cricketers in his active life as a cricketer, and several more as a business man. I know how care he took of me which I never forget. I feel amazed to the commitment shown by Solly Bhai on any issue he takes up, and I often feel mystic about him that he must be the Faristha (Angel) of our times. I wish you and your family good luck! God bless you!!

========

Abdul Jabbar
(Former Indian First-Class Cricketer)
February 22, 2024

I was a regular player in the Tamil Nadu team to play for the Ranji Trophy, and went to UK in 1978 on a cricket tour to play for a private club. Then, I approached my friend and a test cricketer Abid Ali, who then was playing for Lancashire league, to help me finding a club to play in England for a season. Abid Bhai introduced me to Solly Bhai, who was so kind to me that, he signed me with the Meltham CC team to play in the Huddersfield league.

Solly Bhai has a terrific knowledge of the game, and has extensive connections in the cricketing world. Most Indian cricket stars of the late 1960's would know Solly Bhai as their friend, and many club secretaries in the Yorkshire region would approach him for the competent players to play for their clubs.

During my stay in England, I along with my cricket friends used to visit Solly Bhai at his home in Dewsbury, and would receive a homely reception from Solly Bhai and Maryam Bhabhi. We have been treated like his family members, and I am still in touch with him. I am grateful to Solly Bhai for everything that he did to me, and have a high regard for him, for the breaks he had given to me, and to numerous other cricketers.

I look forward for the release of his book, as I am sure that it would be a great read for all the cricket lovers.

May the God bless him and his family!

========

Sue Roberts
(Club Secretary)

October 23, 2022

It was in my role as treasurer of the Heavy Woollen District Challenge Cup (as it was known then) that I first met Solly Adam, and later his lovely wife, Maryam. Throughout the years I have known and worked alongside Solly (in his role of competition sponsor), I have recognised in him the best of the values found in the game of cricket. Solly is a man of great integrity, a true gentleman, a quiet and humble man who does not seek any fame, despite many wonderful things he has done, and continues to do for the game of cricket. Local cricket would not have been what it is today, had it not been for Solly's tireless work and dedication.

Solly makes a number of charitable donations, and yet he does them quietly. He is also committed to his family, and it was evident in the way in which he took care of his wife when she recently fell ill. Solly, I am honoured to know you and Maryam, and to be your friend.

========

Indian cricket team catches up for a dinner at my house in Dewsbury in 1982; a rare picture of cricketers with my family members and friends-Raju Kulkarni, Ghulam Parker, Suru Nayak, Pranab Roy, Gundappa Vishwanath, Sandeep Patil, Ravi Shastri, Shivlal Yadav, Dilip Vengsarkar, Sunil Gavaskar, Syed Kirmani, Dilip Doshi and Ravi Thakkar, and Younus Adam, Asma Adam, Sohail Adam Junior (In my lap), Rashid Desai, Haneef, Mansoor, Ibrahim Naana, and Yakub Vali.

Auctioning Shahid Afridi's bat for his charitable trust.

In a dinner party with Indian Test Cricketers in England (2007 tour)- Sourav Ganguly, Rahul Dravid, Yuvraj Singh and MS Dhoni

With Azharuddin, Dr Rajpura, Shabbir Karolia, Iqbal Khan, and other friends at my house in Dewsbury in 1990's

The Swing of Sultan, Wasim Akram, during 2019 Cricket World Cup in England.

Catching up with Sourav Ganguly during 2019 Cricket World Cup in England

Ghulam Parker (Former Indian Cricketer) and his wife Lubna visits us in Dewsbury. What a humble man he is!

With Younis Khan (Former Pakistan Captain)

Kapil Dev and Azzu play time with my grandson, Mohammad Adam, during IIFA 2007 Celebrity Cricket League - June 08, 2007 at Headingley Stadium, Leeds; Saif Ali Khan in the background. (left), Bollywood Star Salman Khan with my grandson, Mohammad Adam, during IIFA 2007 cricket match. (right)

Legendary crikcet umpire Dickie Bird, Dr Rajpura and I

Sunil likes shopping.(left), Watching a cricket match with Wasim Jaffer, WV Raman and friends at Old Trafoord Stadium, Manchester, during 2019 World Cup. (right)

Sunil, my wife (Maryam) and I, for dinner.

Marshaneil (Pammi) Gavaskar and Maryam on pleasant chat; a sisterhood in deed. (left), Recent visit of Nilesh Kulkarni to Dewsbury. (right)

Abey and his daughter Archana; Abey wouldn't miss visiting us whenever he is in the northern part of England. (left), Catching up with Ashish Nehra (right)

Yousuf Pathan, Mehndi Shaikh (Former Batley CC player) and I

ADAM'S APPLE: with Solly Adam, the expatriate Indian responsible for Yorkshire's offer to Sachin

Sachin Tendulkar hailed as Adam's Apple by the media in Yorkshire (1992).

What's for dinner?... at Durbar restaurant in Leeds

Dinner at Durbar Restaurant in Leeds (1991/92) - Vinod Kambli, Sachin, and my family members (Ebrahim Adam, Maryam and I)

Printed from
THE TIMES OF INDIA

Solly Bhai: Indian cricketers' Man Friday who brought Tendulkar to Yorkshire

PTI | Jul 4, 2019, 08.07 PM IST

LEEDS: Long before Sachin Tendulkar became a name that needed no introduction, a loquacious raconteur from west Yorkshire knew him as the simple teenager, who once messed up his own kitchen while trying his hands at washing clothes.

Meet Suleiman Adam or Solly bhai, a man who is God-send for all Indian cricketers coming to play league or county cricket in the north of England. Solly bhai played a role in bringing Tendulkar to Yorkshire and breaking the county's century-old tradition of not signing a foreign player.

A news article in Times of India in July 2019 that revisits Sachin's signing with Yorkshire County Team in 1992.

Sunil likes to be in Yorkshire.   With Sachin, during a dinner party.

Mount Cricket team visits Vatican City to play against the St. Peter's Cricket Club of Rome in October 2015, and I as its mentor.

During Vatican Tour in 2015 - The then CEO (Mark Arthur) and other officials of the Yorkshire CCC, and ECB; Dr. Rajpura and his wife(Abida), Maryam and I.

Sachin attends the wedding of my eldest son, Ebrahim Adam, in August 1991

Kicking off a new journey with Petrol station Business; my better-half, Maryam, and I

A time to relax; my parents (Ayesha Adam and Saeed Adam) at their comforts, after decades long struggles.

My father, Saeed Adam, who dedicated his life for our family. (left), Angel of our family, Maryam. (right)

My family function at Thornhill in 2022; my family members and friends (Sunil and Chandresh Patel)

Like true siblings; Maryam and Reena Roy, a Bollywood star of our times

Vara Vantapati (the author of my book) with Sunil at our family function.

Solly's delight at Royal party invite

A special dress designed for Maryam by our long-time friend, Mr. Munaf, to attend the garden party at Buckingham Palace in 2015.

"WHEN my dad moved here to work in the mills in 1962, I didn't even know where England was on the map," said Solly Adam this week, at his home in Cowper Street, Savile Town. "And look at this – I'm going to meet the Queen!"

In our recent tour to India in December 2023 - Maryam, Asma (our daughter) and I with Sunil, Dilip Vengsarkar, and Manali vengsarkar.

A treasure to cherish: With mementos and the bats gifted by my friends and legends of the game (Sir Viv Richards, Inzamam-ul-Haq, Kapil Dev, Sachin Tendulkar, Shahid Afridi, Imran Khan, Javed Miandad, Sunil Gavaskar, Vinod Kambli and Sir Ian Botham) at my Solly Sports store in Saville town.

A dream comes true at last; rebuilt the house in December 2023, by clearing off the ruins of our old ancestral home, at Simlak in India where I born.

TIMES

They owe it all to Solly Adam

By Pradeep Vijayakar
The Times of India News Service

LEEDS: One can't come to Yorkshire and go back without getting a whiff of the league cricket here. It is important as hell, for it's the lifeline of their cricket.

For instance, in his Sunday column in the *Yorkshire Post,* former England skipper and coach Ray Illingworth, a famous Yorkshireman, wrote about the good health of the Bradford league. He wrote that he had gone to see his old club Farnsley and was pleased that they were doing well. However, he lamented that today's players were not as ambitious as their predecessors.

"They are content with a total of 500. In our times players would try and reach 1,200 so that they could catch the eye of the selectors of Yorkshire county cricket club." Once that was done, it was only a jump away from Test cricket.

For Indians, the Yorkshire leagues are the most important ones. Sunday's local paper had an action picture of Jatin Paranjpe, the Mumbai batsman. Jatin, whose promising India career suffered a setback due to an ankle injury in Toronto last year, plays for Yorkshire Bank in the Bradford league. He, however, hasn't had a great season so far.

Monday's local paper carried paras on Sammy Dighe and Mohamed Kaif. Sammy is Sameer Dighe, who was once touted as a India material. He scored 83 in Osett's win over Skelmanthorpe in the Heavy Woollen Cup.

Kaif is the under-19 sensation who was the pride of Central Zone in its Duleep trophy triumph. He scored 80 in Lightcliffe's win over Lascelles in the same tournament.

Kaif, like most Indians, owes it all to Solly Adam, who has devoted a lifetime to helping Indian cricketers play professional cricket in the leagues here. He didn't have a pucca contract when he came on the prompting of Mumbai opener Wasim Jaffer, but Solly fixed him up.

Solly, who hails from Surat, came here in 1963. He has helped over 400 players from India and Pakistan in 33 years. But he may not do as much again if he suffers the experience of this season.

He had convinced his club Altofts to sign an Indian and not an Aussie or a New Zealander and Hyderabad allrounder Daniel Manohar was taken. But midway through he received a call for a job interview back home and is going back without fulfilling his commitment, leaving the club and Solly high and dry. And they can't even get a replacement.

The rules have been tightened and players have to be signed well before the start of the season and only one per club. The club may now be regretting not having signed an Aussie or a Kiwi. It's cheaper for them as they can get good jobs as securing work permits is easier for them because of a mutual agreement. For Indians, the club also has to arrange jobs. Solly has had a similar experience earlier too when Maharashtra's Abhijit Kale broke the contract abruptly. He was slapped a life ban from playing. However, Solly helped him out of it.

The fact that an undeterred Solly repeatedly asked me to recommend a promising left-arm spinner-cum-batsman for next year proves his love for Indian players. Even before one could mention the name of Gyanendra Pandey, a fax arrived from India-bound Amay Khurasiya for a contract next season.

A quality player would easily get between 3,000 to 6,000 pounds plus air fare. A player should have played a minimum five first-class games to qualify. The real challenge lies in playing in the Bradford league where the players are mostly pros with one overseas player thrown in. Phil Carrick, a Yorkshire spinner, plays in the league. Along with Jatin there's only Kanwaljit Singh, the evergreen sardar from Hyderabad who plays for Cleckheaton and spun them to a win with a five for 10-wicket haul recently.

Kanwaljit was also brought here by Solly, who takes pride in the fact that Jacob Martin of Vadodara who was recommended by him, created a league record with 11 fifties last year. It is performances like these that make Solly Adam happy as he recalls with pride having helped in their formative years men like Abdul Qadir, Iqbal Qasim, Dilip Doshi, Ajay Jadeja, Abey Kuruvilla, Chandrakant Pandit, Raju Kulkarni, Lalchand Rajput, Vengsarkar and Baroda players Atul Bedade and Tushar Arothe, who are still playing here.

Promising Pakistani opener Suleman Huda has caught his fancy now. He would cherish his first days in England just as Sachin Tendulkar would have during his stint in Yorkshire. That stay was made all the more comfortable because of his stay with Solly. From Gavaskar to Sachin to Suleman Huda, Solly has helped them all in his own way.

Article - 01:
from Times of India,
My Interview with
the media in India

No challenge left for Solly

Article - 02:
from Yorkshire
Press, On my
resignation to
Batley CC, 1987.

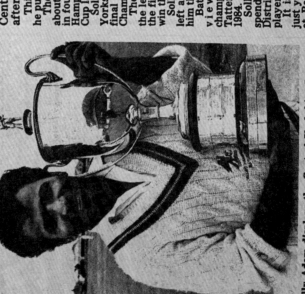

Solly Adam displays the Central Yorkshire League championship trophy before announcing his resignation as Batley captain. — (P.M.).

SOLLY Adam is giving up the captaincy of Central Yorkshire League champions Batley after five years of success.

This week Solly said he was resigning because, as he put it, "There is no challenge left."

The last five years have seen Batley pick up just about every trophy going, winning the league twice in four years, the league knock-out cup, now the Jack Hampshire Trophy, in 1983 and the Heavy Woollen Cup last year after being semi-finalists in 1984.

Solly has also led his team into the semi-final of the Yorkshire Champion of Champions Trophy and the final and semi-final of the Yorkshire Council Championship.

The last five years have also seen Neil Haines win the league bowling prize for Batley, David Dove take the fielding prize and Indian Test star Chaud Pandit win the league batting and wicketkeeping award.

Solly has also played his part with the ball, his slow left arm averaging 40 wickets a season and winning him the club bowling prize in 1984 for his 62 wickets.

Batley's consistency is all the more remarkable in view of the fact that only two of the 1987 championship side — Sean Twohig and David Tattersfield — played in the championship side of 1984.

Solly has been a captain most of his cricketing life, spending ten years as a skipper in the Dewsbury and District League before moving to Thornhill as a player and then Batley as captain.

It is unlikely that he will settle for the sidelines just yet, however. "There is no challenge left for me at Batley but I am considering other offers, especially from Bradford League clubs and I wouldn't rule out being a captain again," he said.

TODAY'S TEAMS

Birstall XI

From

1—A. KARNIK, Captain
2—S. GAVASKAR
3—P. INGHAM
4—R. WRIGHT
5—M. WALMSLEY
6—D. SADLER
7—G. HOBSON
8—W. FINCH
9—A. BORDMAN
10—C. MANBY
11—D. JONES
12—D. JOHNSON
13—M. ELLIS
14—D. GILL

Select League

1—P. HODSON, Captain
(Wakefield)
2—J. WOODFORD
(Liversedge)
3—R. JARRETT (Liversedge)
4—E. LOXTON (Slazengers)
5—A. DENNISON (Morley)
6—S. ADAM (Batley Muslims)
7—B. MASON (Batley)
8—G. PARKES
(Heckmondwike)
9—M. LAIDLER (Wakefield)
10—R. HIRST (Drighlington)
11—B. BURMAN (Meltham)
12—K. GHAVRI (Ramsbottom)

UMPIRES :

PETER MYRES   ALAN STREET

Article 03: Programme Card of the Benefit Match for Avi Karnik (India) at Birstall - August 10, 1980.

365

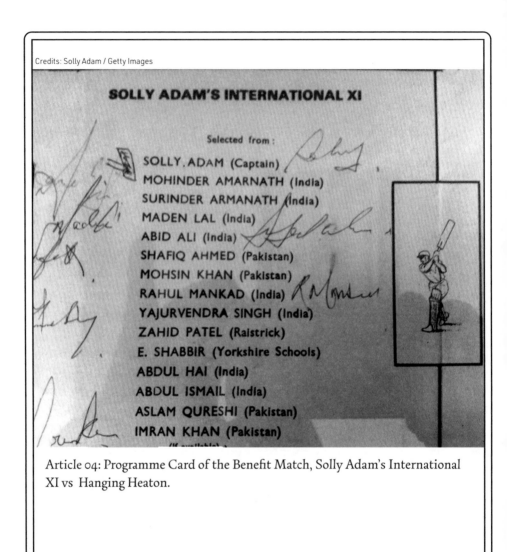

SOLLY ADAM'S INTERNATIONAL XI

Selected from :

SOLLY. ADAM (Captain)
MOHINDER AMARNATH (India)
SURINDER ARMANATH (India)
MADEN LAL (India)
ABID ALI (India)
SHAFIQ AHMED (Pakistan)
MOHSIN KHAN (Pakistan)
RAHUL MANKAD (India)
YAJURVENDRA SINGH (India)
ZAHID PATEL (Raistrick)
E. SHABBIR (Yorkshire Schools)
ABDUL HAI (India)
ABDUL ISMAIL (India)
ASLAM QURESHI (Pakistan)
IMRAN KHAN (Pakistan)

Article 04: Programme Card of the Benefit Match, Solly Adam's International XI vs Hanging Heaton.

RICHARD HADLEE TESTIMONIAL MATCH

Batley International XI	Richard Hadlee's Nottinghamshire XI
1. SOLLY ADAM (Batley)	1. TIM ROBINSON
2. VIVEK JARSINHA (Hyderabad)	2. CHRIS BROAD
3. ABDUL ASEEM (Hyderabad)	3. CLIVE RICE
4. SURECH SKETTY (Bombay)	4. DEREK RANDALL
5. BARRY PETTY (Batley)	5. PAUL JOHNSON
6. DAVID DOVE (Batley)	6. RICHARD HADLEE
7. SEAN TWOHIG (Batley)	7. DUNCAN MARTINDALE
8. MOHAMMAD DADIWALLA (Bombay)	8. BRUCE FRENCH
9. MICHAEL FEN (Batley)	9. EDDIE HEMMINGS
10. JOHN PRENTICE (Batley)	10. KEVIN COOPER
11. ROBERT COOPER (Batley)	11. KEVIN SAXELBY
12. PAUL BLAKLEY (Batley)	12. ANDY PICK
13. ABDUL JABBA (Madras)	13. PETER SUCH

Article 05: Programme Card of the Testimonial Match for Richard Hadlee at Mount Batley, May 5, 1986.

SOLLY ADAM INTERNATIONAL XI

selected from

1. SOLLY ADAM (Captain)
2. RAHUL MANKAD
3. RAJENDRA JADEJA
4. KARSAN GHAVRI
5. MADAN LAL
6. NARASMHA RAO
7. SUBROTO GUHA
8. SURESH SHASTRI
9. RASINDER AMARNATH
10. ABDUL JABBAR
11. HARI HARAN
12. SURYA BAINDOR
13. MAHMOOD DADIEWALA
14. *HAROON RASHID
15. *DILIP DOSHI

* If available

TO-DAY'S RAFFLE PRIZE DONATED BY ⌐

CROWN BATS

— the best Cricket Bat in the world

CROWN — THE PROFESSIONALS CHOICE

Used by Indian, Pakistani, Australian, West Indian, South African
New Zealand and English players

Article 06: Programme Card of the second Testimonial Match at Hanging
Heaton.

Imran's Pakistanis come to the Mount

Pakistan XI 215-9, Batley Select XI 151

A LARGE crowd gathered at Mount Pleasant in the Sunday afternoon sun to watch some of the area's best cricketers take on the Pakistan touring team in a benefit match for Pakistan's captain Imran Khan.

Although the Pakistan team turned up an hour late, the crowds were rewarded with a show of quick-scoring, all-action cricket

Batting first, Pakistan scored 215 runs in less than 30 overs — more than one run per ball

The top batsman in the innings was Asif Mujtaba, who scored 57 before he was stumped by New Zealander Ronnie Hart.

Imran Khan was caught off a ball bowled by Batley Select XI captain Solly Adam with only five runs to his credit.

The Batley XI were off to ba bad start when Indian international Dilip Vengsarkar went for a duck, but the home team still appeared to be in with a chance when Gomersal's Ronnie Hart scored a fast 59.

After this Anwar Khan scored a useful 26, but the team did not have the late-batsman endurance of Pakistan

Pakistan captain Imran Khan is followed by young fans as he enters Batley's Mount Pleasant for the benefit match against a Batley XI. — (0507/1).

PAKISTAN XI

Ijaz Ahmed b Rashid Patel	26
Shoaib Mohammed st. Hart b Tanveer Ali	41
Mansoor Akhtar b Tanveer Ali	21
Manzoor Elahi b Anwar Khan	2
Wasim Akram c Atiqul Rehman b Solly Adam	23
Asif Mujtaba st. Hart b Masood Anwar	57
Imran Khan c Anwar Khan b Solly Adam	5
Salim Yousuf c Masood Anwar b Colin Buzzard	26
Zakir Khan b Masood Anwar	5
Azeem Hafeez not out	1
Iqbal Qasim did not bat	
Extras 8	
Total (for 9 wkts) 215	

Bowling: Rashid Patel 5-0-35-1, Atiqul Rehman 3-0-26-0, Anwar Khan 3-1-7-1, Tanveer Ali 5-1-31-2, Solly Adam 5-0-39-2, Azeem Khan 3-0-26-0, Masood Anwar 3.3-0-33-2, Colin Buzzard 2-0-18-1.

BATLEY SELECT XI

Dilip Vengsarkar c Salim Yousuf b Imran Khan	0
Mohinder Armanath c Salim Yousuf b Wasim Akram	9
Ronnie Hart c Manzoor Elahi b Iqbal Qasim	59
Masood Anwar c Salim Yousuf b Zakir Khan	7
Anwar Khan c Ejaz Ahmed b Manzoor Elahi	26
Rashid Patel b Manzoor Elahi	4
Azeem Khan c Manzoor Elahi b Salim Yousuf	1
Tanveer Ali b Ejaz Ahmed	16
Atiqul Rehman c Ejaz Ahmed b Salim Yousuf	11
Solly Adam run out	5
Colin Buzzard not out	4
Extras 9	
Total 151	

SOLLY Adam (left) tosses up under the watchful eye of Pakistan captain Imran Khan to start Sunday's match at Mount Pleasant, Batley. — (0507/3).

Article 07: from Yorkshire Press, on a Benefit Match for Imran Khan at Mount Batley, July 05, 1987.

Relegated team change captains

SPEN VICTORIA Cricket Club are not going to let their recent relegation from Division One of the Bradford League get them down.

Less than a week after the last ball of the 1988 season has been bowled, Spen are already planning for the summer of 1989.

Solly Adam will be captain for next season, replacing Chris Pickles who will be his vice captain. Solly, a larger than life character, has only been with the club one season, but he has already made an impact on the field and with his slow left arm bowling. This will be the first time he has captained a Bradford League side, but he has plenty of experience, gained mostly with the successful Batley side in the Central Yorkshire League.

DOGGED BY INJURY

Chris Pickles, dogged by injury this year, will be able to concentrate on his undoubted talents as an all rounder. He also hopes to develop his career with Yorkshire, having played in several games for the county this season.

Simon Horkin, who played with Cleckheaton this season, is a new face at Spen for the 1989 season.

Simon, a determined and prolific opening batsman

SOLLY ADAM

makes a welcome return to Spen Lane and the club he started with as a junior. He will replace David Weston who has gone to play with a team in Australia.

NEW FACES

Spen, who were in some respects unlucky to be relegated, will be building a team to make the journey back to the First Division at the first attempt. It is likely that there will be several more new faces signed up for next year.

"I am looking forward to taking Spen back to the First Division next season", says confident new skipper, Solly Adam.

Article 08: from Yorkshire Press, on my selection as the Captain of Spen Victoria, 1989.

Spen in dramatic Cup final triumph

By MIKE POPPLEWELL

SPEN Victoria lifted the Bradford League's Priestley Cup for the first time in almost half a century with a sensational 158-run victory over favourites Pudsey St. Lawrence at Bingley yesterday.

Having knocked off 241 to beat Idle in the semi-final, the Pudsey side were not overwrought at the prospect of chasing Spen's total of 231. But a one-man whirlwind from Wakefield in the form of 20-year-old paceman John Wood quickly wrecked any hopes of success.

From the very start of the Pudsey reply, Wood found something in the wicket no other bowler had and he proceeded to beat the bat time and again.

James Goldthorp fell in his second over and Chris Gott, on whom the Saints' hopes rested heavily, survived an appeal for a bat-pad catch at short leg first ball before helping James Dracup add 27 runs for the second wicket.

Man-of-the-match Wood hit back, however, with a 5-5 spell to remove Gott, Rob Winter, skipper Keith Smith, New Zealand Test star Chris Pringle, and not out specialist Steve Wales.

With the defiant Dracup (19) failing to Gloucestershire second team paceman

Mike Smith, and Martyn Redhead run out by Leeds Grammar schoolboy Tim Walton, Pudsey collapsed to 57 for 8.

Though some brief belligerence from Andrew Langley and Richard Allinson held up the inevitable Spen Victoria victory, Wood, to take his figures to 7-20 in 13 overs, and Smith took the last two wickets to leave Pudsey all out for just 73.

It was a superb all-round effort by Solly Adam's young Spen side with Indian "Tosh" Arothe (57), Steve Foster (44) and Andrew Bethel (36) all making vital contributions in the early part of their innings, while Wood, on a day he could do no wrong, hit 21 at the close.

After the game Adam, revelling in his first major Bradford League success, handed out a warning to the rest of the league: "The next stop is the championship," he declared. "I think we have left it too late this season but just watch out next year. The only enjoyment in cricket to me is winning."

Solly Adam (left), the Spen Victoria captain, holds the Priestley Cup with seven-wicket hero man-of-the-match John Wood. Picture: STEVE RIDING

Article - 09 - from Yorkshire Press, on Spen Victoria winning Priestley Cup, 1990.

RICHARD LUMB'S
YORKSHIRE C.C.C. XI

1. R. G. Lumb (Captain)
2. G. Boycott
3. C. W. J. Athey
4. M. Moxon
5. J. D. Love
6. K. Sharp
7. G. B. Stevenson
8   D. L. Bairstow
9. S. Dennis
10. A. Sidebottom
11. P. Carrick
12. A. Ramage
13. N. Taylor

40 OVER MATCH

Umpires: R. HOLLINGS. D. COCKROFT

BATLEY CRICKET CLUB
SELECT XI

1. S. ADAM (Captain) Batley
2. C. PANDIT (Vice-Captain) Batley & Bombay
3. M. SHAIK Batley & Baroda
4. B. HAIGH Ossett
5. S. LAX Hanging Heaton
6. D. DOSHI India
7. R. HUDSON Hanging Heaton
8. G. GILL Shepley
9. R. KULKARNIE Bombay
10. ALI ZAI
11. J. BURTON Spen Victoria
12. B. BURMAN Batley

Article 10: Programme Card of the Testimonial Match for Richard Lumb, August 19, 1983.

372

> 'I personally believe there aren't any who are good enough. It's nothing do with racial prejudice.'
>
> *Solly Adam.*

Article II: from Yorkshire Press, On my Interview with the media.

Cricket home truth from foreigners

Proud 'Yorkshireman' hits at selectors

DON'T blame the foreigners, learn from them.

That is the message to England's Test selectors from a Dewsbury businessman who has imported nearly 100 Indian and Pakistani cricketers into the English game.

After the team was crushed in the fourth Test yet again, by the West Indies, the chairman of the English selectors, Peter May, laid the blame for the collapse of the national game at the door of overseas players.

It is time, he says, to cut back on foreign imports and give home-grown talent the chance to flourish.

But Mr Solly Adam, an Indian-born Dewsbury businessman who has brought such players as Pakistan Test bowler Abdul Qadir to Yorkshire league cricket, says May is simply looking for excuses.

"He never blames himself, it is always someone else. Now it is the overseas players," said 38-year-old Mr Adam, who has just knocked up 25 years in local league cricket.

"One overseas player does not make a team. If they made such a difference

Somerset would have won the championship every year with Richards and Garner, but they didn't," he said.

"The problem is that clubs do not get the best out of these players. Richard Hadlee has said that in 10 years in English cricket not once has a youngster approached him for advice.

"It should be written into their contracts that they must spend a certain amount of time coaching youngsters," he said.

"English players have the same opportunities to play and coach abroad and many of them do."

Mr Adam came to Britain as a schoolboy in 1963 to settle in Savile Town, Dewsbury. Success in business has brought him a string of garages and a supermarket, but cricket is the real love of his life.

In a five-year spell with Batley in the Central Yorkshire League he won nine trophies, including two championships, the Heavy Woollen Cup and the Jack Hampshire Trophy.

A left arm spinner, he is now with Bowling Old Lane in the Bradford League,

Solly Adam

and returned a five-wicket haul in a recent game against Spen Victoria.

"I might have been born in India, but I consider myself a Yorkshireman, my heart is here, and I love to see Yorkshire do well," he said.

His main reason for introducing Indian and Pakistani cricketers to the Yorkshire Council, Bradford League and Huddersfield League is to improve local cricket, he says.

Pakistan's international spinner Iqbal

Qasim and batsman Mansoor Akhtar, along with Indian bowler Madan Lal were all introduced to English cricket by Mr Adam.

"I don't make money out of it. I do it for the love of the game, to improve local leagues, but they do not get the best out of these overseas players," he said.

"They are happy for them just to turn up for a match and score runs or take wickets,"

Mr Adam says too many English youngsters have too many sports on their minds to become world class in one.

"A lot of the overseas players are just ordinary cricketers when they come here. Players like Imran Khan, Zaheer Abbas and Malcolm Marshall have developed into great players here, but their minds are totally on cricket," he said.

"You find English players have their minds on other things, talking football, golf or snooker during a game of cricket. You must concentrate on one to become a top player."

Mr Adam rates Yorkshire league cricket the best in the world, and the Bradford league best of all, but he would hate to see the County side abandon its Tyke traditions for the sake of success.

"It is not prejudice to have only Yorkshire-born players in the team. Someone from Derbyshire could not play, it is not racial prejudice.

"Yorkshire should stick to tradition. There are some fine players here. They just need to learn from the experience of others."

Article 12: from Yorkshire Press, On my Interview with the media.

Not Enough Chicken Feed!

Solly Adam and his highly talented team of cricketers have been ousted from Chickenly Cricket Club by the Club committee.

This is their reward for rescuing the cricket club three years ago when nobody else wanted it. The Club Secretary Joe Scott announced that Gawthorpe St Marys will now take over the cricket club and asked the Central Yorkshire League (CYL) to allow them to play in the second Division because Gawthorpe's players are not good enough to play first Division cricket. At an emergency meeting the CYL committee accepted Mr. Scott's proposals. All CYL Clubs were invited to this meeting except the existing Chickenley cricket section of which Solly Adam is Chair and Mohammed Ali Lunat, Secretary. Solly knew nothing of this until after the meeting.

This follows the recent announcement by the CYL committee that they did not want 'all Asian' teams playing in the league. However, they made no objections to the 'all white' teams that play in the CYL.

Solly Adam told *AWAAZ* that the cricketers had asked Chickenley for a written contract allowing indefinite stay when they took over the cricket club but the Club committee assured them that this was unnecessary becauses they would allow the team to play as long as they wanted. They had been given such an assurance for the last three seasons.

However last month the Club went back on their word and invited Gawthorpe to take over the cricket team. The reason given to the cricketers was that the 'Club was not making any money at the bar', since they took over because the players did not drink.

"We were informed of the decision in a very underhand way. I received the letter telling us our services were no longer required two weeks after the decision was taken. In the meantime Gawthorpe had already replaced us and the Central Yorkshire League commitee were given notice of this, prompting the emergency meeting of the rest of the clubs to which we were not even invited." said Solly. "But how can an established League call such an important meeting without even receiving an official letter from the Chickenly Club committee. The meeting was called as a result of a verbal request from Joe Scott.

"It seems from what the League have said in the past about not wanting 'all Asian' teams and from Chickenley's attitude towards us over last season there appears to be a conspiracy between the two to stop us playing cricket in their League."

The cricketers had been financing the club themselves because the commitee stopped giving them money after only one season. This, they were happy to do and the CYL committee knew this fact, but they were thrown out anyway.

Article 13: from Yorkshire Press, On a Critique of Chickenly CC.

The Guardian and Herald, Friday, January 3, 1992 17

Guardian & Herald Sport

3-1-92

Spen skipper on building cricket bridges

A SOCIAL occasion tomorrow could build a cricket bridge between local Asian players and the Yorkshire County club, says Solly Adam, captain of the Bradford League club Spen Victoria.

Mr. Adam is an official of two local clubs in the Dewsbury district, Mount Cricket Club and Chickenley which are to hold a combined dinner and prize presentation at Batley tomorrow, an occasion which, he says he looks upon not only as a bridge building exercise but as likely to have far wider significance for

cricket in Yorkshire as a whole.

Most interest will revolve on the attendance of Brian Close, Yorkshire cricket chairman, whose televised remarks in a programme on alleged racism in Yorkshire cricket, caused offence among the ethnic minority.

TOP GUESTS

Other guests who have accepted invitations are Yorkshire president Sir Lawrence Byford, chief executive Chris Hassell, cricket manager Steve Oldham, former captain

Phil Carrick and Dewsbury representative Philip Akroyd as well as YCA secretary Ian Chappell.

Adil Ditta and Ismail Dawood, Yorkshire-born Asians who have been set on the Academy staff, are also expected to attend.

John Holder, the Test umpire, who addressed Central Yorkshire League dinner, will also speak.

About 300 are expected including three representatives from each of the Asian clubs in the Dewsbury League and local Quaid-e-Azam teams as well as prominent members of the Asian

business community.

Chief guest is Mohammed Atif Siddique, the Pakistani Consulate from Bradford.

"The object of the exercise is bridge-building," said Mr. Adam. "We want Yorkshire to tell us the best way for our players to earn a chance of developing to county level while it gives Brian Close the chance to wipe the slate clean.

"In the long term we want to encourage Asian cricket fans to become members of Yorkshire and even stand for the committee.

"It is ridiculous if understandable that many people from Dewsbury prefer to support Lancashire and Derbyshire because Wasim Akram

and Mohammed Azharuddin play for them. We want them to be supporting Yorkshire and we welcome the county opening the way to overseas players.

"We are absolutely delighted that such topranking Yorkshire officials will be coming to the dinner.

"We want to open the door between Asian players and Yorkshire. The sooner we start doing it the sooner there will be more opportunities for the younger generation."

Article 14: from The Guardian and Heralad, On my Role in Building Bridges, January 03, 1992.

Chickenley rescue mounted by Solly

AN all-Asian Dewsbury Cricket League side has come to the rescue of 150-year-old Chickenley club to ensure their future in the Central Yorkshire League.

In a package drawn up this week by Dewsbury businessman Solly Adam, Spen Victoria and former Batley captain:

● Mount will transfer their first team to turn out as Chickenley's second XI with the Batley club continuing to field two teams in the Dewsbury League.

● The best Mount players will be considered for Chickenley's first team while a vigorous recruiting policy has been launched by Mr Adam and Brian Stansfield who has played over 35 years for the club.

● Mr Adam is to be Chickenley's cricket chairman on a new committee comprising representatives of the Ossett Lane club and the Mount on a 50-50 basis.

● And — most exciting of all — Mr Adam has approached Sanchi Tendulkar, the Indian teenage batsman regarded as the best prospect in world cricket, to play this summer.

Although they have been one of the most successful CYL clubs in recent years winning the league in 1986, the HW Cup in 1988 and the Jack Hampshire Trophy last season Chickenley's future has been in doubt most of the winter.

A mass exodus of players has left David Goodlad as the only one of last season's first team intending to play this.

The club are trying to persuade two recently retired top CYL bowlers to return to action while Mr Adam is also hoping to attract the cream of local Asian players especially if he can persuade Tendulkar to come.

Mr Adam, who will continue to captain Spen this season, feels that the gap between Dewsbury League and the CYL first division can be overcome by the Mount's best players such as the Pakwashi cousins and Mohammed Ali Loonat.

Chickenley secretary Joe Scott and treasurer John Foyle are continuing with Mount secretary Hanif Mayet also on the new committee.

By Peter Snape
Sports Editor

Mr Foyle, treasurer for ten years, said: "Things are changing for the good with a cricket committee and proper parent club committee. I am more hopeful for the future than for a long time and immensely pleased by developments".

CYL secretary Don Nicholson said: "Solly Adam has such a lot to offer cricket. We're delighted if he is helping to re-establish such a historic club.

Article 15 - from Yorkshire Press, In Rescue of the Chickenly CC.

Batley dinner helped signing of Tendulkar

JANUARY'S visit to Batley by the Yorkshire CCC top brass was a key factor in the County signing teenage Indian batting prodigy Sachin Tendulkar as their first overseas player.

Solly Adam, Spen Victoria's captain and Chickenley cricket chairman, was instrumental in inviting the Headingley hierarchy to the joint dinner of the Mount and Chickenley clubs as a bridge-building exercise to defuse fears among the ethnic minority that the county's cricket was racist.

Mr Adam, who had tried unsuccessfully to get Tendulkar to play at Chickenley last summer, explained: "When I heard that Craig McDermott, the australian fast bowler, had had to turn down Yorkshire's invitation as he faced an operation I knew Sachin was the right player as there was no big-name fast bowler available.

"If £100,000 was there from Yorkshire TV it was obvious that Yorkshire should go for a number one even if it had to be a batsman, be it Tendulkar, Martin Crowe, Sanjay Manjrekar, Richie Richardson or Azrahuddin.

"I knew Sachin was desperate to come to play league cricket in England, never mind county.

"I got to know Brian Close well when he was a guest at our dinner so I rang him at home and suggested Sachin. When I bring players over here to play league cricket I always look for those with great ability, able to fit in with the dressing room and give 100 per cent.

"Cricket is a business and I knew that Sachin would bring in new Yorkshire spectators and members from the Asian community and in the process dispel the view that Yorkshire was racist.

"Brian said he would put it to the committee, most of whom agreed. When I rang Sachin to tell him the greatest county of all wanted him his first reaction was 'You must be joking'. "He had played five Tests, 12 Benson and Hedges and eight World Cup matches in the last five months in Australia. In October he would be leaving for a tour of South Africa and then India would be entertaining England early next year.

"I told him that he was top name now after the World Cup but if he were to have a less productive winter no-one in county cricket would want to know him.

"So I rang Sunil Gavaskar and asked him to persuade Sachin. Brian invited me to a meeting at Headingley with secretary David Ryder so we talked to chief executive Chris Hassell in South Africa.

"Sachin preferred to discuss details of the deal face-to-face so Chris went to India last weekend to clinch it just in front of Leicestershire.

"I can assure Yorkshire fans that whatever the pressure on Sachin as their first overseas player they will see a very old head on young shoulders as well as a great batsman and no mean bowler.

"A lot of young Asians have told me they will be going to watch him — and that has got to be good for Yorkshire.

"What a difference 12 months make. Last summer at Chickenley we could not afford the £75 per match Sachin wanted. Now he will be earning more than £30,000 this season".

Article 16: from Yorkshire Press, On Signing Sachin Tendulkar to Yorkshire - 1992.

Today's Teams

S. & B.	Overseas XI
Mark Warren (C)	Solly Adam (C)
Ryan Pitts (Wkt)	Samir Dighe
Dave Barlow	Wasim Jaffer
Marlon Black	Amol Mazumdar
Asif Jan	Ameya Khurasia
Colin Maxwell	Amit Dani
Toby Miller	Nishit Shetty
Nick Gallimore	Robin Morris
Simon Sutcliffe	Rajesh Pawar(Wkt)
Neil Rimmer	Atul Ranade
Bryan Strang	Shawn Petafi
	Abey Kuruvilla

Umpires: David Davies and Mike Fletcher

Article 17: Programme Card of the Benefit Match for Abey Kuruvilla at Southport and Birkdale CC, August 20, 2000.

Solly Adam sponsors the Yorkshire Central Cricket League

Dewsbury based businessmen and Cricketing Star Solly Adam has become the first Asian in the history of cricket to sponsor an entire cricket league. A sponsorship deal beginning in April 2001 was struck between the Yorkshire Central Cricket League and one of Solly Adams many businesses, Solly Sports.

Solly Sports is a shop opened in April 2001, based at Solly's Savile Road Service Station. The shop sells everything a keen cricketer might ever need from balls, to bats, to clothing and protective gear. "Professional Cricket is more than just an interest," says Solly, it is almost an addiction and second in my life only to religion". "I find cricket a great way of relaxing and clearing my mind of the stresses of business." Solly has won many coveted awards and trophies for his on field performances. He has played as pro for Cumbria and contributed to the world of sport in many ways.

"It suddenly came to me that I love cricket so why not start up a business in the field, hence the appearance of the Solly Sports shop." He then went one step further in replenishing the Yorkshire Central Cricket league by deciding to sponsor them with the Solly Sports Logo. "Yorkshire has given me so much says Solly, I just wanted to give something back to a community that has given me so much."

By Adeem Younis

SOLLY SPORTS LIMITED

P L A Y   T H E   S P O R T

Article 18: from Yorkshire Press, On my Sponsoring of the Central Yorkshire Cricket League.

380

Dewsbury man makes history

A Dewsbury man made History last month as he organised a game between retired cricket players from Pakistan and India. The proceeds of which, was distributed to providing facilities for orphans and under privileged children.

Mr Solly Adam, who is managing director of Solly Sports in Dewsbury, has incurred notorious achievements in cricket, most notably helping Yorkshire CC sign Sachin Tendulkar a few years ago.

Solly was invited to organise the match by the Shah Satnamji Cricket Academy in Shirsha, Northern India. This was the first time anyone other than the cricket board of India has organised a competitive cricket game in India.

Mr Adam told AWAAZ "I was going to get the current Indian and Pakistani teams to play each other, however both teams were on tour. So I organised a Veterans match. I made personal phone calls to the likes of Waqar Younis, Saeed Anwar, Zaheer Abbas, Heervani, Chohan and many others. They all agreed to take part immediately".

The game was a sell out with over 35,000 people in attendance, whilst the match was also broadcast live by DD Television India. Mr Adam was congratulated by Indian Prime Minister Manmohan Singh, who extended his greetings and good wishes. He also said the game had contributed to the promotion of understanding between the two countries.

Mr Adam has now been asked to organise a match between India and a world 11. He said "It was a great event. I have always wanted to give something back to cricket, and I hope this will go someway towards that. I am looking forward to organising the next match."

AWAAZ would like to congratulate Mr Adam on his important achievement.

A near total view of the pitch

Article 19: from Yorkshire Press, On Organising a Veterans Cricket Match (India Vs Pakistan) in India, December 2004.

How the cricket loving motor mechanic went and graced the Palace lawn

SOLLY ADAM is a name that shouts cricket at you louder than a pace bowlers appeal for an LBW. But behind the man who is now renowned in cricketing circles lay humble beginnings.

The Cricketer

His love for the sport barely has a beginning. In an exclusive interview with Paigaam he told us the passion has always been there. From playing and captaining the school team in Karachi to scouting the legend Sachin Tendulka for Yorkshire, its the love of the game that continues to drive him.

Following his father's initial arrival in the UK Solly came to Dewsbury in 1963. His love for cricket arrived with him and he played for the Victoria School team in his teens.

We asked how he got into playing for a league team. "It's a funny story." He began.

"At first I went for trials to Batley Muslims. I scored 50 and took 3 or 4 wickets, but they told me I had to pay a 20p match fee and £2 for a years subscription. I couldn't afford that because I was still just a school boy."

Instead he went and played for Birstall Trade House who took him on without any charge and after one year there, and because they shut down, Solly went to play for Whitley lower, now upper Hopton.

Batley CC approached Solly in the 1980's to captain the side because they were "like a yoyo." Solly told us. "They never won anything in the Central Yorkshire league. Within a year we won the championship."

He became the first Asian player to play in the first team for Batley CC and led them to two championship victories and won every cup going.

From there he was approached by Spen Victoria to turn their fortunes around and in his first season secured promotion from the second division. In the 1991/2 season Solly led the team to cup success when for the first time in 50 years they won the Priestly Cup.

His playing career doesn't end there. At the age of 42 Solly became the oldest player to sign for first class cricket when he joined Cumberland in the minor counties.

The scout

Famously known as the man with the biggest phone book of international cricketing legends, Solly has been responsible not only for bringing the big names but has been a scout finding league slots for upcoming young talent.

We asked where this link to the big names began. Solly fell into deep thought, and tried to recall.

"I never thought of it." He said with a stunned expression.

"In the early 70's I used to go to the cricket grounds to watch test cricket. I met Gavaskar, Farook Engineer, Imran khan... and I got to know them." These were the players who approached Solly regarding young talented players.

On one occasion Imran khan approached him for Wasim Akram, "He said I have a bowler I want him to play league cricket," he told us adding a number of other names too.

Solly would provide accommodation for the young overseas players as well as setting them up with a league team. In his own words some 9 out of 10 of the players he's helped have gone on to play at international level. He was keen to point out not only has he helped overseas players but also English players who have gone on to play for the national team.

The most famous young cricketer Solly brought to England was of course the master batsman Sachin Tendulka. Just as we arrived he received a message that Tendulka and his wife were due to visit him later that day. Solly told us the story of how he brought the brilliant young Tendulka to Yorkshire.

"Yorkshire never signed any overseas player. Then suddenly they changed their mind and signed an Australian fast bowler but he pulled out.

"Immediately I rang Yorkshire cricket board and said 'you've opened the door, the Australian you signed is not coming, why don't you sign an Indian or a Pakistani to show the people and the world that you're not prejudice."

Solly met the board and advised them to take on this young Indian batsman who "is going to be one of the best in the world."

Solly began to do the necessary for the two to meet. "At the time Tendulka was in Australia. They [Yorkshire board] said if you can talk to him and if he agrees we can go meet him."

Due to business commitments Solly was not able to travel to India for the meet he had arranged, but Yorkshire went ahead with the signing and it opened the door not just for the overseas players but to the many talented young south Asian local players who now have secured positions in the county's teams.

Captain, scout, batsman, bowler is there anything in the team you didn't do? We asked to receive a hearty laugh...."yes anything and everything for cricket." He said.

The Queens Garden Party

In May Solly graced the lawn of Buckingham Place during Her Majesty's Garden Party. He told us "One day I just received a letter. It said we would like to invite you to attend the Queens Garden Party and I thought it was a fake.

"I couldn't believe it. A man who was a motor mechanic, whose father was a mill worker being invited to the Queens Garden Party." It was not until the actual invitation in all its glitz and glamour arrived that he believed it really was happening.

He told us, "In the early 1970's I went to look at Buckingham Palace with my wife standing at a distance. I never knew that one day I would be going into Buckingham Palace with my wife, and go into her garden, looking at the lake and having tea there. It's unbelievable."

When we asked what the day was like with a joy filled breath he said, "Oh it was brilliant!

"I learnt something. She never came a minute earlier. She came bang on time and she was supposed to go back at quarter past 5 but she didn't leave until quarter to six. So her time is not the value the public time is the value. If she starts talking to somebody she'll finish the conversation before she goes to other person.

That I learnt." adding,

"It's a great honour for me and my wife."

In concluding Solly paraphrased his journey, "Its not bad for a boy coming from Simlak village to Dewsbury with a father working in the mill, working as a motor mechanic and went and met the Queen." He said.

Article 20: from Yorkshire Press, On Invitation to the Garden Tea Party at Buckingham Palace.

Palace party dream comes true for Solly

AN adopted Yorkshireman who came to England half a century ago was left bursting with pride after attending a garden party at Buckingham Palace.

Businessman and local league cricket legend Solly Adam received a Royal invite from the Queen.

Father-of-four Solly and wife Maryam, who live in Savile Town, Dewsbury, attended the garden party last Wednesday.

As many as 2,000 people were also there yet the couple were just feet from the Queen as she toured the gardens speaking to guests.

Solly, who came to Dewsbury from Surat in the Indian state of Gujarat in 1963, spoke of his pride and said: "It was a lifetime dream for me.

"I come from a very poor family and I never dreamed something like this would happen.

"I have met many stars and celebrities in my life but the Queen is the ultimate world icon.

"I remember taking my family to Buckingham Palace in 1976 and we were so excited just to take photographs outside.

"This time we went and there were hundreds of tourists outside and we went inside. To see the Queen's house and gardens was unbelievable. There were tears in my eyes I was so proud."

Solly's wife had a dress specially made for the occasion by dressmakers Pankaj and Dhruvi, of Bridal B & Son in Surat.

What surprised and delighted Solly was how the Queen was so generous with her time, speaking to as many people as possible. She stayed 40 minutes longer than scheduled chatting to guests.

"That is something I learned from this, always make time for people," he said. "Often in our own lives we are too busy to talk and listen to others.

"We just run around like headless chickens."

Solly, well-known in local cricket circles, captained Spen Victoria cricket club to many successes in the Bradford League.

Famously, he also brought 19-year-old Indian batsman Sachin Tendulkar to Yorkshire in 1992, making him the first overseas-born player to represent the county. Tendulkar went on to captain India and become one of the greatest cricketers of all time.

Over the years Solly has helped around 400 cricketers in their careers.

Solly, who now runs his own sports store Solly Sports and petrol stations in Savile Town and Heckmondwike, was one of the oldest players still playing first class cricket when he turned out for minor county Cumberland just short of his 43rd birthday.

Solly, who has 10 grandchildren, is coy about his age but still plays the occasional charity match.

"England is my country and I am an adopted Yorkshireman," said Solly. "This country has been good to me and my family and I am proud to call it home."

■ Businessman Solly Adam and wife Maryam at a garden party attended by the Queen at Buckingham Palace.

Article 21: from Yorkshire Press, On my Attending of the Queen's Garden Tea Party at Buckingham Palace .

SUNIL GAVASKAR (left), the record breaking Indian Test batsman who announced his retirement at the end of the World Cup, was in Dewsbury this week visiting Solly Adam (right), the former Batley captain who has moved to Spen Victoria for the new season.

But he was not on a cricketing mission — simply over here to indulge his love for badminton as he took in the All-England championships. "I am a very keen fan and ex-player but our cricket season at home has always prevented me seeing the top players in action", he explained.

Gavaskar, who had one season at Somerset, has no regrets about retiring after a year of mixed fortunes. Last August he achieved his ambition of scoring a century at Lord's in the Bicentenary Test but then saw India surprisingly fall to England in the World Cup semi-final. "You can't have everything", he said. "Nobody can take away the memory of our Cup win at 1983". Now he is concentrating on his business interests including editing a sports magazine and has no intention of donning whites again except for the odd charity match (2203/7).

Article 22: Sunil's interview with the press in Yorkshire on his visit to Dewsbury in 1987.

Wednesday, 25 September 2013

To,

Shri Parmanand Sinha,

London UK

Dear Mr. Sinha,

I have known Mr. Suleiman Adam and his family since the 1970's. Solly, as Suleiman is popularly now has been a great friend of Indian Cricket opening his house to budding young Indian cricketers who go to play in the Yorkshire League.

His wife Mariam has looked after junior as well as senior Indian cricketers providing them with food and accommodation.

I have myself stayed at their house several times and enjoyed their warm hospitality.

I am therefore very happy to invite both Solly and Mariam Bhabhi to visit India this year especially as they love Indian cricket and and to watch Sachin Tendulkar play his 200th test.

Their stay in India will be looked after by me and I hope I will be able to do at least 50% of what they have done for me and other Indian Cricketers.

May I therefore please request you to grant them Visa to travel to India.

Thanking you in advance.

Yours sincerely

Sunil Gavaskar

Article 23: Sunil's letter to Indian Consulate in London, to sanction me a Visa to attend Sachin's farewell test match at Wankhede Stadium in Mumbai in 2013; I'm humbled by his words.

THE PRESS

August 31, 2002

How one of the great Tykes was shamed by a jobsworth gateman.

SOLLY ADAM

I was at Headingly for the first four days of last week's Test match to see India's victory over England. I saw some super cricket and India's triumph has set up a cracking game at the Oval. But while I was there, I saw something that amazed me and left me nothing short of embarrassed.

I remember in the early 1960s going to Headingly and seeing people queuing for half-an-hour just to get the autograph of Fred Trueman.

I know people talk about the likes of Gough, Pollock and Donald but these guys had nothing on Trueman. They are all good bowlers, but Trueman was the greatest.

He was the first bowler to reach 300 Test wickets and had a lovely action which was a pleasure to watch.

In all his cricketing career he only toured four countries - he never strayed far from home - and he was a Yorkshireman through and through.

His 300 wickets would be worth 600 by today's standards, I have no doubt about that.

But how times change! The 1960s seemed so far away when I saw Fred at Headingly last week. Over four days I think I only saw one kid ask for his autograph. It seemed only the older people recognised who he was.

Yorkshire has named rooms at Headingly after some of their greatest heroes - Trueman, Brian Close, Ray Illingworth and Geoffrey Boycott.

I saw with my own eyes how far Trueman's fame has fallen when he was refused entry by a jobsworth gateman.

It takes some guts to come up against Fiery Fred at his worst, but this poor guy didn't know who he was dealing with.

Fred wanted to park his car but there was no way this man was going to let him in. "I don't recognise you," he said. "So, I am not letting you in."

Seconds later Dermot Reeve, the TV commentator, pulled up and the gates were swung open for him, no questions asked.

That was too much for Fred. "Either you let me in or I'm going home," he stormed. Fortunately for the hapless gateman a committee member heard the commotion and quickly ushered a fuming Fred into the car park.

Back in the 1960s gatemen used to salute Fred. Now people refuse to recognise one of the world's greatest bowlers.

I know that if you are hot everybody loves you and when you are down nobody wants to know you but to me Fred deserves better than that.

Also, this week I had the honour to attend a barbecue at Ian Botham's and to have dinner with a host of top stars at Geoffrey Boycott's place.

At Botham's barbecue I had the pleasure of talking with the man himself, Michael Atherton, Michael Holding, David Lloyd and Bob Willis. For a man who played local league cricket all his life it was a privilege to share a table with these people.

It just goes to show the power of television. These ex-players are now commentators and experts who are still mobbed in the street and asked for their autographs.

Yet Trueman, Close - an iron man in the history of cricket- and Ray Illingworth, a great captain, pass by almost unnoticed.

I felt really embarrassed for Fred. He was a hero and deserves more dignity than that gateman gave him.

=======

Daily Pioneer

July 06th, 2019

Meet the Adam of Cricket

Meet the man who has honed cricketers in England. PIONEER SPORT spends an afternoon with Suleiman Adam at his tony Dewsbury home, popular as Solly Adam who brought Sachin Tendulkar to Yorkshire County Cricket Club, to bring you his journey with the game when Indian players would bunk in his house, work for him and enjoy his wife's kitchen delights to learn the art of the game.

As in most relationships in away cricket, this one too kicked off with the craving for Indian food back in the 1970s when Rahul Mankad bumped into Suleiman Adam and got invited for some food at his place. Generations of players down the line have enjoyed the delicious Indian fare cooked up by his stunningly beautiful wife who is now a great grandmother recuperating from a debilitating illness but still not leaving a chance to watch the World Cup live from her bed.

It's been quite a journey between a Dewsbury businessman and the Indian cricketers which has grown at many levels, over three decades and has ended up training the biggest and the best in the desi armoury to become leading Test cricketers. One of them have has even turned in the God of Cricket Sachin Tendulkar to the game's pinnacle of glory.

At 66 now, the man famous for bringing Sachin Tendulkar to the Yorkshire County Cricket and more importantly opening the doors of the 'only for Yorkshire' gates of the respected county, Solly, short for Suleiman, lives on those days when he was kingmaker, guide, father and the unofficial selector of players into the Indian team, especially those who came to him looking for some playing money in pound land, experience and the food of course!

"At the moment people only talk about how I introduced Sachin Tendulkar to Yorkshire. But my association goes back many years and cricketers back. I have introduced a lot of cricketers into league cricket well before Tendulkar," he tells you from the tony back garden of one of his three houses in the posh nook of Dewsbury.

Ask any cab driver at the train station, and he knows the address and the man, taking you straight to his house where the entire family is there to welcome you and talk about cricket. It is the day VVS Laxman, who lived and worked for the family for two long years, has paid a visit to Solly's ailing wife. Some days back, it was Sunil Gavaskar who came calling and recorded a thank you video for the doctor who operated upon the grand old lady of this household. Sachin Tendulkar's wife has been calling up for updates but the little master is yet to come. "He is busy and I know he will be here the moment he gets free from his assignments," Solly says with confidence.

Sounds true, considering Tendulkar's only condition to join Yorkshire club after Gavaskar persuaded him to, had been that he lived next to Solly's house. "I knew Sachin before he came to Yorkshire. Whoever used to come here to play from Bombay would talk about this talented cricketer, like Jatin Paranjape who said, 'one is Sachin and the other Vinod Kambli'. So, when Sachin came here to attend my son's wedding, I asked him if he would like to play league cricket here. He asked for 100 pounds a match. Those days it was 20-25 pounds, so the club said they wouldn't be able to afford him. Sachin

we couldn't afford but we signed Vinod Kambli and he played for my club for 25 pounds a match," Solly tells you.

Sachin, meanwhile, became a Test player and it was while he was playing in Australia that Solly got his second opportunity. Those days, Yorkshire had a rule that anybody born outside of Yorkshire, be he White or Asian, could not play for the club. Suddenly, rules changed and the club signed overseas Australian fast bowler Craig McDermott. But he got injured and the contract fell through.

"The minute I heard that news, I called Yorkshire Cricket Committee (then headed by Geoffrey Boycott) and asked them If I could introduce an Asian to Yorkshire? That would open the door for all the Asians to come and play. 'People reckon that Yorkshire is prejudiced so that will take the stump out of your name', I told them. But they said, 'we don't want that'. I told them that was not right, and I would go to the Press with the story," Solly recalls.

The committee members called him for a discussion. "Next day when I went to the committee, the late Fred Truman was outside. He said, 'Solly I am not happy. We have won so many championships without any overseas player. Up to me, I will not sign'. Indeed, the committee was unhappy. I argued and argued and argued. So, they said ok, if you so insist give me the name. I said, what about Sachin Tendulkar. They said, 'but he is only a young kid'. But have you seen today's news. Don Bradman has said to his wife: 'I watched him play and he reminds me of me playing cricket'. If Bradman says Sachin is as a good as him then he should come and play for Yorkshire'," he told the members who finally agreed.

Sachin was playing a Test series in Australia at that time, but Solly did not waste a minute in calling him. He, however, refused. "I would love to but no Solly bhai but I am playing a lot of cricket. This year I have applied for Ranji and I am playing Test cricket too so it will be too much for me," he told Solly.

"I said, come on Sachin it is not for you. It is for all the Asians. They will come and play for Yorkshire. It will be an honour; people will remember you for it. So, he said 'give me a couple of days I will get back to you on this'. As soon as I put the phone down, I called Sunil Gavaskar who was in the same hotel as Sachin and asked him to persuade him to come here. He said it was a good idea, 'I played for Somerset and it helped me as well. Let me talk to him'. He spoke to him and when two days later I rang up Sachin he said yes but on one condition. 'Only if I will live nearby you'. I found the house nearby mine and he moved there. Rest is history," Solly says after completing in oft-repeated Sachin story. Sachin made an 86 in his maiden appearance for Yorkshire after being scalped by the searing pace of Hampshire's Malcom Marshall just 14 runs short of a ton, and unhappy he did not get his century in his first outing!

Sachin's wife Anjali is in touch with his daughter. Sachin is yet to come and meet him during this tour as he has a packed commentating schedule but Solly is confident he would be at his doorstep the moment he gets time, especially now that his wife has had a brush with death and is battling the loss of a leg from a very rare muscle eating disease, the wife who has been like a mother to cricket's God.

Today, however, it has become different ball game altogether and Solly rues those syrupy old days when cricketers were gentlemen and England the place to be for good money and playing acumen. From Imran Khan who has slept the nights on Solly's living room couch, to Iqbal Qasim, and Mohammad Kaif have all worked and played league and county cricket, thanks to this businessman who has a sports goods shop staring over a closed petrol pump which he owned earlier, in Dewsbury.

Today, he travels to India every year to pick up bats from Punjab, shop from Karol Bagh and visit Mumbai on holidays, not so much to look for new talent. Not many come to him asking for jobs today, not many cricketers that is. "There was no money involved anywhere else but in England back then. Only in Yorkshire they used to pay and paying those days was just 20-30 pounds a match. I introduced cricketers from early 70s plus I have business, a few petrol pumps here. So, they used to play cricket Saturday and Sunday and work for me during the week to get some extra money to take back home. Besides, there were no restaurants or Indian takeaways back then, so my wife used to cook for them and feed them Indian food plus if there was any restaurant they would not have been able to afford eating out as money was very tight for them. It is not just Sachin, Sunil Gavaskar is like a brother to me now, we know each other from the 1970s. Then there was Rahul Mankad, the late Ashok Mankad, Bishan Singh Bedi, Raju Kulkarni, Kuruvilla — cricketers not only from India but a lot of them from Pakistan too who I introduced here, including Imran Khan, Abdul Qadir, Iqbal Qasim to league cricket," he says.

"Those days people loved to come to England, especially to play cricket. It was an honour for them. I remember, before one season I had 10 to 12 first class Indian cricketers sleeping at my place for around two to three weeks before I fixed them in various clubs around here. They became better players once they go back from here," he says, adding that today with big money pouring in from all matches in India, no one wants to spend a hard, cold winter playing cricket in unfriendly conditions at Yorkshire.

But those were the days when Mohammad Kaif worked in his shop. Even Laxman worked hard, slogging away nights at his petrol pump. Kulkarni worked in a mill, cleaning machines. "Nothing wrong with that. They all worked. They had nothing to do Monday to Friday so they did work for some extra money for back home," he says. Solly feels money coming in for cricketers is a good thing, "provided it doesn't go to their heads. As long as they keep their feet on the floor and respect everybody well and good," he adds.

THE SACHIN STORY

Meticulous Sachin

For Sachin playing cricket is a challenge. He doesn't like throwing his wicket away. He was a young kid. Staying in England for four months made him a different person altogether. Everything was earlier done by a servant or parent. Here he was by himself. It made him from boy to a man. He started washing, ironing, cleaning... it helped him a lot in 1991. He was dedicated to cricket. He would play cricket five days a week for the club. As soon as he would finish at 6'o clock he would be at my ground to practice more.

Son, not God

Everybody says he is God of Cricket but for us he was like our son. He treated my wife like a mother and me like a father. He would go out with my children for a pizza or a Kentucky chicken in the evenings. He is family. English people loved him. He was like a Yorkshireman. After a few days when Sachin settled down, 12 of us went to Blackpool and spent a whole day there, he enjoyed every moment of those four months. He would watch old movies on the video cassette, listen to music.

Sachin's mess-ups

Sachin loved my wife's food. He never cooked. He made one or two mess ups in his house so from that day he never did anything. One day he rang my wife and asked how he should wash his clothes. My wife told him there are two machines, a washer and a dryer and how he should use it. In the evening, he called frantically and said his entire kitchen was a pool of soapy bubbles. My wife asked him how much soap he had put into the washing machine and he said: "The entire box"! So, from that day all his clothes were washed and dried and ironed at my place.

Last day of Sachin in Yorkshire

Sachin knew that I went to bed early. But one night, he came at 11 pm, knocking my door and I wondered who it could be. When I opened the door, it was Sachin standing there. He said, "Solly bhai I have to go early tomorrow morning so I have come to touch your and aunty's feet! It was very nice of him. I will remember that as long as I live."

=======

News18

05th July 2019

ICC World Cup 2019 - Meet Adam Solly, the Man who Brought Sachin Tendulkar to Yorkshire

LEEDS: No visit to Leeds for the cricket is complete without tales of Sachin Tendulkar's stint at Yorkshire. The legendary Indian batsman broke multiple records in his career, but becoming the first foreigner to play for Yorkshire was one of his earliest milestones.

And it didn't come easy. Who better than Sulieman Adam to narrate the story of Tendulkar's entry to Yorkshire?

Adam shifted to England from Simlak in Gujarat in 1963 as a schoolboy. He was soon hooked onto cricket, and played at club and league levels in the country. He couldn't make it big on the field, but helped numerous cricketers from India play league or club cricket in England.

Solly, as he is fondly called by many, would host Indian players starved of home food for dinners. He would help many players including Imran Khan, Javed Miandad, Brijesh Patel and Vinod Kambli play league cricket. He would help them get sponsors for equipment. He would even help organise benefit matches. Solly proudly recalls leading players ranging from Imran Khan to Chandrakant Pandit in his club-cricket days.

His biggest signing, though, was the historic deal which got Tendulkar to Yorkshire in 1992.

"I was a member of Yorkshire club. I wanted some Asian to play for Yorkshire," he narrates to *Cricketnext*. "But the rule then was that someone born outside Yorkshire cannot play for the county. Even someone born in say Derbyshire or Lancashire cannot play.

"Yorkshire were reluctant initially but it all changed after he came. Once he signed, it was completely different. He was prompt on practice, never missed training or matches. He was there with full dedication. The way he behaved, he became a Yorkshireman. Local cricketers were snobbish, but he was down to earth and would sign autographs for everyone. He used to play matches, and after the game he would practise with us in the club side. He was unbelievable in dedication.

"He was god-gifted. One day we decided to go to Blackpool where there are lot of fun games. We decided to play billiards. He was first hesitant as he hadn't played billiards before. But within ten minutes, he picked up the game and was better than us. It was same with him in tennis too. But he was down to earth and treated everyone the same. He still respects all of us the same. On the last night before leaving England, he knocked on the door at 11pm and said he came to touch our feet saying we took care of him well. He still respects and treats us the same."

Solly is a reservoir of interesting tales beyond Tendulkar too. He recalls an incident where he had to host wives of many cricketers after the then team manager declined permission for them to stay with the team following a loss in the warm-up game.

He has a story involving Rahul Dravid and Sourav Ganguly's dream Test debut series in 1996 too.

"In 1996, Slazenger gave me 10000 pounds and asked me to sign some Indian players to use their sticker for the England series," he says. "I asked Dada if he would use it for 2000 pounds he was more than happy. He was over the moon. I asked Dravid too for the same amount, he too agreed happily. I was left with 6000 pounds. I was wondering who to sign up. I knew one player very well - Ajay Jadeja - and said I'll sign him up for 6000 pounds because he was an established player, while Dravid and Ganguly were newcomers.

"Dravid and Ganguly were scared how they can carry so much cash from Yorkshire to Nottingham, so my son went and gave them the money. That's how simple they were then."

The likes of VVS Laxman and Madan Lal would work part-time at Solly's petrol stations during their days at club cricket. Laxman in particular has a special place in Solly's heart.

"Laxman and Abey Kuruvilla are very down to earth and unbelievable human beings. My wife was in the hospital last week for an operation. Laxman found out and he came straight to hospital to visit her. He visited today too.

"I was never an agent for any of these cricketers. It was a hobby and purely for the passion of the game. It was the passion for cricket that united us all."

=======

Notes from **David Hopps** (Popular Sports Journalist) book about Sachin and **Solly Adam**

McDermott, only for McDermott to withdraw with a groin injury barely a month before the start of the season. What followed was back-of-an-envelope stuff. On Boycott's suggestion, Yorkshire approached Solly Adam, who was a great provider of overseas players to the local leagues: more than 400, all told. Adam, who also ran a sports shop, had come a long way since he arrived in England in 1963, at a similar age to Tendulkar when he made his debut, with £3 in his pocket. He bought a petrol pump in 1972, stayed open all hours, and eventually, as his business improved, explored his first love and began pumping cricketers into the local economy rather than petrol.

Agents were not so common in cricket in those days and Adam's involvement was voluntary. He loved his connection with the cricketers as they ate at his home, then, homesickness dispelled, made runs on a Saturday. He loved watching them progress into international players and knew if he ever needed a ticket for an international,

no matter how much in demand that match might be, he would have a grateful benefactor able to return the favour. Adam suggested that Yorkshire sign Tendulkar, as he had just signed his school friend Vinod Kambli to play in the Bradford League. He was confident he could persuade Tendulkar that it would be a valuable experience.

Tendulkar was playing Test cricket at the time in Australia and told Adam to give him a week or so to think about it, as he wanted to speak to his parents about the move. Yorkshire, resistant to overseas players for so long, were by now desperate for him to say yes. About a week later, he did just that.

Adam protected and guided him that summer as if he was his own son. He was in the crowd for Tendulkar's farewell Test, in Mumbai. Before he went he told me: "It will be my last glimpse of genius. I'm 68 now and I won't see another Sachin as long as I live. He was put on to this earth to play cricket and to entertain the people."

=======

THE TIMES OF INDIA

04 July 2019

Solly Bhai Indian Cricketers' Man Friday who brought Tendulkar to Yorkshire

LEEDS: Long before Sachin Tendulkar became a name that needed no introduction, a loquacious raconteur from west Yorkshire knew him as the simple teenager, who once messed up his own kitchen while trying his hands at washing clothes.

Meet Suleiman Adam or Solly bhai, a man who is God-send for all Indian cricketers coming to play league or county cricket in the north of England. Solly bhai played a role in bringing Tendulkar to Yorkshire and breaking the county's century-old tradition of not signing a foreign player.

From Sunil Gavaskar and Ashok Mankad in the 1970s to Tendulkar, Yorkshire county's first-ever overseas professional, Solly bhai was their "one-stop solution centre" for years.

"They were never celebrity sportsmen for me. Sunil is like my younger brother. My wife Maryam was in hospital and he came to meet me. VVS (Laxman) is coming today to see her. You know Sachin attended my son's wedding back in 1989 before he played for India," recalls Solly bhai, a raconteur of journeymen Indian cricketers.

He was like the then 18-year-old Tendulkar's local guardian when he signed for Yorkshire in 1992, but the association dates back to late 80s.

"Before Sachin, I had arranged a club contract for Vinod (Kambli) in the high-quality Bradford League. He was being paid 25 pounds per game. Sachin was also in England for Kailash Gattani's club. He asked for 100 pounds per game. I spoke to Chickenley Cricket Club but they couldn't have afforded 100 pounds per game and deal fell through," he remembers.

He was asked how Yorkshire broke their century-old tradition, and Solly bhai had a hearty laugh.

"It's a long story and I believe I had a small role in that as I am a member of Yorkshire CCC. Although I wasn't a part of their cricket committee," he says. "It so happened that I watched the 6 pm news sometime in 1991 where I saw it was announced that Yorkshire was changing the century old rule where no player other than ones born in Yorkshire could play for the county. They had decided on Craig McDermott as their first overseas signing.

"I thought it was a good move and then I suddenly learnt that McDermott is injured and had pulled out. I immediately called a committee member and told them that I can get them a good Asian international player Indian or Pakistani but they were not interested but I was adamant. I said I wanted to speak to the committee," he recollects.

Next day when Fred Trueman, one of the greatest fast bowlers that the game has ever produced, saw Solly entering the Leeds ground, he was livid.

"Freddie said 'I know Solly why you have come but I didn't even want an Australian'. I said that I will place my cards in front of the committee and let them decide. The members asked which name did I have in mind and I promptly said: 'Sachin Tendulkar'."

Those were the days when the concept of sports agent wasn't in vogue in India but Yorkshire did manage to sign Tendulkar after the cricketer was convinced by Gavaskar to take up the challenge.

"Sachin was signed for a very big amount at that time. I know exactly how much it was but I won't reveal it to you. I also got Sachin a bat sponsorship deal with Slazenger," he proudly recalls.

He also had a funny story about Sourav Ganguly and Rahul Dravid's dream debut in England in 1996.

"Slazenger contacted me in 1996 that they have 10,000 pounds and they wanted me to sign a few top cricketers. Sachin told me that he had already signed a big deal with MRF.

"So, there were two young cricketers Sourav and Rahul and one established star, Ajay Jadeja. I was convinced Jadeja will play all three Tests and he got a 6000-pound contract while it was 2000 pound each for Sourav and Rahul.

"These two boys were so simple that they were scared of carrying the whole wad of cash and my son went to Nottingham (before the 3rd Test) and handed them their fees."

Born in Surat, he migrated to England as a school boy in 1963 and worked his way up from being a motor mechanic to owning a chain of petrol pumps. His offsprings (three sons and a daughter) have branched out in different businesses.

"You know cricketers, who played club cricket have worked at my petrol pumps. Because they would be paid 25 pounds for weekend matches. Madan Lal worked at 50 pence an hour, even VVS has worked when he was a teenager and played club cricket. I had few houses and they would stay there."

Content with life, he lives in Dewsbury and owns a sports shop, Solly Sports.

"Me and my wife always felt that these boys were family and they still are. When Laxman came to know that my wife's one leg had to be amputated, he said he is coming to see her. Sunil said he will also be coming. I love them because of my 'keeda' (passion) for cricket," he says.

=======

THE TELEGRAPH

13 November 2013

Sachin Tendulkar's year at Headingley changed Yorkshire cricket forever

Sachin Tendulkar did not rewrite the record books at Yorkshire in 1992, but he certainly left a legacy and made many friends.

By Oliver Brown

A piece of Sachin Tendulkar will remain forever Yorkshire. He depicts his unlikely allegiance with the White Rose, consummated in the heady summer of 1992, as "one of the greatest four-and-a-half months I have spent in my life".

And yet to savour the most exotic flavour of this chapter of Tendulkar the Tyke one needs to plot a course beyond Headingley, to the Texaco garage on Savile Road in Dewsbury, above which Solly Adam still cherishes the memories of when the young Sachin was neither the Little Master nor even a star, but simply the deferential teenage guest at his dining-room table.

"He would come for Indian food at my house, and my wife and sister-in-law would iron his clothes," says Adam, the garrulous businessman and self-made cricketing kingmaker whose extensive web of local-league contacts in old Bombay helped anoint Tendulkar as Yorkshire's first non-white player.

"Whenever he was free we would take him to weddings or the cinema. We would go up to Leeds for Kentucky Fried Chicken - for some reason he loved it."

"With us, he was quite a character, very bubbly," he reflects, negating more recent impressions of Tendulkar the wary diplomat, whose public pronouncements are so charming as to be bloodless. "He mixed with my kids, with my parents, and whatever he took part in he regarded very seriously. I remember that we took him to a snooker hall in Blackpool one weekend. He had never seen one of these tables before but within 30 minutes he was better than the rest of us. It was the same with tennis. An hour later, he would be striking the ball more cleanly than the chap teaching him how to play."

It is a dismally damp day here in West Yorkshire, where Adam runs a thriving cricket suppliers' business from his manic Dewsbury office, but still, he exudes an effervescence befitting his role as the consummate fixer.

For in 1992, Yorkshire County Cricket Club were not exactly the most lavishly hospitable recipients of imported talent. Indeed, Fred Trueman described the very decision to look overseas as a "b—- disgrace".

It had been a cornerstone of policy for seven decades for their team to be resolutely homegrown, until a precipitate decline in form throughout the Eighties forced their hand, prompting Geoffrey Boycott's committee to vote by 18 to one to usher in a fresh age of enlightenment.

As per the wishes of captain Martyn Moxon, Australian fast bowler Craig McDermott was their original choice as foreign player until, just one month before his scheduled debut on Good Friday, he pulled out of the deal citing a groin injury.

Through much gnashing of teeth in the Yorkshire boardroom, the name 'Sachin' finally passed the lips of chairman Sir Lawrence Byford and Adam, who knew Tendulkar and could claim a mutual friend in Gavaskar, took his cue.

"I hadn't brought guys like Imran or Javed over as an agent, but as a hobby," he explains. "It was exactly the same with Sachin.

"I was the captain at Chickenley, here in Dewsbury, and he would ring me to say, 'Solly-bhai - literally, 'Solly, my brother' - I want to play in local league cricket for you. Why haven't you called me?' He was asking for £100 a match. Ultimately, it didn't happen, but when Byford and Brian Close confirmed that they were interested in signing Tendulkar I said that it would be my pleasure.

"Sachin was with the Test team in Australia, but this time he sounded uncertain. 'No, I'm too busy,' he replied. Then, after a pause: 'But let me think about it.' So straight away I called up Gavaskar. He was the one who best understood Sachin's ambitions, and he was going to persuade him." Sure enough, Gavaskar imparted the right solicitous words and Sir Lawrence, with Yorkshire's touring party in South Africa, spoke to Tendulkar in an effort to cement the deal. By April 3 Chris

Hassell, the club's chief executive, had arrived in India with a contract for their man to sign.

A more practical problem was the issue of where Tendulkar, suddenly transplanted from Bombay to the Broad Acres, would live. Adam, who took no commission from the arrangement and insisted he perceived the teenage Sachin 'like a son', offered his own house but Tendulkar, in an early sign of the cultivated manners that would become his trademark, refused on the grounds that he might return too late from away games and disturb his elders.

Thus, it transpired - through the cluster of rented houses that Adam had already acquired for Vinod Kambli and Praveen Amre, two of Tendulkar's World Cup colleagues to have made the journey - that he made 34 Wakefield Crescent, a cream-coloured residence deep in Dewsbury suburbia, his first home on these shores.

His maiden match for Yorkshire was, alas, a trauma. In the teeth of the bowling of Malcolm Marshall, against Hampshire at Headingley, he was out for 86. Adam recalls: "He was so upset when we met afterwards. He had been run out at the non-striker's end and said: 'I'm very disappointed. I always like to score a century in my first match.

Wherever I have made my debut before, I have always done so.'"

Tendulkar's score of 100 not out on his maiden first-class appearance for Bombay, aged 15, bears this out eloquently enough. But if his fleeting career at Yorkshire might be characterised as one of near-misses - given that he was caught short in the 80s three times and in the 90s twice, either side of a solitary century at Chester-Le-Street - his time away from the wicket was exquisitely happy. "Sachin can be a quiet and lonely person, but there were a lot of cricketers from Mumbai here, and my house was like the family home for him," Adam says. "Plus, his girlfriend Anjali, now his wife, would travel over from Gloucester to see him. While he tends to keep himself reserved, I found that he opened up once he thought he knew you. Once he makes friends, he doesn't forget."

Adam discovered that Tendulkar could be strikingly generous with his time, "drinking" the game to such an extent that even after county practice, he would come to support him at his matches for Spen Victoria in the Bradford League. "He respected me like a father and my wife like a mother. He had a great background, as the son of a writer and a teacher. I have always believed that while Brian Lara was a brilliant cricketer, he deteriorated because nobody was there to guide him. But Sachin always knew how to keep his feet on the floor."

Upon leaving Yorkshire, Tendulkar confided to him that the exposure to the English county system "has made me eager to do better". And as India's greatest prepares to take his leave amid the splendour of a five-day carnival in his native city, Adam paints him unambiguously as the man who changed cricket. "Kids in India will ask, 'If Sachin can play at this level at 19 years old, why can't I?' Players will come into the Test side younger than 21 purely because of him. He has transformed the entire tradition."

He is convinced, too, that Tendulkar has chosen a propitious moment to retire, claiming: "I always like it when people say, 'He could have played for another two years', rather than, 'I'm glad he's gone.'" But the most abiding picture for Adam arises not from this week's glorious valediction but from a gesture that his guest made upon leaving Dewsbury. "I will take it with me for as long as I live," he says, visibly emotional. "Sachin had his plane ticket back to India, and he knocked on my door at 11.30 at night. He came in, and he touched my feet. It is a traditional sign of respect in Hinduism. 'Solly-Bhai,' he said. 'I am going tomorrow.' And I gave him my blessing."

=======

LAST WORDS

Once I was an aspiring professional cricketer who played Under-19 age group in the state of Andhra Pradesh in India, and cricket was my lifeworld till 2001. As I was a passionate cricketer, my cricketing potentials attracted the attention of my family members and friends, who encouraged me to pursue cricket as my profession. Accordingly, with a view to embark on the cricketing journey, and to refine my cricketing skills, I travelled all the way from my hometown, Akividu, in the West-Godavari district of Andhra Pradesh, to our state headquarters in Hyderabad, and attended a summer coaching camp at Gymkhana Grounds.

In the Gymkhana Grounds in Hyderabad, I would observe the lower school going kids of about 7-8 years old, playing cricket early in the morning with sophisticated cricket gears, attended by their well-off parents. When I reflected upon the humble financial condition of my family, it began to prick my conscience that whether the profession is at all appropriate for a person of my status. Despite my natural tendency to challenge all odds, as I was a staunch optimist, I took recourse to a pragmatic approach. Knowing that, 'the person who chases two rabbits, catches none,' after poring some deep thoughts about this predicament, I chose to leave cricket to focus on my studies, as I was also good at my studies, consistently ranking among the first three in class. So, I returned to my hometown, Akividu, in the middle of the night. Sensing the apparent question mark on the face of my mother, I told her not to ask me any more about cricket and dumped the kit bag in the corner of the house.

It was the year 2001, and the cricket camp in Hyderabad had brought an incredible shift in my orientation towards my career. I dedicated my time for studies, of course, while helping my hardworking parents in their work during my free time, and eventually, I graduated in Master of Business Administration (Finance) from Andhra University in 2005. With these educational credentials, I worked for several IT firms of international eminence including Kotak Mahindra Bank, TCS (Kolkata and Mexico), Wipro, Wm Morrisons (Bradford), Network Rail UK, NHS, etc., and by 2010, I migrated to UK to make England my home.

Despite my professional pursuits in business administration in finance, my love for cricket would often linger in my mind, which I would douse with great difficulty, and never touched the bat again. Then I happened to meet my close friend and a brother figure, Syed Shahabuddin (Shabu), who was a former Captain of the Andhra Ranji Cricket Team, and the one who had also played for the IPL Mumbai Indians Team. We were so happy to meet each other, and from our conversation, I learnt that Shabu then was playing for league cricket in England. Thereafter, Shabu and I would meet up frequently, and I would visit him to watch him playing cricket matches. Upon learning about my absolute disconnect from cricket, Shabu tried to rekindle my interest in cricket. But I shied away from it, as it had been over a decade since I had lost my connection to the game.

Meanwhile, I developed an interest in reading and writing, particularly I extended my assistance to my friends in writing journals on cricket and films, while continuing to hold focus on my IT consulting job. It was during this phase of my voracious reading that I came across a small, yet a significant, reference of Solly Bhai in the autobiography of Sachin Tendulkar, *Playing It My Way,* where Sachin lauded Solly Bhai for his remarkable contribution in mentoring and fostering numerous

Asian cricketers in England. Like any cricket enthusiast, and most importantly as the cricket history buff that I am, this sparked my curiosity to delve deeper into the life and deeds of Solly Bhai.

Eventually, I revived my interest of cricket, and in 2019, I finally took a plunge again into the cricketing arena; I joined Trafford Metrovics Cricket Club (TMV CC) in Manchester which plays for Cheshire County Cricket League. It is a real joy playing the game which I always loved, yet left untouched for over a decade, and now I feel that I returned to those wonderful old days.

It was during this phase of my reviving interest in cricket, and my active engagement with the game, that I met Solly Bhai several times in his sports shoppe and bought sports equipment both for myself and for some of my teammates. Since, I had already read about Solly Bhai first from Sachin' book, and then from newspaper archives, I took an initiative to begin my conversation with him, merely out of my curiosity to know more about him. In our conversation, what really captivated me was that, more than his cricketing achievements, he had this extraordinary capacity to face the most adverse challenge from his childhood, to emerge as one of the pioneering Asians to make successful ordeals in more than one fields—business, league cricket, mentoring, and philanthropic deeds. It is an inspirational story, and I began to think of writing his biography.

I continued visiting him at his sport shoppe, and eventually, our relationship deepened. This was around the time I began contemplating on quitting my IT profession to pursue something that would be true to my heart. I began recounting this inspiring story of Solly Bhai to my better-half, Ammu (Aruna), as always, she is the first person with whom I share my views and experiences, and then with my always supportive elder brother in India, Ayyanna Babu. Seeing their curiosity and enthusiasm, I told them about my idea and plan of writing this biography, and they were glad about it.

Consequently, I resigned my IT consultant job, prepared a blueprint of my book proposal, designed questionnaire for each chapter, and presented the same to Solly Bhai on March 25, 2022. To my delight, Solly Bhai found this exciting, and gave his enthusiastic nod to my intended project. Since then, my life has been shuttling three times a week between Bradford, the place of my residence, to the Solly Sports in Dewsbury. He took the pains of graciously recording every detail of his life and times, as planned, in a digital voice recorder, and patiently provided me with all the necessary information. Solly Bhai would take a close reading of each draft of each chapter I put down on paper, which would be verified and refined multiple times, until his final approval. It is a rare case for biography writing, in which the man himself equally played his part in writing this book, alongside me, so we resolved to write this biography in first person narrative, with me as its author. I also feel that I must express my heartfelt thanks to Bhabhi (Maryam Bhabhi) and all the family members of Solly Bhai for their kind reception at their home. Hence, I would like to express my gratitude to Solly Bhai, as the first and foremost thing, for keeping his trust on me to write his biography, and for all his endeavours to join me in this difficult ordeal.

Throughout this journey, I also have had the privilege of speaking to numerous cricketers and friends of Solly Bhai, that include great legends and star cricketers like Sunil Gavaskar, Javed Miandad, VVS Laxman, Iqbal Qasim, Sairaj Bahuthule, Avinash Karnik (who unfortunately passed away recently), Amin Lakhani, David Byrne, and Sean Twohig, among others. They generously shared their insights about their association and friendship with Solly Bhai. I am deeply grateful to each one of them for extending their valuable time, and for providing me with valuable information that was of great help.

ACKNOWLEDGEMENTS

Given Solly Bhai's acquaintance with hundreds of cricketers, the task of collecting data on each player, analysing each event in its historical context, and weaving them into an authentic narrative, indeed, has been a herculean task. Nonetheless, I took all the pains in delving into the cricket archives in different websites, and read numerous articles and books, to shape this book into this final form. Throughout this process, many of my friends joined me to extend their warm support. This book stands out to be a testament to the power of collaboration and friendship, as many of my friends and well-wishers extended their contributions and warm support, throughout the period of this project, and I am indebted to each one of them.

Among the contributors of the book, a special note of gratitude must be extended to my scholar friend and a brother figure, Kotesh Devulapally from India. Dr. Kotesh has been with me all through the two years of my engagement, right from its inception to its idea formulation, interpretation of the data, and of course, even in drafting and editing the book into its final form. Hours of discussions with him sharpened my theoretical grasp over the subject of my study, and his profound insights, which were based on his cultural analysis and philosophical view towards understanding the world at large, has been a great asset for me. I wish him good luck in all his future endeavours, and I hope that our friendship lasts for ever. A special mention must also be made of my childhood friend, Satyanarayana Gorgi, for his invaluable assistance in collecting and documenting the necessary data as per my requirements. The support of the above two friends has been instrumental in making this project a reality.

I am a firm believer in the power of human emotions and bonding with the members of the family, friends, and colleagues, which makes our life so happy and beautiful. In fact, I am fortunate to receive the boundless love and support from my family throughout my life. My late mother, Subbalakshmi (Ammulu), had been a pillar of support for me throughout, and she took care of all our sibling with all her warmth of love and with her mighty boldness. I extend my love for my father, Shri Venkateshwara Rao, my eldest brother, Naga Shankar Babu, my second eldest brother, V.N. Ayyanna Babu (Director of Sri Medha College, Attapur, Hyderabad), and all my family members for their consistent support and love throughout this journey. Here is my love and my life, Ammu (Aruna). Ammu has been the first person who read the manuscript of each chapter, has left her comments, besides looking after my three loving kids, Nirvana (Late), Mayukha, and Nirvaan. Without encouragement and support of Ammu, and the atmosphere of cheerfulness created by my children, this project would not have been possible. I express my love for my wife and children.

There are also several of my friends who made my life so happy and meaningful. A mention must be made of a few of them who have been closest to my heart, who became my extended family. I express my gratitude to my former colleagues, and presently intimate friends, to begin with, Kalyan Chukkapalli, Chanukya Rajagopala, Sreentath Halaharvi, Gowtham Varma Alluri, Kalyan Krishna Doddapaneni (Former Deccan Chargers – IPL Player), Bhanu Bhaskarala, Dr. Gurram Seetaramulu, Anna Llinares Sanchez, Sammy Khan, Deepa Chukkapalli, Steve Beech, John Chandra, Sreelu Karatam, Rama Rajesh, Michael Lingam, KV Sai Krishna, Venkatesh Chittajallu, Kavitha Manickam, Ramesh Penmatsa, Prasanth Kesireddy, Suresh Geddam, Bhimavarapu Shafi, Manikandan Kathirvel, Simon McDermott and all my cricket teammates at Trafford Metrovics CC who indisputably stand as my well-wishers.

I also extend sincere thanks to my supporters who have been there to encourage me in my personal and professional career; they include Shri Dr. Mathukumalli Vidyasagar (Former Executive Vice-President of TCS, and a fellow of the Royal Society), Shri Giri S.V (Former DY GM